Python Deep Learn

MW00723384

9 projects demystifying neural network and deep learning models for building intelligent systems

Matthew Lamons
Rahul Kumar
Abhishek Nagaraja

BIRMINGHAM - MUMBAI

Python Deep Learning Projects

Commissioning Editor: Pravin Dhandre
Acquisition Editor: Karan Jain
Content Development Editor: Karan Thakkar
Technical Editor: Nilesh Sawakhande
Copy Editor: Safis Editing
Project Coordinator: Nidhi Joshi
Proofreader: Safis Editing
Indexer: Aishwarya Gangawane
Graphics: Jisha Chirayil
Production Coordinator: Nilesh Mohite

First published: October 2018

Production reference: 1311018

Published by Packt Publishing Ltd.
Livery Place
35 Livery Street
Birmingham
B3 2PB, UK.

ISBN 978-1-78899-709-6

www.packtpub.com

To my wife Kristine for her impatience with unintelligent technology and superhuman patience with me. The first provided me with the goal to study and apply deep learning to everyday problems, the second the time!

To my children Ethan and Margarete & husband Derek, and colleagues at The Intelligence Factory and Skejul Inc., for your support & encouragement as we work together to be the architects of the future and not it's victims.

– Matthew Lamons

To my mom, dad and sister for constant support and motivation. To Late Prof. Pervez Ahmed for his wisdom and guidance which helped me to build my foundation and all my teachers for showing me the way.

To my friends for discussing ideas. And to the amazing team at Jatana.ai and BotSupply.ai. for pushing the boundaries of what I could achieve while creating technology products that drive innovation for a better future.

– Rahul Kumar

To my mom, Nagarathna, and my dad, Nagaraja for your support, love, and for always being there for me. To my sisters Deepthi and Madhuri for always encouraging and guiding me all the way. To my amazing colleagues at Skejul Inc., for your constant support and believing in me. To Matthew Lamons for his guidance and for this opportunity.

– Abhishek Nagaraja

mapt.io

Mapt is an online digital library that gives you full access to over 5,000 books and videos, as well as industry leading tools to help you plan your personal development and advance your career. For more information, please visit our website.

Why subscribe?

- Spend less time learning and more time coding with practical eBooks and Videos from over 4,000 industry professionals
- Improve your learning with Skill Plans built especially for you
- Get a free eBook or video every month
- Mapt is fully searchable
- Copy and paste, print, and bookmark content

Packt.com

Did you know that Packt offers eBook versions of every book published, with PDF and ePub files available? You can upgrade to the eBook version at www.packt.com and as a print book customer, you are entitled to a discount on the eBook copy. Get in touch with us at customercare@packtpub.com for more details.

At www.packt.com, you can also read a collection of free technical articles, sign up for a range of free newsletters, and receive exclusive discounts and offers on Packt books and eBooks.

Contributors

About the authors

Matthew Lamons's background is in experimental psychology and deep learning. Founder and CEO of Skejul—the AI platform to help people manage their activities. Named by Gartner, Inc. as a "Cool Vendor" in the "Cool Vendors in Unified Communication, 2017" report. He founded The Intelligence Factory to build AI strategy, solutions, insights, and talent for enterprise clients and incubate AI tech startups based on the success of his Applied AI MasterMinds group. Matthew's global community of more than 85 K are leaders in AI, forecasting, robotics, autonomous vehicles, marketing tech, NLP, computer vision, reinforcement, and deep learning. Matthew invites you to join him on his mission to simplify the future and to build AI for good.

Rahul Kumar is an AI scientist, deep learning practitioner, and independent researcher. His expertise in building multilingual NLU systems and large-scale AI infrastructures has brought him to Copenhagen, where he leads a large team of AI engineers as Chief AI Scientist at Jatana.ai.
Often invited to speak at AI conferences, he frequently travels between India, Europe, and the US where, among other research initiatives, he collaborates with The Intelligence Factory as NLP data science fellow. Keen to explore the ramifications of emerging technologies for his next book, he's currently involved in various research projects on Quantum Computing (QC), high-performance computing (HPC), and the brain-computer interaction (BCI).

Abhishek Nagaraja was born and raised in India. Graduated Magna Cum Laude from the University of Illinois at Chicago, United States, with a Masters Degree in Mechanical Engineering with a concentration in Mechatronics and Data Science. Abhishek specializes in Keras and TensorFlow for building and evaluation of custom architectures in deep learning recommendation models. His deep learning skills and interest span computational linguistics and NLP to build chatbots to computer vision and reinforcement learning. He has been working as a Data Scientist for Skejul Inc. building an AI-powered activity forecast engine and engaged as a Deep Learning Data Scientist with The Intelligence Factory building solutions for enterprise clients.

About the reviewers

Doug Ortiz is the founder of Illustris, LLC and is an experienced enterprise cloud, big data, data analytics, and solutions architect who has architected, designed, developed, re-engineered, and integrated enterprise solutions. His other areas of expertise include Amazon Web Services, Azure, Google Cloud, Business Intelligence, Hadoop, Spark, NoSQL Databases, and SharePoint, to name but a few.

Huge thanks to my wonderful wife, Milla, Maria, and Nikolay, and to my children, for all their support.

Juan Tomás Oliva Ramos is an environmental engineer from University of Guanajuato, Mexico, with a master's degree in administrative engineering and quality. He is working Know in the Instituto Tecnologico Superior de Purísima del Rincón Guanajuato, México. He has more than 5 years of experience in management and development of patents, technological innovation projects, and technological solutions through the statistical control of processes. He has been a teacher of statistics, entrepreneurship, and technological development since 2011. He has developed prototypes via programming and automation technologies for the improvement of operations, which have been registered for patents.

I want to thank God for giving me the wisdom and humility to review this book. I thank Packt for giving me the opportunity to review this amazing book and to collaborate with a group of committed people. I want to thank my beautiful wife, Brenda, our two magic princesses
(Maria Regina and Maria Renata), and Angel Tadeo. All of you give me the strength, happiness, and joy to start a new day. Thanks for being my family.

Packt is searching for authors like you

If you're interested in becoming an author for Packt, please visit `authors.packtpub.com` and apply today. We have worked with thousands of developers and tech professionals, just like you, to help them share their insight with the global tech community. You can make a general application, apply for a specific hot topic that we are recruiting an author for, or submit your own idea.

Table of Contents

Preface   1

Chapter 1: Building Deep Learning Environments   9
  Building a common DL environment   9
    Get focused and into the code!   10
  DL environment setup locally   10
    Downloading and installing Anaconda   11
      Installing DL libraries   12
  Setting up a DL environment in the cloud   13
  Cloud platforms for deployment   14
    Prerequisites   14
    Setting up the GCP   14
  Automating the setup process   15
  Summary   18

Chapter 2: Training NN for Prediction Using Regression   19
  **Building a regression model for prediction using an MLP deep
  neural network**   20
  Exploring the MNIST dataset   21
  Intuition and preparation   23
    Defining regression   24
    Defining the project structure   24
  Let's code the implementation!   25
    Defining hyperparameters   25
    Model definition   26
    Building the training loop   29
      Overfitting and underfitting   34
    Building inference   36
  Concluding the project   39
  Summary   40

Chapter 3: Word Representation Using word2vec   41
  Learning word vectors   42
    Loading all the dependencies   43
      Preparing the text corpus   44
      Defining our word2vec model   45
      Training the model   47
      Analyzing the model   47
      Plotting the word cluster using the t-SNE algorithm   49
  **Visualizing the embedding space by plotting the model on
  TensorBoard**   51

Building language models using CNN and word2vec   54
   Exploring the CNN model   55
      Understanding data format   61
      Integrating word2vec with CNN   63
      Executing the model   63
   Deploy the model into production   64
Summary   64

Chapter 4: Building an NLP Pipeline for Building Chatbots   67
   Basics of NLP pipelines   68
      Tokenization   69
      Part-of-Speech tagging   70
         Extracting nouns   71
         Extracting verbs   72
      Dependency parsing   73
      NER   73
   Building conversational bots   74
      What is TF-IDF?   74
         Preparing the dataset   74
         Implementation   75
            Creating the vectorizer   76
            Processing the query   77
            Rank results   77
      Advanced chatbots using NER   77
         Installing Rasa   78
         Preparing dataset   79
         Training the model   80
         Deploying the model   81
   Serving chatbots   83
   Summary   84

Chapter 5: Sequence-to-Sequence Models for Building Chatbots   87
   Introducing RNNs   88
      RNN architectures   90
   Implementing basic RNNs   91
      Importing all of the dependencies   92
      Preparing the dataset   92
      Hyperparameters   94
      Defining a basic RNN cell model   94
      Training the RNN Model   97
      Evaluation of the RNN model   99
   LSTM architecture   100
   Implementing an LSTM model   102
      Defining our LSTM model   102
      Training the LSTM model   103
      Evaluation of the LSTM model   106
   Sequence-to-sequence models   106

Data preparation   108
Defining a seq2seq model   109
Hyperparameters   111
Training the seq2seq model   112
Evaluation of the seq2seq model   113
Summary   114

Chapter 6: Generative Language Model for Content Creation   117
LSTM for text generation   118
Data pre-processing   119
Defining the LSTM model for text generation   120
Training the model   121
Inference and results   123
Generating lyrics using deep (multi-layer) LSTM   124
Data pre-processing   125
Defining the model   128
Training the deep TensorFlow-based LSTM model   130
Inference   133
Output   134
Generating music using a multi-layer LSTM   135
Pre-processing data   136
Defining the model and training   141
Generating music   144
Summary   146

Chapter 7: Building Speech Recognition with DeepSpeech2   149
Data preprocessing   150
Corpus exploration   151
Feature engineering   153
Data transformation   157
DS2 model description and intuition   158
Training the model   162
Testing and evaluating the model   167
Summary   168

Chapter 8: Handwritten Digits Classification Using ConvNets   169
Code implementation   170
Importing all of the dependencies   170
Exploring the data   170
Defining the hyperparameters   172
Building and training a simple deep neural network   173
Fitting a model   176
Evaluating a model   177
MLP – Python file   179
Convolution   180
Convolution in Keras   181

Fitting the model   184
Evaluating the model   184
Convolution – Python file   186
Pooling   187
Fitting the model   191
Evaluating the model   192
Convolution with pooling – Python file   194
Dropout   195
Fitting the model   197
Evaluating the model   198
Convolution with pooling – Python file   200
Going deeper   201
Compiling the model   202
Fitting the model   203
Evaluating the model   204
Convolution with pooling and Dropout – Python file   206
Data augmentation   207
Using ImageDataGenerator   208
Fitting ImageDataGenerator   210
Compiling the model   211
Fitting the model   211
Evaluating the model   212
Augmentation – Python file   214
Additional topic – convolution autoencoder   216
Importing the dependencies   217
Generating low-resolution images   218
Scaling   218
Defining the autoencoder   218
Fitting the autoencoder   221
Loss plot and test results   221
Autoencoder – Python file   224
Conclusion   226
Summary   227

Chapter 9: Object Detection Using OpenCV and TensorFlow   229
Object detection intuition   230
Improvements in object detection models   232
Object detection using OpenCV   233
A handcrafted red object detector   234
Installing dependencies   234
Exploring image data   235
Normalizing the image   237
Preparing a mask   238
Post-processing of a mask   239
Applying a mask   241
Object detection using deep learning   242
Quick implementation of object detection   242
Installing all the dependencies   242
Implementation   244

Deployment   247
Object Detection In Real-Time Using YOLOv2   250
    Preparing the dataset   250
        Using the pre-existing COCO dataset   251
        Using the custom dataset   252
    Installing all the dependencies   253
    Configuring the YOLO model   254
    Defining the YOLO v2 model   255
    Training the model   256
    Evaluating the model   261
Image segmentation   264
    Importing all the dependencies   264
    Exploring the data   265
        Images   265
        Annotations   267
    Preparing the data   269
        Normalizing the image   270
        Encoding   271
        Model data   272
    Defining hyperparameters   273
    Define SegNet   274
        Compiling the model   277
        Fitting the model   277
        Testing the model   278
Conclusion   280
Summary   280

Chapter 10: Building Face Recognition Using FaceNet   281
Setup environment   283
    Getting the code   283
    Building the Docker image   283
    Downloading pre-trained models   286
Building the pipeline   288
Preprocessing of images   290
    Face detection   290
    Aligning faces   291
    Feature extraction   295
    Execution on Docker   297
Training the classifier   297
Evaluation   298
Summary   300

Chapter 11: Automated Image Captioning   301
Data preparation   302
    Initialization   303
    Download and prepare the MS-COCO dataset   303
    Data preparation for a deep CNN encoder   305

Performing feature extraction 306
Data prep for a language generation (RNN) decoder 307
Setting up the data pipeline 309
Defining the captioning model 310
Attention 310
CNN encoder 311
RNN decoder 311
Loss function 312
Training the captioning model 312
Evaluating the captioning model 315
Deploying the captioning model 318
Summary 321

Chapter 12: Pose Estimation on 3D models Using ConvNets 323
Code implementation 324
Importing the dependencies 325
Exploring and pre-processing the data 326
Preparing the data 336
Cropping 336
Resizing 338
Plotting the joints and limbs 339
Transforming the images 340
Defining hyperparameters for training 342
Building the VGG16 model 343
Defining the VGG16 model 343
Training loop 347
Plot training and validation loss 350
Predictions 351
Scripts in modular form 353
Module 1 – crop_resize_transform.py 354
Module 2 – plotting.py 356
Module 3 – test.py 358
Module 4 – train.py 360
Conclusion 365
Summary 366

Chapter 13: Image Translation Using GANs for Style Transfer 367
Let's code the implementation! 369
Importing all of the dependencies 369
Exploring the data 370
Preparing the data 372
Type conversion, centering, and scaling 372
Masking/inserting noise 373
Reshaping 375
MNIST classifier 375
Defining hyperparameters for GAN 378
Building the GAN model components 378

Defining the generator 379
Defining the discriminator 382
Defining the DCGAN 383
Training GAN 384
Plotting the training – part 1 384
Plotting the training – part 2 386
Training loop 388
Predictions 397
CNN classifier predictions on the noised and generated images 397
Scripts in modular form 399
Module 1 – train_mnist.py 399
Module 2 – training_plots.py 400
Module 3 – GAN.py 400
Module 4 – train_gan.py 401
The conclusion to the project 403
Summary 404

Chapter 14: Develop an Autonomous Agent with Deep R Learning 405
Let's get to the code! 407
Deep Q-learning 407
Importing all of the dependencies 407
Exploring the CartPole game 408
Interacting with the CartPole game 408
Loading the game 408
Resetting the game 409
Playing the game 410
Q-learning 412
Defining hyperparameters for Deep Q Learning (DQN) 413
Building the model components 414
Defining the agent 414
Defining the agent action 416
Defining the memory 416
Defining the performance plot 417
Defining replay 418
Training loop 420
Testing the DQN model 422
Deep Q-learning scripts in modular form 423
Module 1 – hyperparameters_dqn.py 424
Module 2 – agent_replay_dqn.py 424
Module 3 – test_dqn.py 425
Module 4 – train_dqn.py 426
Deep SARSA learning 427
SARSA learning 427
Importing all of the dependencies 428
Loading the game environment 428
Defining the agent 429
Training the agent 429
Testing the agent 430
Deep SARSA learning script in modular form 432

The conclusion to the project 433
Summary 434
Chapter 15: Summary and Next Steps in Your Deep Learning Career 435
  Python deep learning – building the foundation – two projects 435
    Chapter 1 – Building the Deep Learning Environment 436
    Chapter 2 – Training NN for Prediction Using Regression 436
  Python deep learning – NLP – 5 projects 437
    Chapter 3 – Word Representations Using word2vec 437
    Chapter 4 – Build an NLP Pipeline for Building Chatbots 437
    Chapter 5 – Sequence-to-Sequence Models for Building Chatbots 438
    Chapter 6 – Generative Language Model for Content Creation 439
    Chapter 7 – Building Speech Recognition with DeepSpeech2 439
  Deep learning – computer vision – 6 projects 440
    Chapter 8 – Handwritten Digit Classification Using ConvNets 440
    Chapter 9 – Object Detection Using OpenCV and TensorFlow 441
    Chapter 10 – Building Facial Recognition Using OpenFace 442
    Chapter 11 – Automated Image Captioning 442
    Chapter 12 – Pose Estimation on 3D Models Using ConvNets 443
    Chapter 13 – Image Translation Using GANs for Style Transfer 443
  Python deep learning – autonomous agents – 1 project 444
    Chapter 14 – Develop an Autonomous Agent with Deep Reinforcement Learning 444
  Next steps – AI strategy and platforms 445
    AI strategy 445
    Deep learning platforms – TensorFlow Extended (TFX) 446
  Conclusion and thank you! 446
Other Books You May Enjoy 447
Index 451

Preface

Have you ever tried to get something novel out of a computer? I can ask you to make up a story or look at a picture and tell me what's in it. How would you make a computer program behave like this in contrast to the digital storage and transfer unit we've used them for these past 30+ yrs?

If you had perfect knowledge and all the time in the world, you could write all the rules by which a computer program would need to operate. Of course, if you had all the knowledge to define the operational rules, you wouldn't need the computer to do anything! So what do you do if you need a computer to function in complex ways (making predictions, classifications, optimizing processes, generating content, responding to interactions, performing robotic controls), but don't have all the heuristic rules defined?

You build an algorithmically-based application that can learn the rules, find the pattern, or determine the signal, from data that comes from the domain space in question. You set up the training such that it iterates incredibly fast and with a great number of cycles (we call them epochs) to provide the "experience" to incrementally train the model in a process that would not be possible in a human lifetime.

When we build these algorithmic architectures in layers, we create deep learning models that can learn features (for example, dogs have tails and cars have wheels) and these learned features are powerful! What we really find in *Python Deep Learning Projects* is that we can ask profound questions not possible before. It's these questions that drive our deep learning technologies to solve problems that range from healthcare diagnostics in radiology to cancer screening. Deep learning applications drive chatbot experiences, facial recognition, autonomous vehicles, recommendation engines, and marketing tech. The hard sciences of physics, biology, and chemistry are incorporating deep learning skills training just as they have in the past with regard to statistics and microscopes.

Who this book is for

This book is perfect for you if you've undertaken at least one course in machine learning and have a modest functional proficiency in Python (meaning you can create programs in Python when supported by examples). Many of our readers will be undergraduates at university studying computer science, statistics, mathematics, physics, biology, chemistry, marketing, and business. Deep learning technologies are being applied to all the professions that these degrees prepare you for, and this book is a great way to learn skills that will be applicable to your success. Postgraduates will appreciate the instruction level, too, as the projects selected are directly applicable to the modern job market, from tech start-ups to enterprise applications.

Python Deep Learning Projects is focused at the core of the data science pipeline – model building, training, evaluation, and validation. Additional pre- and post-data science engineering processes are required in the data pipeline for production applications that we cannot address here due to space considerations, but that we are looking to address in a future publication.

What this book covers

Chapter 1, *Building Deep Learning Environments*, in this chapter we will establish a common workspace for our projects with core technologies such as Ubuntu, Anaconda, Python, TensorFlow, Keras, and **Google Cloud Platform** (**GCP**).

Chapter 2, *Training a Neural Net for Prediction Using Regression*, in this chapter we will build a 2 layer (minimally deep) neural network in TensorFlow and train it on the classic MNIST dataset of handwritten digits for a restaurant patron text notification business use case.

Chapter 3, *Word Representations Using word2vec*, in this chapter we will learn and use word2vec to transform words into dense vectors (that is, tensors) creating embedding representations for a corpus, then create a **convolutional neural network** (**CNN**) to build a language model for sentiment analysis in a text exchange business use case.

Chapter 4, *Build a NLP Pipeline for Building Chatbots*, in this chapter we will create an NLP pipeline to tokenized a corpus, tag parts of speech, determine relationships between words with dependency parsing, and that conducts Named Entity Recognition. Use TF-IDF to vectorize the features in the document to create a simple FAQ type chatbot. Enhance this chatbot with NER and implementation of Rasa NLU to build a chatbot which understands the context (intent) to provide an accurate response.

Chapter 5, *Sequence-to-sequence Models for Building Chatbots*, in this chapter we will use Chapter 4, *Build a NLP Pipeline for Building Chatbots*, chatbots to build a more advanced chatbot combining learnings from earlier projects in a number of technologies to make a chatbot that is more contextually aware and robust. We avoided some of the limitations of CNNs in chatbots by building a **recurrent neural network (RNN)** model with **long short-term memory (LSTM)** units specifically designed to capture the signal represented in sequences of characters or words.

Chapter 6, *Generative Language Model for Content Creation*, in this chapter we implement a generative model to generate content using the **long short-term memory (LSTM)**, variational autoencoders, and **Generative Adversarial Networks (GANs)**. You will effectively implement models for both text and music which can generate song lyrics, scripts, and music for artists and various creative businesses.

Chapter 7, *Building Speech Recognition with DeepSpeech2*, in this chapter we build and train an **automatic speech recognition (ASR)** system to accept then convert an audio call to text that could then be used as the input into a text-based chatbot. Work with speech and spectrograms to build an end-to-end speech recognition system with a **Connectionist Temporal Classification (CTC)** loss function, batch normalization and SortaGrad for the RNNs. This chapter is the capstone in the Natural Language Processing section of the *Python Deep Learning Projects* Book.

Chapter 8, *Handwritten Digit Classification Using ConvNets*, in this chapter we will teach the fundamentals of **Convolutional Neural Networks (ConvNets)** in an examination of the convolution operation, pooling, and dropout regularization. These are the levers you'll adjust in tuning your models in your career. See the value of deploying a more complex and deeper model in the performance results compared to an earlier *Python Deep Learning Project* in Chapter 2, *Training a Neural Net for Prediction Using Regression*.

Chapter 9, *Object Detection Using OpenCV and TensorFlow*, in this chapter we will learn to master object detection and classification while using significantly more informationally complex data than previous projects, to produce impressive outcomes. Learn to use the deep learning package YOLOv2 and gain experience how this model architecture gets deeper and more complex and produces good results.

Chapter 10, *Building Facial Recognition Using FaceNet*, in this chapter we will be using FaceNet to build a model that looks at a picture and identifies all the possible faces in it, then performs face extraction to understand the quality of the face part of the image. Performing feature extraction on the face identified parts of the image provides the basis for comparison to another data point (a labeled image of the person's face). This *Python Deep Learning Project* demonstrates the exciting potential for this technology in applications from social media to security.

Chapter 11, *Automated Image Captioning*, in this chapter we will combine the current state-of-the-art techniques we've learned so far in *Python Deep Learning Projects* in both *computer vision* and *natural language processing* to form a complete image description approach. The clever idea that makes this possible is to replace the Encoder (RNN layer) in an Encoder-Decoder architecture with a deep **Convolutional Neural Network (CNN)** trained to classify objects in images. This model is capable of constructing computer-generated natural language descriptions of any image provided.

Chapter 12, *Pose Estimation on 3D Models Using ConvNets*, in this chapter we will successfully build a deep convolution neural network/VGG16 model in Keras on **Frames Labeled In Cinema (FLIC)** images. Get hands-on experience in preparing the images for modeling. Successfully implement transfer learning and test the modified VGG16 model performance on unseen data to determined success.

Chapter 13, *Image Translation Using GANs for Style Transfer*, in this chapter you will build a neural network that fills in the missing part of a handwritten digit. Focusing on the model creation -the generation/reconstruction of the missing sections of a digit with the help of neural inpainting with GANs, you will then reconstruct (generate back) the missing parts of the handwritten numbers so that the classifier can receive clear handwritten numbers for conversion into digits.

Chapter 14, *Develop an Autonomous Agent with Deep R Learning*, in this chapter we will build a deep reinforcement learning model to successfully play the game of CartPole-v1 from OpenAI Gym. Learn and demonstrate professional competency in the Gym toolkit, Q and SARSA learning, how to code the reinforcement learning model and define hyperparameters, build the training loop and test the model.

Chapter 15, *Summary and Next Steps in Your Deep Learning Career*, in this chapter you will find reviews key learnings, with a summary of deep learning projects intuition and looks to what could be next in your deep learning career.

To get the most out of this book

We approach deep learning projects from a very practical point of view. In thinking about how to share what we know, our experiences, the strategies that we've learned, and the tactics we employ, it was natural for us to format this book as if you (the reader) were a member of our Applied AI Engineering team here at The Intelligence Factory.

To get the most out of these projects, you should have at least an average working knowledge of Python and some familiarity with deep learning concepts. This *Python Deep Learning Projects* book is primarily a technical instruction book with content related to the intuition side of deep learning as required in order to learn the code that will produce functioning models. It is outside the scope of this book to dive deep into the calculus that is the foundation for these technologies.

Each chapter is like participating in the AI team's weekly standup. As you engage with the material, you will hopefully do the following:

- See the big picture
    - What's the real-world use case and the goal of the project?
    - What's the impact of success?
    - What's our strategy to achieve the goal?
- Get focused and into the code!
    - Identify specific tactics to achieve the project goal
    - Why is this the right approach?
    - Loop through executing the tactics
        - What are the inputs or establishing context?
        - Code examples
        - Outputs and success criteria
    - Questions and answers
        - What questions did we have?
        - What questions might you have?
- Expand back out to the big picture
    - Let's confirm that we have achieved our goal
    - What intuition can we gain from the experience?
    - How to generalize this successful experience in relation to new use cases?

Explaining Python deep learning is as easy as 1-2-3! But talking about deep learning isn't the same thing as doing, and that's what this book is about. What follows are a few thought provoking and exciting experiences. We will be using the most sophisticated Python libraries and advanced technologies available to empower you (our newest Applied AI Engineering team member) to contribute in your career using the projects we've created in this book. We're happy to have you in our weekly AI team standup.

Now let's learn a bunch, have some fun, and do great work in these Python deep learning projects!

Download the example code files

You can download the example code files for this book from your account at `www.packt.com`. If you purchased this book elsewhere, you can visit `www.packt.com/support` and register to have the files emailed directly to you.

You can download the code files by following these steps:

1. Log in or register at `www.packt.com`.
2. Select the **SUPPORT** tab.
3. Click on **Code Downloads & Errata**.
4. Enter the name of the book in the **Search** box and follow the onscreen instructions.

Once the file is downloaded, please make sure that you unzip or extract the folder using the latest version of:

- WinRAR/7-Zip for Windows
- Zipeg/iZip/UnRarX for Mac
- 7-Zip/PeaZip for Linux

The code bundle for the book is also hosted on GitHub at **`https://github.com/PacktPublishing/Python-Deep-Learning-Projects`**. In case there's an update to the code, it will be updated on the existing GitHub repository.

We also have other code bundles from our rich catalog of books and videos available at `https://github.com/PacktPublishing/`. Check them out!

Download the color images

We also provide a PDF file that has color images of the screenshots/diagrams used in this book. You can download it here: `http://www.packtpub.com/sites/default/files/downloads/9781788997096_ColorImages.pdf`.

Conventions used

There are a number of text conventions used throughout this book.

`CodeInText`: Indicates code words in text, database table names, folder names, filenames, file extensions, pathnames, dummy URLs, user input, and Twitter handles. Here is an example: "Once you have Docker installed, you should be able to use the `docker` command in Terminal."

A block of code is set as follows:

```
import sys
import dlib
from skimage import io
```

When we wish to draw your attention to a particular part of a code block, the relevant lines or items are set in bold:

```
# Create a HOG face detector using the built-in dlib class
face_detector = dlib.get_frontal_face_detector()
```

Any command-line input or output is written as follows:

```
curl https://get.docker.com | sh
```

Warnings or important notes appear like this.

Tips and tricks appear like this.

Get in touch

Feedback from our readers is always welcome.

General feedback: If you have questions about any aspect of this book, mention the book title in the subject of your message and email us at `customercare@packtpub.com`.

Errata: Although we have taken every care to ensure the accuracy of our content, mistakes do happen. If you have found a mistake in this book, we would be grateful if you would report this to us. Please visit www.packt.com/submit-errata, selecting your book, clicking on the Errata Submission Form link, and entering the details.

Piracy: If you come across any illegal copies of our works in any form on the internet, we would be grateful if you would provide us with the location address or website name. Please contact us at copyright@packt.com with a link to the material.

If you are interested in becoming an author: If there is a topic that you have expertise in, and you are interested in either writing or contributing to a book, please visit authors.packtpub.com.

Reviews

Please leave a review. Once you have read and used this book, why not leave a review on the site that you purchased it from? Potential readers can then see and use your unbiased opinion to make purchase decisions, we at Packt can understand what you think about our products, and our authors can see your feedback on their book. Thank you!

For more information about Packt, please visit packt.com.

1
Building Deep Learning Environments

Welcome to the applied AI deep-learning team, and to our first project—*Building a Common Deep Learning Environment*! We're excited about the projects we've assembled in this book. The foundation of a common working environment will help us work together and learn very cool and powerful **deep learning** (**DL**) technologies, such as **computer vision** (**CV**) and **natural language processing** (**NLP**), that you will be able to use in your professional career as a data scientist.

The following topics will be covered in this chapter:

- Components in building a common DL environment
- Setting up a local DL environment
- Setting up a DL environment in the cloud
- Using the cloud for deployment for DL applications
- Automating the setup process to reduce errors and get started quickly

Building a common DL environment

Our main goal to achieve by the end of this chapter is to standardize the toolsets to work together and achieve consistently accurate results.

In the process of building applications using DL algorithms that can also scale for production, it's very important to have the right kind of setup, whether local or on the cloud, to make things work end to end. So, in this chapter, we will learn how to set up a DL environment that we will be using to run all the experiments and finally take the AI models into production.

First, we will discuss the major components required to code, build, and deploy the DL models, then various ways to do this, and finally, look at a few code snippets that will help to automate the whole process.

The following is the list of required components that we need to build DL applications:

- Ubuntu 16.04 or greater
- Anaconda Package
- Python 2.x/3.x
- TensorFlow/Keras DL packages
- CUDA for GPU support
- Gunicorn for deployment at scale

Get focused and into the code!

We'll start by setting up your local DL environment. Much of the work that you'll do can be done on local machines. But with large datasets and complex model architectures, processing time slows down dramatically. This is why we are also setting up a DL environment in the cloud, because the processing time for these complex and repetitive calculations just becomes too long to be able to efficiently get things done otherwise.

We will work straight through the preceding list, and by the end (and with the help of a bit of automated script), you'll have everything set up!

DL environment setup locally

Throughout this book, we will be using Ubuntu OS to run all the experiments, because there is great community support for Linux and mostly any DL application can be set up easily on Linux. For any assistance on installation and setup related to Ubuntu, please refer to the tutorials at `https://tutorials.ubuntu.com/`. On top of that, this book will use the Anaconda package with Python 2.7+ to write our code, train, and test. Anaconda comes with a huge list of pre-installed Python packages, such as `numpy`, `pandas`, `sklearn`, and so on, which are commonly used in all kinds of data science projects.

Why do we need Anaconda? Can't we use Vanilla Python?
Anaconda is a generic bundle that contains iPython Notebook, editor, and lots of Python libraries preinstalled, which saves a lot of time on setting up everything. With Anaconda, we can quickly get started on solving the data science problem, instead of configuring the environment.
But, yes, you can use the default Python—it's totally the reader's choice, and we will learn at the end of this chapter how to configure `python env` using script.

Downloading and installing Anaconda

Anaconda is a very popular data science platform for people using Python to build machine learning and DL models, and deployable applications. The Anaconda marketing team put it best on their *What is Anaconda?* page, available at `https://www.anaconda.com/what-is-anaconda/`. To install Anaconda, perform the following steps:

1. Click **Anaconda** on the menu, then click **Downloads** to go to the download page at `https://www.anaconda.com/download/#linux`
2. Choose the download suitable for your platform (Linux, OS X, or Windows):
    1. Choose Python 3.6 version*
    2. Choose the Graphical Installer
3. Follow the instructions on the wizard, and in 10 to 20 minutes, your Anaconda environment (Python) setup will be ready

Once the installation process is completed, you can use following command to check the Python version on your Terminal:

```
python -V
```

You should see the following output:

```
Python 3.6 :: Anaconda,Inc.
```

If the command does not work, or returns an error, please check the documentation for help for your platform.

Installing DL libraries

Now, let's install the Python libraries used for DL, specifically, TensorFlow and Keras.

What is TensorFlow?
TensorFlow is a Python library developed and maintained by Google. You can implement many powerful machine learning and DL architectures in custom models and applications using TensorFlow. To find out more, visit https://www.tensorflow.org/.

Install the TensorFlow DL library (for all OS except Windows) by typing the following command:

```
conda install -c conda-forge tensorflow
```

Alternatively, you may choose to install using pip and a specific version of TensorFlow for your platform, using the following command:

```
pip install tensorflow==1.6
```

You can find the installation instructions for TensorFlow at https://www.tensorflow.org/get_started/os_setup#anaconda_installation.

Now we will install keras using the following command:

```
pip install keras
```

To validate the environment and the version of the packages, let's write the following script, which will print the version numbers of each library:

```
# Import the tensorflow library
import tensorflow
# Import the keras library
import keras

print('tensorflow: %s' % tensorflow.__version__)
print('keras: %s' % keras.__version__)
```

Save the script as dl_versions.py. Run the script by typing the following command:

```
python dl_version.py
```

You should see the following output:

```
tensorflow: 1.6.0
Using TensorFlow backend.
keras: 2.1.5
```

Voila! Now our Python development environment is ready for us to write some awesome DL applications in our local.

Setting up a DL environment in the cloud

All the steps we performed up to now remain the same for the cloud as well, but there are a few additional modules required to configure the cloud virtual machines to make your DL applications servable and scalable. So, before setting up your server, follow the instructions from the preceding section.

To deploy your DL applications in the cloud, you will need a server good enough to train your models and serve at the same time. With huge development in the sphere of DL, the need for cloud servers to practice and deploy projects has increased drastically, and so have the options on the market. The following is a list of some of the best options on offer:

- Paperspace (https://www.paperspace.com/)
- FloydHub (https://www.floydhub.com)
- Amazon Web Services (https://aws.amazon.com/)
- Google Cloud Platform (https://cloud.google.com/)
- DigitalOcean (https://cloud.digitalocean.com/)

All of these options have their own pro and cons, and the final choice totally depends on your use case and preferences, so feel free to explore more. In this book, we will build and deploy our models mostly on **Google Compute Engine** (**GCE**), which is a part of **Google Cloud Platform** (**GCP**). Follow the steps mentioned in this chapter to spin up a VM server and get started.

 Google has released an internal notebook platform, **Google Colab** (https://colab.research.google.com/), which is pre-installed with all the DL packages and other Python libraries. You can write all of your ML/DL applications on the Google Cloud, leveraging free GPUs for 10 hours.

Cloud platforms for deployment

The main idea behind this book is to empower you to build and deploy DL applications. In this section, we will discuss some critical components required to make your applications accessible to millions of users.

The best way to make your application accessible is to expose it as a web service, using REST or SOAP APIs. To do so, we have many Python web frameworks to choose from, such as web.py, Flask, Bottle, and many more. These frameworks allow us to easily build web services and deploy them.

Prerequisites

You should have a Google Cloud (https://cloud.google.com/) account. Google is promoting the usage of its platform right now, and is giving away $300 dollars of credit and 12 months as a free tier user.

Setting up the GCP

Follow these instructions to set up your GCP:

1. **Creating a new project**: Click on the three dots, as shown in the following screenshot, and then click on the + sign to create a new project:

2. **Spinning a VM instance**: Click on the three lines on the upper-left corner of the screen, select the **compute** option, and click on **Compute Engine**. Now choose **Create new instance**. Name the VM instance, and select your zone as **us-west2b**. Choose the **machine type** size.

   Choose your boot disk as **Ubuntu 16.04 LTS**. In firewall options, choose both the **http** and **https** option (it's important to make it accessible from the outer world). To opt for GPU options, you can click on **customize** button, and find the GPU options. You can choose between two NVIDIA GPUs. Check both **Allow HTTP traffic** and **Allow HTTPS traffic**.

   Now click on **Create**. Boom! your new VM is getting ready.

3. **Modify the firewall settings**: Now click on the **Firewall rules** setting under **Networking**. Under Protocols and Ports, we need to select the port that we will use to export our APIs. We have chosen `tcp:8080` as our port number. Now click on the **Save** button. This will assign a rule in the firewall of your VM to access the applications from the external world.

4. **Boot your VM**: Now start your VM instance. When you see the green tick, click on **SSH**—this will open a command window, and you are now inside the VM. You can also use `gcloud cli` to log in and access your VMs.

5. Then follow the same steps as we performed to set up the local environment, or read further to learn how to create an automation script that will perform all the setup automatically.

Now we need a web framework to write our DL applications as web services—again, there are lots of options, but to make it simple, we will be using a combination of `web.py` and Gunicorn.

 If you want to know which web framework to choose based on memory consumption, CPU utilization, and so on, you can have a look at the comprehensive list of benchmarks at `http://klen.github.io/py-frameworks-bench`.

Let's install them using following commands:

```
pip install web.py
pip install gunicorn
```

Now we are ready to deploy our DL solution as a web service, and scale it to production level.

Automating the setup process

Installing of Python packages and DL libraries can be a tedious process, requiring lots of time and repetitive effort. So, to ease the job, we will create a bash script that can be used to install everything using a single command.

The following is a list of components that will get installed and configured:

- Java 8
- Bazel for building
- Python and associated dependencies
- TensorFlow
- Keras
- Git
- Unzip
- Dependencies for all of the aforementioned services (see the script for exact details)

You can simply download the automation script to your server or locally, execute it, and you're done. Here are the steps to follow:

1. Save the script to your home directory, by cloning the code from the repository:

```
git clone
https://github.com/PacktPublishing/Python-Deep-Learning-Projects
```

2. Once you have the copy of the complete repository, move to the Chapter01 folder, which will contain a script file named setupDeepLearning.sh. This is the script that we will execute to start the setup process, but, before execution, we will have to make it executable using the chmod command:

```
cd Python-Deep-Learning-Projects/Chapter01/
chmod +x setupDeepLearning.sh
```

3. Once this is done, we are ready to execute it as follows:

```
./setupDeepLearning.sh
```

Follow any instructions that appear (basically, say yes to everything and accept Java's license). It should take about 10 to 15 minutes to install everything. Once it has finished, you will see the list of Python packages being installed, as shown in the following screenshot:

```
Ready to run TensorFlow!
***Listing modules***
absl-py (0.1.13)
astor (0.6.2)
backports.weakref (1.0.post1)
bleach (1.5.0)
boto (2.38.0)
chardet (2.3.0)
crcmod (1.7)
enum34 (1.1.6)
funcsigs (1.0.2)
futures (3.2.0)
gast (0.2.0)
google-compute-engine (2.7.5)
grpcio (1.10.1)
gunicorn (19.7.1)
html5lib (0.9999999)
Markdown (2.6.11)
mock (2.0.0)
numpy (1.14.2)
pandas (0.22.0)
pbr (4.0.1)
Pillow (5.1.0)
pip (8.1.1)
protobuf (3.5.2.post1)
python-dateutil (2.7.2)
pytz (2018.4)
requests (2.9.1)
scikit-learn (0.19.1)
scipy (1.0.1)
setuptools (20.7.0)
six (1.10.0)
sklearn (0.0)
tensorboard (1.7.0)
tensorflow (1.7.0)
termcolor (1.1.0)
urllib3 (1.13.1)
web.py (0.39)
Werkzeug (0.14.1)
wheel (0.29.0)
```

Listed packages with TensorFlow and other Python dependencies

There are a couple of other options, too, such as getting Docker images from TensorFlow and other DL packages, which can set up fully functional DL machines for large-scale and production-ready environments. You can find out more about Docker at `https://www.docker.com/what-docker`. Also, for a quick-start guide, follow the instructions on this repository for an all-in-one Docker image for DL at `https://github.com/floydhub/dl-docker`.

Summary

In this chapter, we worked to get the team set up in a common environment with a standardized toolset. We are looking to deploy our project applications by utilizing Gunicorn and CUDA. Those projects will rely on highly advanced and effective DL libraries, such as TensorFlow and Keras running in Python 2.x/3.x. We'll write our code using the resources in the Anaconda package, and all of this will be running on Ubuntu 16.04 or greater.

Now we are all set to perform experiments and deploy our DL models in production!

2
Training NN for Prediction Using Regression

Welcome to our first proper project in Python deep learning! What we'll be doing today is building a classifier to solve the problem of identifying specific handwriting samples from a dataset of images. We've been asked (in this hypothetical use case) to do this by a restaurant chain that has the need to accurately classify handwritten numbers into digits. What they have their customers do is write their phone numbers in a simple iPad application. At the time when they can be seated, the guest will get a text prompting them to come and see the restaurant's host. We need to accurately classify the handwritten numbers, so that the output from the app will be accurately predicted labels for the digits of a phone number. This can then be sent to their (hypothetical) auto dialer service for text messages, and the notice gets to the right hungry customer!

 Define success: A good practice is to define the criteria for success at the beginning of a project. What metric should we use for this project? Let's use a global accuracy test as a percentage to measure our performance in this project.

The data science approach to the problem of classification can be configured in a number of ways. In fact, later in this book, we'll look at how to increase accuracy in image classification with convolutional neural networks.

Transfer learning: This means pretraining a deep learning model on a different (but quite similar) dataset to speed up the rate of learning and accuracy on another (often smaller) dataset. In this project and our hypothetical use case, the pretraining of our deep learning **multi-layer perceptron** (**MLP**) on the MNIST dataset would enable the deployment of a production system of handwriting classification, without having a huge period of time where we were collecting data samples in a live but non-functional system. Python deep learning projects are cool!

Let's start with the baseline deep neural network model architecture. We will get our intuition and skills firmly established, and this will prepare us for learning more complex architectures to solve a wider variety of problems as we go progress through the projects in this book.

What we'll learn in this chapter includes the following:

- What is an MLP?
- Exploring a common open source handwriting dataset—the MNIST dataset
- Building our intuition and preparations for model architecture
- Coding the model and defining hyperparameters
- Building the training loop
- Testing the model

Building a regression model for prediction using an MLP deep neural network

In any real job working in an AI team, one of the primary goals will be to build regression models that can make predictions in non-linear datasets. Because of the complexity of the real world and the data that you'll be working with, simple linear regression models won't provide the predictive power you're seeking. That is why, in this chapter, we will discuss how to build world-class prediction models using MLP. More information can be found at http://www.deeplearningbook.org/contents/mlp.html, and an example of the MLP architecture is shown here:

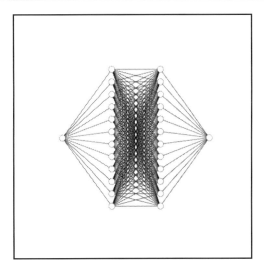

An MLP with two hidden layers

We will implement a neural network with a simple architecture of only two layers, using TensorFlow, that will perform regression on the MNIST dataset (`http://yann.lecun.com/exdb/mnist/`) that we will provide. We can (and will) go deeper in architecture in later projects! We assume that you are already familiar with backpropagation (if not, please read article on backpropagation by Michal Nielsen at `http://neuralnetworksanddeeplearning.com/chap2.html`). We'll not spend much time on how TensorFlow works, but you can refer to the official tutorial, available at `https://www.tensorflow.org/versions/r0.10/get_started/basic_usage.html`, if you are interested in looking under the hood of that technology.

Exploring the MNIST dataset

Before we jump into building our awesome neural network, let's first have a look at the famous MNIST dataset. So let's visualize the MNIST dataset in this section.

Words of wisdom: You must know your data and how it has been preprocessed, in order to know why the models you build perform the way they do. This section reviews the significant work that has been done in preparation on the dataset, to make our current job of building the MLP easier. Always remember: data science begins with DATA!

Let's start therefore by downloading the data, using the following commands:

```
from tensorflow.examples.tutorials.mnist import input_data
mnist = input_data.read_data_sets("/tmp/data/", one_hot=True)
```

If we examine the `mnist` variable content, we can see that it is structured in a specific format, with three major components—**TRAIN**, **TEST**, and **VALIDATION**. Each set has handwritten images and their respective labels. The images are stored in a flattened way as a single vector:

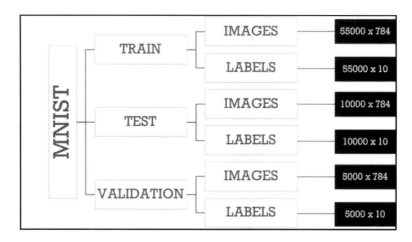

The format of the MNIST dataset

Let's extract one image from the dataset and plot it. Since the stored shape of a single image matrix is `[1,784]`, we need to reshape these vectors into `[28,28]` to visualize the original image:

```
sample_image = mnist.train.images[0].reshape([28,28])
```

Once we have the image matrix, we will use `matplotlib` to plot it, as follows:

```
import matplotlib.pyplot as plt
plt.gray()
plt.imshow(sample_image)
```

The output will be as follows:

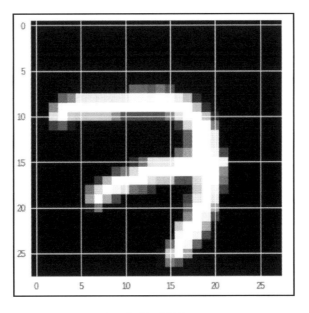

A sample of the MNIST dataset

In the same vein as this image, there are a total of 55,000 similar images of handwritten digits [0-9]. The labels in the MNIST dataset are the true value of the digits present in the image. Our objective, then, is to train a model with this set of images and labels, so that it can predict the labels of any image provided from the MNIST dataset.

 Be a deep learning explorer: If you are interested in playing around with the dataset, you can try the Colab Notebook, available at `https://drive.google.com/file/d/1-GVlob72EyiJyQpk8EL2fg2mvzaEayJ_/view?usp=sharing.`

Intuition and preparation

Let's build our intuition around this project. What we need to do is build a deep learning technology that accurately assigns class labels to an input image. We're using a deep neural network, known as an MLP, to do this. The core of this technology is the mathematics of regression. The specific calculus proofs are outside the scope of this book, but in this section, we provide a foundational basis for your understanding. We also outline the structure of the project, so that it's easy to understand the primary steps needed to create our desired results.

Defining regression

Our first task is to define the model that will perform regression on the provided MNIST dataset. So, we will create a TensorFlow model with two hidden layers as part of a fully connected neural network. You may also hear it referred to as MLP.

The model will perform the operation that will fit the following equation, where y is the label, x is the image, W is the weight that the model will learn, and b is the bias, which will also be learned by the model, following is the regression equation for the model:

$$y = nonlinearity(xW + b)$$

The regression equation for the model

Supervised learning: When you have data and accurate labels for the training set (that is, you know the answer), you are in a supervised deep learning paradigm. Model training is a mathematical process by which the features of the data are learned and associated with the proper labels, so that when a new data point (test data) is presented, the accurate output class label can be produced. In other words, when you present a new data point and do not have the label (that is, you don't know the answer), your model can produce it for you with a highly reliable class prediction.

Each iteration will try to generalize the values of weight and bias and reduce the error rate. Also, keep in mind that we need to ensure that the model is not overfitting, which may lead to wrong predictions for the unseen dataset. We'll show you how to code this and visualize the progress to aid in your intuition of model performance.

Defining the project structure

Let's structure our project as shown in the following pattern:

- hy_param.py: All the hyperparameters and other configurations are defined here
- model.py: The definition and architecture of the model are defined here
- train.py: The code to train the model is written here
- inference.py: The code to execute the trained model and make predictions is defined here
- /runs: This folder will store all of the checkpoints that get created during the training process

You can clone the code from the repository—the code for this can be found in the `Chapter02` folder, available at `https://github.com/PacktPublishing/Python-Deep-Learning-Projects/`.

Let's code the implementation!

To code the implementation, we'll start by defining the hyperparameters, then we will define the model, followed by building and executing the training loop. We conclude by checking to see if our model is overfitting and build an inference code that loads the latest checkpoints and then makes predictions on the basis of learned parameters.

Defining hyperparameters

We will define all of the required hyperparameters in the `hy_param.py` file and then import it as a module in our other codes. This makes it easy in deployment, and is good practice to make your code as modular as possible. Let's look into the hyperparameter configurations that we have in our `hy_param.py` file:

```python
#!/usr/bin/env python2

# Hyperparameters and all other kind of params

# Parameters
learning_rate = 0.01
num_steps = 100
batch_size = 128
display_step = 1


# Network Parameters
n_hidden_1 = 300 # 1st layer number of neurons
n_hidden_2 = 300 # 2nd layer number of neurons
num_input = 784 # MNIST data input (img shape: 28*28)
num_classes = 10 # MNIST total classes (0-9 digits)

#Training Parameters
checkpoint_every = 100
checkpoint_dir = './runs/'
```

We will be using these values throughout our code, and they're totally configurable.

As a Python deep learning projects exploration opportunity, we invite you, our project teammate and reader, to try different values of learning rate and numbers of hidden layers to experiment and build better models!

Since the flat vectors of images shown previously are of a size of [1 x 786], the `num_input=784` is fixed in this case. In addition, the class count in the MNIST dataset is `10`. We have digits from 0-9, so obviously we have `num_classes=10`.

Model definition

First, we will load the Python modules; in this case, the TensorFlow package and the hyperparameters that we defined previously:

```
import tensorflow as tf
import hy_param
```

Then, we define the placeholders that we will be using to input data into the model. `tf.placeholder` allows us to feed input data to the computational graph. We can define constraints with the shape of the placeholder to only accept a tensor of a certain shape. Note that it is common to provide `None` for the first dimension, which allows us to the size of the batch at runtime.

 Master your craft: Batch size can often have a big impact on the performance of deep learning models. Explore different batch sizes in this project. What changes as a result? What's your intuition? Batch size is another tool in your data science toolkit!

We have also assigned names to the placeholders, so that we can use them later on while building our inference code:

```
X = tf.placeholder("float", [None, hy_param.num_input],name="input_x")
Y = tf.placeholder("float", [None, hy_param.num_classes],name="input_y")
```

Now we will define variables that will hold values for weights and bias. `tf.Variable` allows us to store and update tensors in our graph. To initialize our variables with random values from a normal distribution, we will use `tf.random_normal()` (more details can be found at `https://www.tensorflow.org/api_docs/python/tf/random_normal`). The important thing to notice here is the mapping variable size between layers:

```
weights = {
  'h1': tf.Variable(tf.random_normal([hy_param.num_input,
hy_param.n_hidden_1])),
```

```
 'h2': tf.Variable(tf.random_normal([hy_param.n_hidden_1,
hy_param.n_hidden_2])),
 'out': tf.Variable(tf.random_normal([hy_param.n_hidden_2,
hy_param.num_classes]))
 }
 biases = {
 'b1': tf.Variable(tf.random_normal([hy_param.n_hidden_1])),
 'b2': tf.Variable(tf.random_normal([hy_param.n_hidden_2])),
 'out': tf.Variable(tf.random_normal([hy_param.num_classes]))
 }
```

Now, let's set up the operation that we defined in the equation earlier in this chapter. This is the logistic regression operation:

```
layer_1 = tf.add(tf.matmul(X, weights['h1']), biases['b1'])
layer_2 = tf.add(tf.matmul(layer_1, weights['h2']), biases['b2'])
logits = tf.matmul(layer_2, weights['out']) + biases['out']
```

The logistic values are converted into the probabilistic values using `tf.nn.softmax()`. The softmax activation squashes the output values of each unit to a value between zero and one:

```
prediction = tf.nn.softmax(logits, name='prediction')
```

Next, let's use `tf.nn.softmax_cross_entropy_with_logits` to define our cost function. We will optimize our performance using the Adam Optimizer. Finally, we can use the built-in `minimize()` function to calculate the **stochastic gradient descent (SGD)** update rule for each parameter in our network:

```
loss_op =
tf.reduce_mean(tf.nn.softmax_cross_entropy_with_logits(logits=logits,
labels=Y))
optimizer = tf.train.AdamOptimizer(learning_rate=hy_param.learning_rate)
train_op = optimizer.minimize(loss_op)
```

Next, we make our prediction. These functions are needed to calculate and capture the accuracy values in a batch:

```
correct_pred = tf.equal(tf.argmax(prediction, 1), tf.argmax(Y, 1))
accuracy = tf.reduce_mean(tf.cast(correct_pred, tf.float32)
,name='accuracy')
```

The complete code is as follows:

```
#!/usr/bin/env python2
# -*- coding: utf-8 -*-

import tensorflow as tf
```

```
import hy_param


## Defining Placeholders which will be used as inputs for the model
X = tf.placeholder("float", [None, hy_param.num_input],name="input_x")
Y = tf.placeholder("float", [None, hy_param.num_classes],name="input_y")


# Defining variables for weights & bias
weights = {
    'h1': tf.Variable(tf.random_normal([hy_param.num_input,
hy_param.n_hidden_1])),
    'h2': tf.Variable(tf.random_normal([hy_param.n_hidden_1,
hy_param.n_hidden_2])),
    'out': tf.Variable(tf.random_normal([hy_param.n_hidden_2,
hy_param.num_classes]))
}
biases = {
    'b1': tf.Variable(tf.random_normal([hy_param.n_hidden_1])),
    'b2': tf.Variable(tf.random_normal([hy_param.n_hidden_2])),
    'out': tf.Variable(tf.random_normal([hy_param.num_classes]))
}


# Hidden fully connected layer 1 with 300 neurons
layer_1 = tf.add(tf.matmul(X, weights['h1']), biases['b1'])
# Hidden fully connected layer 2 with 300 neurons
layer_2 = tf.add(tf.matmul(layer_1, weights['h2']), biases['b2'])
# Output fully connected layer with a neuron for each class
logits = tf.matmul(layer_2, weights['out']) + biases['out']

# Performing softmax operation
prediction = tf.nn.softmax(logits, name='prediction')

# Define loss and optimizer
loss_op = tf.reduce_mean(tf.nn.softmax_cross_entropy_with_logits(
    logits=logits, labels=Y))
optimizer = tf.train.AdamOptimizer(learning_rate=hy_param.learning_rate)
train_op = optimizer.minimize(loss_op)

# Evaluate model
correct_pred = tf.equal(tf.argmax(prediction, 1), tf.argmax(Y, 1))
accuracy = tf.reduce_mean(tf.cast(correct_pred, tf.float32)
,name='accuracy')
```

Hurray! The heavy lifting part of the code is done. We save the model code in the model.py file. So, up until now, we've defined the simple two-hidden-layer model architecture, with 300 neurons in each layer, which will try to learn the best weight distribution using the Adam Optimizer and predict the probability of ten classes. These layers are shown in the following diagram:

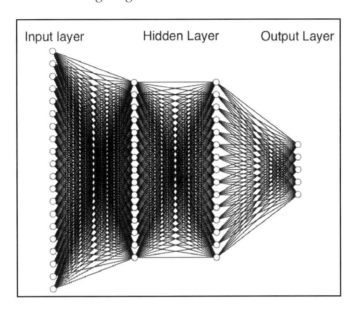

An illustration of the model that we created

Building the training loop

The next step is to utilize the model for training, and record the learned model parameters, which we will accomplish in train.py.

Let's start by importing the dependencies:

```
import tensorflow as tf
import hy_param

# MLP Model which we defined in previous step
import model
```

Then, we define the variables that we require to be fed into our MLP:

```
# This will feed the raw images
X = model.X
# This will feed the labels associated with the image
Y = model.Y
```

Let's create the folder to which we will save our checkpoints. Checkpoints are basically the intermediate steps that capture the values of W and b in the process of learning. Then, we will use the tf.train.Saver() function (more details on this function can be found at https://www.tensorflow.org/api_docs/python/tf/train/Saver) to save and restore checkpoints:

```
checkpoint_dir = os.path.abspath(os.path.join(hy_param.checkpoint_dir,
"checkpoints"))
checkpoint_prefix = os.path.join(checkpoint_dir, "model")
if not os.path.exists(checkpoint_dir):
    os.makedirs(checkpoint_dir)

# We only keep the last 2 checkpoints to manage storage
saver = tf.train.Saver(tf.global_variables(), max_to_keep=2)
```

In order to begin training, we need to create a new session in TensorFlow. In this session, we'll initialize the graph variables and feed the model operations the valid data:

```
# Initialize the variables
init = tf.global_variables_initializer()

# Start training
with tf.Session() as sess:

    # Run the initializer
    sess.run(init)

    for step in range(1, hy_param.num_steps+1):
        # Extracting
        batch_x, batch_y = mnist.train.next_batch(hy_param.batch_size)
        # Run optimization op (backprop)
        sess.run(model.train_op, feed_dict={X: batch_x, Y: batch_y})
        if step % hy_param.display_step == 0 or step == 1:
            # Calculate batch loss and accuracy
            loss, acc = sess.run([model.loss_op, model.accuracy],
feed_dict={X: batch_x,
                                                                Y:
batch_y})
            print("Step " + str(step) + ", Minibatch Loss= " + \
                "{:.4f}".format(loss) + ", Training Accuracy= " + \
```

```
                    "{:.3f}".format(acc))
        if step % hy_param.checkpoint_every == 0:
            path = saver.save(
                    sess, checkpoint_prefix, global_step=step)
            print("Saved model checkpoint to {}\n".format(path))

    print("Optimization Finished!")
```

We will extract batches of 128 training image-label pairs from the MNIST dataset and feed them into the model. After subsequent steps or epochs, we will store the checkpoints using the `saver` operation:

```python
#!/usr/bin/env python2
# -*- coding: utf-8 -*-


from __future__ import print_function

# Import MNIST data
import os
from tensorflow.examples.tutorials.mnist import input_data
mnist = input_data.read_data_sets("/tmp/data/", one_hot=True)

import tensorflow as tf
import model
import hy_param


## tf Graph input
X = model.X
Y = model.Y



checkpoint_dir = os.path.abspath(os.path.join(hy_param.checkpoint_dir,
"checkpoints"))
checkpoint_prefix = os.path.join(checkpoint_dir, "model")
if not os.path.exists(checkpoint_dir):
    os.makedirs(checkpoint_dir)
saver = tf.train.Saver(tf.global_variables(), max_to_keep=2)
#loss = tf.Variable(0.0)
# Initialize the variables
init = tf.global_variables_initializer()
all_loss = []
# Start training
with tf.Session() as sess:
    writer_1 = tf.summary.FileWriter("./runs/summary/",sess.graph)
    sum_var = tf.summary.scalar("loss", model.accuracy)
```

```
    write_op = tf.summary.merge_all()

    # Run the initializer
    sess.run(init)

    for step in range(1, hy_param.num_steps+1):
        # Extracting
        batch_x, batch_y = mnist.train.next_batch(hy_param.batch_size)
        # Run optimization op (backprop)
        sess.run(model.train_op, feed_dict={X: batch_x, Y: batch_y})
        if step % hy_param.display_step == 0 or step == 1:
            # Calculate batch loss and accuracy
            loss, acc, summary = sess.run([model.loss_op, model.accuracy,
write_op], feed_dict={X: batch_x,
                                                                    Y:
batch_y})
            all_loss.append(loss)
            writer_1.add_summary(summary, step)
            print("Step " + str(step) + ", Minibatch Loss= " + \
                    "{:.4f}".format(loss) + ", Training Accuracy= " + \
                    "{:.3f}".format(acc))
        if step % hy_param.checkpoint_every == 0:
            path = saver.save(
                        sess, checkpoint_prefix, global_step=step)
# print("Saved model checkpoint to {}\n".format(path))

    print("Optimization Finished!")

    # Calculate accuracy for MNIST test images
    print("Testing Accuracy:", \
        sess.run(model.accuracy, feed_dict={X: mnist.test.images,
                                            Y: mnist.test.labels}))
```

Once we have executed the `train.py` file, you will see the progress on your console, as shown in the preceding screenshot. This depicts the loss being reduced after every step, along with accuracy increasing over each step:

```
Step 68, Minibatch Loss= 306.3990, Training Accuracy= 0.852
Step 69, Minibatch Loss= 300.6138, Training Accuracy= 0.844
Step 70, Minibatch Loss= 179.9460, Training Accuracy= 0.867
Step 71, Minibatch Loss= 228.6768, Training Accuracy= 0.844
Step 72, Minibatch Loss= 138.8158, Training Accuracy= 0.938
Step 73, Minibatch Loss= 175.2319, Training Accuracy= 0.906
Step 74, Minibatch Loss= 231.0065, Training Accuracy= 0.867
Step 75, Minibatch Loss= 229.3589, Training Accuracy= 0.883
Step 76, Minibatch Loss= 273.3831, Training Accuracy= 0.891
Step 77, Minibatch Loss= 205.3752, Training Accuracy= 0.891
Step 78, Minibatch Loss= 203.4548, Training Accuracy= 0.844
Step 79, Minibatch Loss= 195.2928, Training Accuracy= 0.883
Step 80, Minibatch Loss= 213.9747, Training Accuracy= 0.859
Step 81, Minibatch Loss= 284.2013, Training Accuracy= 0.836
Step 82, Minibatch Loss= 205.6791, Training Accuracy= 0.859
Step 83, Minibatch Loss= 221.5348, Training Accuracy= 0.875
Step 84, Minibatch Loss= 106.9436, Training Accuracy= 0.875
Step 85, Minibatch Loss= 209.3381, Training Accuracy= 0.867
Step 86, Minibatch Loss= 243.1940, Training Accuracy= 0.867
Step 87, Minibatch Loss= 161.6641, Training Accuracy= 0.859
Step 88, Minibatch Loss= 224.7084, Training Accuracy= 0.844
Step 89, Minibatch Loss= 211.0281, Training Accuracy= 0.875
Step 90, Minibatch Loss= 146.3944, Training Accuracy= 0.883
Step 91, Minibatch Loss= 94.1382, Training Accuracy= 0.898
Step 92, Minibatch Loss= 134.1990, Training Accuracy= 0.938
Step 93, Minibatch Loss= 232.2369, Training Accuracy= 0.867
Step 94, Minibatch Loss= 253.5543, Training Accuracy= 0.898
Step 95, Minibatch Loss= 260.2030, Training Accuracy= 0.859
Step 96, Minibatch Loss= 155.0190, Training Accuracy= 0.914
Step 97, Minibatch Loss= 239.0048, Training Accuracy= 0.828
Step 98, Minibatch Loss= 322.0966, Training Accuracy= 0.836
Step 99, Minibatch Loss= 167.7812, Training Accuracy= 0.883
Step 100, Minibatch Loss= 80.1014, Training Accuracy= 0.914
Optimization Finished!
Testing Accuracy: 0.8742
```

The training epoch's output with minibatch loss and training accuracy parameters

Also, you can see in the plot of minibatch loss, shown in the following diagram, that it approaches toward the minima with each step:

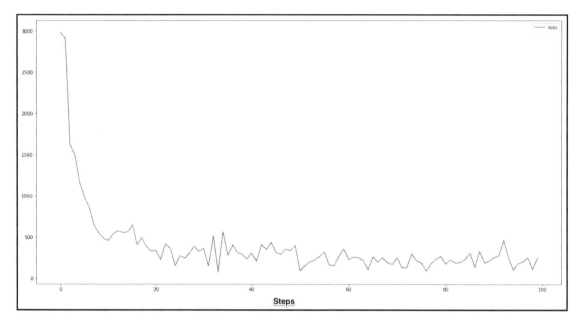

Plotting the loss values computed at each step

It is very important to visualize how your model is performing, so that you can analyze and prevent it from underfitting or overfitting. Overfitting is a very common scenario when you are dealing with the deeper models. Let's spend some time getting to understand them in detail and learning a few tricks to overcome them.

Overfitting and underfitting

With great power comes great responsibility and with deeper models come deeper problems. A fundamental challenge with deep learning is striking the right balance between generalization and optimization. In the deep learning process, we are tuning hyperparameters and often continuously configuring and tweaking the model to produce the best results, based on the data we have for training. This is **optimization**. The key question is, how well does our model generalize in performing predictions on unseen data?

As professional deep learning engineers, our goal is to build models with good real-world generalization. However, generalization is subjective to the model architecture and the training dataset. We work to guide our model for maximum utility by reducing the likelihood that it learns irrelevant patterns or simple similar patterns found in the data used for training. If this is not done, it can affect the generalization process. A good solution is to provide the model with more information that is likely to have a better (that is, more complete and often complex) signal of what you're trying to actually model, by getting more data to train on and to work to optimize the model architecture. Here are few quick tricks that can improve your model by preventing overfitting:

- Getting more data for training
- Reducing network capacity by altering the number of layers or nodes
- Employing L2 (and trying L1) weight regularization techniques
- Adding dropout layers or polling layers in the model

 L1 regularization, where the cost added is proportional to the absolute value of the weights coefficients, is also known as *L1 norm*. L2 regularization, where the cost added is proportional to the square of the value of the weight's coefficients, is also known as *L2 norm* or *weight decay.*

When the model gets trained completely, its output, as checkpoints, will get dumped into the /runs folder, which will contain the binary dump of checkpoints, as shown in the following screenshot:

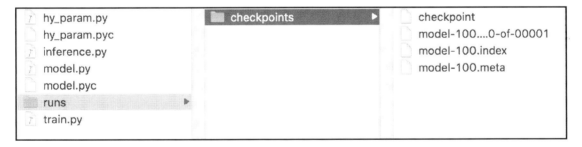

The checkpoint folder after the training process is completed

Building inference

Now, we will create an inference code that loads the latest checkpoints and then makes predictions on the basis of learned parameters. For that, we need to create a `saver` operation that will pick the latest checkpoints and load the metadata. Metadata contains the information regarding the variables and the nodes that we created in the graph:

```
# Pointing the model checkpoint
checkpoint_file =
tf.train.latest_checkpoint(os.path.join(hy_param.checkpoint_dir,
'checkpoints'))
saver = tf.train.import_meta_graph("{}.meta".format(checkpoint_file))
```

We know the importance of this, because we want to load similar variables and operations back from the stored checkpoint. We load them into memory using `tf.get_default_graph().get_operation_by_name()`, by passing the operation name in the parameter that we defined in the model:

```
# Load the input variable from the model
input_x =
tf.get_default_graph().get_operation_by_name("input_x").outputs[0]

# Load the Prediction operation
prediction =
tf.get_default_graph().get_operation_by_name("prediction").outputs[0]
```

Now, we need to initialize the session and pass data for a test image to the operation that makes the prediction, as follows:

```
# Load the test data
test_data = np.array([mnist.test.images[0]])

with tf.Session() as sess:
    # Restore the model from the checkpoint
    saver.restore(sess, checkpoint_file)
    # Execute the model to make predictions
    data = sess.run(prediction, feed_dict={input_x: test_data })
    print("Predicted digit: ", data.argmax() )
```

Following is the full code:

```
#!/usr/bin/env python2
# -*- coding: utf-8 -*-


from __future__ import print_function
```

```python
import os
import numpy as np
import tensorflow as tf
import matplotlib.pyplot as plt

import hy_param

from tensorflow.examples.tutorials.mnist import input_data
mnist = input_data.read_data_sets("/tmp/data/", one_hot=True)

# Pointing the model checkpoint
checkpoint_file =
tf.train.latest_checkpoint(os.path.join(hy_param.checkpoint_dir,
'checkpoints'))
saver = tf.train.import_meta_graph("{}.meta".format(checkpoint_file))

# Loading test data
test_data = np.array([mnist.test.images[6]])

# Loading input variable from the model
input_x =
tf.get_default_graph().get_operation_by_name("input_x").outputs[0]

# Loading Prediction operation
prediction =
tf.get_default_graph().get_operation_by_name("prediction").outputs[0]


with tf.Session() as sess:
    # Restoring the model from the checkpoint
    saver.restore(sess, checkpoint_file)
    # Executing the model to make predictions
    data = sess.run(prediction, feed_dict={input_x: test_data })
    print("Predicted digit: ", data.argmax() )


# Display the feed image
print ("Input image:")
plt.gray()
plt.imshow(test_data.reshape([28,28]))
```

And with that, we are done with our first project that predicts the digits provided in a handwritten image! Here are some of the results that the model predicted when provided with the test image from the MNIST dataset:

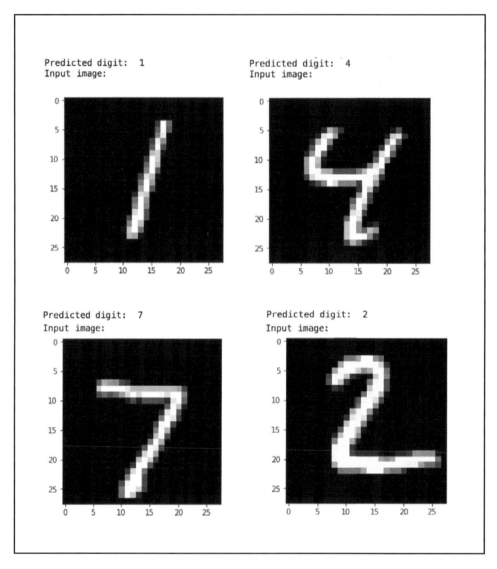

The output of the model. depicting the prediction of the model and the input image

Concluding the project

Today's project was to build a classifier to solve the problem of identifying specific handwriting samples from a dataset of images. Our hypothetical use case was to apply deep learning to enable customers of a restaurant chain to write their phone numbers in a simple iPad application, so that they could get a text notification that their party was ready to be seated. Our specific task was to build the intelligence that would drive this application.

 Revisit our success criteria: How did we do? Did we succeed? What was the impact of our success? Just as we defined success at the beginning of the project, these are the key questions that we need to ask as deep learning data scientists, as we look to wrap up a project.

Our MLP model accuracy hit 87.42%! Not bad, given the depth of the model and the hyperparameters that we chose at the beginning. See if you can tweak the model to get an even higher test set accuracy.

What are the implications of this accuracy? Let's calculate the incidence of an error occurring that would result in a customer service issue (that is, the customer not getting the text that their table is ready, and getting upset due to an excessively long wait time at the restaurant).

Each customer's phone number is ten digits long. Let's say that our hypothetical restaurant has an average of 30 tables at each location, and those tables turn over two times per night during the rush hour, when the system is likely to be used, and finally, the restaurant chain has 35 locations. This means that each day of operation, there are approximately 21,000 handwritten numbers captured (30 tables x 2 turns/day x 35 locations x 10 digit phone number).

Obviously, all digits must be correctly classified for the text to get to the waiting restaurant patron. So, any single digit misclassification causes a failure. A model accuracy of 87.42% would improperly classify 2,642 digits per day in our example. The worst case for the hypothetical scenario would be if there occurred only one improperly classified digit in each phone number. Since there are only 2,100 patrons and corresponding phone numbers, this would mean that every phone number had an error in classification (a 100% failure rate), and not a single customer would get their text notification that their party could be seated! The best case, in this scenario, would be if all 10 digits were misclassified in each phone number, which would result in 263 wrong phone numbers out of 2,100 (a 12.5% failure rate). This is still not a level of performance that the restaurant chain would be likely be happy with.

Words of wisdom: Model performance may not equal system or app performance. Many factors contribute to a system being robust or fragile in the real world. Model performance is a key factor, but other items with individual fault tolerances definitely play a part. Know how your deep learning models integrate into the larger project so that you can set proper expectations!

Summary

In the project in this chapter, we successfully built an MLP to produce a regression classification prediction, based on handwritten digits. We gained experience with the MNIST dataset and a deep neural network model architecture, which gave us the added opportunity to define some key hyperparameters. Finally, we looked at the model performance in testing and determined whether we succeeded in achieving our goals.

3
Word Representation Using word2vec

Our *Python Deep Learning Projects* team is doing good work, and our (hypothetical) business use case has expanded! In the last project, we were asked to accurately classify handwritten digits to generate a phone number so that an *available table notification* text could be sent out to patrons of a restaurant chain. What we learned after the project was that the text that the restaurant sent out had a message that was friendly and well received. The restaurant was actually getting texts back!

The notification text was: *We're excited that you're here and your table is ready! See the greeter, and we'll seat you now.*

Response texts were varied and usually short, but the responses were noticed by the greeter and the restaurant management, who started thinking that maybe they could use this simple system to get feedback on the dining experience. This feedback would provide useful business intelligence on how the food tasted, how the service was delivered, and the overall quality of the experience.

 Define success: The goal of this project is to build a computational linguistic model, using word2vec, that can take a text response (as identified in our hypothetical use case for this chapter) and output a sentiment classification that is meaningful.

In this chapter, we introduce the foundational knowledge of **deep learning** (DL) for computational linguistics.

We present the role of the dense vector representation of words in various computational linguistic tasks and how to construct them from an unlabeled monolingual corpus.

We'll then present the role of language models in various computational linguistic tasks, such as text classification, and how to construct them from an unlabeled monolingual corpus using **convolutional neural networks** (**CNNs**). We'll also explore CNN architecture for language modeling.

While working with machine learning/DL, the structure of data is very important. Unfortunately, raw data is often very unclean and unstructured, especially in the practice of **natural language processing** (**NLP**). When working with textual data, we cannot feed strings as input in most DL algorithms; hence, **word embedding** methods come to the rescue. Word embedding is used to transform the textual data into dense vector (tensors) form, which we can feed to the learning algorithm.

There are several ways in which we can perform word embeddings, such as one-hot encoding, GloVe, word2vec, and many more, and each of them have their own pros and cons. Our current favorite is word2vec because it has been proven to be the most efficient approach when it comes to learning high quality features.

If you have ever worked on a use case where the input data is in text form, then you know that it's a really messy affair because you have to teach a computer about the irregularities of human language. Language has lots of ambiguities, and you have to teach sort of like hierarchical and the sparse nature of grammar. So these are the kinds of problems that word vectors solve by removing the ambiguities and making all different kinds of concepts similar.

In this chapter, we will learn how to build word2vec models and analyze what characteristics we can learn about the provided corpus. Also, we will learn how to build a language model that utilizes a CNN with trained word vectors.

Learning word vectors

To implement a fully functional word embedding model, we will perform the following steps:

1. Loading all the dependencies
2. Preparing the text corpus

3. Defining the model
4. Training the model
5. Analyzing the model
6. Plotting the word cluster using the **t-Distributed Stochastic Neighbor Embedding (t-SNE)** algorithm
7. Plotting the model on TensorBoard

Let's make some world-class word embedding models!

The code for this section is available at `https://github.com/PacktPublishing/Python-Deep-Learning-Projects/blob/master/Chapter03/create_word2vec.ipynb`.

Loading all the dependencies

In this chapter, we will be using the `gensim` module (`https://github.com/RaRe-Technologies/gensim`) to train our `word2vec` model. Gensim provides large-scale multi-core processing support to many popular algorithms, including **Latent Dirichlet Allocation (LDA)**, **Hierarchical Dirichlet Process (HDP)**, and word2vec. There are other approaches that we could take, such as the use of TensorFlow (`https://github.com/tensorflow/models/blob/master/tutorials/embedding/word2vec_optimized.py`) to define our own computation graph and build the model—this is something that we will look into later on.

Know the code! Python dependencies are quite manageable. You can learn more at `https://packaging.python.org/tutorials/managing-dependencies/`.

This tutorial walks you through the use of Pipenv to manage dependencies for an application. It will show you how to install and use the necessary tools and make strong recommendations on best practices. Keep in mind that Python is used for a great many different purposes, and precisely how you want to manage your dependencies may change based on how you decide to publish your software. The guidance presented here is most directly applicable to the development and deployment of network services (including web applications), but is also very well suited to managing development and testing environments for any kind of project.

We will be using the `seaborn` package to plot the word clusters, `sklearn` to implement the t-SNE algorithm, and `tensorflow` for building TensorBoard plots:

```
import multiprocessing
import os , json , requests
import re
import nltk
import gensim.models.word2vec as w2v
import sklearn.manifold
import pandas as pd
import seaborn as sns
import tensorflow as tf
from tensorflow.contrib.tensorboard.plugins import projector
```

Preparing the text corpus

We will use the previously trained **Natural Language Toolkit** (**NLTK**) tokenizer (`http://www.nltk.org/index.html`) and stop words for the English language to clean our corpus and extract relevant unique words from the corpus. We will also create a small module to clean the provided collection, with a list of unprocessed sentences, to output the list of words:

```
"""**Download NLTK tokenizer models (only the first time)**"""

nltk.download("punkt")
nltk.download("stopwords")

def sentence_to_wordlist(raw):
    clean = re.sub("[^a-zA-Z]"," ", raw)
    words = clean.split()
    return map(lambda x:x.lower(),words)
```

Since we haven't yet captured the data from the text responses in our hypothetical business use case, let's collect a good quality dataset that's available on the web. Demonstrating our understanding and skills with this corpus will prepare us for the hypothetical business use case data. You can also use your own dataset, but it's important to have a huge amount of words so that the `word2vec` model can generalize well. So, we will load our data from the Project Gutenberg website, available at `Gutenberg.org`.

Then we tokenize the raw corpus into the list of unique clean words, as shown in the following diagram:

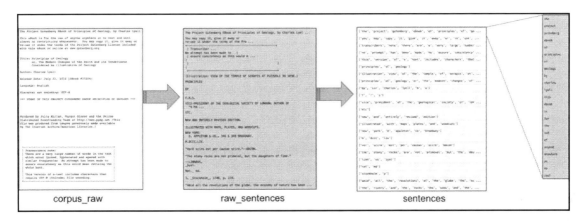

This process depicts the data transformation, from raw data, to the list of words that will be fed into the word2vec model

Here we will download the text data from the URL and process them as shown in the preceding figure:

```
# Article 0on earth from Gutenberg website
filepath = 'http://www.gutenberg.org/files/33224/33224-0.txt

corpus_raw = requests.get(filepath).text

tokenizer = nltk.data.load('tokenizers/punkt/english.pickle')

raw_sentences = tokenizer.tokenize(corpus_raw)

#sentence where each word is tokenized
sentences = []
for raw_sentence in raw_sentences:
    if len(raw_sentence) > 0:
        sentences.append(sentence_to_wordlist(raw_sentence))
```

Defining our word2vec model

Now let's use `gensim` in our definition of the `word2vec` model. To begin, let's define a few hyperparameters for our model, such as the dimension, which means how many low-level features we want to learn. Each dimension will learn a unique concept of gender, objects, age, and so on.

Computational linguistics model tip #1: Increasing the number of dimensions leads to better generalization... but it also adds more computational complexity. The right number is an empirical question for you to determine as an applied AI deep learning engineer!

Computational linguistics model tip #2: Pay attention to context_size. This is important because it sets the upper limit for the distance between the current and target word prediction within a sentence. This helps the model in learning the deeper relationships between a word and the other nearby words.

Using the gensim instance, we will define our model, including all the hyperparameters:

```
num_features = 300

# Minimum word count threshold.
min_word_count = 3

# Number of threads to run in parallel.

#more workers, faster we train
num_workers = multiprocessing.cpu_count()

# Context window length.
context_size = 7

# Downsample setting for frequent words. 0 - 1e-5 is good for this
downsampling = 1e-3

seed = 1

model2vec = w2v.Word2Vec(
        sg=1,
        seed=seed,
        workers=num_workers,
        size=num_features,
        min_count=min_word_count,
        window=context_size,
        sample=downsampling
     )
model2vec.build_vocab(sentences)
```

Training the model

Once we have configured the `gensim word2vec` object, we need to give the model some training. Be prepared, as this might take some time depending on the amount of data and the computation power you have. In this process, we have to define the number of epochs we need to run, which can vary depending on your data size. You can play around with these values and evaluate your `word2vec` model's performance.

Also, we will save the trained model so that we can use it later on while building our language models:

```
"""**Start training, this might take a minute or two...**"""

model2vec.train(sentences ,total_examples=model2vec.corpus_count ,
epochs=100)

"""**Save to file, can be useful later**"""

if not os.path.exists(os.path.join("trained",'sample')):
    os.makedirs(os.path.join("trained",'sample'))

model2vec.save(os.path.join("trained",'sample', ".w2v"))
```

Once the training process is complete, you can see a binary file stored in `/trained/sample.w2v`. You can share the `sample.w2v` file with others and they can use this word vectors in their NLP usecases and load it later into any other NLP task.

Analyzing the model

Now that we have trained our `word2vec` model, let's explore what our model was able to learn. We will use `most_similar()` to explore the relations between various words. In the following example, you see that the model was able to learn that the word `earth` is related to `crust`, `globe`, and other words. It is interesting to see that we only provided the raw data and the model was able to learn all of these relations and concepts automatically! The following is the example:

```
model2vec.most_similar("earth")

[(u'crust', 0.6946468353271484),
 (u'globe', 0.6748907566070557),
 (u'inequalities', 0.6181437969207764),
 (u'planet', 0.6092090606689453),
 (u'orbit', 0.6079996824264526),
 (u'laboring', 0.6058655977249146),
```

```
(u'sun', 0.5901342630386353),
(u'reduce', 0.5893668532371521),
(u'moon', 0.5724939107894897),
(u'eccentricity', 0.5709577798843384)]
```

Let's try to find words related to human and see what the model has learned:

```
model2vec.most_similar("human")

[(u'art', 0.6744576692581177),
(u'race', 0.6348963975906372),
(u'industry', 0.6203593611717224),
(u'man', 0.6148483753204346),
(u'population', 0.6090731620788574),
(u'mummies', 0.5895125865936279),
(u'gods', 0.5859177112579346),
(u'domesticated', 0.5857442021369934),
(u'lives', 0.5848811864852905),
(u'figures', 0.5809590816497803)]
```

 Critical thinking tip: It's interesting to observe that art, race, and industry are the most similar outputs. Remember that these similarities are based on the corpus of text that we used for training, and they should be thought of in that context. Generalization, and its unwanted sidekick, bias, can come into play when similarities from outdated or dissimilar training corpora are used to train a model that is applied to a new set of language data or cultural norms.

Even when we try to derive an analogy by using two positive vectors, earth and moon, and a negative vector, orbit, the model predicts the word sun, which makes sense because there is a semantic relation between the moon orbiting around the earth, and the earth orbiting around the sun:

```
model2vec.most_similar_cosmul(positive=['earth','moon'],
negative=['orbit'])

(u'sun', 0.8161555624008179)
```

So, we learned that by using the word2vec model we can derive valuable information from raw unlabeled data. This process is crucial in terms of learning the grammar of a language and the semantic correlations between words.

Later, we will learn how to use these `word2vec` features as an input for the classification model, which helps in boosting the model's accuracy and performance.

Plotting the word cluster using the t-SNE algorithm

So, after our analysis, we know that our `word2vec` model has learned some concepts from the provided corpus, but how do we visualize it? Because we have created a 300-dimensional space to learn the features, it's practically impossible for us to visualize. To make it possible, we will use a dimension reduction algorithm, called t-SNE, which is very well known for reducing a high dimensional space into more humanly understandable two or three-dimensional space.

> *"t-Distributed Stochastic Neighbor Embedding (t-SNE)* (`https://lvdmaaten.github.io/tsne/`) *is a (prize-winning) technique for dimensionality reduction that is particularly well suited for the visualization of high-dimensional datasets. The technique can be implemented via Barnes-Hut approximations, allowing it to be applied on large real-world datasets. We applied it on data sets with up to 30 million examples."*
>
> *– Laurens van der Maaten*

To implement this, we will use the `sklearn` package, and define `n_components=2`, which means we want to have 2-D space as the output. Next, we will perform the transformation by feeding the word vectors into the t-SNE object.

After this step, we now have a set of values for each word that we can use as `x` and `y` coordinates, respectively, to plot it on the 2D plane. Let's prepare a `DataFrame` to store all the words and their `x` and `y` coordinates in the same variable, as shown in the following screenshot, and take data from there to create a scatter plot:

```
tsne = sklearn.manifold.TSNE(n_components=2, random_state=0)

all_word_vectors_matrix = model2vec.wv.vectors

all_word_vectors_matrix_2d = tsne.fit_transform(all_word_vectors_matrix)

points = pd.DataFrame(
    [
        (word, coords[0], coords[1])
        for word, coords in [
            (word,
all_word_vectors_matrix_2d[model2vec.wv.vocab[word].index])
            for word in model2vec.wv.vocab
```

```
        ]
    ],
    columns=["word", "x", "y"]
)

sns.set_context("poster")
ax = points.plot.scatter("x", "y", s=10, figsize=(20, 12))
fig = ax.get_figure()
```

This is our `DataFrame` containing words and coordinates for both `x` and `y`:

	word	x	y
0	writings	-7.430655	-2.197504
1	grossier	-6.101781	6.286809
2	yellow	0.267137	9.981658
3	four	9.251252	1.031454
4	woods	1.035477	13.307897
5	preface	-9.289152	0.782565
6	woody	-0.714374	-6.950973
7	increase	4.004862	0.776931
8	granting	1.398124	5.031035
9	electricity	8.233945	-7.784630

Our word list with the coordinate values obtained using t-SNE

This is what the entire cluster looks like after plotting 425,633 tokens on the 2D plane. Each point is positioned after learning the features and correlations between the nearby words, as shown:

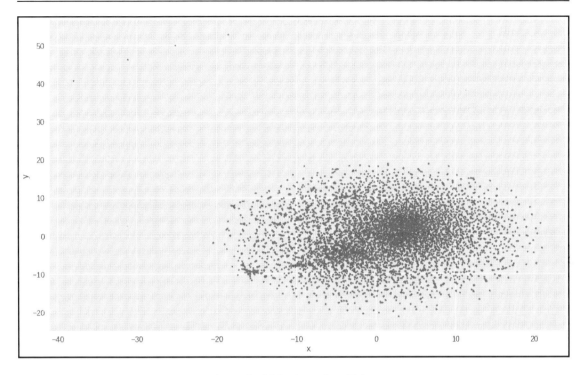

A scatter plot of all the unique words on a 2D plane

Visualizing the embedding space by plotting the model on TensorBoard

There is no benefit to visualization if you cannot make use of it, in terms of understanding how and what the model has learned. To gain a better intuition of what the model has learned, we will be using TensorBoard.

TensorBoard is a powerful tool that can be used to build various kinds of plots to monitor your models while in the training process, as well as building DL architectures and word embeddings. Let's build a TensorBoard embedding projection and make use of it to do various kinds of analysis.

To build an embedding plot in TensorBoard, we need to perform the following steps:

1. Collect the words and the respective tensors (300-D vectors) that we learned in previous steps.
2. Create a variable in the graph that will hold the tensors.
3. Initialize the projector.
4. Include an appropriately named embedding layer.
5. Store all the words in a `.tsv` formatted metadata file. These file types are used by TensorBoard to load and display words.
6. Link the `.tsv` metadata file to the projector object.
7. Define a function that will store all of the summary checkpoints.

The following is the code to complete the preceding seven steps:

```
vocab_list = points.word.values.tolist()
embeddings = all_word_vectors_matrix


embedding_var = tf.Variable(all_word_vectors_matrix, dtype='float32',
name='embedding')
projector_config = projector.ProjectorConfig()


embedding = projector_config.embeddings.add()
embedding.tensor_name = embedding_var.name

LOG_DIR='./'
metadata_file = os.path.join("sample.tsv")

with open(os.path.join(LOG_DIR, metadata_file), 'wt') as metadata:
    metadata.writelines("%s\n" % w.encode('utf-8') for w in vocab_list)

embedding.metadata_path = os.path.join(os.getcwd(), metadata_file)

# Use the same LOG_DIR where you stored your checkpoint.
summary_writer = tf.summary.FileWriter(LOG_DIR)

# The next line writes a projector_config.pbtxt in the LOG_DIR. TensorBoard
will
# read this file during startup.
projector.visualize_embeddings(summary_writer, projector_config)

saver = tf.train.Saver([embedding_var])

with tf.Session() as sess:
```

```
# Initialize the model
sess.run(tf.global_variables_initializer())

saver.save(sess, os.path.join(LOG_DIR, metadata_file+'.ckpt'))
```

Once the TensorBoard preparation module is executed, the binaries, metadata, and checkpoints get stored in the disk, as shown in the following screenshot:

```
checkpoint   projector_config.pbtxt                 sample.tsv.ckpt.index  url.txt
datalab      sample.tsv                             sample.tsv.ckpt.meta
nltk_data    sample.tsv.ckpt.data-00000-of-00001   trained
```

The outputs created by TensorBoard

To visualize the TensorBoard, execute the following command in the Terminal:

```
tensorboard --logdir=/path/of/the/checkpoint/
```

Now, in the browser, open http://localhost:6006/#projector, you should see TensorBoard with all the data points projected in 3D space. You can zoom in, zoom out, look for specific words, as well as retrain the model using t-SNE, and visualize the cluster formation of the dataset:

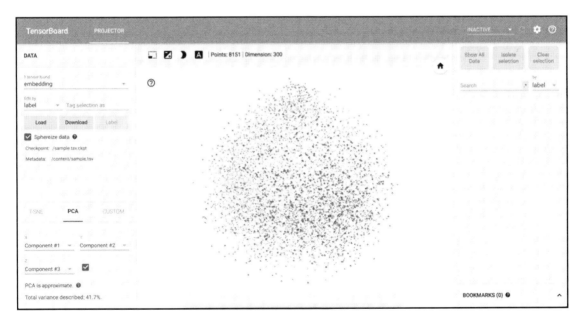

The TensorBoard embedding projection

Data visualization helps you tell your story! TensorBoard is very cool! Your business use case stakeholders love impressive dynamic data visualizations. They help with your model intuition, and with generating new hypotheses to test.

Building language models using CNN and word2vec

Now that we have learned the core concepts of computational linguistics, and trained relations from the provided dataset, we can use this learning to implement a language model that can perform a task.

In this section, we will build a text classification model to perform sentiment analysis. For classification, we will be using a combination of CNN and a pre-trained word2vec model, which we learned about in the previous section of this chapter.

This task is the simulation of our hypothetical business use case of taking text responses from restaurant patrons and classifying what they text back into meaningful classes for the restaurant.

We have been inspired by Denny Britz's (https://twitter.com/dennybritz) work on *Implementing a CNN for Text Classification in TensorFlow* (http://www.wildml.com/2015/12/implementing-a-cnn-for-text-classification-in-tensorflow/) in our own CNN and text classification build. We invite you to review the blog he created to gain a more complete understanding of the internal mechanisms that make CNNs useful for text classification.

As an overview, this architecture starts with an input embedding step, then a 2D convolution utilizing max pooling with multiple filters, and a softmax activation layer producing the output.

Exploring the CNN model

You might be asking yourself, how do you use CNNs to classify text when they are most commonly used in image processing?

> There are many discussions in the literature, linked at the bottom of this tip, which have proven that CNNs are a generic feature extraction function that can compute **location invariance** and **compositionality**. The location invariance property helps the model to capture the context of words, irrespective of their occurrence in the corpus. Compositionality helps to derive higher-level representations using lower-level features:

> - Convolutional Neural Networks for Sentence Classification (https://arxiv.org/abs/1408.5882)
>
> - A CNN Based Scene Chinese Text Recognition Algorithm with Synthetic Data Engine (https://arxiv.org/abs/1604.01891)
>
> - Text-Attentional Convolutional Neural Networks for Scene Text Detection (https://arxiv.org/pdf/1510.03283.pdf)

So instead of sending pixel values for an image into the model, we feed one-hot encoded word vectors or the word2vec matrix, which represent a word or a character (for character-based models). Denny Britz's implementation has two filters each in three region sizes of two, three, and four. The convolution operation is performed by these filters as it processes over the sentence matrix to generate feature maps. Downsampling is performed by a max pooling operation over each activation map. Finally, all the outputs are concatenated and passed into the softmax classifier.

Because we are performing sentiment analysis, there will be both a positive and a negative output class target. The softmax classifier will output probabilities for each class, as shown:

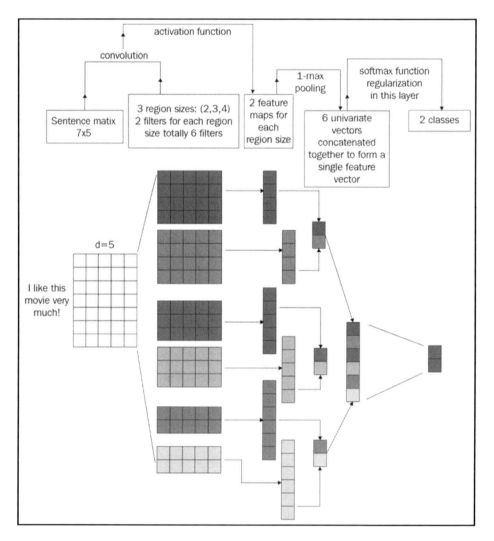

This diagram is taken from Denny Britz's blog post describing the functioning of the CNN language model

Let's look into the implementation of the model. We have modified the existing implementation by adding the input of the previously trained word2vec model component.

The code for this project can be found at `https://github.com/PacktPublishing/Python-Deep-Learning-Projects/tree/master/Chapter03/sentiment_analysis`.

The model resides in `text_cnn.py`. We created a class, named `TextCNN`, which takes a few parameters as an input for the model's configuration, also known as hyperparameters. The following is a list of hyperparameters:

- `sequence_length`: The fixed sentence length
- `num_classes`: The number of output classes that will be produced by the softmax activation (positive and negative)
- `vocab_size`: The count of unique words in our embeddings
- `embedding_size`: Embedding dimensionality that we created
- `filter_sizes`: The convolutional filter will cover this many words
- `num_filters`: Each filter size will have this many filters
- `pre_trained`: Integrates the `word2vec` representation that has been previously trained

Following is the declaration of the `TextCNN()` class with the `init()` function initializing all the hyperparameter values:

```
import tensorflow as tf
import numpy as np


class TextCNN(object):
    """
    A CNN for text classification.
    Uses an embedding layer, followed by a convolutional, max-pooling and
softmax layer.
    """

    def __init__(self,
                 sequence_length,
                 num_classes,
                 vocab_size,
                 embedding_size,
                 filter_sizes,
                 num_filters,
                 l2_reg_lambda=0.0,
                 pre_trained=False):
```

The code is divided into six main parts:

1. **Placeholders for inputs**: All the placeholders that we need to contain the input values for our model are defined first. In this case, inputs are the sentence vector and associated labels (either positive or negative). `input_x` holds the sentence, `input_y` holds the value of label, and we use `dropout_keep_prob` for the probability that we keep a neuron in the dropout layer. The following code shows an example of this:

```
# Placeholders for input, output and dropout
self.input_x = tf.placeholder(
    tf.int32, [
        None,
        sequence_length,
    ], name="input_x")
self.input_y = tf.placeholder(
    tf.float32, [None, num_classes], name="input_y")
self.dropout_keep_prob = tf.placeholder(
    tf.float32, name="dropout_keep_prob")
# Keeping track of l2 regularization loss (optional)
l2_loss = tf.constant(0.0)
```

2. **Embedding**: Our model's first layer, in which we feed the word representations learned in the process of training the `word2vec` model, is the embedding layer. We will modify the baseline code that's in the repository to use our pre-trained embedding model, instead of learning the embedding from scratch. This will enhance the model accuracy. It is also a kind of a `transfer learning`, where we transfer the general knowledge learned from a generic Wikipedia or social media corpus. The embedding matrix that is initialized with the `word2vec` model is named `W`, as seen as follows:

```
# Embedding layer
with tf.device('/cpu:0'), tf.name_scope("embedding"):
    if pre_trained:
        W_ = tf.Variable(
            tf.constant(0.0, shape=[vocab_size, embedding_size]),
            trainable=False,
            name='W')
        self.embedding_placeholder = tf.placeholder(
            tf.float32, [vocab_size, embedding_size],
            name='pre_trained')
        W = tf.assign(W_, self.embedding_placeholder)
    else:
        W = tf.Variable(
            tf.random_uniform([vocab_size, embedding_size], -1.0,
1.0),
```

```
                    name="W")
        self.embedded_chars = tf.nn.embedding_lookup(W, self.input_x)
        self.embedded_chars_expanded = tf.expand_dims(
            self.embedded_chars, -1)
```

3. **Convolution with maxpooling:** Defining the convolution layer is done with `tf.nn.conv2d()`. This takes, as inputs, the previous embedding layer's weight (`W`—filter matrix) and applies a nonlinear ReLU activation function. Further max polling is performed over each filter size using `tf.nn.max_pool()`. Results are concatenated, creating a single vector that will become the inputs for the following layer of the model:

```
# Create a convolution + maxpool layer for each filter size
pooled_outputs = []
for i, filter_size in enumerate(filter_sizes):
    with tf.name_scope("conv-maxpool-%s" % filter_size):
        # Convolution Layer
        filter_shape = [filter_size, embedding_size, 1,
num_filters]
        W = tf.Variable(
            tf.truncated_normal(filter_shape, stddev=0.1),
name="W")
        b = tf.Variable(
            tf.constant(0.1, shape=[num_filters]), name="b")
        conv = tf.nn.conv2d(
            self.embedded_chars_expanded,
            W,
            strides=[1, 1, 1, 1],
            padding="VALID",
            name="conv")
        # Apply nonlinearity
        h = tf.nn.relu(tf.nn.bias_add(conv, b), name="relu")
        # Maxpooling over the outputs
        pooled = tf.nn.max_pool(
            h,
            ksize=[1, sequence_length - filter_size + 1, 1, 1],
            strides=[1, 1, 1, 1],
            padding='VALID',
            name="pool")
        pooled_outputs.append(pooled)

# Combine all the pooled features
num_filters_total = num_filters * len(filter_sizes)
self.h_pool = tf.concat(pooled_outputs, 3)
self.h_pool_flat = tf.reshape(self.h_pool, [-1, num_filters_total])
```

4. **Dropout layer**: To regularize CNN and prevent the model from overfitting, a minor percentage of signals from neurons are blocked. This forces the model to learn more unique or individual features:

```
# Add dropout
with tf.name_scope("dropout"):
    self.h_drop = tf.nn.dropout(self.h_pool_flat,
                                self.dropout_keep_prob)
```

5. **Prediction**: A TensorFlow wrapper performs the $W * x + b$ metric multiplications, where x is the output of the previous layer. This computation will compute the values for the scores and the predictions will be produced by tf.argmax():

```
# Final (unnormalized) scores and predictions
with tf.name_scope("output"):
    W = tf.get_variable(
        "W",
        shape=[num_filters_total, num_classes],
        initializer=tf.contrib.layers.xavier_initializer())
    b = tf.Variable(tf.constant(0.1, shape=[num_classes]),
name="b")
    l2_loss += tf.nn.l2_loss(W)
    l2_loss += tf.nn.l2_loss(b)
    self.scores = tf.nn.xw_plus_b(self.h_drop, W, b, name="scores")
    self.predictions = tf.argmax(self.scores, 1,
name="predictions")
```

6. **Accuracy**: We can define the loss function with our scores. Remember that the measurement of the error our network makes is called **loss**. As good DL engineers, we want to minimize this and make our model more accurate. For the problem of categorization, the cross-entropy loss (http://cs231n.github.io/linear-classify/#softmax) is the standard loss function used:

```
# CalculateMean cross-entropy loss
with tf.name_scope("loss"):
    losses = tf.nn.softmax_cross_entropy_with_logits(
        labels=self.input_y, logits=self.scores)
    self.loss = tf.reduce_mean(losses) + l2_reg_lambda * l2_loss

# Accuracy
with tf.name_scope("accuracy"):
    correct_predictions = tf.equal(self.predictions,
                                   tf.argmax(self.input_y, 1))
    self.accuracy = tf.reduce_mean(
        tf.cast(correct_predictions, "float"), name="accuracy")
```

That's it, we're done with our model. Let's use TensorBoard to visualize the network and improve our intuition, as shown:

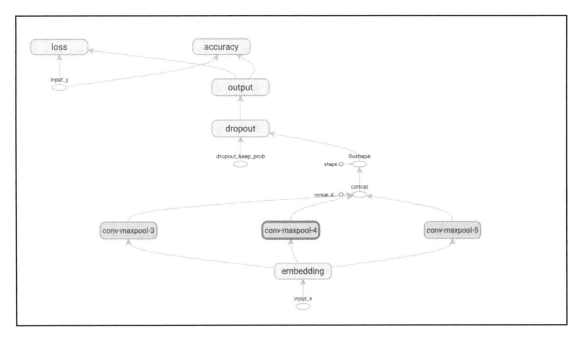

The CNN model architecture definition

Understanding data format

An interesting dataset, *Movie Review Data* from Rotten Tomatoes (http://www.cs.cornell.edu/people/pabo/movie-review-data/), was used in this case. Half of the reviews are positive, the other half negative, and there are about 10,000 sentences in total. There are around 20,000 different words in the vocabulary. The dataset is stored in the data folder.

It contains two files: one, `rt-polarity.neg`, contains all the negative sentences, and another, `rt-polarity.pos`, contains only positive sentences. To perform classification, we need to associate them with the labels. Each positive sentence is associated with a one-hot encoded label, [0, 1], and each negative sentence is associated with [1, 0], as shown in the following screenshot:

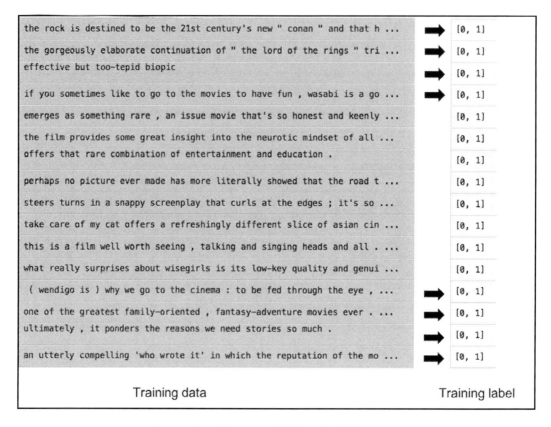

A sample of few positive sentences and the label associated with the sentence

Pre-processing the text data is done with these four steps:

1. **Load**: Make sure to load both the positive and negative sentence data files
2. **Clean**: Use regex to remove punctuation and other special characters
3. **Pad**: Make each sentence the same size by appending <PAD> tokens
4. **Index**: Map each word to an integer in an index so that each sentence can become a vector of integers

Now that we have our data formatted as vectors, we can feed them into our model.

Integrating word2vec with CNN

So, the last time we created our `word2vec` model, we dumped that model into a binary file. Now it's time to use that model as part of our CNN model. We perform this by initializing the `W` weights in the embeddings to these values.

Since we trained on a very small corpus in our previous `word2vec` model, let's choose the `word2vec` model that was pre-trained on the huge corpus. A good strategy is to use fastText embedding, which is trained on documents available online and for 294 languages (`https://github.com/facebookresearch/fastText/blob/master/pretrained-vectors.md`). We do this as follows:

1. We will download the English Embedding fastText dataset (`https://s3-us-west-1.amazonaws.com/fasttext-vectors/wiki.en.zip`)
2. Next, extract the vocab and embedding vectors into a separate file
3. Load them into the `train.py` file

That's it—by introducing this step, we can now feed the embedding layer with the pre-training `word2vec` model. This incorporation of information has a sufficient amount of features to improve the learning process of the CNN model.

Executing the model

Now it's time to train our model with the provided dataset and the pre-trained embedding model. A few hyperparameters will need fine-tuning to achieve good results. But once we have executed the `train.py` file with reasonably good configurations, we can demonstrate that the model is able to distinguish well between the positive and negative sentences when classifying.

As we can see in the following graph, the performance metric of accuracy is tending towards 1 and the loss factor is reducing towards 0 over each iteration:

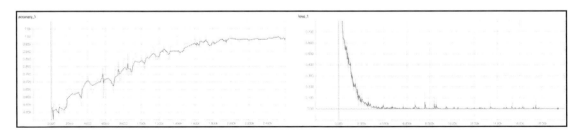

A plot of the performance metrics accuracy and loss of the CNN model during the training process

Voila! We just used the pre-trained embedding model to train our CNN classifier with an average loss of 6.9 and accuracy of 72.6%.

Once the model training is completed successfully, the output of the model will have the following:

- The checkpoints stored in `/runs/folder`. We will use these checkpoints to make predictions.
- A summary with all the loss, accuracy, histogram, and gradient value distribution captured during the training process. We can visualize it using the TensorBoard.

Deploy the model into production

Now that we have our model binaries stored in the `/runs/` folder, we just need to write a restful API, for which you can use Flask, and then call the `sentiment_engine()` defined in the `model_inference.py` code.

Always make sure that you use the checkpoints of the best model and the correct embedding file, which is defined as the following:

```
checkpoint_dir = "./runs/1508847544/"
embedding = np.load('fasttext_embedding.npy')
```

Summary

Today's project was to build a DL computational linguistics model using word2vec to accurately classify text in a sentiment analysis paradigm. Our hypothetical use case was to apply DL to enable the management of a restaurant chain to understand the general sentiment of text responses their customers made, in response to a phone text question asking about their experience after dining. Our specific task was to build the natural language processing model that would create business intelligence from the data obtained in this simple (hypothetical) application.

 Revisit our success criteria: How did we do? Did we succeed? What is the impact of success? Just as we defined success at the beginning of the project, these are the key questions we ask as DL data scientists as we look to wrap up a project.

Our CNN model, which was built on the trained `word2vec` model created earlier in the chapter, reached an accuracy of 72.6%! This means that we were able to reasonably accurately classify the unstructured text sentences as positive or negative.

What are the implications of this accuracy? In our hypothetical example, this means that we can take a body of data that is difficult to summarize outside of this DL NLP model and summarize it to produce actionable insights for the restaurant management. With summary data points of positive or negative sentiment to the questions asked in a phone text, the restaurant chain can track performance over time, make adjustments, and possibly even reward staff for improvements.

In this chapter's project, we learned how to build `word2vec` models and analyze what characteristics we can learn about the provided corpus. We also learned how to build a language model with CNN, using the trained word embeddings.

Finally, we looked at the model performance in testing and determined whether we succeeded in achieving our goals. In the next chapter's project, we're going to leverage even more power from our computational linguistic skills to create a natural language pipeline that will power a chatbot for open domain question answering. This is exciting work—let's see what next!

4
Building an NLP Pipeline for Building Chatbots

Our project has expanded once again, thanks to the good work that we've been doing. We started off working for a restaurant chain, helping them to classify handwritten digits for use in a text notification system, used to alert their waiting guests that their table was ready. Based on this success, and when the owners realized that their customers were actually responding to the texts, we were asked to contribute a deep learning solution using **Natural Language Processing** (**NLP**) to accurately classify text into a meaningful sentiment category that would give the owners an indication as to their satisfaction with the dining experience.

 Do you know what happens to deep learning engineers that do good work? They get asked to do more!

This project for the next business use case is pretty cool. What we're being asked to do is to create a natural language pipeline that would power a chatbot for open domain question answering. The (hypothetical) restaurant chain has a website with their menu, history, location, hours, and other information, and they would like to add the ability for a website visitor to ask a question in a query box, and have our deep learning NLP chatbot find the relevant information and present that back. They think that getting the right information back to the website visitor quickly would help drive in-store visits and improve the general customer experience.

Named Entity Recognition (**NER**) is the approach we will be using, which will give us the power we need to quickly classify the input text, which we can then match to the relevant content for a response. It's a great way to take advantage of a large corpus of unstructured data that changes without using hardcoded heuristics.

In this chapter, we will learn about the building blocks of the NLP model, including pre-processing, tokenizing, and tagging parts of speech. We will use this understanding to build a system able to read an unstructured piece of text, in order to formulate an answer for a specific question. We will also describe how to include this deep learning component in a classic NLP pipeline to retrieve information, in order to provide an open-domain question answering system that doesn't require a structured knowledge base.

In this chapter, we will do the following:

- Build a basic FAQ-based chatbot using statistical modeling in a framework, capable of detecting intents and entities for answering open-domain questions
- Learn to generate dense representations of sentences
- Build a document reader for extracting answers from unstructured text
- Learn how to integrate deep learning models into a classic NLP pipeline

Define the goal: To build a chatbot that understands the context (intent) and can also extract the entities. To do this, we need an NLP pipeline that can perform intent classification, along with NER extraction to then provide an accurate response.

Skills learned: You will learn how to build an open-domain question answering system using a classic NLP pipeline, with a document reader component that uses deep learning techniques to generate sentence representations.

Let's get started!

Basics of NLP pipelines

Textual data is a very large source of information, and properly handling it is crucial to success. So, to handle this textual data, we need to follow some basic text processing steps.

Most of the processing steps covered in this section are commonly used in NLP and involve combining a number of steps into one executable flow. This is what we refer to as the NLP pipeline. This flow can be a combination of tokenization, stemming, word frequency, parts of speech tagging, and many more elements.

Let's look into the details on how to implement the steps in the NLP pipeline and, specifically, what each stage of processing does. We will use the **Natural Language Toolkit (NLTK)** package—an NLP toolkit written in Python, which you can install with the following:

```
import nltk
nltk.download('punkt')
nltk.download('averaged_perceptron_tagger')
```

The code for this project is available at `https://github.com/PacktPublishing/Python-Deep-Learning-Projects/blob/master/Chapter04/Basic%20NLP%20Pipeline.ipynb`.

Tokenization

Tokenization separates a corpus into sentences, words, or tokens. Tokenization is needed to make our texts ready for further processing and is the first step in creating an NLP pipeline. A token can vary according to the task we are performing or the domain in which we are working, so keep an open mind as to what you consider as a token!

Know the code: NLTK is powerful, as much of the hard coding work is already done in the library. You can read more about NLTK tokenization at `http://www.nltk.org/api/nltk.tokenize.html#nltk.tokenize.api.TokenizerI.tokenize_sents`.

Let's try to load a corpus and use NLTK tokenizer to first tokenize the raw corpus into sentences, and then tokenize each sentence further into words:

```
text = u"""
Dealing with textual data is very crucial so to handle these text data we
need some
basic text processing steps. Most of the processing steps covered in this
section are
commonly used in NLP and involve the combination of several steps into a
single
executable flow. This is usually referred to as the NLP pipeline. These
flow
can be a combination of tokenization, stemming, word frequency, parts of
speech tagging, etc.
"""

# Sentence Tokenization
sentenses = nltk.sent_tokenize(text)
```

```
# Word Tokenization
words = [nltk.word_tokenize(s) for s in sentenses]
```

OUTPUT:
SENTENCES:
```
[u'\nDealing with textual data is very crucial so to handle these text data
we need some \nbasic text processing steps.',
u'Most of the processing steps covered in this section are \ncommonly used
in NLP and involve the combination of several steps into a single
\nexecutable flow.',
u'This is usually referred to as the NLP pipeline.',
u'These flow \ncan be a combination of tokenization, stemming, word
frequency, parts of \nspeech tagging, etc.']
```

WORDS:
```
[[u'Dealing', u'with', u'textual', u'data', u'is', u'very', u'crucial',
u'so', u'to', u'handle', u'these', u'text', u'data', u'we', u'need',
u'some', u'basic', u'text', u'processing', u'steps', u'.'], [u'Most',
u'of', u'the', u'processing', u'steps', u'covered', u'in', u'this',
u'section', u'are', u'commonly', u'used', u'in', u'NLP', u'and',
u'involve', u'the', u'combination', u'of', u'several', u'steps', u'into',
u'a', u'single', u'executable', u'flow', u'.'], [u'This', u'is',
u'usually', u'referred', u'to', u'as', u'the', u'NLP', u'pipeline', u'.'],
[u'These', u'flow', u'can', u'be', u'a', u'combination', u'of',
u'tokenization', u',', u'stemming', u',', u'word', u'frequency', u',',
u'parts', u'of', u'speech', u'tagging', u',', u'etc', u'.']]
```

Part-of-Speech tagging

Some words have multiple meanings, for example, *charge* is a noun, but can also be a verb, *(to) charge*. Knowing a **Part-of-Speech** (**POS**) can help to disambiguate the meaning. Each token in a sentence has several attributes that we can use for our analysis. The POS of a word is one example: nouns are a person, place, or thing; verbs are actions or occurrences and adjectives are words that describe nouns. Using these attributes, it becomes straightforward to create a summary of a piece of text by counting the most common nouns, verbs, and adjectives:

```
tagged_wt = [nltk.pos_tag(w)for w in words]

[[('One', 'CD'), ('way', 'NN'), ('to', 'TO'), ('extract', 'VB'),
('meaning', 'VBG'), ('from', 'IN'), ('text', 'NN'), ('is', 'VBZ'), ('to',
'TO'), ('analyze', 'VB'), ('individual', 'JJ'), ('words', 'NNS'), ('.',
'.')], [('The', 'DT'), ('processes', 'NNS'), ('of', 'IN'), ('breaking',
'VBG'), ('up', 'RP'), ('a', 'DT'), ('text', 'NN'), ('into', 'IN'),
('words', 'NNS'), ('is', 'VBZ'), ('called', 'VBN'), ('tokenization', 'NN'),
```

```
('--', ':'), ('the', 'DT'), ('resulting', 'JJ'), ('words', 'NNS'), ('are',
'VBP'), ('referred', 'VBN'), ('to', 'TO'), ('as', 'IN'), ('tokens', 'NNS'),
('.', '.')], [('Punctuation', 'NN'), ('marks', 'NNS'), ('are', 'VBP'),
('also', 'RB'), ('tokens', 'NNS'), ('.', '.')], [('Each', 'DT'), ('token',
'NN'), ('in', 'IN'), ('a', 'DT'), ('sentence', 'NN'), ('has', 'VBZ'),
('several', 'JJ'), ('attributes', 'IN'), ('we', 'PRP'), ('can', 'MD'),
('use', 'VB'), ('for', 'IN'), ('analysis', 'NN'), ('.', '.')]]


patternPOS= []
for tag in tagged_wt:
  patternPOS.append([v for k,v in tag])

[['CD', 'NN', 'TO', 'VB', 'VBG', 'IN', 'NN', 'VBZ', 'TO', 'VB', 'JJ',
'NNS', '.'], ['DT', 'NNS', 'IN', 'VBG', 'RP', 'DT', 'NN', 'IN', 'NNS',
'VBZ', 'VBN', 'NN', ':', 'DT', 'JJ', 'NNS', 'VBP', 'VBN', 'TO', 'IN',
'NNS', '.'], ['NN', 'NNS', 'VBP', 'RB', 'NNS', '.'], ['DT', 'NN', 'IN',
'DT', 'NN', 'VBZ', 'JJ', 'IN', 'PRP', 'MD', 'VB', 'IN', 'NN', '.'], ['DT',
'NN', 'IN', 'NN', 'IN', 'DT', 'NN', 'VBZ', 'CD', 'NN', ':', 'NNS', 'VBP',
'DT', 'NN', ',', 'NN', ',', 'CC', 'NN', ':', 'NNS', 'VBP', 'NNS', 'CC',
'NNS', ':', 'NNS', 'VBP', 'NNS', 'IN', 'NN', 'NNS', '.'], ['VBG', 'DT',
'NNS', ',', 'PRP', 'VBZ', 'JJ', 'TO', 'VB', 'DT', 'NN', 'IN', 'DT', 'NN',
'IN', 'NN', 'IN', 'VBG', 'DT', 'RBS', 'JJ', 'NNS', ',', 'NNS', ',', 'CC',
'NNS', '.']]
```

Extracting nouns

Let's extract all of the nouns present in the corpus. This is very useful practice when you want to extract something specific. We are using NN, NNS, NNP, and NNPS tags to extract the nouns:

```
nouns = []
for tag in tagged_wt:
nouns.append([k for k,v in tag if v in ['NN','NNS','NNP','NNPS']])

[['way', 'text', 'words'], ['processes', 'text', 'words', 'tokenization',
'words', 'tokens'], ['Punctuation', 'marks', 'tokens'], ['token',
'sentence', 'analysis'], ['part', 'speech', 'word', 'example', 'nouns',
'person', 'place', 'thing', 'verbs', 'actions', 'occurences', 'adjectives',
'words', 'describe', 'nouns'], ['attributes', 'summary', 'piece', 'text',
'nouns', 'verbs', 'adjectives']]
```

Extracting verbs

Let's extract all of the verbs present in the corpus. In this case, we are using VB, VBD, VBG, VBN, VBP, and VBZ as verb tags:

```
verbs = []
for tag in tagged_wt:
verbs.append([k for k,v in tag if v in
['VB','VBD','VBG','VBN','VBP','VBZ']])

[['extract', 'meaning', 'is', 'analyze'], ['breaking', 'is', 'called',
'are', 'referred'], ['are'], ['has', 'use'], ['is', 'are', 'are', 'are'],
['Using', "'s", 'create', 'counting']]
```

Now, let's use spacy to tokenize a piece of text and access the POS attribute for each token. As an example application, we'll tokenize the previous paragraph and count the most common nouns with the following code. We'll also lemmatize the tokens, which gives the root form a word, to help us standardize across forms of a word:

```
! pip install -q spacy
! pip install -q tabulate
! python -m spacy download en_core_web_lg



from collections import Counter
import spacy
from tabulate import tabulate
nlp = spacy.load('en_core_web_lg')

doc = nlp(text)
noun_counter = Counter(token.lemma_ for token in doc if token.pos_ ==
'NOUN')

print(tabulate(noun_counter.most_common(5), headers=['Noun', 'Count']))
```

Following is the output:

```
Noun          Count
----------    -------
step          3
combination   2
text          2
processing    2
datum         2
```

Dependency parsing

Dependency parsing is a way to understand the relationships between words in a sentence. Dependency relations are a more fine-grained attribute, available to help build the model's understanding of the words through their relationships in a sentence:

```
doc = nlp(sentenses[2])
spacy.displacy.render(doc,style='dep', options={'distance' : 140},
jupyter=True)
```

These relationships between words can get complicated, depending on how sentences are structured. The result of dependency-parsing a sentence is a tree data structure, with the verb as the root, as shown in the following diagram:

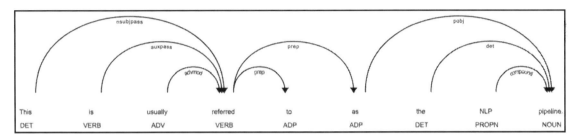

The tree structure of the dependency parsing of a sentence, with the verb as the root.

NER

Finally, there's NER. Named entities are the proper nouns of sentences. Computers have gotten pretty good at figuring out if they're in a sentence and at classifying what type of entity they are. `spacy` handles NER at the document level, since the name of an entity can span several tokens:

```
doc = nlp(u"My name is Jack and I live in India.")
entity_types = ((ent.text, ent.label_) for ent in doc.ents)
print(tabulate(entity_types, headers=['Entity', 'Entity Type']))
```

Output:
```
Entity     Entity Type
--------   -------------
Jack       PERSON
India      GPE
```

So, we just saw some of the basic building blocks of the NLP pipeline. These pipelines are consistently used in various NLP projects, be it in machine learning or in the deep learning space.

Does something look familiar?

We used a few of these NLP pipeline building blocks in the previous chapter, Chapter 3, *Word Representation Using word2vec*, to build our word2vec models. This more in-depth explanation of the building blocks of the NLP pipeline helps us take the next step in our projects, as we look to deploy more and more complex models!

As with everything in this book on *Python Deep Learning Projects*, we encourage you to also try your own combinations of the previous processes for the use cases you work on in your data science career. Now, let's implement a chatbot using these pipelines!

Building conversational bots

In this section, we will learn about some basic statistical modeling approaches to build an information retrieval system using **term frequency-inverse document frequency (TF-IDF)**, which we can use with the NLP pipelines to build fully functional chatbots. Also, later on, we will learn to build a much more advanced conversational bot that can extract a specific piece of information, such as location, capture time, and so on, using NER.

What is TF-IDF?

TF-IDFs are a way to represent documents as feature vectors. But what are they? TF-IDFs can be understood as a modification of the raw **term frequency (TF)** and **inverse document frequency (IDF)**. The TF is the count of how often a particular word occurs in a given document. The concept behind the TF-IDF is to downweight terms proportionally to the number of documents in which they occur. Here, the idea is that terms that occur in many different documents are likely to be unimportant, or don't contain any useful information for NLP tasks, such as document classification.

Preparing the dataset

If we think about building a chatbot with the TF-IDF approach, we first need to form a data structure that supports training data with labels. Now, let's take an example of a chatbot built to answer questions from users.

In this case, using historical data, we can form a dataset where we have two columns, one of which is the question, and the second of which is the answer to that question, as shown in the following table:

Question	Answer
When does your shop open?	Our shop timings are 9:00 A.M-9:00 P.M on weekdays and 11:00 A.M-12:00 midnight on weekends.
What is today's special?	Today, we have a variety of Italian pasta, with special sauce and a lot more other options in the bakery.
What is the cost of an Americano?	Americano with a single shot will cost $1.4 and the double shot will cost $2.3.
Do you sell ice-creams?	We do have desserts such as ice-cream, brownies, and pastries.

Let's take the previous example, and consider it a sample dataset. It is a very small example and, in the original hypothetical scenario, we will have a much larger dataset to work with. The typical process will be as follows: the user will interact with the bot and write a random query about the store. The bot will simply send that query to the NLP engine, using an API, and then it is up to the NLP model to decide what to return for a new query (test data). In reference to our dataset, all of the questions are the training data and the answers are labels. In the event of a new query, the TF-IDF algorithm will match it to one of the questions with a confidence score, which tells us that the new question asked by the user is close to some specific question from the dataset, and the answer against that question is the answer that our bots return.

Let's take the preceding example even further. When the user queries, "Can I get an Americano, btw how much it will cost?", we can see that words like *I*, *an*, and *it* are the ones that will have a higher occurrence frequency in other questions as well.

Now, if we match our remaining important words, we will see that this question is most close to: "What is the cost of an Americano?" So, our bot will respond back with the historical answer to this type of question: "Americano with a single shot will cost $1.4 and the double shot will cost $2.3."

Implementation

After creating the data structure in tabular format, as mentioned previously, we will be calculating the predicted answer to a question every time a user queries our bot. We load all of the question-answer pairs from the dataset.

Let's load our CSV file using `pandas`, and perform some pre-processing on the dataset:

```
import pandas as pd

filepath = 'sample_data.csv'
csv_reader=pd.read_csv(filepath)

question_list = csv_reader[csv_reader.columns[0]].values.tolist()
answers_list = csv_reader[csv_reader.columns[1]].values.tolist()

query= 'Can I get an Americano, btw how much it will cost ?'
```

 The code for this project can be found at `https://github.com/PacktPublishing/Python-Deep-Learning-Projects/tree/master/Chapter04/tfidf_version`.

Creating the vectorizer

Now, let's initialize the TF-IDF vectorizer and define a few parameters:

- `min_df`: When building the vocabulary, ignore terms that have a document frequency strictly lower than the given threshold
- `ngram_range`: Configures our vectorizer to capture *n*-words at a time
- `norm`: This is used to normalize term vectors using L1 or L2 norms
- `encoding`: Handles Unicode characters

There are many more parameters that you can look into, configure, and play around with:

```
from sklearn.feature_extraction.text import TfidfVectorizer

vectorizer = TfidfVectorizer(min_df=0, ngram_range=(2, 4),
strip_accents='unicode',norm='l2' , encoding='ISO-8859-1')
```

Now, we train the model on the questions:

```
# We create an array for our train data set (questions)
X_train = vectorizer.fit_transform(np.array([''.join(que) for que in
question_list]))

# Next step is to transform the query sent by user to bot (test data)
X_query=vectorizer.transform(query)
```

Processing the query

To process the query, we find out its similarity with other questions. We do this by taking a dot product of the training data matrix with a transpose of the query data:

```
XX_similarity=np.dot(X_train.todense(), X_query.transpose().todense())
```

Now, we take out the similarity between the query and train data as a list:

```
XX_sim_scores= np.array(XX_similarity).flatten().tolist()
```

Rank results

We create a sorted dictionary of similarities for a query:

```
dict_sim= dict(enumerate(XX_sim_scores))

sorted_dict_sim = sorted(dict_sim.items(), key=operator.itemgetter(1),
reverse =True)
```

Finally, in the sorted dictionary, we check for the index of the most similar question, and the response with the value at that index in the answers column. If nothing is found, then we can return our default answer:

```
if sorted_dict_sim[0][1]==0:
        print("Sorry I have no answer, please try asking again in a nicer
way :)")
elif sorted_dic_sim[0][1]>0:
        print answer_list [sorted_dic_sim[0][0]]
```

Advanced chatbots using NER

We just created a very basic chatbot that can understand the user's query and then respond to the customer accordingly. But it is not yet capable of understanding the context, because it can not extract information such as the product name, places, or any other entities.

To build a bot that understands the context (intent) and can also extract the entities, we need an NLP pipeline that can perform intent classification, along with NER extraction, and then provide an accurate response.

Keep your eyes on the goal! This is the goal of our open-domain question answering bot.

To do that, we will use an open source project called Rasa NLU (`https://github.com/RasaHQ/rasa_nlu`).

Rasa NLU is a **Natural Language Understanding** tool for understanding a text; in particular, what is being said in short pieces of text. For example, imagine that the system is given a short message like the following:

```
"I'm looking for an Italian restaurant in the center of town"
```

In such a case, the system returns the following:

```
intent: search_restaurant
entities:
      - cuisine : Italian
      - location : center of town
```

So, by harnessing the power of RASA, we can build a chatbot that can do intent classification and NER extraction.

Great, let's do it!

 The code for this project can be found at `https://github.com/PacktPublishing/Python-Deep-Learning-Projects/tree/master/Chapter04/rasa_version`

Installing Rasa

Let's install Rasa in our local environment or server using these commands:

```
pip install rasa_nlu
pip install coloredlogs sklearn_crfsuite spacy
python -m spacy download en
```

If it fails to install, then you can look into a detailed approach at `https://nlu.rasa.com/installation.html`.

Rasa uses a variety of NLP pipelines such as `spacy`, `sklearn`, or MITIE. You can use any one of them or build your own custom pipelines, which can include any deep model, such as CNN with word2vec, which we created in the previous chapter. In our case, we will be using `spacy` with `sklearn`.

Preparing dataset

In our previous project, we created a dataset in a CSV file with two columns for question and answer pairs. We need to do this again, but in a different format. In this case, we need questions associated with its intent, as shown in the following diagram, so we have a query as **hello** with its intent labeled as **greet**. Similarly, we will label all of the questions with their respective intents.

Once we have all of the forms of questions and intents ready, we need to label the entities. In this case, as shown in the following diagram, we have a **location** entity with a **centre** value, and a **cuisine** entity with the value as **mexican**:

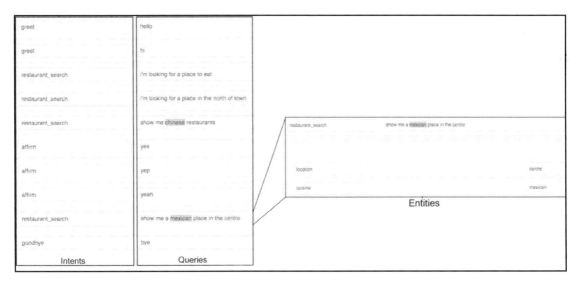

The figure illustrated the content of the data what we are preparing for the chatbot. Lest most is the list of all intents which we need out bot to understand. Then we have respective sample utterneces for each intent. And the right most part represents the annotation of the specific entity with its label 'location' and 'cuisine' in this case.

To feed data into Rasa, we need to store this information in a specific JSON format, which looks like the following:

```
# intent_list : Only intent part
[
  {
    "text": "hey",
    "intent": "greet"
  },
  {
    "text": "hello",
    "intent": "greet"
  }
```

```
]

# entity_list : Intent with entities
[{
  "text": "show me indian restaurants",
  "intent": "restaurant_search",
  "entities": [
    {
      "start": 8,
      "end": 15,
      "value": "indian",
      "entity": "cuisine"
    }
  ]
},
]
```

The final version of the JSON should have this structure:

```
{
  "rasa_nlu_data": {
    "entity_examples": [entity_list],
    "intent_examples": [intent_list]
  }
}
```

> To make it simple, there is an online tool into which you can feed and annotate all of the data, and download the JSON version of it. You can run the editor locally by following the instructions from https://github.com/RasaHQ/rasa-nlu-trainer or simply use the online version of it from https://rasahq.github.io/rasa-nlu-trainer/.

Save this JSON file as restaurant.json in the current working directory.

Training the model

Now we're going to create a configuration file. This configuration file will define the pipeline that is to be used in the process of training and building of the model.

Create a file called config_spacy.yml in your working directory, and insert the following code into it:

```
language: "en"
pipeline: "spacy_sklearn"
fine_tune_spacy_ner: true
```

Know the code: spaCy configuration customization is there for a reason. Other data scientists have found some utility in the ability to change values here, and it's good practice to explore this as you get more familiar with this technology. There is a huge list of configurations, which you can look into at `https://nlu.rasa.com/config.html`.

This configuration states that we will be using English language models, and the pipeline running on the backend will be spaCy with scikit-learn. Now, to begin the training process, execute the following command:

```
python -m rasa_nlu.train \
    --config config_spacy.yml \
    --data restaurant.json \
    --path projects
```

This takes the configuration file and the training data file as input. The `--path` parameter is the location where the trained model will be stored.

Once the model training process is completed, you'll see a new folder named in the `projects/default/model_YYYYMMDD-HHMMSS` format, with the timestamp when the training finished. The complete project structure will look as shown in the following screenshot:

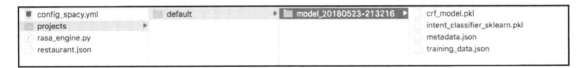

The folder structure after the training process is completed. The model folder will contain all the binary files and metadata which was learned during the training process.

Deploying the model

Now it's the moment to make your bot go live! While using Rasa, you don't need to write any API services—everything is available in the package itself. So, to expose the trained model as a service, you need to execute the following command, which takes the path of the stored trained model:

```
python -m rasa_nlu.server --path projects
```

If everything goes fine, then a RESTful API will be exposed at port 5000, and you should see this log on the console screen:

```
2018-05-23 21:34:23+0530 [-] Log opened.
2018-05-23 21:34:23+0530 [-] Site starting on 5000
2018-05-23 21:34:23+0530 [-] Starting factory <twisted.web.server.Site
instance at 0x1062207e8>
```

To access the API, you can use the following command. We are querying the model, making a statement such as "I am looking for Mexican food":

```
curl -X POST localhost:5000/parse -d '{"q":"I am looking for Mexican
food"}' | python -m json.tool
```

```
Output:
{
  "entities": [
    {
      "confidence": 0.5348393725109971,
      "end": 24,
      "entity": "cuisine",
      "extractor": "ner_crf",
      "start": 17,
      "value": "mexican"
    }
  ],
  "intent": {
    "confidence": 0.7584285478135262,
    "name": "restaurant_search"
  },
  "intent_ranking": [
    {
      "confidence": 0.7584285478135262,
      "name": "restaurant_search"
    },
    {
      "confidence": 0.11009204166074991,
      "name": "goodbye"
    },
    {
      "confidence": 0.08219245368495268,
      "name": "affirm"
    },
    {
      "confidence": 0.049286956840770876,
      "name": "greet"
    }
```

```
    ],
    "model": "model_20180523-213216",
    "project": "default",
    "text": "I am looking for Mexican food"
}
```

So here, we can see that model has performed quite accurately with the intent classification and the entity extraction process. It is able to classify the intent as `restaurant_search` with 75.8% of accuracy, and is also able to detect the `cuisine` entity with the value as `mexican`.

Serving chatbots

Up to now, we have seen how to build chatbots using the two methods of TF-IDF and Rasa NLU. Let's expose both of them as APIs. The architecture of this simple chatbot framework will look like this:

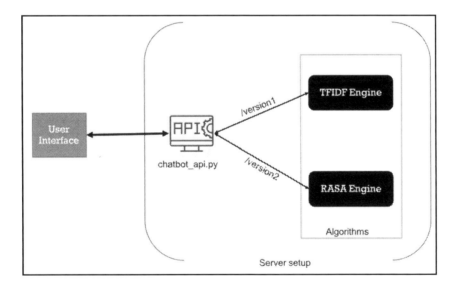

This chatbot pipeline illustrates that we can have any User Interface (Slack, Skype, and so on) integrated with the chatbot_api which we exposed . And under the hood we can setup any number of algorithms 'TFIDF' and 'RASA'

Refer to the Packt repository for this chapter (available at `https://github.com/PacktPublishing/Python-Deep-Learning-Projects/tree/master/Chapter04`) for the API code and look into the `chatbot_api.py` file. Here, we have implemented a common API that can load both versions of bot, and you can now build a whole framework on top of this.

To execute the serving of the APIs, follow these steps:

1. Enter the chapter directory using the following command:

   ```
   cd Chapter04/
   ```

2. This will expose the Rasa module at `localhost:5000`. If you have not trained the Rasa engine, then please apply the following command:

   ```
   python -m rasa_nlu.server --path ./rasa_version/projects
   ```

3. In a separate console, execute the following command. This will expose an API at `localhost:8080`:

   ```
   python chatbot_api.py
   ```

4. Now your chatbot is ready to be accessed via API. Try the following:

   - Call the following API to execute the TFIDF version:

     ```
     curl http://localhost:8080/version1?query=Can I get an
     Americano
     ```

   - Call the following API to execute the Rasa version:

     ```
     http://localhost:8080/version2?query=where is Indian cafe
     ```

Summary

In this project, we were asked to create a natural language pipeline that would power a chatbot for open domain question answering. A (hypothetical) restaurant chain has much text-based data on their website, including their menu, history, location, hours, and other information, and they would like to add the ability for a website visitor to ask a question in a query box. Our deep learning NLP chatbot would then find the relevant information and present that back to the visitor.

We got started by showing how we could build a simple FAQ chatbot that took in random queries, matched that up to predefined questions, and returned a response with a confidence score that indicated the similarity between the input question and the question in our database. But this was only a stepping stone to our real goal, which was to create a chatbot that could capture the intent of the question and prepare an appropriate response.

We explored an NER approach to give us the added power that we needed to quickly classify input text, which we could then match to the relevant content for a response. This was determined to fit our goal of allowing for open-domain question answering and to take advantage of a large corpus of unstructured data that changes without using hardcoded heuristics (as in our hypothetical restaurant example).

We learned to use the building blocks of the NLP model, including pre-processing, tokenizing, and tagging POS. We used this understanding to build a system able to read an unstructured text in order to comprehend an answer to a specific question.

Specifically, we gained these skills in this project:

- Building a basic FAQ-based chatbot using statistical modeling in a framework capable of detecting intents and entities for answering open-domain questions
- Generating a dense representation of sentences
- Building a document reader for extracting answers from unstructured text
- Learned how to integrate deep learning models into a classic NLP pipeline

These skills will come very much in handy in your career, as you see similar business use cases, and also as conversational user interfaces continue to gain in popularity. Well done—let's see what's in store for our next deep learning project in Python!

5
Sequence-to-Sequence Models for Building Chatbots

We're learning a lot and doing some valuable work! In the evolution of our hypothetical business use case, this chapter builds directly on `Chapter 4`, *Building an NLP Pipeline for Building Chatbots*, where we created our **Natural Language Processing** (**NLP**) pipeline. The skills we learned so far in computational linguistics should give us the confidence to expand past the training examples in this book and tackle this next project. We're going to build a more advanced chatbot for our hypothetical restaurant chain to automate the process of fielding call-in orders.

This requirement would mean that we'd have to combine a number of technologies that we've learned so far. But for this project, we'll be interested in learning how to make a chatbot that is more contextually aware and robust, so that we could integrate it into a larger system in this hypothetical. By demonstrating mastery on this training example, we'll have the confidence to execute this in a real situation.

In the previous chapters, we learned about representational learning methods, such as word2vec, and how to use them in combination with a type of deep learning algorithm called a **Convolutional Neural Network** (**CNN**). But there are few constraints while using CNNs to build language models, such as the following:

- The model will not be able to preserve the state information
- The length of sentences needs to be of a fixed size for both input values and output values
- CNNs are sometimes unable to adequately handle complex sequential contexts
- **Recurrent Neural Networks** (**RNNs**) do better at modeling information in sequence

So, to overcome all of these problems, we have an alternative algorithm, which is specially designed to handle input data that comes in the form of sequences (including sequences of words, or of characters). This class of algorithm is called RNN.

In this chapter, we will do the following:

- Learn about RNN and its various forms
- Create a language model implementation using RNN
- Build our intuition on the **Long Short-Term Memory** (**LSTM**) model
- Create an LSTM language model implementation and compare it to the RNN model
- Implement an encoder-decoder RNN, based on the LSTM unit, for a simple sequence of question-answer tasks

 Define the goal: Build a more robust chatbot with memory to provide more contextually correct responses to questions.

Let's get started!

Introducing RNNs

RNN is a deep learning model architecture specifically designed for sequential data. The purpose of this type of model is to extract relevant features of words and characters of text by using a small window that traverses the corpus.

RNN applies a non-linear function to each item in the sequence. This is called the RNN *cell* or *step* and, in our case, the items are words or characters in the sequence. The layer's output in an RNN is derived from the output of the RNN cell, which is applied to each element in the sequence. With regard to NLP and chatbots that use text data as input, the outputs of the model are successive characters or words.

 Each RNN cell holds an internal memory that summarizes the history of the sequence it has seen so far.

This diagram helps us to visualize the RNN model architecture:

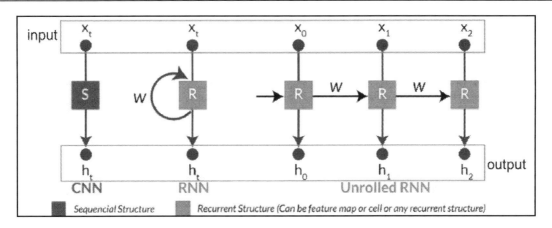

Vanilla version of RNN model architecture.

At the heart of the purpose of an RNN was the idea to introduce a feedback mechanism that enables context modeling through the use of fixed-weight feedback structures. What this does is build a connection between the features in the current mapping to the previous version. Basically, it employs a strategy of using an earlier version of a sequence to instruct a later version.

This is quite clever; however, it's not without its challenges. Exploding and vanishing gradients make it extremely frustrating to train these types of modes in instances where the problem is of a complex time series nature.

 A great reference to dive into that expertly outlines the vanishing and exploding gradient problem, and gives a technical explanation of viable solutions, can be found in Sepp's work from 1998 (`https://dl.acm.org/citation.cfm?id=355233`).

A second problem that was discovered was that RNNs were picking up only one of two temporal structures: either the short-term or long-term structures. But what was needed for the best model performance was a model that was able to learn from both types of features (short-term and long-term) at the same time. The solution came in changing the basic RNN cell for a **Gated Recurrent Unite (GRU)** or LSTM cell.

 For additional information on the GRU refer to `http://www.wildml.com/2015/10/recurrent-neural-network-tutorial-part-4-implementing-a-grulstm-rnn-with-python-and-theano/` or, to learn more on the LSTM, refer to `http://colah.github.io/posts/2015-08-Understanding-LSTMs/`.

We'll explore the LSTM architecture in detail later in this chapter. Let's gain some intuition on the value of LSTM that will help us achieve our goal first.

RNN architectures

We will mostly use the LSTM cell, since it has proven better in most NLP tasks. The principle benefit of the LSTM in RNN architectures is that it enables model training over long sequences, while retaining memory. To solve the gradient problem, LSTMs include more gates that effectively control access to the cell state.

 We've found that Colah's blog post (`http://colah.github.io/posts/2015-08-Understanding-LSTMs/`) is a great place to go to obtain a good understand the working of LSTMs.

These small LSTM units of RNN can be combined in multiple forms to solve various kinds of use-cases. RNNs are quite flexible in terms of combining the different input and output patterns, as follows:

- **Many to one**: The model takes a complete input sequence to make a single prediction. This is used in sentiment models.
- **One to many**: This model transforms a single input, such as a numerical date, to generate a sequence string such as "day", "month", or "year".
- **Many to many**: This is a **sequence-to-sequence (seq2seq)** model, which takes the entire sequence as input into a second sequence form, as Q/A systems do.

This diagram maps out these relationships nicely:

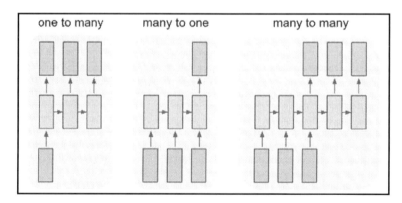

In this chapter, we will focus on the **many to many** relationship, also known as seq2seq architecture, to build a question-answer chatbot. The standard RNN approach to solving the seq2seq problem involves three primary components:

- **Encoders**: These transform the input sentences into some abstract encoded representation
- **Hidden layer**: Encoded sentence transformation representations are manipulated here
- **Decoders**: These output a decoded target sequence

Let's have a look at the following diagram:

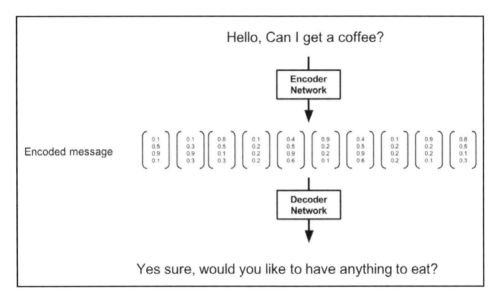

The illustration of building the encode decoder model which takes input text (question) in the encoder. it gets transformed in the intermediate step and gets mapped with the decoder which represents the respective text (answer).

Let's build our intuition on RNNs by first implementing basic forms of RNN models.

Implementing basic RNNs

In this section, we will implement a language model, using a basic RNN to perform sentiment classification. Code files for the model can found at `https://github.com/PacktPublishing/Python-Deep-Learning-Projects/blob/master/Chapter05/1.%20rnn.py`.

Importing all of the dependencies

This code imports TensorFlow and key dependencies for our RNN:

```
from utils import *
import tensorflow as tf
from sklearn.cross_validation import train_test_split
import time
```

Preparing the dataset

The dataset we'll use in this project is the *Movie Review Data* from Rotten Tomatoes (`http:/`
`/www.cs.cornell.edu/people/pabo/movie-review-data/`). It contains 10,662 example
review sentences, with approximately half of them positive and half negative. The dataset
has a vocabulary of around 20,000 words. We will use the `sklearn` wrapper to load the
dataset from a raw file and then a `separate_dataset()` helper function to clean the
dataset and transform it from its raw form to the separate list structure:

```
#Helper function
def separate_dataset(trainset,ratio=0.5):
    datastring = []
     datatarget = []
     for i in range(int(len(trainset.data)*ratio)):
         data_ = trainset.data[i].split('\n')
         data_ = list(filter(None, data_))
         for n in range(len(data_)):
             data_[n] = clearstring(data_[n])
         datastring += data_
         for n in range(len(data_)):
             datatarget.append(trainset.target[i])
    return datastring, datatarget
```

Here, `trainset` is an object that stores all of the text data and the sentiment label data:

```
trainset = sklearn.datasets.load_files(container_path = './data', encoding
= 'UTF-8')
trainset.data, trainset.target = separate_dataset(trainset,1.0)
print (trainset.target_names)
print ('No of training data' , len(trainset.data))
print ('No. of test data' , len(trainset.target))

# Output:
['negative', 'positive']
No of training data 10662
No of test data 10662
```

Now we will transform the labels into the one-hot encoding.

It's important to understand the dimensions of the one-hot encoding vector. Since we have `10662` separate sentences, and two sentiments, `negative` and `positive`, our one-hot vector size will be of a size of [*10662, 2*].

We will be using a popular `train_test_split()` sklearn wrapper to randomly shuffle the data and divide the dataset into two parts: the `training` set and the `test` set. Further, with another `build_dataset()` helper function, we will create the vocabulary using a word-count-based approach:

```
ONEHOT = np.zeros((len(trainset.data),len(trainset.target_names)))
ONEHOT[np.arange(len(trainset.data)),trainset.target] = 1.0
train_X, test_X, train_Y, test_Y, train_onehot, test_onehot =
train_test_split(trainset.data, trainset.target,
ONEHOT, test_size = 0.2)


concat = ' '.join(trainset.data).split()
vocabulary_size = len(list(set(concat)))
data, count, dictionary, rev_dictionary = build_dataset(concat,
vocabulary_size)
print('vocab from size: %d'%(vocabulary_size))
print('Most common words', count[4:10])
print('Sample data', data[:10], [rev_dictionary[i] for i in data[:10]])


# OUTPUT:
vocab from size: 20465
'Most common words', [(u'the', 10129), (u'a', 7312), (u'and', 6199),
(u'of', 6063), (u'to', 4233), (u'is', 3378)]

'Sample data':
[4, 662, 9, 2543, 8, 22, 4, 3558, 18064, 98] -->
[u'the', u'rock', u'is', u'destined', u'to', u'be', u'the', u'21st',
u'centurys', u'new']
```

You can also try to feed any embedding model in here to make the model more accurate.

There are a few important things to remember while preparing the dataset for the RNN models. We need to add explicitly special tags in the vocabulary to keep track of the start of sentences, extra padding, the ends of sentences, and any unknown words. Hence, we have reserved the following positions for special tags in our vocabulary dictionary:

```
# Tag to mark the beginning of the sentence
'GO' = 0th position
# Tag to add extra padding in the sentence
'PAD'= 1st position
# Tag to mark the end of the sentence
'EOS'= 2nd position
# Tag to mark the unknown word
'UNK'= 3rd position
```

Hyperparameters

We will define some of the hyperparameters for our model, as follows:

```
size_layer = 128
num_layers = 2
embedded_size = 128
dimension_output = len(trainset.target_names)
learning_rate = 1e-3
maxlen = 50
batch_size = 128
```

Defining a basic RNN cell model

Now we will create the RNN model, which takes a few input parameters, including the following:

- `size_layer`: The number of units in the RNN cell
- `num_layers`: The number of hidden layers
- `embedded_size`: The size of the embedding
- `dict_size`: The vocabulary size
- `dimension_output`: The number of classes we need to classify
- `learning_rate`: The learning rate of the optimization algorithm

The architecture of our RNN model consists of the following parts:

1. Two placeholders; one to feed sequence data into the model and the second for the output
2. A variable to store the embedding lookup from the dictionary
3. Then, add the RNN layer with multiple basic RNN cells
4. Create weight and bias variables
5. Compute `logits`
6. Compute loss
7. Add the Adam Optimizer
8. Calculate prediction and accuracy

This model is similar to the CNN model created in the previous chapter, Chapter 4, *Building an NLP Pipeline for Building Chatbots*, except for the RNN cell part:

```
class Model:
    def __init__(self, size_layer, num_layers, embedded_size,
                 dict_size, dimension_output, learning_rate):
        def cells(reuse=False):
            return tf.nn.rnn_cell.BasicRNNCell(size_layer,reuse=reuse)
        self.X = tf.placeholder(tf.int32, [None, None])
        self.Y = tf.placeholder(tf.float32, [None, dimension_output])

        encoder_embeddings = tf.Variable(tf.random_uniform([dict_size,
embedded_size], -1, 1))
        encoder_embedded = tf.nn.embedding_lookup(encoder_embeddings,
self.X)

        rnn_cells = tf.nn.rnn_cell.MultiRNNCell([cells() for _ in
range(num_layers)])
        outputs, _ = tf.nn.dynamic_rnn(rnn_cells, encoder_embedded, dtype =
tf.float32)

        W = tf.get_variable('w',shape=(size_layer,
dimension_output),initializer=tf.orthogonal_initializer())
        b =
tf.get_variable('b',shape=(dimension_output),initializer=tf.zeros_initializ
er())

        self.logits = tf.matmul(outputs[:, -1], W) + b
        self.cost =
tf.reduce_mean(tf.nn.softmax_cross_entropy_with_logits(logits =
self.logits, labels = self.Y))
        self.optimizer = tf.train.AdamOptimizer(learning_rate =
learning_rate).minimize(self.cost)
```

```
        correct_pred = tf.equal(tf.argmax(self.logits, 1),
tf.argmax(self.Y, 1))
        self.accuracy = tf.reduce_mean(tf.cast(correct_pred, tf.float32))
```

In this model, the data flows from the variables that we created in *Step 1*. Then, it moves to the embedding layer defined in *Step 2*, followed by our RNN layer, which performs the computation in two hidden layers of RNN cells. Later, `logits` are computed by performing a matrix multiplication of the weight, the output from the RNN layer, and addition of bias. The last step is that we define the `cost` function; we will be using the `softmax_cross_entropy` function.

This is what the complete model looks like after computation:

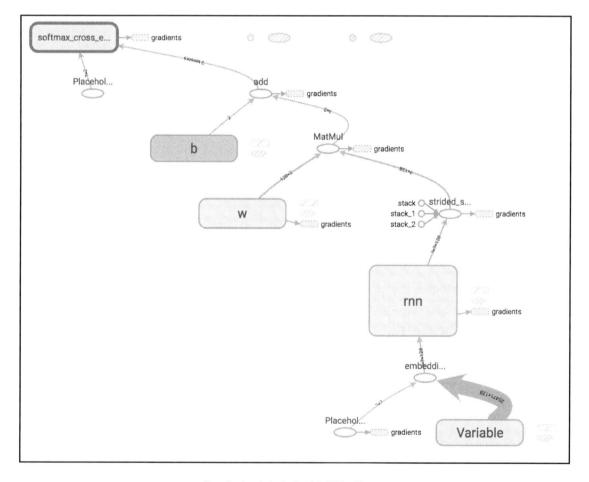

TensorBoard graph visualization of the RNN architecture

The following diagram represents the structure of the RNN block from the preceding screenshot. In this architecture, we have two RNN cells incorporated in hidden layers:

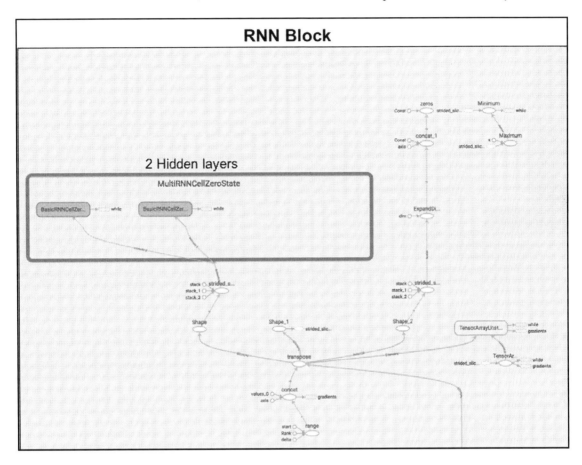

TensorBoard visualization of the RNN block containing 2 hidden layers as defined in the code

Training the RNN Model

Now that we have our model architecture defined, let's train our model. We begin with a TensorFlow graph initialization and execute the training steps as follows:

```
tf.reset_default_graph()
sess = tf.InteractiveSession()
model =
Model(size_layer,num_layers,embedded_size,vocabulary_size+4,dimension_outpu
```

```
t,learning_rate)
sess.run(tf.global_variables_initializer())


EARLY_STOPPING, CURRENT_CHECKPOINT, CURRENT_ACC, EPOCH = 5, 0, 0, 0
while True:
    lasttime = time.time()
    if CURRENT_CHECKPOINT == EARLY_STOPPING:
        print('break epoch:%d\n'%(EPOCH))
        break
    train_acc, train_loss, test_acc, test_loss = 0, 0, 0, 0
    for i in range(0, (len(train_X) // batch_size) * batch_size,
batch_size):
        batch_x = str_idx(train_X[i:i+batch_size],dictionary,maxlen)
        acc, loss, _ = sess.run([model.accuracy, model.cost,
model.optimizer],
                        feed_dict = {model.X : batch_x, model.Y :
train_onehot[i:i+batch_size]})
        train_loss += loss
        train_acc += acc
    for i in range(0, (len(test_X) // batch_size) * batch_size,
batch_size):
        batch_x = str_idx(test_X[i:i+batch_size],dictionary,maxlen)
        acc, loss = sess.run([model.accuracy, model.cost],
                        feed_dict = {model.X : batch_x, model.Y :
train_onehot[i:i+batch_size]})
        test_loss += loss
        test_acc += acc
    train_loss /= (len(train_X) // batch_size)
    train_acc /= (len(train_X) // batch_size)
    test_loss /= (len(test_X) // batch_size)
    test_acc /= (len(test_X) // batch_size)
    if test_acc > CURRENT_ACC:
        print('epoch: %d, pass acc: %f, current acc:
%f'%(EPOCH,CURRENT_ACC, test_acc))
        CURRENT_ACC = test_acc
        CURRENT_CHECKPOINT = 0
    else:
        CURRENT_CHECKPOINT += 1
    print('time taken:', time.time()-lasttime)
    print('epoch: %d, training loss: %f, training acc: %f, valid loss: %f,
valid acc: %f\n'%(EPOCH,train_loss, train_acc,test_loss,test_acc))
    EPOCH += 1
```

While the RNN model is being trained, we can see the logs of each epoch, shown as follows:

```
Future major versions of TensorFlow will allow gradients to flow
into the labels input on backprop by default.

See @{tf.nn.softmax_cross_entropy_with_logits_v2}.

epoch: 0, pass acc: 0.000000, current acc: 0.502441
time taken: 11.038581609725952
epoch: 0, training loss: 0.702008, training acc: 0.542614, valid loss: 0.723523, valid acc: 0.502441

time taken: 11.019535303115845
epoch: 1, training loss: 0.623813, training acc: 0.653883, valid loss: 0.795169, valid acc: 0.487305

epoch: 2, pass acc: 0.502441, current acc: 0.506836
time taken: 10.916295766830444
epoch: 2, training loss: 0.515812, training acc: 0.746449, valid loss: 0.937421, valid acc: 0.506836

time taken: 10.991063356399536
epoch: 3, training loss: 0.379528, training acc: 0.833333, valid loss: 1.163410, valid acc: 0.501953

time taken: 10.905569076538086
epoch: 4, training loss: 0.270475, training acc: 0.891927, valid loss: 1.482876, valid acc: 0.499512

time taken: 10.94543194770813
epoch: 5, training loss: 0.169099, training acc: 0.939512, valid loss: 1.838352, valid acc: 0.495605

epoch: 6, pass acc: 0.506836, current acc: 0.508789
time taken: 10.955822944641113
epoch: 6, training loss: 0.112769, training acc: 0.960346, valid loss: 2.379099, valid acc: 0.508789

time taken: 10.9817533493042
epoch: 7, training loss: 0.063998, training acc: 0.975379, valid loss: 2.511583, valid acc: 0.498047

time taken: 10.956014394760132
epoch: 8, training loss: 0.037480, training acc: 0.987098, valid loss: 2.797244, valid acc: 0.494629

time taken: 10.966387510299683
epoch: 9, training loss: 0.022739, training acc: 0.994081, valid loss: 3.233259, valid acc: 0.499023

time taken: 10.951802968978882
epoch: 10, training loss: 0.015956, training acc: 0.995028, valid loss: 3.160137, valid acc: 0.482422

time taken: 10.971746683120728
epoch: 11, training loss: 0.008966, training acc: 0.997751, valid loss: 3.295206, valid acc: 0.486816

break epoch:12
```

Evaluation of the RNN model

Let's look at our results. Once the model is trained, we can feed the test data that we prepared earlier in this chapter and evaluate the predictions. In this case, we will use a few different metrics to evaluate our model: precision, recall, and F1-scores.

To evaluate your model, it is important to choose the right kind of metrics—F1-scores are considered more practical compared to the accuracy score.

Some key points to help you understand them in simple terms are as follows:

- **Accuracy**: The count of correct predictions, divided by the count of total examples that have been evaluated.
- **Precision**: High precision means you identified nearly all positives appropriately; a low precision score means you often incorrectly predicted a positive when there was none.
- **Recall**: High recall means you correctly predicted almost all of the real positives present in the data; a low score means you frequently missed positives that were present.
- **F1-score**: The balanced harmonic mean of recall and precision, giving both metrics equal weight. The higher the F-measure, the better.

Now we will execute the model by feeding the test data with vocabulary and the max length of the text. This will produce the `logits` values which we will use to generate the evaluation metrics:

```
logits = sess.run(model.logits,
feed_dict={model.X:str_idx(test_X,dictionary,maxlen)})
print(metrics.classification_report(test_Y, np.argmax(logits,1),
target_names = trainset.target_names))
```

The output is as follows:

	precision	recall	f1-score	support
negative	0.65	0.73	0.69	1079
positive	0.68	0.59	0.64	1054
avg / total	0.67	0.66	0.66	2133

So here, we can see that our average `f1-score` is 66% while using basic RNN cells. Let's see if this can be improved on by using other variations of RNN architectures.

LSTM architecture

The desire to model sequential data more effectively, without the limitations of the gradient problem, led researchers to create the LSTM variant of the previous RNN model architecture. LSTM achieves better performance because it incorporates gates to control the process of memory in the cell. The following diagram shows an LSTM cell:

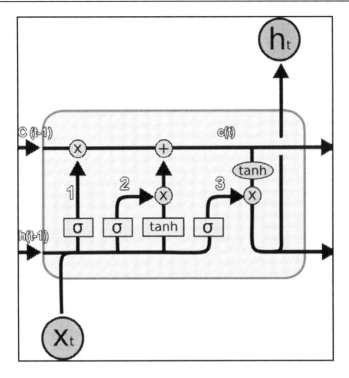

An LSTM unit (source: http://colah.github.io/posts/2015-08-Understanding-LSTMs)

LSTM consist of three primary elements, labeled as **1**, **2**, and **3** in the preceding diagram:

1. **The forget gate f(t)**: This gate provides the ability, in the LSTM cell architecture, to forget information that is not needed. The sigmoid activation accepts the inputs $X(t)$ and **h(t-1)**, and effectively decides to remove pieces of old output information by passing a 0. The output of this gate is $f(t)*c(t-1)$.

2. Information from the new input, $X(t)$, that is determined to be retained needs to be stored in the next step in the cell state. A sigmoid activation is used in this process to update or ignore parts of the new information. Next, a vector of all possible values for the new input is created by a **tanh** activation function. The new cell state is the product of these two values, then this new memory is added to the old memory, **c(t-1)**, to give **c(t)**.

3. The last process of the LSTM cell is to determine the final output. A sigmoid layer decides which parts of the cell state to output. We then put the cell state through a **tanh** activation to generate all of the possible values, and multiply it by the output of the sigmoid gate, to produce desired outputs according to a non-linear function.

These three steps in the LSTM cell process produce a significant result, that being that the model can be trained to learn which information to retain in long-term memory and which information to forget. Genius!

Implementing an LSTM model

The process that we performed previously, to build the basic RNN model, will remain the same, except for the model definition part. So, let's implement this and check the performance of the new model.

The code for the model can be viewed at `https://github.com/PacktPublishing/Python-Deep-Learning-Projects/blob/master/Chapter05/2.%20rnn_lstm.py`.

Defining our LSTM model

Again, most of the code will remain same—the only the major change will be to use `tf.nn.rnn_cell.LSTMCell()`, instead of `tf.nn.rnn_cell.BasicRNNCell()`. While initializing the LSTM cell, we are using an orthogonal initializer that will generate a random orthogonal matrix, which is an effective way of combating exploding and vanishing gradients:

```
class Model:
    def __init__(self, size_layer, num_layers, embedded_size,
                 dict_size, dimension_output, learning_rate):
        def cells(reuse=False):
            return
tf.nn.rnn_cell.LSTMCell(size_layer,initializer=tf.orthogonal_initializer(),
reuse=reuse)
        self.X = tf.placeholder(tf.int32, [None, None])
        self.Y = tf.placeholder(tf.float32, [None, dimension_output])

        encoder_embeddings = tf.Variable(tf.random_uniform([dict_size,
embedded_size], -1, 1))
        encoder_embedded = tf.nn.embedding_lookup(encoder_embeddings,
self.X)

        rnn_cells = tf.nn.rnn_cell.MultiRNNCell([cells() for _ in
range(num_layers)])
        outputs, _ = tf.nn.dynamic_rnn(rnn_cells, encoder_embedded, dtype =
tf.float32)

        W = tf.get_variable('w',shape=(size_layer,
```

```
dimension_output),initializer=tf.orthogonal_initializer())
        b =
tf.get_variable('b',shape=(dimension_output),initializer=tf.zeros_initializ
er())

        self.logits = tf.matmul(outputs[:, -1], W) + b
        self.cost =
tf.reduce_mean(tf.nn.softmax_cross_entropy_with_logits(logits =
self.logits, labels = self.Y))
        self.optimizer = tf.train.AdamOptimizer(learning_rate =
learning_rate).minimize(self.cost)

        correct_pred = tf.equal(tf.argmax(self.logits, 1),
tf.argmax(self.Y, 1))
        self.accuracy = tf.reduce_mean(tf.cast(correct_pred, tf.float32))
```

So this is what the architecture of the LSTM model looks like—almost the same, compared to the previous basic model, except with the addition of the LSTM cells in the **RNN Block**:

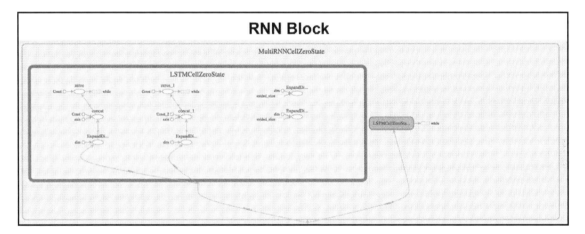

Training the LSTM model

Now that we've established our LSTM intuition and built the model, let's train it as follows:

```
EARLY_STOPPING, CURRENT_CHECKPOINT, CURRENT_ACC, EPOCH = 5, 0, 0, 0
while True:
    lasttime = time.time()
    if CURRENT_CHECKPOINT == EARLY_STOPPING:
        print('break epoch:%d\n'%(EPOCH))
        break
    train_acc, train_loss, test_acc, test_loss = 0, 0, 0, 0
```

```
    for i in range(0, (len(train_X) // batch_size) * batch_size,
batch_size):
        batch_x = str_idx(train_X[i:i+batch_size],dictionary,maxlen)
        acc, loss, _ = sess.run([model.accuracy, model.cost,
model.optimizer],
                        feed_dict = {model.X : batch_x, model.Y :
train_onehot[i:i+batch_size]})
        train_loss += loss
        train_acc += acc
    for i in range(0, (len(test_X) // batch_size) * batch_size,
batch_size):
        batch_x = str_idx(test_X[i:i+batch_size],dictionary,maxlen)
        acc, loss = sess.run([model.accuracy, model.cost],
                        feed_dict = {model.X : batch_x, model.Y :
train_onehot[i:i+batch_size]})
        test_loss += loss
        test_acc += acc
    train_loss /= (len(train_X) // batch_size)
    train_acc /= (len(train_X) // batch_size)
    test_loss /= (len(test_X) // batch_size)
    test_acc /= (len(test_X) // batch_size)
    if test_acc > CURRENT_ACC:
        print('epoch: %d, pass acc: %f, current acc:
%f'%(EPOCH,CURRENT_ACC, test_acc))
        CURRENT_ACC = test_acc
        CURRENT_CHECKPOINT = 0
    else:
        CURRENT_CHECKPOINT += 1
    print('time taken:', time.time()-lasttime)
    print('epoch: %d, training loss: %f, training acc: %f, valid loss: %f,
valid acc: %f\n'%(EPOCH,train_loss,
train_acc,test_loss,
test_acc))
    EPOCH += 1
```

While the LSTM model is being trained, we can see the logs of each epoch as shown in the following screenshot:

```
epoch: 0, pass acc: 0.000000, current acc: 0.503418
time taken: 24.84701442718506
epoch: 0, training loss: 0.678766, training acc: 0.566998, valid loss: 0.731442, valid acc: 0.503418

epoch: 1, pass acc: 0.503418, current acc: 0.507324
time taken: 25.422342777252197
epoch: 1, training loss: 0.583385, training acc: 0.689749, valid loss: 0.985936, valid acc: 0.507324

time taken: 25.386239051818848
epoch: 2, training loss: 0.434628, training acc: 0.801136, valid loss: 1.419970, valid acc: 0.502441

time taken: 25.27470636367798
epoch: 3, training loss: 0.299446, training acc: 0.878433, valid loss: 1.933248, valid acc: 0.501953

time taken: 25.538538455963135
epoch: 4, training loss: 0.199658, training acc: 0.923651, valid loss: 2.140550, valid acc: 0.496582

time taken: 25.40754723548889
epoch: 5, training loss: 0.122418, training acc: 0.954545, valid loss: 2.092578, valid acc: 0.495605

time taken: 25.391931295394897
epoch: 6, training loss: 0.086722, training acc: 0.968395, valid loss: 2.719897, valid acc: 0.506348

break epoch:7
```

Following is the output:

```
('time taken:', 18.061596155166626)
epoch: 10, training loss: 0.015714, training acc: 0.994910, valid loss:
4.252270, valid acc: 0.500000

('time taken:', 17.786305904388428)
epoch: 11, training loss: 0.011198, training acc: 0.995975, valid loss:
4.644272, valid acc: 0.502441

('time taken:', 19.031064987182617)
epoch: 12, training loss: 0.009245, training acc: 0.996686, valid loss:
4.575824, valid acc: 0.499512

('time taken:', 16.996762990951538)
epoch: 13, training loss: 0.006528, training acc: 0.997751, valid loss:
4.449901, valid acc: 0.501953

('time taken:', 17.008245944976807)
epoch: 14, training loss: 0.011770, training acc: 0.995739, valid loss:
4.282045, valid acc: 0.499023

break epoch:15
```

You will notice that, even after using the same configurations of the model, the training time required for the LSTM-based model will be greater than the RNN model.

Evaluation of the LSTM model

Now, let's again compute the metrics and compare the performance:

```
logits = sess.run(model.logits,
feed_dict={model.X:str_idx(test_X,dictionary,maxlen)})
print(metrics.classification_report(test_Y, np.argmax(logits,1),
target_names = trainset.target_names))
```

The computed outputs are shown as follows:

	precision	recall	f1-score	support
negative	0.76	0.62	0.69	1034
positive	0.70	0.82	0.75	1099
avg / total	0.73	0.72	0.72	2133

So, we can clearly see the boost in the performance of the model! Now, with the LSTM, the f1-score is bumped to 72% whereas, in our previous basic RNN model, it was 66%, which is quite a good improvement of 7%.

Sequence-to-sequence models

In this section, we'll implement a seq2seq model (an encoder-decoder RNN), based on the LSTM unit, for a simple sequence-to-sequence question-answer task. This model can be trained to map an input sequence (questions) to an output sequence (answers), which are not necessarily of the same length as each other.

This type of seq2seq model has shown impressive performance in various other tasks such as speech recognition, machine translation, question answering, **Neural Machine Translation** (**NMT**), and image caption generation.

The following diagram helps us visualize our seq2seq model:

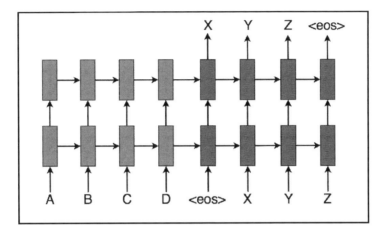

The illustration of the sequence to sequence (seq2seq) model. Each rectangle box is the RNN cell in which blue ones are the encoders and Red been the Decoders.

In the encoder-decoder structure, one RNN (blue) **encodes** the input sequence. The encoder emits the context **C**, usually as a simple function of its final hidden state. And the second RNN (red) **decoder** calculates the target values and generates the output sequence. One essential step is to let the encoder and decoder communicate. In the simplest approach, you use the last hidden state of the encoder to initialize the decoder. Other approaches let the decoder attend to different parts of the encoded input at different timesteps in the decoding process.

So, let's get started with data preparation, model building, training, tuning, and evaluating our seq2seq model, and see how it performs.

The model file can be found at https://github.com/PacktPublishing/Python-Deep-Learning-Projects/blob/master/Chapter05/3.%20rnn_lstm_seq2seq.py.

Data preparation

Here, we will build our question-answering system. For the project, we need a dataset with question and answer pairs, as shown in the following screenshot. Both of the columns contain sequences of words, which is what we need to feed into our seq2seq model. Also, note that our sentences can be of dynamic length:

Question	Answer
hi	hi there
good morning	good morning
good afternoon	good afternoon
good evening	good evening
good night	good night have a nice dream
how are you	i am fine thank you
how are you doing	doing good thank you
what is your name	my name is papaya and what do you want me to call you dear sir or mada ...
whats your name	my name is papaya may i also have your name please
may i have your name	sure my name is papaya may i also have your name please
are you a boy or a girl	i am a boy
are you a man or a woman	i am still a boy
are you a woman or a man	i am a boy
where do you live	miami florida
in which city do you live	i live in miami florida
in which country do you live	i live in the united states
where are you	currently i am in miami florida
where are you now	i am in miami florida
why are we here	we are here to communicate with each other
whats up	not much
what a nice day it is	yes it is
another	why are ets eyes so big he saw the phone bill for phoning home no free ...
thats really a funny joke	i think youre making that joke

The dataset which we prepared with set of questions and answers

Let's load them and perform the same data processing using `build_dataset()`. In the end, we will have a dictionary with words as keys, where the associated values are the counts of the word in the respective corpus. Also, we have four extras values that we talked about before in this chapter:

```
import numpy as np
import tensorflow as tf
import collections
from utils import *


file_path = './conversation_data/'

with open(file_path+'from.txt', 'r') as fopen:
    text_from = fopen.read().lower().split('\n')
with open(file_path+'to.txt', 'r') as fopen:
    text_to = fopen.read().lower().split('\n')
print('len from: %d, len to: %d'%(len(text_from), len(text_to)))


concat_from = ' '.join(text_from).split()
vocabulary_size_from = len(list(set(concat_from)))
data_from, count_from, dictionary_from, rev_dictionary_from =
build_dataset(concat_from, vocabulary_size_from)


concat_to = ' '.join(text_to).split()
vocabulary_size_to = len(list(set(concat_to)))
data_to, count_to, dictionary_to, rev_dictionary_to =
build_dataset(concat_to, vocabulary_size_to)


GO = dictionary_from['GO']
PAD = dictionary_from['PAD']
EOS = dictionary_from['EOS']
UNK = dictionary_from['UNK']
```

Defining a seq2seq model

In this section, we will outline the TensorFlow seq2seq model definition. We employed an embedding layer to go from integer representation to the vector representation of the input. This seq2seq model has four major components: the embedding layer, encoders, decoders, and cost/optimizers.

You can see the model in graphical form in the following diagram:

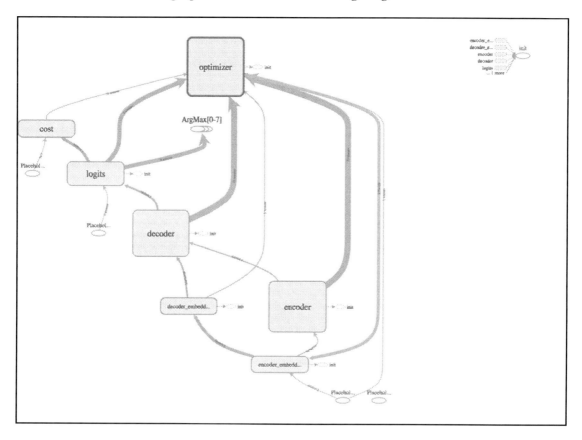

The TensorBoard visualization of the seq2seq model. This graph shows the connection between the encode and the decoder with other relevent components like the optimizer.

The following is a formal outline of the TensorFlow seq2seq model definition:

```
class Chatbot:
  def __init__(self, size_layer, num_layers, embedded_size,
  from_dict_size, to_dict_size, learning_rate, batch_size):

  def cells(reuse=False):
  return
tf.nn.rnn_cell.LSTMCell(size_layer,initializer=tf.orthogonal_initializer(),
reuse=reuse)

  self.X = tf.placeholder(tf.int32, [None, None])
  self.Y = tf.placeholder(tf.int32, [None, None])
  self.X_seq_len = tf.placeholder(tf.int32, [None])
```

```
self.Y_seq_len = tf.placeholder(tf.int32, [None])

with tf.variable_scope("encoder_embeddings"):
encoder_embeddings = tf.Variable(tf.random_uniform([from_dict_size,
embedded_size], -1, 1))
encoder_embedded = tf.nn.embedding_lookup(encoder_embeddings, self.X)
main = tf.strided_slice(self.X, [0, 0], [batch_size, -1], [1, 1])

with tf.variable_scope("decoder_embeddings"):
decoder_input = tf.concat([tf.fill([batch_size, 1], GO), main], 1)
decoder_embeddings = tf.Variable(tf.random_uniform([to_dict_size,
embedded_size], -1, 1))
decoder_embedded = tf.nn.embedding_lookup(encoder_embeddings,
decoder_input)

with tf.variable_scope("encoder"):
rnn_cells = tf.nn.rnn_cell.MultiRNNCell([cells() for _ in
range(num_layers)])
_, last_state = tf.nn.dynamic_rnn(rnn_cells, encoder_embedded,
dtype = tf.float32)
with tf.variable_scope("decoder"):
rnn_cells_dec = tf.nn.rnn_cell.MultiRNNCell([cells() for _ in
range(num_layers)])
outputs, _ = tf.nn.dynamic_rnn(rnn_cells_dec, decoder_embedded,
initial_state = last_state,
dtype = tf.float32)
with tf.variable_scope("logits"):
self.logits = tf.layers.dense(outputs,to_dict_size)
print(self.logits)
masks = tf.sequence_mask(self.Y_seq_len, tf.reduce_max(self.Y_seq_len),
dtype=tf.float32)
with tf.variable_scope("cost"):
self.cost = tf.contrib.seq2seq.sequence_loss(logits = self.logits,
targets = self.Y,
weights = masks)
with tf.variable_scope("optimizer"):
self.optimizer = tf.train.AdamOptimizer(learning_rate =
learning_rate).minimize(self.cost)
```

Hyperparameters

Now that we have our model definition ready, we will define the hyperparameters. We will keep most of the configurations the same as in the previous one:

```
size_layer = 128
num_layers = 2
```

```
embedded_size = 128
learning_rate = 0.001
batch_size = 32
epoch = 50
```

Training the seq2seq model

Now, let's train the model. We will need some helper functions for the padding of the sentence and to calculate the accuracy of the model:

```
def pad_sentence_batch(sentence_batch, pad_int):
    padded_seqs = []
    seq_lens = []
    max_sentence_len = 50
    for sentence in sentence_batch:
        padded_seqs.append(sentence + [pad_int] * (max_sentence_len -
len(sentence)))
        seq_lens.append(50)
    return padded_seqs, seq_lens

def check_accuracy(logits, Y):
    acc = 0
    for i in range(logits.shape[0]):
        internal_acc = 0
        for k in range(len(Y[i])):
            if Y[i][k] == logits[i][k]:
                internal_acc += 1
        acc += (internal_acc / len(Y[i]))
    return acc / logits.shape[0]
```

We initialize our model and iterate the session for the defined number of epochs:

```
tf.reset_default_graph()
sess = tf.InteractiveSession()
model = Chatbot(size_layer, num_layers, embedded_size, vocabulary_size_from
+ 4,
                vocabulary_size_to + 4, learning_rate, batch_size)
sess.run(tf.global_variables_initializer())

for i in range(epoch):
 total_loss, total_accuracy = 0, 0
 for k in range(0, (len(text_from) // batch_size) * batch_size,
batch_size):
 batch_x, seq_x = pad_sentence_batch(X[k: k+batch_size], PAD)
 batch_y, seq_y = pad_sentence_batch(Y[k: k+batch_size], PAD)
 predicted, loss, _ = sess.run([tf.argmax(model.logits,2), model.cost,
```

```
model.optimizer],
 feed_dict={model.X:batch_x,
 model.Y:batch_y,
 model.X_seq_len:seq_x,
 model.Y_seq_len:seq_y})
 total_loss += loss
 total_accuracy += check_accuracy(predicted,batch_y)
 total_loss /= (len(text_from) // batch_size)
 total_accuracy /= (len(text_from) // batch_size)
 print('epoch: %d, avg loss: %f, avg accuracy: %f'%(i+1, total_loss,
total_accuracy))
```

OUTPUT:

```
epoch: 47, avg loss: 0.682934, avg accuracy: 0.000000
epoch: 48, avg loss: 0.680367, avg accuracy: 0.000000
epoch: 49, avg loss: 0.677882, avg accuracy: 0.000000
epoch: 50, avg loss: 0.678484, avg accuracy: 0.000000
 .
 .
 .
epoch: 1133, avg loss: 0.000464, avg accuracy: 1.000000
epoch: 1134, avg loss: 0.000462, avg accuracy: 1.000000
epoch: 1135, avg loss: 0.000460, avg accuracy: 1.000000
epoch: 1136, avg loss: 0.000457, avg accuracy: 1.000000
```

Evaluation of the seq2seq model

So, after running the training process for few hours on a GPU, you can see that the accuracy has reached a value of 1.0, and loss has significantly reduced to 0.00045. Let's see how the model performs when we ask some generic questions.

To make predictions, we will create a predict() function that will take the raw text of any size as input and return the response to the question that we asked. We did a quick fix to handle the **Out Of Vocab (OOV)** words by replacing them with the PAD:

```
def predict(sentence):
    X_in = []
    for word in sentence.split():
        try:
            X_in.append(dictionary_from[word])
        except:
            X_in.append(PAD)
            pass
    test, seq_x = pad_sentence_batch([X_in], PAD)
    input_batch = np.zeros([batch_size,seq_x[0]])
    input_batch[0] =test[0]
```

```
log = sess.run(tf.argmax(model.logits,2),
                              feed_dict={
                                      model.X:input_batch,
                                      model.X_seq_len:seq_x,
                                      model.Y_seq_len:seq_x
                                      }
                      )
result=' '.join(rev_dictionary_to[i] for i in log[0])
return result
```

When the model was trained for the first 50 epochs, we had the following result:

```
>> predict('where do you live')
>> i PAD PAD PAD PAD PAD PAD PAD PAD PAD PAD PAD PAD PAD PAD PAD PAD PAD
PAD PAD PAD PAD PAD PAD PAD PAD PAD PAD PAD PAD PAD PAD PAD PAD PAD PAD
PAD PAD PAD PAD PAD PAD PAD PAD PAD PAD PAD PAD PAD

>> print predict('how are you ?')
>> i am PAD PAD PAD PAD PAD PAD PAD PAD PAD PAD PAD PAD PAD PAD PAD PAD PAD
PAD PAD PAD PAD PAD PAD PAD PAD PAD PAD PAD PAD PAD PAD PAD PAD PAD PAD
PAD PAD PAD PAD PAD PAD PAD PAD PAD PAD PAD
```

When the model was trained for 1,136 epochs:

```
>> predict('where do you live')
>> miami florida PAD PAD PAD PAD PAD PAD PAD PAD PAD PAD PAD PAD PAD PAD
PAD PAD PAD PAD PAD PAD PAD PAD PAD PAD PAD PAD PAD PAD PAD PAD PAD PAD
PAD PAD PAD PAD PAD PAD PAD PAD PAD PAD PAD PAD PAD

>> print predict('how are you ?')
>> i am fine thank you PAD PAD PAD PAD PAD PAD PAD PAD PAD PAD PAD PAD PAD
PAD PAD PAD PAD PAD PAD PAD PAD PAD PAD PAD PAD PAD PAD PAD PAD PAD PAD PAD
PAD PAD PAD PAD PAD PAD PAD PAD PAD PAD PAD PAD
```

Well! That's impressive, right? Now your model is not just able to understand the context, but can also generate answers word by word.

Summary

In this chapter, we covered basic RNN cells, LSTM cells, and the seq2seq model in building a language model that can be used for multiple NLP tasks. We implemented a chatbot, from scratch, to answer questions by generating a sequence of words from the provided dataset.

The experience in this exercise demonstrates the value of LSTM as an often necessary component of the RNN. With the LSTM, we were able to see the following improvements over past CNN models:

- The LSTM was able to preserve state information
- The length of sentences for both inputs and outputs could be variable and different
- The LSTM was able to adequately handle complex context

Specifically, in this chapter, we did the following:

- Gained an intuition about the RNN and its primary forms
- Implemented a language model using RNN
- Learned about the LSTM model
- Implemented the LSTM language model and compared it to the RNN
- Implemented an encoder-decoder RNN based on the LSTM unit for a simple sequence-to-sequence question-answer task

With the right training data, it would be possible to use this model to achieve the goal of the hypothetical client (the restaurant chain) of building a robust chatbot (in combination with other computational linguistic technologies that we've explored) that could automate the over-the-phone food ordering process.

Well done!

6
Generative Language Model for Content Creation

This work is certainly getting exciting, and the word is out that we're demonstrating a professional set of deep learning capabilities by producing solutions for a wide range of business use cases! As data scientists, we understand the transferability of our skills. We know that we can provide value by employing core skills when working on problems that we know are similar in structure but that may seem different at first glance. This couldn't be more true than in the next deep learning project. Next, we're (hypothetically) going to be working on a project in which a creative group has asked us to help produce some original content for movie scripts, song lyrics, and even music!

How can we leverage our experience in solving problems for restaurant chains to such a different industry? Let's explore what we know and what we're going to be asked to do. In past projects, we demonstrated that we could take an image as input and output a class label (Chapter 2, *Training NN for Prediction Using Regression*); we trained a model to take text input and output sentiment classifications (Chapter 3, *Word Representation Using word2vec*); we built a NLP pipeline for an open domain question and answering chatbot where we took text as input and identified text in a corpus to present as the appropriate output (Chapter 4, *Building an NLP Pipeline for Building Chatbots*); and we expanded that chatbot's functionality so that it was able to serve a restaurant with an automated ordering system (Chapter 5, *Sequence-to-Sequence Models for Building Chatbots*).

Define the goal: In this next project, we're going to take the next step in our computational linguistics journey in *Python Deep Learning Projects* and generate new content for our client. We need to help them by providing a deep learning solution that generates new content that can be used in movie scrips, song lyrics, and music.

In this chapter, we will implement a generative model that can generate content using **long short-term memory** (**LSTM**), variational autoencoders, and **Generative Adversarial Networks** (**GANs**). We will be implementing models for both text and images, which can then generate images and text for artists and various businesses.

In this chapter, we'll cover the following topics:

- Text generation with LSTM
- Additional power of a bi-directional LSTM for text generation
- Deep (multi-layer) LSTM to generate lyrics for a song
- Deep (multi-layer) LSTM music generation for a song

LSTM for text generation

In this section, we'll explore a popular deep learning model: the **recurrent neural network** (**RNN**), and how it can be used in the generation of sequence data. The universal way to create sequence data in deep learning is to train a model (usually a RNN or a ConvNet) to predict the next token or next few tokens in a series, based on the previous tokens as input. For instance, let's imagine that we're given the sentence with these words as input: `I love to work in deep learning`. We will train the network to predict the next character as our target.

 When working with textual data, tokens are typically words or characters, and any network that can model the probability of the next token given the previous ones is called a language model that can capture the latent space of language.

Upon training the language model, we can then proceed to feed some initial text and ask it to generate the next token, then add the generated token back into the language model to predict more tokens. For our hypothetical use case, our creative client will use this model and later provide examples of text that we would then be asked to create novel content for in that style.

The first step in building the generative model for text is to import all the modules required. Keras APIs will be used in this project to create the models and Keras utils will be used to download the dataset. In order to build text generation modules, we need a significant amount of simple text data.

You can find the code file for this at `https://github.com/PacktPublishing/Python-Deep-Learning-Projects/blob/master/Chapter06/Basics/generative_text.py`:

```python
import keras
import numpy as np
from keras import layers
# Gather data
path = keras.utils.get_file(
    'sample.txt',
    origin='https://s3.amazonaws.com/text-datasets/nietzsche.txt')
text = open(path).read().lower()
print('Number of words in corpus:', len(text))
```

Data pre-processing

Let's perform the data pre-processing to convert the raw data into its encoded form. We will extract fixed length sentences, encode them using a one-hot encoding process, and finally build a tensor of the (`sequence`, `maxlen`, `unique_characters`) shape, as shown in the following diagram. At the same time, we will prepare the target vector, y, to contain the associated next character that follows each extracted sequence.

The following is the code we'll use to pre-process the data:

```python
# Length of extracted character sequences
maxlen = 100

# We sample a new sequence every 5 characters
step = 5

# List to hold extracted sequences
sentences = []

# List to hold the target characters
next_chars = []

# Extracting sentences and the next characters.
for i in range(0, len(text) - maxlen, step):
    sentences.append(text[i: i + maxlen])
    next_chars.append(text[i + maxlen])
print('Number of sequences:', len(sentences))

# List of unique characters in the corpus
chars = sorted(list(set(text)))

# Dictionary mapping unique characters to their index in `chars`
```

```
char_indices = dict((char, chars.index(char)) for char in chars)

# Converting characters into one-hot encoding.
x = np.zeros((len(sentences), maxlen, len(chars)), dtype=np.bool)
y = np.zeros((len(sentences), len(chars)), dtype=np.bool)
for i, sentence in enumerate(sentences):
    for t, char in enumerate(sentence):
        x[i, t, char_indices[char]] = 1
    y[i, char_indices[next_chars[i]]] = 1
```

Following is how data preprocessing looks like. We have transformed the raw data into the tensors which we will further use for the training purpose:

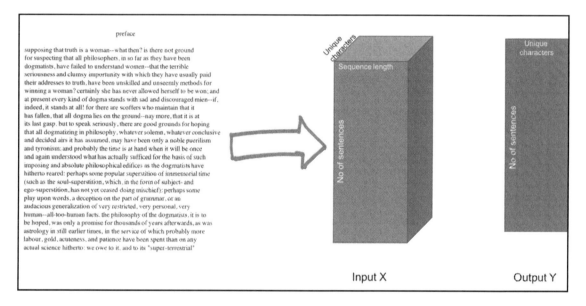

Defining the LSTM model for text generation

This deep model is a network that's made up of one hidden LSTM layer with `128` memory units, followed by a `Dense` classifier layer with a `softmax` activation function over all possible characters. Targets are one-hot encoded, and this means that we'll train the model using `categorical_crossentropy` as the `loss` function.

The following code block defines the model's architecture:

```
model = keras.models.Sequential()
model.add(layers.LSTM(128, input_shape=(maxlen, len(chars))))
model.add(layers.Dense(len(chars), activation='softmax'))


optimizer = keras.optimizers.RMSprop(lr=0.01)
model.compile(loss='categorical_crossentropy', optimizer=optimizer)
```

The following diagram helps us visualize the model's architecture:

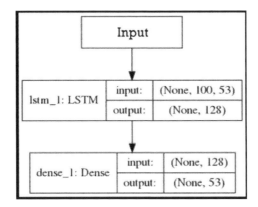

Training the model

In text generation, the way we choose the succeeding character is crucial. The most common way (greedy sampling) leads to repetitive characters that does not produce a coherent language. This is why we use a different approach called **stochastic sampling**. This adds a degree of randomness to the prediction probability distribution.

Use the following code to re-weight the prediction probability distribution and sample a character index:

```
def sample(preds, temperature=1.0):
    preds = np.asarray(preds).astype('float64')
    preds = np.log(preds) / temperature
    exp_preds = np.exp(preds)
    preds = exp_preds / np.sum(exp_preds)
    probas = np.random.multinomial(1, preds, 1)
    return np.argmax(probas)
```

Now, we iterate the training and text generation, beginning with 30 training epochs and then fitting the model for 1 iteration. Then, perform a random selection of the seed text, convert it into one-hot encoding format, and perform predictions of 100 characters. Finally, append the newly generated character to the seed text in each iteration.

After each epoch, generation is performed by utilizing a different temperature from a range of values. This makes it possible to see and understand the evolution of the generated text at model convergence, and the consequences of temperature in the sampling strategy.

 Temperature is an LSTM hyperparameter that is used to influence prediction randomness by logit scaling before applying softmax.

We need to execute the following code so that we can train the model:

```
for epoch in range(1, 30):
    print('epoch', epoch)
    # Fit the model for 1 epoch
    model.fit(x, y, batch_size=128, epochs=1, callbacks=callbacks_list)

    # Select a text seed randomly
    start_index = random.randint(0, len(text) - maxlen - 1)
    generated_text = text[start_index: start_index + maxlen]
    print('---Seeded text: "' + generated_text + '"')

    for temperature in [0.2, 0.5, 1.0, 1.2]:
        print('------ Selected temperature:', temperature)
        sys.stdout.write(generated_text)

        # We generate 100 characters
        for i in range(100):
            sampled = np.zeros((1, maxlen, len(chars)))
            for t, char in enumerate(generated_text):
                sampled[0, t, char_indices[char]] = 1.

            preds = model.predict(sampled, verbose=0)[0]
            next_index = sample(preds, temperature)
            next_char = chars[next_index]

            generated_text += next_char
            generated_text = generated_text[1:]

            sys.stdout.write(next_char)
            sys.stdout.flush()
        print()
```

Inference and results

This gets us to the exciting part of our generative language model—creating custom content! The inference step in deep learning is where we take a trained model and expose it to new data to make predictions or classifications. In the current context of this project, we're looking for model outputs, that is, new sentences, which will be our novel custom content. Let's see what our deep learning model can do!

We will use the following code to store and load the checkpoints into a binary file that stores all of the weights:

```python
from keras.callbacks import ModelCheckpoint

filepath="weights-{epoch:02d}-{loss:.4f}.hdf5"
checkpoint = ModelCheckpoint(filepath, monitor='loss', verbose=1,
save_best_only=True, mode='min')
callbacks_list = [checkpoint]
```

Now, we will use the trained model and generate new text:

```python
seed_text = 'i want to generate new text after this '
print (seed_text)

# load the network weights
filename = "weights-30-1.545.hdf5"
model.load_weights(filename)
model.compile(loss='categorical_crossentropy', optimizer='adam')

for temperature in [0.5]:
        print('------ temperature:', temperature)
        sys.stdout.write(seed_text)

        # We generate 400 characters
        for i in range(40):
            sampled = np.zeros((1, maxlen, len(chars)))
            for t, char in enumerate(seed_text):
                sampled[0, t, char_indices[char]] = 1.

            preds = model.predict(sampled, verbose=0)[0]
            next_index = sample(preds, temperature)
            next_char = chars[next_index]

            seed_text += next_char
            seed_text = seed_text[1:]

            sys.stdout.write(next_char)
```

```
            sys.stdout.flush()
        print()
```

After successfully training the model, we will see the following results at the 30th epoch:

```
--- Generating with seed:
the "good old time" to which it belongs, and as an expressio"
------ temperature: 0.2
the "good old time" to which it belongs, and as an expression of the sense
of the stronger and subli
------ temperature: 0.5
and as an expression of the sense of the stronger and sublication of
possess and more spirit and in
------ temperature: 1.0
e stronger and sublication of possess and more spirit and instinge, and it:
he ventlumentles, no dif
------ temperature: 1.2
d more spirit and instinge, and it: he ventlumentles, no differific and
does amongly domen--whete ac
```

We find that, with low values for the `temperature` hyperparameter, the model is able to generate more practical and realistic words. When we use higher temperatures, the generated text becomes more interesting and unusual—some might even say creative. Sometimes, the model will even invent new words that often sound vaguely credible. So, the idea of using low temperature is more reasonable for business use cases where you need to be realistic, while higher temperature values can be used in more creative and artistic use cases.

The art of deep learning and generative linguistic models is a balance between the learned structure and randomness, which makes the output interesting.

Generating lyrics using deep (multi-layer) LSTM

Now that we have built a basic LSTM model for text generation and learned its value, let's move one step further and create a deep LSTM model suited for the task of generating music lyrics. We now have a new goal: to build and train a model that outputs entirely new and original lyrics that is in the style of an arbitrary number of artists.

Let's begin. You can refer to the code file found at `Lyrics-ai` (`https://github.com/PacktPublishing/Python-Deep-Learning-Projects/tree/master/Chapter06/Lyrics-ai`) for this exercise.

Data pre-processing

To build a model that can generate lyrics, we will need a huge amount of lyric data, which can easily be extracted from various sources. We collected lyrics from around 10,000 songs and stored them in a text file called `lyrics_data.txt`. You can find the data file in our GitHub repository (`https://github.com/PacktPublishing/Python-Deep-Learning-Projects/blob/master/Chapter06/Lyrics-ai/lyrics_data.txt`).

Now that we have our data, we need to convert this raw text into the one-hot encoding version:

```python
import numpy as np
import codecs

# Class to perform all preprocessing operations
class Preprocessing:
    vocabulary = {}
    binary_vocabulary = {}
    char_lookup = {}
    size = 0
    separator = '->'
# This will take the data file and convert data into one hot encoding and
dump the vocab into the file.
    def generate(self, input_file_path):
        input_file = codecs.open(input_file_path, 'r', 'utf_8')
        index = 0
        for line in input_file:
            for char in line:
                if char not in self.vocabulary:
                    self.vocabulary[char] = index
                    self.char_lookup[index] = char
                    index += 1
        input_file.close()
        self.set_vocabulary_size()
        self.create_binary_representation()

# This method is to load the vocab into the memory
    def retrieve(self, input_file_path):
        input_file = codecs.open(input_file_path, 'r', 'utf_8')
        buffer = ""
        for line in input_file:
```

```
        try:
            separator_position = len(buffer) +
line.index(self.separator)
            buffer += line
            key = buffer[:separator_position]
            value = buffer[separator_position + len(self.separator):]
            value = np.fromstring(value, sep=',')

            self.binary_vocabulary[key] = value
            self.vocabulary[key] = np.where(value == 1)[0][0]
            self.char_lookup[np.where(value == 1)[0][0]] = key

            buffer = ""
        except ValueError:
            buffer += line
    input_file.close()
    self.set_vocabulary_size()

# Below are some helper functions to perform pre-processing.
    def create_binary_representation(self):
        for key, value in self.vocabulary.iteritems():
            binary = np.zeros(self.size)
            binary[value] = 1
            self.binary_vocabulary[key] = binary

    def set_vocabulary_size(self):
        self.size = len(self.vocabulary)
        print "Vocabulary size: {}".format(self.size)

    def get_serialized_binary_representation(self):
        string = ""
        np.set_printoptions(threshold='nan')
        for key, value in self.binary_vocabulary.iteritems():
            array_as_string = np.array2string(value, separator=',',
max_line_width=self.size * self.size)
            string += "{}{}{}\n".format(key.encode('utf-8'),
self.separator, array_as_string[1:len(array_as_string) - 1])
        return string
```

The overall objective of the pre-processing module is to convert the raw text data into one-hot encoding, as shown in the following diagram:

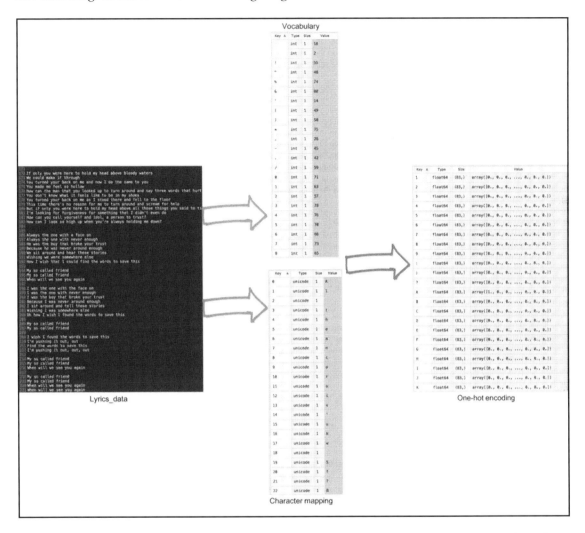

This figure represents the data preprocessing part. The law lyrics data is used to build the vocabulary mapping which is further been transformed into the on-hot encoding.

After the successful execution of the pre-processing module, a binary file will be dumped as `{dataset_filename}.vocab`. This `vocab` file is one of the mandatory files that needs to be fed into the model during the training process, along with the dataset.

Defining the model

We will be using a approach from the Keras model that we used earlier in this project to build this model. To build a more complex model, we will use TensorFlow to write each layer from scratch. TensorFlow gives us, as data scientists and deep learning engineers, more fine-tuned control over our model's architecture.

For this model, we will use the code in the following block to create two placeholders that will store the input and output values:

```
import tensorflow as tf
import pickle
from tensorflow.contrib import rnn

    def build(self, input_number, sequence_length, layers_number,
units_number, output_number):
        self.x = tf.placeholder("float", [None, sequence_length,
input_number])
        self.y = tf.placeholder("float", [None, output_number])
        self.sequence_length = sequence_length
```

Next, we need to store the weights and bias in the variables that we've created:

```
        self.weights = {
            'out': tf.Variable(tf.random_normal([units_number,
output_number]))
        }
        self.biases = {
            'out': tf.Variable(tf.random_normal([output_number]))
        }

        x = tf.transpose(self.x, [1, 0, 2])
        x = tf.reshape(x, [-1, input_number])
        x = tf.split(x, sequence_length, 0)
```

We can build this model by using multiple LSTM layers, with the basic LSTM cells assigning each layer with the specified number of cells, as shown in the following diagram:

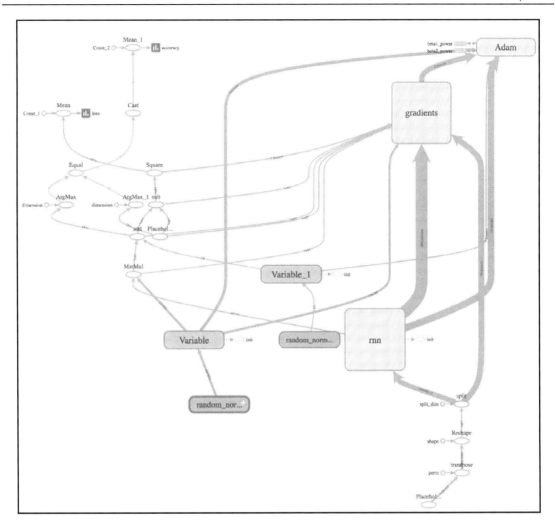

Tensorboard visualization of the LSTM architecture

The following is the code for this:

```
lstm_layers = []
for i in range(0, layers_number):
    lstm_layer = rnn.BasicLSTMCell(units_number)
    lstm_layers.append(lstm_layer)

deep_lstm = rnn.MultiRNNCell(lstm_layers)

self.outputs, states = rnn.static_rnn(deep_lstm, x,
dtype=tf.float32)
```

```
        print "Build model with input_number: {}, sequence_length: {},
layers_number: {}, " \
            "units_number: {}, output_number: {}".format(input_number,
sequence_length, layers_number,
                                                    units_number,
output_number)
# This method is using to dump the model configurations
        self.save(input_number, sequence_length, layers_number,
units_number, output_number)
```

Training the deep TensorFlow-based LSTM model

Now that we have the mandatory inputs, that is, the dataset file path, the `vocab` file path, and the model name, we will initiate the training process. Let's define all of the hyperparameters for the model:

```
import os
import argparse
from modules.Model import *
from modules.Batch import *

def main():
    parser = argparse.ArgumentParser()
    parser.add_argument('--training_file', type=str, required=True)
    parser.add_argument('--vocabulary_file', type=str, required=True)
    parser.add_argument('--model_name', type=str, required=True)

    parser.add_argument('--epoch', type=int, default=200)
    parser.add_argument('--batch_size', type=int, default=50)
    parser.add_argument('--sequence_length', type=int, default=50)
    parser.add_argument('--log_frequency', type=int, default=100)
    parser.add_argument('--learning_rate', type=int, default=0.002)
    parser.add_argument('--units_number', type=int, default=128)
    parser.add_argument('--layers_number', type=int, default=2)
    args = parser.parse_args()
```

Since we are batch training the model, we will divide the dataset into batches of a defined `batch_size` using the `Batch` module:

```
batch = Batch(training_file, vocabulary_file, batch_size, sequence_length)
```

Each batch will return two arrays. One will be the input vector of the input sequence, which will have a shape of [`batch_size`, `sequence_length`, `vocab_size`], and the other array will hold the label vector, which will have a shape of [`batch_size`, `vocab_size`].

Now, we initialize our model and create the optimizer function. In this model, we used the Adam Optimizer.

 The Adam Optimizer is a powerful tool. You can read up on it from the official TensorFlow documentation at `https://www.tensorflow.org/api_docs/python/tf/train/AdamOptimizer`.

Then, we will train our model and perform the optimization over each batch:

```
# Building model instance and classifier
    model = Model(model_name)
    model.build(input_number, sequence_length, layers_number, units_number,
classes_number)
    classifier = model.get_classifier()

# Building cost functions
    cost = tf.reduce_mean(tf.square(classifier - model.y))
    optimizer =
tf.train.AdamOptimizer(learning_rate=learning_rate).minimize(cost)

# Computing the accuracy metrics
    expected_prediction = tf.equal(tf.argmax(classifier, 1),
tf.argmax(model.y, 1))
    accuracy = tf.reduce_mean(tf.cast(expected_prediction, tf.float32))

# Preparing logs for Tensorboard
    loss_summary = tf.summary.scalar("loss", cost)
    acc_summary = tf.summary.scalar("accuracy", accuracy)
    train_summary_op = tf.summary.merge_all()
    out_dir = "{}/{}".format(model_name, model_name)
    train_summary_dir = os.path.join(out_dir, "summaries")

##

# Initializing the session and executing the training

init = tf.global_variables_initializer()
with tf.Session() as sess:
        sess.run(init)
        iteration = 0

        while batch.dataset_full_passes < epoch:
            iteration += 1
            batch_x, batch_y = batch.get_next_batch()
            batch_x = batch_x.reshape((batch_size, sequence_length,
input_number))
```

```
                    sess.run(optimizer, feed_dict={model.x: batch_x, model.y:
        batch_y})
                    if iteration % log_frequency == 0:
                        acc = sess.run(accuracy, feed_dict={model.x: batch_x,
        model.y: batch_y})
                        loss = sess.run(cost, feed_dict={model.x: batch_x, model.y:
        batch_y})
                        print("Iteration {}, batch loss: {:.6f}, training accuracy:
        {:.5f}".format(iteration * batch_size,
        loss, acc))
                batch.clean()
```

Once the model completes its training, the checkpoints are stored. We can use later on for inferencing. The following is a graph of the accuracy and the loss that occurred during the training process:

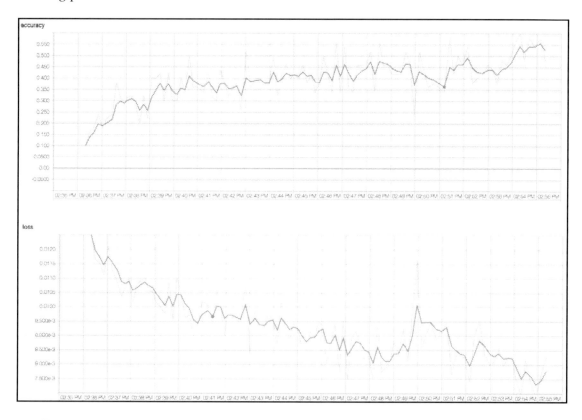

The accuracy (top) and the loss (bottom) plot with respect to the time. We can see that accuracy getting increased and loss getting reduced over the period of time.

Inference

Now that the model is ready, we can use it to make predictions. We will start by defining all of the parameters. While building inference, we need to provide some seed text, just like we did in the previous model. Along with that, we will also provide the path of the `vocab` file and the output file in which we will store the generated lyrics. We will also provide the length of the text that we need to generate:

```
import argparse
import codecs
from modules.Model import *
from modules.Preprocessing import *
from collections import deque

def main():
    parser = argparse.ArgumentParser()
    parser.add_argument('--model_name', type=str, required=True)
    parser.add_argument('--vocabulary_file', type=str, required=True)
    parser.add_argument('--output_file', type=str, required=True)

    parser.add_argument('--seed', type=str, default="Yeah, oho ")
    parser.add_argument('--sample_length', type=int, default=1500)
    parser.add_argument('--log_frequency', type=int, default=100)
```

Next, we will load the model by providing the name of model that we used in the training step in the preceding code, and we will restore the vocabulary from the file:

```
model = Model(model_name)
model.restore()
classifier = model.get_classifier()

vocabulary = Preprocessing()
vocabulary.retrieve(vocabulary_file)
```

We will be using the stack methods to store the generated characters, append the stack, and then use the same stack to feed it into the model in an interactive fashion:

```
# Preparing the raw input data
for char in seed:
    if char not in vocabulary.vocabulary:
        print char,"is not in vocabulary file"
        char = u' '
    stack.append(char)
    sample_file.write(char)

# Restoring the models and making inferences
    with tf.Session() as sess:
```

```
tf.global_variables_initializer().run()

saver = tf.train.Saver(tf.global_variables())
ckpt = tf.train.get_checkpoint_state(model_name)

if ckpt and ckpt.model_checkpoint_path:
    saver.restore(sess, ckpt.model_checkpoint_path)

    for i in range(0, sample_length):
        vector = []
        for char in stack:
            vector.append(vocabulary.binary_vocabulary[char])
        vector = np.array([[vector]])
        prediction = sess.run(classifier, feed_dict={model.x:
vector})
        predicted_char =
vocabulary.char_lookup[np.argmax(prediction)]

        stack.popleft()
        stack.append(predicted_char)
        sample_file.write(predicted_char)

        if i % log_frequency == 0:
            print "Progress: {}%".format((i * 100) / sample_length)

    sample_file.close()
    print "Sample saved in {}".format(output_file)
```

Output

After successful execution, we will get our own freshly brewed, AI generated lyrics reviewed and published. The following is one sample of such lyrics. We have modified some of the spelling so that the sentence makes sense:

```
Yeah, oho once upon a time, on ir intasd

I got monk that wear your good
So heard me down in my clipp

Cure me out brick
Coway got baby, I wanna sheart in faic

I could sink awlrook and heart your all feeling in the firing of to the
still hild, gavelly mind, have before you, their lead
Oh, oh shor,s sheld be you und make
```

```
Oh, fseh where sufl gone for the runtome
Weaaabe the ligavus I feed themust of hear
```

Here, we can see that the model has learned in the way it has generated the paragraphs and sentences with appropriate spacing. It still lacks perfection and also doesn't make sense.

 Seeing signs of success: The first task is to create a model that can learn, and then the second one is used to improve on that model. This can be obtained by training the model with a larger training dataset and longer training durations.

Generating music using a multi-layer LSTM

Our (hypothetical) creative agency client loves what we've done in how we can generate music lyrics. Now, they want us to create some music. We will be using multiple layers of LSTMs, as shown in the following diagram:

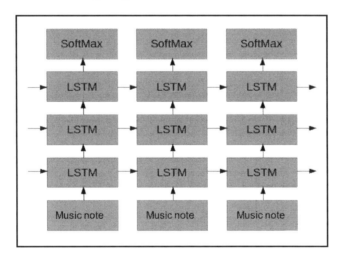

By now, we know that RNNs are good for sequential data, and we can also represent a music track as notes and chord sequences. In this paradigm, notes become data objects containing octave, offset, and pitch information. Chords become data container objects holding information for the combination of notes played at one time.

Pitch is the sound frequency of a note. Musicians represent notes with letter designations [A, B, C, D, E, F, G], with G being the lowest and A being the highest.

Octave identifies the set of pitches used at any one time while playing an instrument.

Offset identifies the location of a note in the piece of music.

Let's explore the following section to build our intuition on how to generate music by first processing the sound files, converting them into the sequential mapping data, and then using the RNN to train the model.

Let's do it. You can refer to the Music-ai code for this exercise, which can be found at https://github.com/PacktPublishing/Python-Deep-Learning-Projects/tree/master/Chapter06/Music-ai.

Pre-processing data

To generate music, we will need a good size set of training data of music files. These will be used to extract sequences while building our training dataset. To simplify this process, in this chapter, we are using the soundtrack of a single instrument. We collected some melodies and stored them in MIDI files. The following sample of a MIDI file shows you what this looks like:

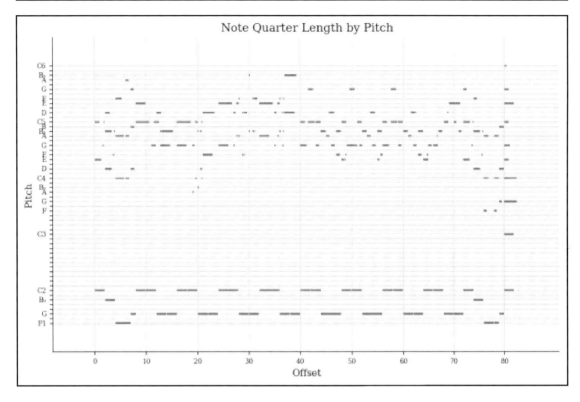

The image represents the pitch and note distribution for a sample MIDI file

We can see the intervals between notes, the offset for each note, and the pitch.

To extract the contents of our dataset, we will be using music21. This also takes the output of the model and translates it into musical notation. Music21 (`http://web.mit.edu/music21/`) is a very helpful Python toolkit that's used for computer-aided musicology.

To get started, we will load each file and use the `converter.parse(file)` function to create a music21 `stream` object. We will get a list of all of the notes and chords in the file by using this `stream` object later. Because the most salient features of a note's pitch can be recreated from string notation, we'll append the pitch of every note. To handle chords, we will encode the ID of every note in the chord as a single string, where each note is separated by a dot, and append this to the chord. This encoding process makes it possible for us to decode the model generated output with ease into the correct notes and chords.

We will load the data from the MIDI files into an array, as you can see in the following code snippet:

```
from music21 import converter, instrument, note, chord
import glob

notes = []

for file in glob.glob("/data/*.mid"):
    midi = converter.parse(file)
    notes_to_parse = None
    parts = instrument.partitionByInstrument(midi)
    if parts: # file has instrument parts
        notes_to_parse = parts.parts[0].recurse()
    else: # file has notes in a flat structure
        notes_to_parse = midi.flat.notes
    for element in notes_to_parse:
        if isinstance(element, note.Note):
            notes.append(str(element.pitch))
        elif isinstance(element, chord.Chord):
            notes.append('.'.join(str(n) for n in element.normalOrder))
```

The next step is to create input sequences for the model and the corresponding outputs, as shown in the following diagram:

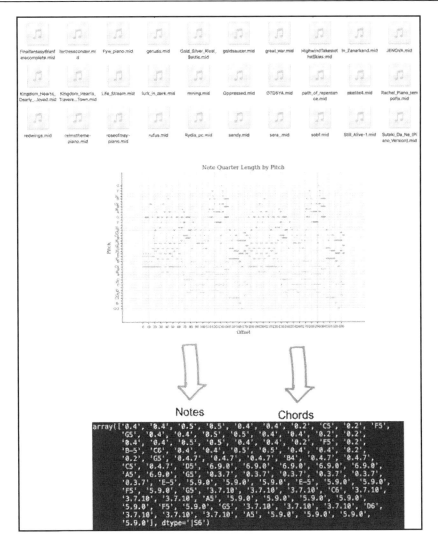

The overview of data processing part in which we take the MIDI files, extract the notes and chords from each file and strore them as an array.

The model outputs a note or chord for each input sequence. We use the first note or chord, following the input sequence in our list of notes. To complete the final step in data preparation for our network, we need to one-hot encode the output. This normalizes the input for the next iteration.

We can do this with the following code:

```
sequence_length = 100
# get all pitch names
```

```
pitchnames = sorted(set(item for item in notes))

# create a dictionary to map pitches to integers
note_to_int = dict((note, number) for number, note in
enumerate(pitchnames))
network_input = []
network_output = []
# create input sequences and the corresponding outputs
for i in range(0, len(notes) - sequence_length, 1):
    sequence_in = notes[i:i + sequence_length]
    sequence_out = notes[i + sequence_length]
    network_input.append([note_to_int[char] for char in sequence_in])
    network_output.append(note_to_int[sequence_out])
n_patterns = len(network_input)
# reshape the input into a format compatible with LSTM layers
network_input = numpy.reshape(network_input, (n_patterns, sequence_length,
1))
# normalize input
network_input = network_input / float(n_vocab)
network_output = np_utils.to_categorical(network_output)
```

Now that we have all the notes and chords extracted. We will create our training data X and Y as shown in the following figure:

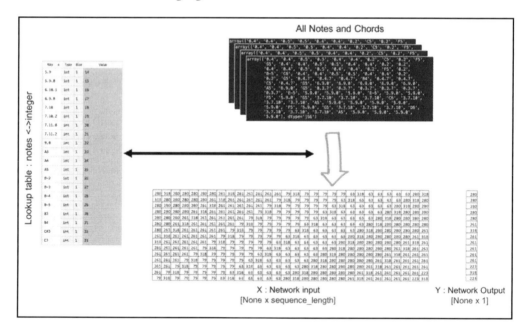

The captured notes any chords in the array is further transformed into a one-hot encoding vector by mapping the values from the vocabulary. So we will fed the sequences in X matrix and expect the model to learn to predict Y for the given sequence.

Defining the model and training

Now, we are getting to the part that all deep learning engineers love: designing the model's architecture! We will be using four distinctive types of layers in our model architecture:

- **LSTM**: This is a type of RNN layer.
- **Dropout**: A technique for regularization. This helps prevent the model from overfitting by randomly dropping some nodes.
- **Dense:** This is a fully connected layer where every input node is connected to every output node.
- **Activation**: This determines the `activation` function that's going to be used to produce the node's output.

We will again employ the Keras APIs to make the implementation quick:

```
model = Sequential()
model.add(LSTM(
    256,
    input_shape=(network_input.shape[1], network_input.shape[2]),
    return_sequences=True
))
model.add(Dropout(0.5))
model.add(LSTM(512, return_sequences=True))
model.add(Dropout(0.3))
model.add(LSTM(256))
model.add(Dense(256))
model.add(Dropout(0.3))
model.add(Dense(n_vocab))
model.add(Activation('softmax'))
model.compile(loss='categorical_crossentropy',
              optimizer='rmsprop',
              metrics=['accuracy'])
```

The generative model architecture we designed has three LSTM layers, three `Dropout` layers, two `Dense` layers, and one `Activation` layer, as shown in the following diagram:

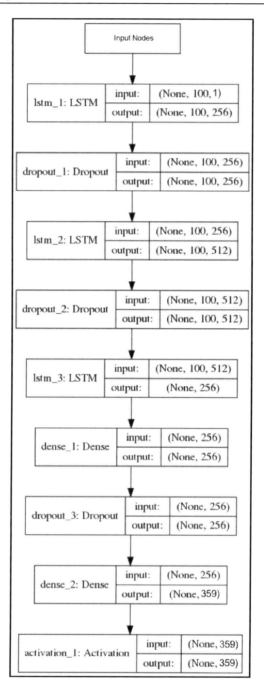

The model architecture for music generation

Categorical cross entropy will be used to calculate the loss for each iteration of the training. We will once again use the Adam optimizer in this network. Now that we have our deep learning model architecture configured, it's time to train the model. We have decided to train the model for 200 epochs, each with 25 batches, by using `model.fit()`. We also want to track the reduction in loss over each epoch and will use checkpoints for this purpose.

Now we will perform the training operation and dump the model in the file mentioned in the following code:

```
filepath = "weights-{epoch:02d}-{loss:.4f}.hdf5"
checkpoint = ModelCheckpoint(
    filepath,
    monitor='loss',
    verbose=0,
    save_best_only=True,
    mode='min'
)
callbacks_list = [checkpoint]

history = model.fit(network_input, network_output, epochs=200,
batch_size=64, callbacks=callbacks_list)
```

The performance of the model can be seen as follows:

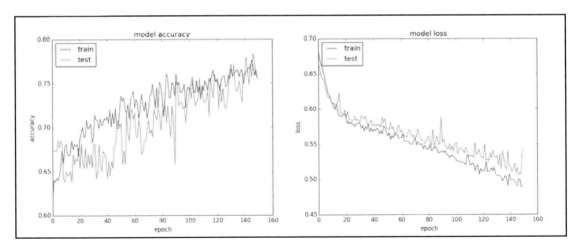

The accuracy and the loss plot over the epochs

Now that the training process is completed, we will load the trained models and generate our own music.

Generating music

It's time for the real fun! Let's generate some instrumental music. We will use the code from the model setup and training, but instead of executing the training (as our model is already trained), we will insert the learned weights that we obtained in earlier training.

The following code block executes these two steps:

```
model = Sequential()
model.add(LSTM(
    512,
    input_shape=(network_input.shape[1], network_input.shape[2]),
    return_sequences=True
))
model.add(Dropout(0.5))
model.add(LSTM(512, return_sequences=True))
model.add(Dropout(0.3))
model.add(LSTM(512))
model.add(Dense(256))
model.add(Dropout(0.3))
model.add(Dense(n_vocab))
model.add(Activation('softmax'))
model.compile(loss='categorical_crossentropy', optimizer='adam')

# Load the weights to each node
model.load_weights('weights_file.hdf5')
```

By doing this, we created the same model, but this time for prediction purposes, and added one extra line of code to load the weights into memory.

Because we need a seed input so that the model can start generating music, we chose to use a random sequence of notes that we obtained from our processed files. You can also send your own nodes as long as you can ensure that the sequence length is precisely 100:

```
# Randomly selected a note from our processed data
start = numpy.random.randint(0, len(network_input)-1)
pattern = network_input[start]

int_to_note = dict((number, note) for number, note in
enumerate(pitchnames))

prediction_output = []

# Generate 1000 notes of music
for note_index in range(1000):
    prediction_input = numpy.reshape(pattern, (1, len(pattern), 1))
    prediction_input = prediction_input / float(n_vocab)
```

```
prediction = model.predict(prediction_input, verbose=0)

index = numpy.argmax(prediction)
result = int_to_note[index]
prediction_output.append(result)

pattern.append(index)
pattern = pattern[1:len(pattern)]
```

We iterated the model generation 1,000 times, which created 1,000 notes using the network, producing approximately five minutes of music. The process we used to select the next sequence for each iteration was that we'd start with the first sequence to submit, since it was of the sequence of notes that was at the starting index. For subsequent input sequences, we removed the first note and appended the output from the previous iteration at the end of the sequence. This is a very crude way to do this and is known as the sliding window approach. You can play around and add some randomness to each sequence we select, which could give more creativity to the music that is generated.

It is at this point that we have an array of all of the encoded representations of the notes and chords. To turn this array back into `Note` and `Chord` objects, we need to decode it.

When we detect that the pattern is that of a `Chord` object, we will separate the string into an array of notes. We will then loop through the string's representation of each note to create a `Note` object for each item. The `Chord` object is then created, which contains each of these notes.

When the pattern is that of a `Note` object, we will use the string representation of the pitch pattern to create a `Note` object. At the end of each iteration, we increase the offset by `0.5`, which can again be changed and randomness can be introduced to it.

The following function is responsible for determining whether the output is a `Note` or `Chord` object. Finally, can we use the music21 output `stream` object to create the MIDI file. Here are a few samples of generated music: `https://github.com/PacktPublishing/ Python-Deep-Learning-Projects/tree/master/Chapter06/Music-ai/generated_music`.

To execute these steps, you can make use of this `helper` function, as shown in the following code block:

```
def create_midi_file(prediction_output):
    """ convert the output from the prediction to notes and create a midi
file"""
    offset = 0
    output_notes = []

    for pattern in prediction_output:
```

```
# pattern is a chord
if ('.' in pattern) or pattern.isdigit():
    notes_in_chord = pattern.split('.')
    notes = []
    for current_note in notes_in_chord:
        new_note = note.Note(int(current_note))
        new_note.storedInstrument = instrument.Piano()
        notes.append(new_note)
    new_chord = chord.Chord(notes)
    new_chord.offset = offset
    output_notes.append(new_chord)
# pattern is a note
else:
    new_note = note.Note(pattern)
    new_note.offset = offset
    new_note.storedInstrument = instrument.Piano()
    output_notes.append(new_note)

# increase offset each iteration so that notes do not stack
offset += 0.5

midi_stream = stream.Stream(output_notes)

midi_stream.write('midi', fp='generated.mid')
```

Summary

Wow, that's an impressive set of practical examples of using deep learning projects in Python to build solutions in a creative space! Let's revisit the goals we set up for ourselves.

Defining the goal:

In this project, we're going to take the next step in our computational linguistics journey in deep learning projects in Python and generate new content for our client. We need to help them by providing a deep learning solution that generates new content that can be used in movie scripts, song lyrics, and music.

Deep learning generated content for creative purposes is obviously very tricky. Our realistic goal in this chapter was to demonstrate and train you on the skills and architecture needed to get started on these types of projects. Producing acceptable results takes interacting with the data, the model, and the outputs and testing it with the appropriate audiences. The key takeaway to remember is that the outputs of your models can be quite personalized to the task at hand and that you can expand your thinking of what types of business use cases you should feel comfortable working on in your career.

In this chapter, we implemented a generative model, which generated content with the use of LSTMs. We implemented models for both text and audio that generated content for artists and various businesses in the creative space (hypothetically): the music and movie industries.

What we learned in this chapter was the following:

- Text generation with LSTM
- The additional power of a Bi-directional LSTM for text generation
- Deep (multi-layer) LSTM to generate lyrics for a song
- Deep (multi-layer) LSTM to generate the music for a song

This is some exciting work regarding deep learning, and it keeps on coming in the next chapter. Let's see what's in store!

Building Speech Recognition with DeepSpeech2

7

It's been a great journey, building awesome deep learning projects in Python using image, text, and sound data.

We've been working quite heavily on language models in building chatbots in our previous chapters. Chatbots are a powerful tool for customer engagement and the automation of a wide range of business processes from customer service to sales. Chatbots enable the automation of repetitive and/or redundant interactions such as frequently asked questions or product-ordering workflows. This automation saves time and money for businesses and enterprises. If we've done our job well as deep-learning engineers, it also means that the consumers are receiving a much-improved **user experience** (**UX**) as a result.

The new interaction between a business and its customers via a chatbot is very effective in each party receiving value. Let's look at the interaction scenario and see if we can identify any constraints that should be the focus of our next project. Up until now, all of our chat interactions have been through text. Let's think about what this means for the consumer. Text interactions are often (but not exclusively) initiated via mobile devices. Secondly, chatbots open up a new **user interaction** (**UI**)—for conversational UI. Part of the power of conversational UI is that it can remove the constraint of the physical keyboard and open the range of locations and devices that are now possible for this interaction to take place.

 Conversational UI is made possible by speech recognition systems working through popular devices, such as your smartphone with Apple's Siri, Amazon's Echo, and Google Home. It's very cool technology, consumers love it, and businesses that adopt this technology gain an advantage over those in their industry that do not keep up with the times.

In this chapter, we will build a system that recognizes English speech, using the **DeepSpeech2** (**DS2**) model.

You will learn the following:

- To work with speech and spectrograms
- To build an end-to-end speech recognition system
- The **Connectionist Temporal Classification** (**CTC**) loss function
- Batch normalization and SortaGrad for **recurrent neural networks** (**RNNs**)

Let's get started and deep dive into the speech data, learn to feature engineer the speech data, extract various kinds of features from it, and then build a speech recognition system that can detect your or a registered user's voice.

Define the goal: The goal of this project is to build and train an **automatic speech recognition** (**ASR**) system to take in and convert an audio call to text that could then be used as input for a text-based chatbot that could understand and respond.

Data preprocessing

In this project, we will use *LibriSpeech ASR corpus* (`http://www.openslr.org/12/`), which is 1,000 hours of 16 kHz-read English speech.

Let's use the following commands to download the corpus and unpack the LibriSpeech data:

```
mkdir -p data/librispeech
cd data/librispeech
wget http://www.openslr.org/resources/12/train-clean-100.tar.gz
wget http://www.openslr.org/resources/12/dev-clean.tar.gz
wget http://www.openslr.org/resources/12/test-clean.tar.gz
mkdir audio
cd audio
tar xvzf ../train-clean-100.tar.gz LibriSpeech/train-clean-100 --strip-components=1
tar xvzf ../dev-clean.tar.gz LibriSpeech/dev-clean --strip-components=1
tar xvzf ../test-clean.tar.gz LibriSpeech/test-clean --strip-components=1
```

This will take a while and once the process is completed, we will have the `data` folder structure, as shown in the following screenshot:

```
.
|── audio
|   |── train-clean-100
|   |   |── 12722
|   |   |   |── 1281042
|   |   |   |   |── 12722-1281042-0000.flac
|   |   |   |   |── 12722-1281042-0001.flac
|   |   |   |   |── 12722-1281042-00030.flac
|   |   |   |   |── 12722-1281042-trans.txt
|   |── dev-clean
|   |   |── 1272
|   |   |   |── 128104
|   |   |   |   |── 1272-128104-0000.flac
|   |   |   |   |── 1272-128104-0001.flac
|   |   |   |   |── 1272-128104-0002.flac
|   |   |   |   |── 1272-128104-0013.flac
|   |   |   |   |── 1272-128104-trans.txt
|   |── test-clean
|   |   |── 12722
|   |   |   |── 1281042
|   |   |   |   |── 12722-1281042-0000.flac
|   |   |   |   |── 12722-1281042-0001.flac
|   |   |   |   |── 12722-1281042-trans.txt
|── dev-clean.tar.gz
|── train-clean-100.tar.gz
`── test-clean.tar.gz
```

We now have three folders named as `train-clean-100`, `dev-clean`, and `test-clean`. Each folder will have subfolders that are the associated IDs used for mapping the small segment of the transcript and the audio. All the audio files are in the `.flac` extension, and all the folders will have one `.txt` file, which is the transcript for the audio files.

Corpus exploration

Let's explore the dataset in detail. First, let's look into the audio file by reading it from the file and plotting it. To read the audio file, we will use the `pysoundfile` package with the following command:

```
pip install pysoundfile
```

Next, we will import the modules, read the audio files, and plot them with the following code block:

```python
import soundfile as sf
import matplotlib.pyplot as plt


def plot_audio(audio):
    fig, axs = plt.subplots(4, 1, figsize=(20, 7))
    axs[0].plot(audio[0]);
    axs[0].set_title('Raw Audio Signals')
    axs[1].plot(audio[1]);
    axs[2].plot(audio[2]);
    axs[3].plot(audio[3]);

audio_list =[]
for i in xrange(4):
    file_path = 'data/128684/911-128684-000{}.flac'.format(i+1)
    a, sample_rate = sf.read(file_path)
    audio_list.append(a)
plot_audio(audio_list)
```

The following is the frequency representation of each segment of speech:

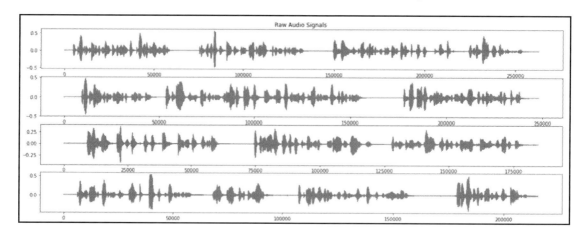

The raw audio signal plot from the audio MIDI file

Now let's look into the content of the transcript text file. It's a clean version of the text with the audio file IDs in the beginning and the associated text following:

911-128684-0001 OR CONCENTRATING ITSELF IN THE SHAPE OF PASSION OR EMOTION CAN BE DIRECTLY FELT AS THE SPIRITUAL ACTIVITY WHICH IT IS AND KNOWN IN CONTRAST WITH THE SPACE FI
911-128684-0002 IN OPPOSITION TO THIS DUALISTIC PHILOSOPHY I TRIED IN THE FIRST ESSAY TO SHOW THAT THOUGHTS AND THINGS ARE ABSOLUTELY HOMOGENEOUS AS TO THEIR MATERIAL AND TH
911-128684-0003 THERE IS NO THOUGHT STUFF DIFFERENT FROM THING STUFF I SAID BUT THE SAME IDENTICAL PIECE OF PURE EXPERIENCE WHICH WAS THE NAME I GAVE TO THE MATERIA PRIMA OF
911-128684-0004 CAN STAND ALTERNATELY FOR A FACT OF CONSCIOUSNESS OR FOR A PHYSICAL REALITY ACCORDING AS IT IS TAKEN IN ONE CONTEXT OR IN ANOTHER FOR THE RIGHT UNDERSTANDING

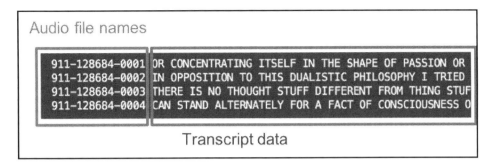

The transcript data is stored a specific format. Left numbers are the midi file name and the right part is the actually transcript. This helps in building the mapping between the midi file and its respective transcript.

What we see is that each audio file is the narration of the transcript contained in the file. Our model will try to learn this sequence pattern. But before we work on the model, we need to extract some features from the audio file and convert the text into one-hot encoding format.

Feature engineering

So, before we feed the raw audio data into our model, we need to transform the data into numerical representations that are features. In this section, we will explore various techniques to extract features from the speech data that we can use to feed into the model. The accuracy and performance of the model vary based on the type of features we use. As an inquisitive deep-learning engineer, it's your opportunity to explore and learn the features with these techniques and use the best one for the use case at hand.

The following table gives us a list of techniques and their properties:

Techniques	Properties
Principal component analysis (PCA)	• Eigenvector-based method • Non-linear feature extraction method • Supported to linear map • Faster than other techniques • Good for Gaussian data
Linear discriminate analysis (LDA)	• Linear feature extraction method • Supported to the supervised linear map • Faster than other techniques • Better than PCA for classification
Independent component analysis (ICA)	• Blind course separation method • Support to linear map • Iterative in nature • Good for non-Gaussian data

Cepstral analysis	• Static feature extraction method • Power spectrum method • Used to represent spectral envelope
Mel-frequency scale analysis	• Static feature extraction method • Spectral analysis method • Mel scale is calculated
Mel-frequency cepstral coefficient (MFFCs)	• Power spectrum is computed by performing Fourier Analysis • Robust and dynamic method for speech feature extraction
Wavelet technique	• Better time resolution than Fourier transform • Real-time factor is minimum

The MFCC technique is the most efficient and is often used for the extraction of speech features for speech recognition. The MFCC is based on the known variation of the human ear's critical bandwidth frequencies, with filters spaced linearly at low frequencies. The process of MFCC is shown in the following diagram:

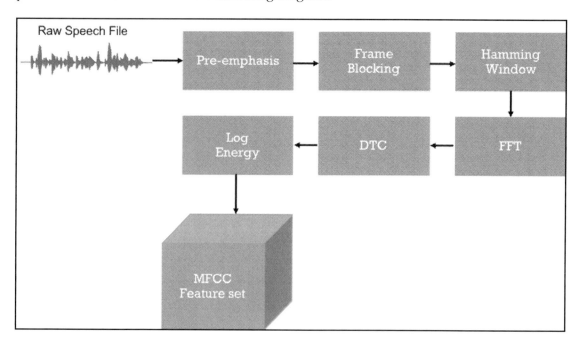

Block diagram of MFCC process

For our implementation purposes, we are not going to perform each step; instead, we will use a Python package called `python_speech_features` that provides common speech features for ASR, including MFCCs and filterbank energies.

Let's `pip install` the package with the following command:

```
pip install python_speech_features
```

So, let's define a function that will normalize the audio time series data and extract the MFCC features:

```
from python_speech_features import mfcc

def compute_mfcc(audio_data, sample_rate):
    ''' Computes the MFCCs.
    Args:
        audio_data: time series of the speech utterance.
        sample_rate: sampling rate.
    Returns:
        mfcc_feat:[num_frames x F] matrix representing the mfcc.
    '''

    audio_data = audio_data - np.mean(audio_data)
    audio_data = audio_data / np.max(audio_data)
    mfcc_feat = mfcc(audio_data, sample_rate, winlen=0.025, winstep=0.01,
                    numcep=13, nfilt=26, nfft=512, lowfreq=0,
highfreq=None,
                    preemph=0.97, ceplifter=22, appendEnergy=True)
    return mfcc_feat
```

Let's plot the audio and MFCC features and visualize them:

```
audio, sample_rate = sf.read(file_path)
feats[audio_file] = compute_mfcc(audio, sample_rate)
plot_audio(audio,feats[audio_file])
```

The following is the output of the spectrogram:

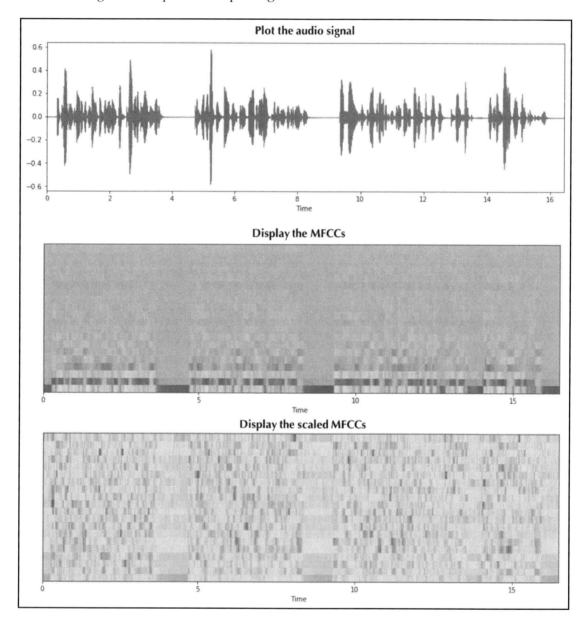

Data transformation

Once we have all the features that we need to feed into the model, we will transform the raw NumPy tensors into the TensorFlow specific format called TFRecords.

In the following code snippet, we are creating the folders to store all the processed records. The make_example() function creates the sequence example for a single utterance given the sequence length, MFCC features, and corresponding transcript. Multiple sequence records are then written into TFRecord files using the tf.python_io.TFRecordWriter() function:

```
if os.path.basename(partition) == 'train-clean-100':
    # Create multiple TFRecords based on utterance length for training
    writer = {}
    count = {}
    print('Processing training files...')
    for i in range(min_t, max_t+1):
        filename = os.path.join(write_dir, 'train' + '_' + str(i) +
                                '.tfrecords')
        writer[i] = tf.python_io.TFRecordWriter(filename)
        count[i] = 0

    for utt in tqdm(sorted_utts):
        example = make_example(utt_len[utt], feats[utt].tolist(),
                               transcripts[utt])
        index = int(utt_len[utt]/100)
        writer[index].write(example)
        count[index] += 1

    for i in range(min_t, max_t+1):
        writer[i].close()
    print(count)

    # Remove bins which have fewer than 20 utterances
    for i in range(min_t, max_t+1):
        if count[i] < 20:
            os.remove(os.path.join(write_dir, 'train' +
                                   '_' + str(i) + '.tfrecords'))
else:
    # Create single TFRecord for dev and test partition
    filename = os.path.join(write_dir, os.path.basename(write_dir) +
                            '.tfrecords')
    print('Creating', filename)
    record_writer = tf.python_io.TFRecordWriter(filename)
    for utt in sorted_utts:
        example = make_example(utt_len[utt], feats[utt].tolist(),
                               transcripts[utt])
```

```
        record_writer.write(example)
    record_writer.close()
    print('Processed '+str(len(sorted_utts))+' audio files')
```

All the data-processing code is written in the `preprocess_LibriSpeech.py` file, which will perform all the previously mentioned data manipulation part, and once the operation is complete, the resulting processed data gets stored at the `data/librispeech/processed/` location. Use the following command to run the file:

```
python preprocess_LibriSpeech.py
```

DS2 model description and intuition

DS2 architecture is composed of many layers of recurrent connections, convolutional filters, and non-linearities, as well as the impact of a specific instance of batch normalization, applied to RNNs, as shown here:

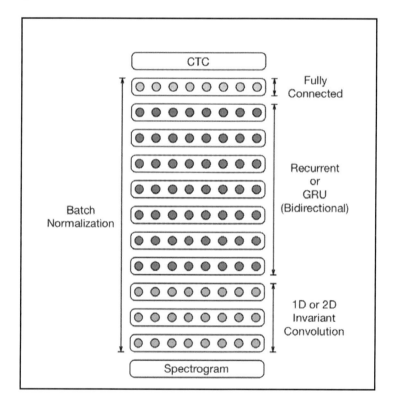

To learn from datasets with a large amount of data, DS2 model's capacity is increased by adding more depth. The architectures are made up to 11 layers of many bidirectional recurrent layers and convolutional layers. To optimize these models successfully, batch normalization for RNNs and a novel optimization curriculum called SortaGrad were used.

The training data is a combination of input sequence x(i) and the transcript y(i), whereas the goal of the RNN layers is to learn the features between x(i) and y(i):

```
training set X =  {(x(1), y(1)), (x(2), y(2)), . . .}
utterance =  x(i)
label = y(i)
```

The spectrogram of power normalized audio clips are used as the features to the system and the outputs of the network are the graphemes of each language. In terms of adding non-linearity, the clipped **rectified linear unit (ReLU)** function $\sigma(x) = min\{max\{x, 0\}, 20\}$ was used. After the bidirectional recurrent layers, one or more fully connected layers are placed and the output layer L is a softmax, computing a probability distribution over characters.

Now let's look into the implementation of the DS2 architecture. You can find the full code https://github.com/PacktPublishing/Python-Deep-Learning-Projects/tree/master/Chapter07.

The following is what the model looks like in TensorBoard:

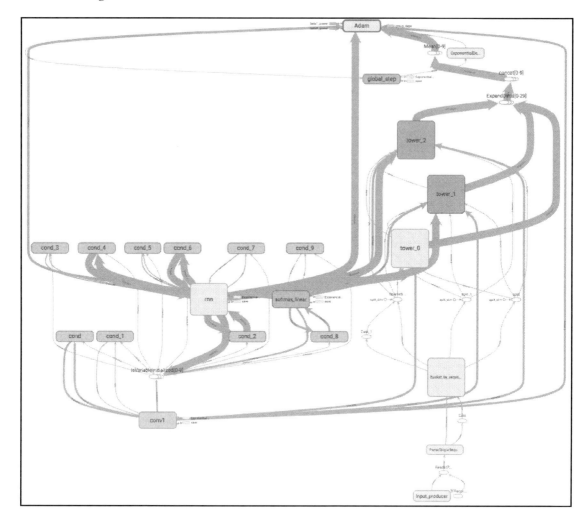

For the convolution layers, we have the kernel of size [11, input_seq_length, number_of_filter] followed by the 2D convolution operation on the input sequence, and then dropout is applied to prevent overfitting.

The following code segment executes these steps:

```
with tf.variable_scope('conv1') as scope:
    kernel = _variable_with_weight_decay(
        'weights',
        shape=[11, feat_len, 1, params.num_filters],
```

```
                wd_value=None, use_fp16=params.use_fp16)

        feats = tf.expand_dims(feats, dim=-1)
        conv = tf.nn.conv2d(feats, kernel,
                            [1, params.temporal_stride, 1, 1],
                            padding='SAME')
        biases = _variable_on_cpu('biases', [params.num_filters],
                                  tf.constant_initializer(-0.05),
                                  params.use_fp16)
        bias = tf.nn.bias_add(conv, biases)
        conv1 = tf.nn.relu(bias, name=scope.name)
        _activation_summary(conv1)

        # dropout
        conv1_drop = tf.nn.dropout(conv1, params.keep_prob)
```

Then, we next have the recurrent layer, where we reshape the output of the convolution layer to fit the data into the RNN layer. Then, the custom RNN cells are created based on the hyperparameter called `rnn_type`, which can be of two types, uni-directional or bi-directional, followed by the dropout cells.

The following code block creates the RNN part of the model:

```
    with tf.variable_scope('rnn') as scope:

        # Reshape conv output to fit rnn input
        rnn_input = tf.reshape(conv1_drop, [params.batch_size, -1,
                                            feat_len*params.num_filters])
        # Permute into time major order for rnn
        rnn_input = tf.transpose(rnn_input, perm=[1, 0, 2])
        # Make one instance of cell on a fixed device,
        # and use copies of the weights on other devices.
        cell = rnn_cell.CustomRNNCell(
            params.num_hidden, activation=tf.nn.relu6,
            use_fp16=params.use_fp16)
        drop_cell = tf.contrib.rnn.DropoutWrapper(
            cell, output_keep_prob=params.keep_prob)
        multi_cell = tf.contrib.rnn.MultiRNNCell(
            [drop_cell] * params.num_rnn_layers)

        seq_lens = tf.div(seq_lens, params.temporal_stride)
        if params.rnn_type == 'uni-dir':
            rnn_outputs, _ = tf.nn.dynamic_rnn(multi_cell, rnn_input,
                                               sequence_length=seq_lens,
                                               dtype=dtype,
                                   time_major=True,

                                               scope='rnn',
                                               swap_memory=True)
```

```
else:
    outputs, _ = tf.nn.bidirectional_dynamic_rnn(
        multi_cell, multi_cell, rnn_input,
        sequence_length=seq_lens, dtype=dtype,
        time_major=True, scope='rnn',
        swap_memory=True)
    outputs_fw, outputs_bw = outputs
    rnn_outputs = outputs_fw + outputs_bw
_activation_summary(rnn_outputs)
```

Further more, the linear layer is created to perform the CTC loss function and output from the softmax layer:

```
with tf.variable_scope('softmax_linear') as scope:
    weights = _variable_with_weight_decay(
        'weights', [params.num_hidden, NUM_CLASSES],
        wd_value=None,
        use_fp16=params.use_fp16)
    biases = _variable_on_cpu('biases', [NUM_CLASSES],
                                tf.constant_initializer(0.0),
                                params.use_fp16)
    logit_inputs = tf.reshape(rnn_outputs, [-1, cell.output_size])
    logits = tf.add(tf.matmul(logit_inputs, weights),
                    biases, name=scope.name)
    logits = tf.reshape(logits, [-1, params.batch_size, NUM_CLASSES])
    _activation_summary(logits)
```

Production scale tip: Training a single model at these scales requires tens of exaFLOPs that would take three to six weeks to execute on a single GPU. This makes model exploration a very time-consuming exercise, so the developers of DeepSpeech have built a highly optimized training system that uses eight or 16 GPUs to train one model, as well as synchronous **stochastic gradient descent (SGD)**, which is easier to debug while testing new ideas, and also converges faster for the same degree of data parallelism.

Training the model

Now that we understand the data that we are using and the DeepSpeech model architecture, let's set up the environment to train the model. There are some preliminary steps to create a virtual environment for the project that are optional, but always recommended to use. Also, it's recommended to use GPUs to train these models.

Along with Python Version 3.5 and TensorFlow version 1.7+, the following are some of the prerequisites:

- `python-Levenshtein`: To compute **character error rate** (**CER**), basically the distance
- `python_speech_features`: To extract MFCC features from raw data
- `pysoundfile`: To read FLAC files
- `scipy`: Helper functions for windowing
- `tqdm`: For displaying a progress bar

Let's create the virtual environment and install all the dependencies:

```
conda create -n 'SpeechProject' python=3.5.0
source activate SpeechProject
```

Install the following dependencies:

```
(SpeechProject)$ pip install python-Levenshtein
(SpeechProject)$ pip install python_speech_features
(SpeechProject)$ pip install pysoundfile
(SpeechProject)$ pip install scipy
(SpeechProject)$ pip install tqdm
```

Install TensorFlow with GPU support:

```
(SpeechProject)$ conda install tensorflow-gpu
```

If you see a `sndfile` error, use the following command:

```
(SpeechProject)$ sudo apt-get install libsndfile1
```

Now you will need to clone the repository that contains all the code:

```
(SpeechRecog)$ git clone https://github.com/FordSpeech/deepSpeech.git
(SpeechRecog)$ cd deepSpeech
```

Let's move the TFRecord files that we created in the *Data transformation* section. The computed MFCC features are stored inside the `data/librispeech/processed/` directory:

```
cp -r ./data/librispeech/audio /home/deepSpeech/data/librispeech
cp -r ./data/librispeech/processed /home/deepSpeech/librispeech
```

Once we have all the data files in place, it's time to train the model. We are defining four hyperparameters as `num_rnn_layers` set to 3, `rnn_type` set to `bi-dir`, `max_steps` is set to `30000`, and `initial_lr` is set to `3e-4`:

```
(SpeechRecog)$python deepSpeech_train.py --num_rnn_layers 3 --rnn_type 'bi-
dir' --initial_lr 3e-4 --max_steps 30000 --train_dir ./logs/
```

 Also, if you want to resume the training using the pre-trained models from `https://drive.google.com/file/d/1E65g4H1QU666RhgY712Sn6FuU2wvZTnQ/view`, you can download and unzip them to the `logs` folder:
```
(SpeechRecog)$python deepSpeech_train.py --checkpoint_dir
./logs/ --max_steps 40000
```

Note that during the first epoch, the cost will increase and it will take longer to train on later steps because the utterances are presented in a sorted order to the network.

The following are the steps involved during the training process:

```
# Learning rate set up from the hyper-param.
learning_rate, global_step = set_learning_rate()

# Create an optimizer that performs gradient descent.
optimizer = tf.train.AdamOptimizer(learning_rate)

# Fetch a batch worth of data for each tower to train.
data = fetch_data()

# Construct loss and gradient ops.
loss_op, tower_grads, summaries = get_loss_grads(data, optimizer)

# Calculate the mean of each gradient. Note that this is the
synchronization point across all towers.
grads = average_gradients(tower_grads)

# Apply the gradients to adjust the shared variables.
apply_gradient_op = optimizer.apply_gradients(grads,
                                              global_step=global_step)

# Track the moving averages of all trainable variables.
variable_averages = tf.train.ExponentialMovingAverage(
    ARGS.moving_avg_decay, global_step)
variables_averages_op = variable_averages.apply(
    tf.trainable_variables())

# Group all updates to into a single train op.
```

```
train_op = tf.group(apply_gradient_op, variables_averages_op)

# Build summary op.
summary_op = add_summaries(summaries, learning_rate, grads)

# Create a saver.
saver = tf.train.Saver(tf.all_variables(), max_to_keep=100)

# Start running operations on the Graph with allow_soft_placement set to
True
# to build towers on GPU.
sess = tf.Session(config=tf.ConfigProto(
    allow_soft_placement=True,
    log_device_placement=ARGS.log_device_placement))

# Initialize vars depending on the checkpoints.
if ARGS.checkpoint is not None:
    global_step = initialize_from_checkpoint(sess, saver)
else:
    sess.run(tf.initialize_all_variables())

# Start the queue runners.
tf.train.start_queue_runners(sess)

# Run training loop.
run_train_loop(sess, (train_op, loss_op, summary_op), saver)
```

While the training process happens, we can see significant improvements, as shown in the following plots. Following graph shows the accuracy of the plot after 50k steps:

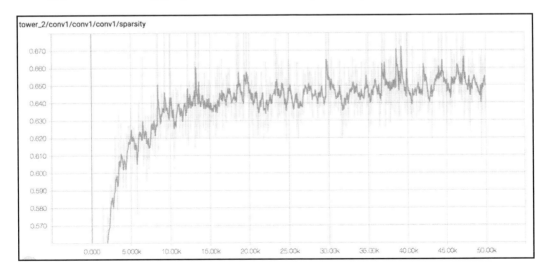

Here are the loss plots over 50k steps:

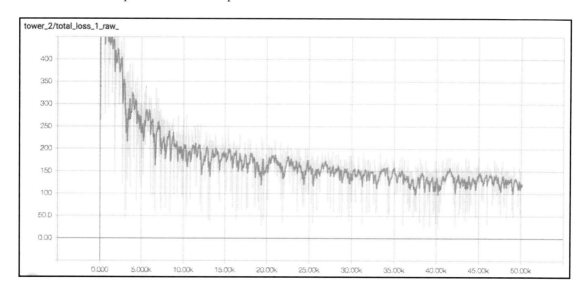

The learning rate is slowing down over the period of time:

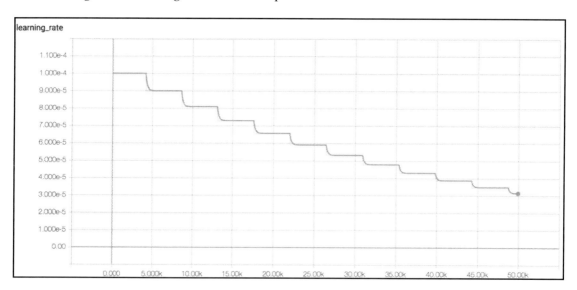

Testing and evaluating the model

Once the model is trained, you can perform the following command to execute the `test` steps using the `test` dataset:

```
(SpeechRecog)$python deepSpeech_test.py --eval_data 'test' --checkpoint_dir
./logs/
```

We evaluate its performance by testing it on previously unseen utterances from a `test` set. The model generates sequences of probability vectors as outputs, so we need to build a decoder to transform the model's output into word sequences. Despite being trained on character sequences, DS2 models are still able to learn an implicit language model and are already quite adept at spelling out words phonetically, as shown in the following table. The model's spelling performance is typically measured using CERs calculated using the Levenshtein distance (`https://en.wikipedia.org/wiki/Levenshtein_distance`) at the character level:

Ground truth	Model output
This had some effect in calming him	This had some offectind calming him
He went in and examined his letters but there was nothing from carrier	He went in an examined his letters but there was nothing from carry
The design was different but the thing was clearly the same	The design was differampat that thing was clarly the same

Although the model exhibit excellent CERs, their tendency to spell out words phonetically results in relatively high word-error rates. You can improve the model's performance **word-error rate** (**WER**) by allowing the decoder to incorporate constraints from an external lexicon and language model.

We have observed that many of the errors in the model's predictions occur in words that do not appear in the training set. It is thus reasonable to expect that the overall CER would continue to improve as we increased the size of the training set and training steps. It achieved 15% CERs after 30k steps or training.

Summary

We dove right into this deep-learning project in Python, creating and training an ASR model that understands speech data. We learned to feature engineer the speech data to extract various kinds of features from it and then build a speech recognition system that could detect a user's voice.

We're happy to have achieved our stated goal!

In this chapter, we built a system that recognizes English speech, using the DS2 model.

You learned following:

- To work with speech and spectrograms
- To build an end-to-end speech recognition system
- The CTC loss function
- Batch normalization and SortaGrad for RNNs

This caps off a major section of the deep-learning projects in this Python book that explores chatbots, NLP, and speech recognition with RNNs (uni and bi-directional, with and without LSTM components), and CNNs. We've seen the power of these technologies to provide intelligence to existing business processes and to create entirely new and smart systems. This is exciting work at the cutting edge of applied AI using deep learning! In the remaining half of the book, we'll explore deep-learning projects in Python that are generally grouped into computer vision technologies.

Let's turn the page and get started!

8
Handwritten Digits Classification Using ConvNets

Welcome to this chapter on using **convolution neural networks (ConvNets)** for the classification of handwritten digits. In `Chapter 2`, *Training NN for Prediction Using Regression,* we built a simple neural network for classifying handwritten digits. This was 87% accurate, but we were not happy with its performance. In this chapter, we will understand what convolution is and build a ConvNet for classifying the handwritten digits to help the restaurant chain become more accurate in sending text messages to the right person. If you have not been through `Chapter 2`, *Training NN for Prediction Using Regression*, please go through it once so that you can get an understanding of the use case.

The following topics will be covered in this chapter:

- Convolution
- Pooling
- Dropout
- Training the model
- Testing the model
- Building deeper models

It would be better if you implement the code snippets as you go through this chapter, either in a Jupyter Notebook or any source code editor. This will make it easier for you to follow along as well as understand how the different sections of the code work.

All of the Python files and the Jupyter Notebook files for this chapter can be found at `https://github.com/PacktPublishing/Python-Deep-Learning-Projects/tree/master/Chapter08`.

Code implementation

In this exercise, we will be using the Keras deep learning library, which is a high-level neural network API capable of running on top of TensorFlow, Theano, and CNTK.

Know the code! We will not spend time understanding how Keras works, but if you are interested, refer to this easy-to-understand official documentation from Keras at https://keras.io/.

Importing all of the dependencies

We will be using the `numpy`, `matplotlib`, `keras`, `scipy`, and `tensorflow` packages in this exercise. Here, TensorFlow is used as the backend for Keras. You can install these packages with `pip`. For the MNIST data, we will be using the dataset available in the `keras` module with a simple `import`:

```
import numpy as np
```

It is important that you set `seed` for reproducibility:

```
# set seed for reproducibility
seed_val = 9000
np.random.seed(seed_val)
```

Exploring the data

Let's import the `mnist` module that's available in `keras` with the following code:

```
from keras.datasets import mnist
```

Then, unpack the `mnist` train and test images with the following code:

```
# unpack mnist data
(X_train, y_train), (X_test, y_test) = mnist.load_data()
```

Now that the data has been imported, let's explore these digits:

```
print('Size of the training_set: ', X_train.shape)
print('Size of the test_set: ', X_test.shape)
print('Shape of each image: ', X_train[0].shape)
print('Total number of classes: ', len(np.unique(y_train)))
print('Unique class labels: ', np.unique(y_train))
```

The following is the output of the preceding code:

```
('Size of the training_set: ', (60000, 28, 28))
('Size of the test_set: ', (10000, 28, 28))
('Shape of each image: ', (28, 28))
('Total number of classes: ', 10)
('Unique class labels: ', array([0, 1, 2, 3, 4, 5, 6, 7, 8, 9], dtype=uint8))
```

Figure 8.1: Printout information of the data

From the preceding screenshot, we can see that we have 60000 train images, 10000 test images with each image being 28*28 in size, and a total of 10 predictable classes.

Now, let's plot 9 handwritten digits. Before that, we will need to import matplotlib for plotting:

```
import matplotlib.pyplot as plt
# Plot of 9 random images
for i in range(0, 9):
    plt.subplot(331+i) # plot of 3 rows and 3 columns
    plt.axis('off') # turn off axis
    plt.imshow(X_train[i], cmap='gray') # gray scale
```

The following is the output of the preceding code:

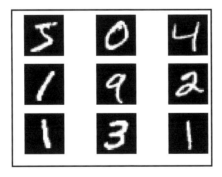

Figure 8.2: Visualizing MNIST digits

Print out the maximum and minimum pixel value of the pixels in the training_set:

```
# maximum and minimum pixel values
print('Maximum pixel value in the training_set: ', np.max(X_train))
print('Minimum pixel value in the training_set: ', np.min(X_train))
```

The following is the output of the preceding code:

```
('Maximum pixel value in the training_set: ', 255)
('Minimum pixel value in the training_set: ', 0)
```

Figure 8.3: Printout of the maximum and minimum pixel value in the data

We can see that the maximum and minimum pixel values in the training set are 255 and 0.

Defining the hyperparameters

The following are some of the hyperparameters that we will be using throughout our code. These are totally configurable:

```
# Number of epochs
epochs = 20

# Batchsize
batch_size = 128

# Optimizer for the generator
from keras.optimizers import Adam
optimizer = Adam(lr=0.0001)

# Shape of the input image
input_shape = (28,28,1)
```

If you look back at Chapter 2, *Training NN for Prediction Using Regression,* you'll see that the optimizer used there was Adam. Therefore, we will import the Adam optimizer from the keras module and set its learning rate, as shown in the preceding code. For most cases that will follow, we will be training for 20 epochs for ease of comparison.

To learn more about the optimizers and their APIs in Keras, visit https://keras.io/optimizers/.

Experiment with different learning rates, optimizers, and batch sizes to see how these factors affect the quality of your model. If you get better results, show this to the deep learning community.

Building and training a simple deep neural network

Now that we have loaded the data into memory, we need to build a simple neural network model to predict the MNIST digits. We will use the same architecture we used in Chapter 2, *Training NN for Prediction Using Regression*.

We will be building a Sequential model. So, let's import it from Keras and initialize it with the following code:

```
from keras.models import Sequential
model = Sequential()
```

 To learn more about the Keras Model API, visit https://keras.io/models/model/.

The next thing that we need to do is define the Dense/Perceptron layer. In Keras, this can be done by importing the Dense layer, as follows:

```
from keras.layers import Dense
```

Then, we need to add the Dense layer to the Sequential model as follows:

```
model.add(Dense(300, input_shape=(784,), activation = 'relu'))
```

 To learn more about the Keras Dense API call, visit https://keras.io/layers/core/.

The add command performs the job of appending a layer to the Sequential model, in this case, Dense.

In the Dense layer in the preceding code, we have defined the number of neurons in the first hidden layer, which is 300. We have also defined the input_shape parameter as being equal to (784,) to indicate to the model that it will be accepting input arrays of the shape (784,). This means that the input layer will have 784 neurons.

The type of activation function that needs to be applied to the result can be defined with the `activation` parameter. In this case, this is `relu`.

Add another `Dense` layer of 300 neurons by using the following code:

```
model.add(Dense(300, activation='relu'))
```

And the final `Dense` layer with the following code:

```
model.add(Dense(10, activation='softmax'))
```

Here, the final layer has 10 neurons as we need it to predict scores for 10 classes. The `activation` function that has been chosen here is `softmax` so that we can limit the scores between 0 and 1, and the sum of scores to 1.

Compiling the model in Keras is super-easy and can be done with following code:

```
# compile the model
model.compile(loss = 'sparse_categorical_crossentropy', optimizer=optimizer
, metrics = ['accuracy'])
```

All you need to do to compile the model is call the `compile` method of the model and specify the `loss`, `optimizer`, and `metrics` parameters, which in this case are `sparse_categorical_crossentropy`, Adam, and `['accuracy']`.

> To learn more about the Keras Model's `compile` method, visit `https://keras.io/models/model/`.

The metrics that need to be monitored during this learning process must be specified as a list to the `metrics` parameter of the `compile` method.

Print out the summary of the model with the following code:

```
# print model summary
model.summary()
```

The following is the output of the preceding code:

```
Layer (type)                    Output Shape              Param #
=================================================================
dense_1 (Dense)                 (None, 300)               235500
_____
dense_2 (Dense)                 (None, 300)               90300
_____
dense_3 (Dense)                 (None, 10)                3010
=================================================================
Total params: 328,810
Trainable params: 328,810
Non-trainable params: 0
_____
```

Figure 8.4: Summary of the multilayer Perceptron model

Notice that this model has 328,810 trainable parameters, which is reasonable.

Now, split the train data into train and validation data by using the train_test_split function that we imported from sklearn:

```
from sklearn.model_selection import train_test_split

# create train and validation data
X_train, X_val, y_train, y_val = train_test_split(X_train, y_train,
stratify = y_train, test_size = 0.08333, random_state=42)

X_train = X_train.reshape(-1, 784)
X_val = X_val.reshape(-1, 784)
X_test = X_test.reshape(-1, 784)

print('Training Examples', X_train.shape[0])
print('Validation Examples', X_val.shape[0])
print('Test Examples', X_test.shape[0])
```

We have split the data so that we end up with 55,000 training examples and 5,000 validation examples.

You will also see that we have reshaped the arrays so that each image is of shape (784,). This is because we have defined the model to accept images/arrays of shape (784,).

Like we did in Chapter 2, *Training NN for Prediction Using Regression*, we will now train our model on 55,000 training examples, validate on 5,000 examples, and test on 10,000 examples.

Assigning the fit to a variable stores relevant information inside it, such as train and validation loss and accuracy at each `epoch`, which can then be used for plotting the learning process.

Fitting a model

To fit a model in Keras, along with train digits and train labels, call the `fit` method of the model with the following parameters:

- `epochs`: The number of epochs
- `batch_size`: The number of images in each batch
- `validation_data`: The tuple of validation images and validation labels

Look at the *Defining the hyperparameters* section of the chapter for the defined values of `epochs` and `batch_size`:

```
# fit the model
history = model.fit(X_train, y_train, epochs = epochs,
batch_size=batch_size, validation_data=(X_val, y_val))
```

The following is the output of the preceding code:

```
Train on 55000 samples, validate on 5000 samples
Epoch 1/20
55000/55000 [==============================] - 4s 66us/step - loss: 9.1007 - acc: 0.4256 - val_loss: 7.3798 - val_acc: 0.5342
Epoch 2/20
55000/55000 [==============================] - 3s 54us/step - loss: 6.4443 - acc: 0.5922 - val_loss: 5.3994 - val_acc: 0.6572
Epoch 3/20
55000/55000 [==============================] - 3s 54us/step - loss: 5.3398 - acc: 0.6625 - val_loss: 5.3888 - val_acc: 0.6578
Epoch 4/20
55000/55000 [==============================] - 3s 55us/step - loss: 5.1974 - acc: 0.6723 - val_loss: 5.3200 - val_acc: 0.6624
```

The following is the output at the end of the code's execution:

```
Epoch 19/20
55000/55000 [==============================] - 4s 69us/step - loss: 1.7686 - acc: 0.8871 - val_loss: 2.0171 - val_acc: 0.8696
Epoch 20/20
55000/55000 [==============================] - 4s 67us/step - loss: 1.7533 - acc: 0.8889 - val_loss: 1.9683 - val_acc: 0.8728
```

Figure 8.5: Metrics printed out during the training of MLP

Evaluating a model

To evaluate the model on test data, you can call the `evaluate` method of the `model` by feeding the test images and test labels:

```
# evaluate the model
loss, acc = model.evaluate(X_test, y_test)
print('Test loss:', loss)
print('Accuracy:', acc)
```

The following is the output of the preceding code:

```
10000/10000 [==================================] - 1s 95us/step
Test loss: 1.9103740268349634
Accuracy: 0.8764
```

Figure 8.6: Printout of the evaluation of MLP

From the validation and test accuracy, we can see that after 20 epochs of training, we have reached the same level of accuracy as we did in Chapter 2, *Training NN for Prediction Using Regression,* but with very few lines of code.

Now, let's define a function to plot the train and validation loss and accuracy that we have stored in the `history` variable:

```
import matplotlib.pyplot as plt

def loss_plot(history):
    train_acc = history.history['acc']
    val_acc = history.history['val_acc']

    plt.figure(figsize=(9,5))
    plt.plot(np.arange(1,21),train_acc, marker = 'D', label = 'Training
Accuracy')
    plt.plot(np.arange(1,21),val_acc, marker = 'o', label = 'Validation
Accuracy')
    plt.xlabel('Epochs')
    plt.ylabel('Accuracy')
    plt.title('Train/Validation Accuracy')
    plt.legend()
    plt.margins(0.02)
    plt.show()

    train_loss = history.history['loss']
    val_loss = history.history['val_loss']
```

```
    plt.figure(figsize=(9,5))
    plt.plot(np.arange(1,21),train_loss, marker = 'D', label = 'Training
Loss')
    plt.plot(np.arange(1,21),val_loss, marker = 'o', label = 'Validation
Loss')
    plt.xlabel('Epochs')
    plt.ylabel('Loss')
    plt.title('Train/Validation Loss')
    plt.legend()
    plt.margins(0.02)
    plt.show()
# plot training loss
loss_plot(history)
```

The following is the output of the preceding code:

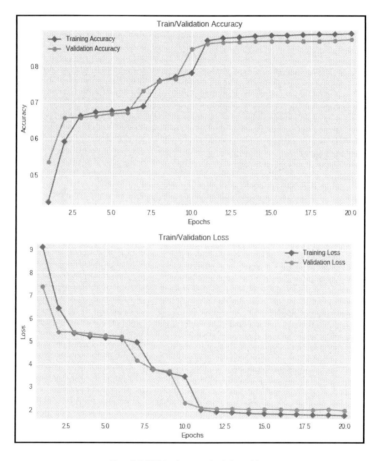

Figure 8.7: MLP loss/accuracy plot during training

MLP – Python file

This module implements training and evaluation of a simple MLP:

```python
"""This module implements a simple multi layer perceptron in keras."""
import numpy as np
from keras.datasets import mnist
from keras.models import Sequential
from keras.layers import Dense
import matplotlib.pyplot as plt

from sklearn.model_selection import train_test_split
from loss_plot import loss_plot

# Number of epochs
epochs = 20
# Batchsize
batch_size = 128
# Optimizer for the generator
from keras.optimizers import Adam
optimizer = Adam(lr=0.0001)
# Shape of the input image
input_shape = (28,28,1)

(X_train, y_train), (X_test, y_test) = mnist.load_data()

X_train, X_val, y_train, y_val = train_test_split(X_train, y_train,
                                                  stratify = y_train,
                                                  test_size = 0.08333,
                                                  random_state=42)

X_train = X_train.reshape(-1, 784)
X_val = X_val.reshape(-1, 784)
X_test = X_test.reshape(-1, 784)

model = Sequential()
model.add(Dense(300, input_shape=(784,), activation = 'relu'))
model.add(Dense(300, activation='relu'))
model.add(Dense(10, activation='softmax'))
model.compile(loss = 'sparse_categorical_crossentropy',
optimizer=optimizer,
              metrics = ['accuracy'])

history = model.fit(X_train, y_train, epochs = epochs,
batch_size=batch_size,
                    validation_data=(X_val, y_val))

loss,acc = model.evaluate(X_test, y_test)
```

```
print('Test loss:', loss)
print('Accuracy:', acc)

loss_plot(history)
```

Convolution

Convolution can be defined as the process of striding a small kernel/filter/array over a target array and obtaining the sum of element-wise multiplication between the kernel and a subset of equal size of the target array at that location.

Consider the following example:

```
array = np.array([0, 1, 0, 1, 0, 1, 0, 1, 0, 1])
kernel = np.array([-1, 1, 0])
```

Here, you have a target `array` of length 10 and a `kernel` of length 3.

When you start the convolution, implement the following steps:

1. The `kernel` will be multiplied with the subset of the target `array` within indices 0 through 2. This will be between [-1,1,0] (kernel) and [0,1,0] (from index 0 through to 2 of the target array). The result of this element-wise multiplication will then be summed up to obtain what is called the result of convolution.
2. The `kernel` will then be stridden by 1 unit and then multiplied with the subset of the target `array` within the indices 1 through 3, just like in *Step 1*, and the result is obtained.
3. *Step 2* is repeated until a subset equal to the length of the `kernel` is not possible at a new stride location.

The result of convolution at each stride is stored in an `array`. This `array` that's holding the result of the convolution is called the feature map. The length of the 1-D feature map (with step/stride of 1) is equal to the difference in length of the `kernel` and the target `array` plus 1.

Only in this case, we need to take the following equation into account:

length of the feature map = length of the target array - length of the kernel + 1

Here is a code snippet implementing 1-D convolution:

```
array = np.array([0, 1, 0, 1, 0, 1, 0, 1, 0, 1])
kernel = np.array([-1, 1, 0])

# empty feature map
conv_result = np.zeros(array.shape[0] - kernel.shape[0] +1).astype(int)

for i in range(array.shape[0] - kernel.shape[0] +1):
    # convolving
    conv_result[i] = (kernel * array[i:i+3]).sum()
    print(kernel, '*', array[i:i+3], '=', conv_result[i])
print('Feature Map :', conv_result)
```

The following is the output of the preceding code:

```
[-1  1  0] * [0 1 0] = 1
[-1  1  0] * [1 0 1] = -1
[-1  1  0] * [0 1 0] = 1
[-1  1  0] * [1 0 1] = -1
[-1  1  0] * [0 1 0] = 1
[-1  1  0] * [1 0 1] = -1
[-1  1  0] * [0 1 0] = 1
[-1  1  0] * [1 0 1] = -1
Feature Map : [ 1 -1  1 -1  1 -1  1 -1]
```

Figure 8.8: Printout of example feature map

Convolution in Keras

Now that you have an understanding of how convolution works, let's put it into use and build a CNN classifier on MNIST digits.

For this, import the `Conv2D` API from the `layers` module of Keras. You can do this with the following code:

```
from keras.layers import Conv2D
```

Since the convolution will be defined to accept images of shape $28*28*1$, we need to reshape all the images to be of $28*28*1$:

```
# reshape data
X_train = X_train.reshape(-1,28,28,1)
X_val = X_val.reshape(-1,28,28,1)
```

```
X_test = X_test.reshape(-1,28,28,1)

print('Train data shape:', X_train.shape)
print('Val data shape:', X_val.shape)
print('Test data shape:', X_test.shape)
```

The following is the output of the preceding code:

```
Train data shape: (55000, 28, 28, 1)
Val data shape: (5000, 28, 28, 1)
Test data shape: (10000, 28, 28, 1)
```

Figure 8.9: Shape of data after reshaping

To build the `model`, just like we did previously, we need to initialize the `model` as `Sequential`:

```
model = Sequential()
```

Now, add the `Conv2D` layer to the `model` with the following code:

```
model.add(Conv2D(32, kernel_size=(3,3), input_shape=input_shape, activation = 'relu'))
```

In the `Conv2D` API, we have defined the following parameters:

- `units`: 32 (number of kernels/filters)
- `kernel_size`: (3,3) (size of each kernel)
- `input_shape`: 28*28*1 (shape of the input array it will receive)
- `activation`: relu

 For additional information on the `Conv2D` API, visit `https://keras.io/layers/convolutional/`.

The result of the preceding convolution is 32 feature maps of size 26*26. These 2-D feature maps now have to be converted into a 1-D feature map. This can be done in Keras with the following code:

```
from keras.layers import Flatten
model.add(Flatten())
```

The result of the preceding snippet is just like a layer of neurons in a simple neural network. The `Flatten` function converts all of the 2-D feature maps into a single `Dense` layer. In this layer, will we add a `Dense` layer with `128` neurons:

```
model.add(Dense(128, activation = 'relu'))
```

Since we need to get scores for each of the `10` possible classes, we must add another `Dense` layer with `10` neurons, with `softmax` as the `activation` function:

```
model.add(Dense(10, activation = 'softmax'))
```

Now, just like in the case of the simple dense neural network we built in the preceding code, we will compile and fit the model:

```
# compile model
model.compile(loss = 'sparse_categorical_crossentropy',
optimizer=optimizer, metrics = ['accuracy'])

# print model summary
model.summary()
```

The following is the output of the preceding code:

Layer (type)	Output Shape	Param #
conv2d_10 (Conv2D)	(None, 26, 26, 32)	320
flatten_6 (Flatten)	(None, 21632)	0
dense_36 (Dense)	(None, 128)	2769024
dense_37 (Dense)	(None, 10)	1290

```
Total params: 2,770,634
Trainable params: 2,770,634
Non-trainable params: 0
```

Figure 8.10: Summary of the convolution classifier

From the model's summary, we can see that this convolution classifier has $2,770,634$ parameters. This is a lot of parameters compared to the Perceptron model. Let's fit this model and evaluate its performance.

Fitting the model

Fit the convolution neural network model on the data with the following code:

```
# fit model
history = model.fit(X_train, y_train, epochs = epochs,
batch_size=batch_size, validation_data=(X_val, y_val))
```

The following is the output of the preceding code:

```
Train on 55000 samples, validate on 5000 samples
Epoch 1/20
55000/55000 [==============================] - 7s 124us/step - loss: 2.8752 - acc: 0.7995 - val_loss: 1.9732 - val_acc: 0.8614
Epoch 2/20
55000/55000 [==============================] - 6s 105us/step - loss: 1.2099 - acc: 0.8994 - val_loss: 0.3333 - val_acc: 0.9404
Epoch 3/20
55000/55000 [==============================] - 6s 105us/step - loss: 0.1757 - acc: 0.9643 - val_loss: 0.1891 - val_acc: 0.9592
```

The following is the output from the end of the code's execution:

```
Epoch 19/20
55000/55000 [==============================] - 6s 104us/step - loss: 0.0170 - acc: 0.9964 - val_loss: 0.1326 - val_acc: 0.9786
Epoch 20/20
55000/55000 [==============================] - 6s 108us/step - loss: 0.0132 - acc: 0.9971 - val_loss: 0.1381 - val_acc: 0.9772
```

Figure 8.11: Metrics printed out during the training of the convolution classifier

We can see that the convolution classifier's accuracy is 97.72% on the validation data.

Evaluating the model

You can evaluate the convolution model on the test data with the following code:

```
# evaluate model
loss,acc = model.evaluate(X_test, y_test)
print('Test loss:', loss)
print('Accuracy:', acc)
```

The following is the output of the preceding code:

```
10000/10000 [==============================] - 2s 175us/step
Test loss: 0.1275109763626777
Accuracy: 0.9792
```

Figure 8.12: Printout of the evaluation of the convolution classifier

We can see that the model is 97.92% accurate on test data, 97.72% on validation data, and 99.71% on train data. It is clear from the loss as well that the model is slightly overfitting on the train data. We will talk about how to handle overfitting later.

Now, let's plot the train and validation metrics to see how the training has progressed:

```
# plot training loss
loss_plot(history)
```

The following is the output of the preceding code:

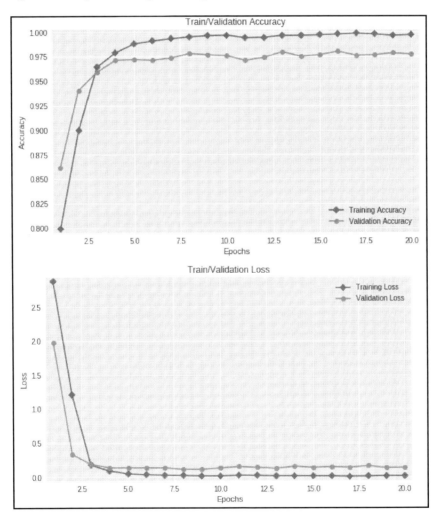

Figure 8.13: Loss/accuracy plot of the convolution classifier during training

Convolution – Python file

This module implements the training and evaluation of a convolution classifier:

```python
"""This module implements a simple convolution classifier."""
import numpy as np
from keras.datasets import mnist
from keras.models import Sequential
from keras.layers import Dense, Conv2D, Flatten
import matplotlib.pyplot as plt

from sklearn.model_selection import train_test_split
from loss_plot import loss_plot

# Number of epochs
epochs = 20
# Batchsize
batch_size = 128
# Optimizer for the generator
from keras.optimizers import Adam
optimizer = Adam(lr=0.0001)
# Shape of the input image
input_shape = (28,28,1)

(X_train, y_train), (X_test, y_test) = mnist.load_data()

X_train, X_val, y_train, y_val = train_test_split(X_train, y_train,
                                        stratify = y_train,
                                        test_size = 0.08333,
                                        random_state=42)

X_train = X_train.reshape(-1,28,28,1)
X_val = X_val.reshape(-1,28,28,1)
X_test = X_test.reshape(-1,28,28,1)

model = Sequential()
model.add(Conv2D(32, kernel_size=(3,3), input_shape=input_shape,
                activation = 'relu'))
model.add(Flatten())
model.add(Dense(128, activation = 'relu'))
model.add(Dense(10, activation='softmax'))
model.compile(loss = 'sparse_categorical_crossentropy',
optimizer=optimizer,
                metrics = ['accuracy'])

history = model.fit(X_train, y_train, epochs = epochs,
batch_size=batch_size,
                    validation_data=(X_val, y_val))
```

```
loss,acc = model.evaluate(X_test, y_test)
print('Test loss:', loss)
print('Accuracy:', acc)

loss_plot(history)
```

Pooling

Max pooling can be defined as the process of summarizing a group of values with the maximum value within that group. Similarly, if you computed the average, it would be average pooling. Pooling operations are usually performed on the generated feature maps after convolution to reduce the number of parameters.

Let's take the example array we considered for convolution:

```
array = np.array([0, 1, 0, 1, 0, 1, 0, 1, 0, 1])
```

Now, if you were to perform max pooling on this `array` with the pool size set to size 1*2 and a stride of 2, the result would be an array of [1,1,1,1,1]. The `array` of size 1*10 has been reduced to a size of 1*5 due to max pooling.

Here, since the pool size is of shape 1*2, you would take the subset of the target `array` from index 0 to index 2, which will be [0,1], and compute the maximum of this subset as 1. You would do the same for the subset from index 2 to index 4, from index 4 to index 6, index 6 to index 8, and finally index 8 to 10.

Similarly, average pooling can be implemented by computing the average value of the pooled section. In this case, it would result in the array [0.5, 0.5, 0.5, 0.5, 0.5].

The following are a couple of code snippets that are implementing max and average pooling:

```
# 1D Max Pooling
array = np.array([0, 1, 0, 1, 0, 1, 0, 1, 0, 1])
result = np.zeros(len(array)//2)
for i in range(len(array)//2):
    result[i] = np.max(array[2*i:2*i+2])
result
```

The following is the output of the preceding code:

```
array([1., 1., 1., 1., 1.])
```

Figure 8.14: Max pooling operation's result on an array

The following is the code snippet for average pooling:

```
# 1D Average Pooling
array = np.array([0, 1, 0, 1, 0, 1, 0, 1, 0, 1])
result = np.zeros(len(array)//2)
for i in range(len(array)//2):
    result[i] = np.mean(array[2*i:2*i+2])
result
```

The following is the output of the preceding code:

```
array([0.5, 0.5, 0.5, 0.5, 0.5])
```

Figure 8.15: Average pooling operation's result on an array

The following is a diagram explaining the max pooling operation:

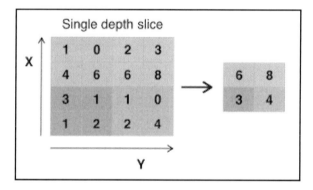

Figure 8.16: 2*2 max pooling with stride 2 (Source: https://en.wikipedia.org/wiki/Convolutional_neural_network)

Consider the following code for a digit:

```
plt.imshow(X_train[0].reshape(28,28), cmap='gray')
```

The following is the output of the preceding code:

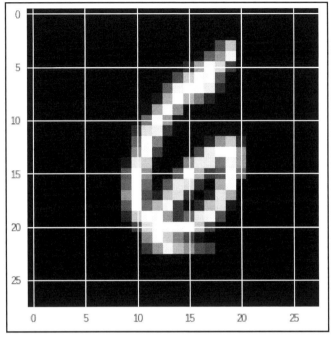

Figure 8.17: Random MNIST digit

This image is of shape 28*28. Now, if you were to perform a 2*2 max pooling operation of this, the resulting image would have a shape of 14*14.

Now, let's write a function to implement a 2*2 max pooling operation on a MNIST digit:

```
def square_max_pool(image, pool_size=2):
    result = np.zeros((14,14))
    for i in range(result.shape[0]):
        for j in range(result.shape[1]):
            result[i,j] = np.max(image[i*pool_size : i*pool_size+pool_size,
j*pool_size : j*pool_size+pool_size])
    return result

# plot a pooled image
plt.imshow(square_max_pool(X_train[0].reshape(28,28)), cmap='gray')
```

The following is the output of the preceding code:

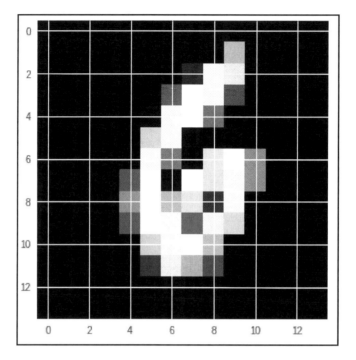

Figure 8.18: Random MNIST digit after max pooling

You may have noticed that the convolution classifier that we built in the previous section has around 2.7 million parameters. It has been proven that having a lot of parameters can lead to overfitting in a lot of cases. This is where pooling comes in. It helps us to retain the important features in the data as well as reduce the number of parameters.

Now, let's implement a convolution classifier with max pooling.

Import the max pool operation from Keras with the following code:

```
from keras.layers import MaxPool2D
```

Then, define and compile the model:

```
# model
model = Sequential()
model.add(Conv2D(32, kernel_size=(3,3), input_shape=input_shape, activation
= 'relu'))
model.add(MaxPool2D(2,2))
model.add(Dropout(0.2))
```

```
model.add(Flatten())
model.add(Dense(128, activation = 'relu'))
model.add(Dense(10, activation = 'softmax'))

# compile model
model.compile(loss = 'sparse_categorical_crossentropy', optimizer=
optimizer, metrics = ['accuracy'])

# print model summary
model.summary()
```

The following is the output of the preceding code:

Layer (type)	Output Shape	Param #
conv2d_12 (Conv2D)	(None, 26, 26, 32)	320
max_pooling2d_10 (MaxPooling	(None, 13, 13, 32)	0
flatten_8 (Flatten)	(None, 5408)	0
dense_43 (Dense)	(None, 128)	692352
dense_44 (Dense)	(None, 10)	1290

```
Total params: 693,962
Trainable params: 693,962
Non-trainable params: 0
```

Figure 8.19: Summary of the convolution classifier with max pooling

From the summary, we can see that with a pooling filter of 2*2 with stride 2, the number of parameters has come down to $693,962$, which is $1/4^{th}$ of the number of parameters in the convolution classifier.

Fitting the model

Now, let's fit the model on the data:

```
# fit model
history = model.fit(X_train, y_train, epochs = epochs,
batch_size=batch_size, validation_data=(X_val, y_val))
```

The following is the output of the preceding code:

```
Train on 55000 samples, validate on 5000 samples
Epoch 1/20
55000/55000 [==============================] - 6s 117us/step - loss: 1.5566 - acc: 0.8555 - val_loss: 0.4041 - val_acc: 0.9416
Epoch 2/20
55000/55000 [==============================] - 5s 97us/step - loss: 0.2344 - acc: 0.9603 - val_loss: 0.2542 - val_acc: 0.9596
Epoch 3/20
55000/55000 [==============================] - 5s 95us/step - loss: 0.1293 - acc: 0.9742 - val_loss: 0.2171 - val_acc: 0.9634
```

The following is the output at the end of the code's execution:

```
Epoch 19/20
55000/55000 [==============================] - 5s 91us/step - loss: 0.0092 - acc: 0.9983 - val_loss: 0.1411 - val_acc: 0.9788
Epoch 20/20
55000/55000 [==============================] - 5s 90us/step - loss: 0.0113 - acc: 0.9974 - val_loss: 0.1630 - val_acc: 0.9772
```

Figure 8.20: Metrics printed out during the training of the convolution classifier with max pooling

We can see that the convolution classifier with max pooling has an accuracy of 97.72% on the validation data.

Evaluating the model

Now, evaluate the convolution model with max pooling on the test data:

```
# evaluate model
loss, acc = model.evaluate(X_test, y_test)
print('Test loss:', loss)
print('Accuracy:', acc)
```

The following is the output of the preceding code:

```
10000/10000 [==============================] - 1s 111us/step
Test loss: 0.13552795079282295
Accuracy: 0.9788
```

Figure 8.21: Printout of the evaluation of the convolution classifier with max pooling

We can see that the model is 97.88% accurate on the test data, 97.72% on the validation data, and 99.74% on the train data. The convolution model with pooling gives the same level of performance as the convolution model without pooling, but with four times less parameters.

In this case, we can clearly see from the loss that the model is slightly overfitting on the train data.

Just like we did previously, plot the train and validation metrics to see how the training has progressed:

```
# plot training loss
loss_plot(history)
```

The following is the output of the preceding code:

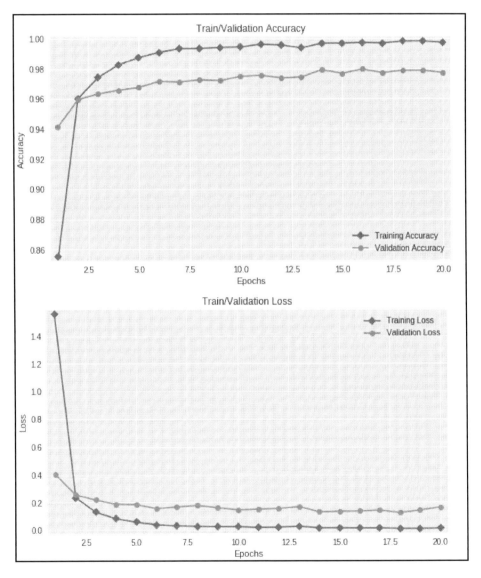

Figure 8.22: Loss/accuracy plot of the convolution classifier with max pooling during training

Convolution with pooling – Python file

This module implements the training and evaluation of a convolution classifier with the pooling operation:

```python
"""This module implements a convolution classifier with maxpool
operation."""
import numpy as np
from keras.datasets import mnist
from keras.models import Sequential
from keras.layers import Dense, Conv2D, Flatten, MaxPool2D
import matplotlib.pyplot as plt

from sklearn.model_selection import train_test_split
from loss_plot import loss_plot

# Number of epochs
epochs = 20
# Batchsize
batch_size = 128
# Optimizer for the generator
from keras.optimizers import Adam
optimizer = Adam(lr=0.0001)
# Shape of the input image
input_shape = (28,28,1)

(X_train, y_train), (X_test, y_test) = mnist.load_data()

X_train, X_val, y_train, y_val = train_test_split(X_train, y_train,
                                                  stratify = y_train,
                                                  test_size = 0.08333,
                                                  random_state=42)

X_train = X_train.reshape(-1,28,28,1)
X_val = X_val.reshape(-1,28,28,1)
X_test = X_test.reshape(-1,28,28,1)

model = Sequential()
model.add(Conv2D(32, kernel_size=(3,3), input_shape=input_shape,
                 activation='relu'))
model.add(MaxPool2D(2,2))
model.add(Flatten())
model.add(Dense(128, activation = 'relu'))
model.add(Dense(10, activation='softmax'))
model.compile(loss = 'sparse_categorical_crossentropy',
optimizer=optimizer,
              metrics = ['accuracy'])
```

```
history = model.fit(X_train, y_train, epochs = epochs,
batch_size=batch_size,
                    validation_data=(X_val, y_val))

loss,acc = model.evaluate(X_test, y_test)
print('Test loss:', loss)
print('Accuracy:', acc)

loss_plot(history)
```

Dropout

Dropout is a regularization technique used to prevent overfitting. During training, it is implemented by randomly sampling a neural network from the original neural network during each forward and backward propagation, and then training this subset network on the batch of input data. During testing, no dropout is implemented. The test results are obtained as an ensemble of all of the sampled networks:

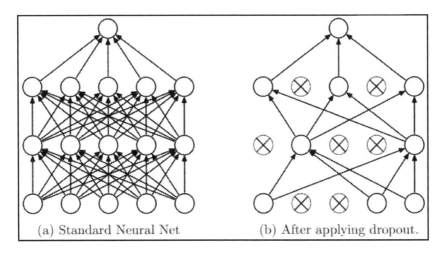

Figure 8.23: Dropout. as shown in the Dropout: A Simple Way to Prevent Neural Networks from Overfitting paper (Source: http://www.cs.toronto.edu/~rsalakhu/papers/srivastava14a.pdf)

In Keras, implementing `Dropout` is easy. First, import it from the `layers` module of `keras`:

```
from keras.layers import Dropout
```

Then, place the layer where needed. In the case of our CNN, we will place one after the max pool operation and one after the `Dense` layer, as shown in the following code:

```
# model
model = Sequential()
model.add(Conv2D(32, kernel_size=(3,3), input_shape=input_shape, activation
= 'relu'))
model.add(MaxPool2D(2,2))
model.add(Dropout(0.2))
model.add(Flatten())
model.add(Dense(128, activation = 'relu'))
model.add(Dropout(0.2))
model.add(Dense(10, activation = 'softmax'))

# compile model
model.compile(loss = 'sparse_categorical_crossentropy', optimizer=
optimizer, metrics = ['accuracy'])

# model summary
model.summary()
```

The following is the output of the preceding code:

```
Layer (type)                 Output Shape              Param #
=================================================================
conv2d_13 (Conv2D)           (None, 26, 26, 32)        320

max_pooling2d_11 (MaxPooling (None, 13, 13, 32)        0

dropout_11 (Dropout)         (None, 13, 13, 32)        0

flatten_9 (Flatten)          (None, 5408)              0

dense_45 (Dense)             (None, 128)               692352

dropout_12 (Dropout)         (None, 128)               0

dense_46 (Dense)             (None, 10)                1290
=================================================================
Total params: 693,962
Trainable params: 693,962
Non-trainable params: 0
```

Figure 8.24: Summary of the convolution classifier

Since `Dropout` is a regularization technique, adding it to a model will not result in a change in the number of trainable parameters.

Fitting the model

Again, train the model on the standard 20 `epochs`:

```
# fit model
history = model.fit(X_train, y_train, epochs = epochs,
batch_size=batch_size, validation_data=(X_val, y_val))
```

The following is the output of the preceding code:

```
Train on 55000 samples, validate on 5000 samples
Epoch 1/20
55000/55000 [==============================] - 7s 128us/step - loss: 1.8460 - acc: 0.7737 - val_loss: 0.3178 - val_acc: 0.9122
Epoch 2/20
55000/55000 [==============================] - 6s 107us/step - loss: 0.4344 - acc: 0.8889 - val_loss: 0.1863 - val_acc: 0.9468
Epoch 3/20
55000/55000 [==============================] - 6s 108us/step - loss: 0.2815 - acc: 0.9251 - val_loss: 0.1443 - val_acc: 0.9584
```

The following is the output at the end of the code's execution:

```
Epoch 19/20
55000/55000 [==============================] - 6s 105us/step - loss: 0.0255 - acc: 0.9916 - val_loss: 0.0671 - val_acc: 0.9860
Epoch 20/20
55000/55000 [==============================] - 6s 102us/step - loss: 0.0228 - acc: 0.9926 - val_loss: 0.0677 - val_acc: 0.9852
```

Figure 8.25: Metrics printed out during the training of the convolution classifier with max pooling and dropout

We see that the convolution classifier with max pooling and dropout is 98.52% accurate on the validation data.

Evaluating the model

Now, let's evaluate the model and capture the loss and the accuracy:

```
# evaluate model
loss, acc = model.evaluate(X_test, y_test)
print('Test loss:', loss)
print('Accuracy:', acc)
```

The following is the output of the preceding code:

```
10000/10000 [====================================] - 1s 128us/step
Test loss: 0.06125994629900379
Accuracy: 0.9842
```

Figure 8.26: Printout of the evaluation of the convolution classifier with max pooling and dropout

We can see that the model is 98.42% accurate on the test data, 98.52% on the validation data, and 99.26% on the train data. The convolution model with pooling and dropout gives the same level of performance as the convolution model without pooling, but with four times fewer parameters. If you look at the `loss` as well, this model was able to reach a better minima than the other models we have trained before.

Plot the metrics to understand how the training has progressed:

```
# plot training loss
loss_plot(history)
```

The following is the output of the preceding code:

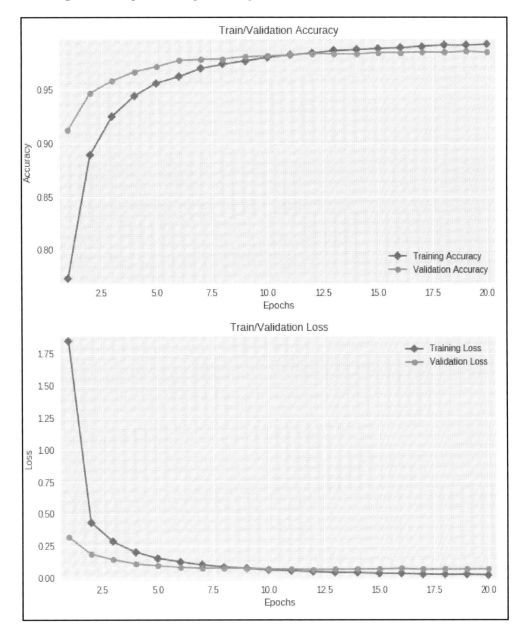

Figure 8.27: Loss/accuracy plot of the convolution classifier with max pooling and dropout during training

Convolution with pooling – Python file

This module implements the training and evaluation of a convolution classifier with the max pool and `Dropout` operations:

```python
"""This module implements a deep conv classifier with max pool and
dropout."""
import numpy as np
from keras.datasets import mnist
from keras.models import Sequential
from keras.layers import Dense, Conv2D, Flatten, MaxPool2D, Dropout
import matplotlib.pyplot as plt

from sklearn.model_selection import train_test_split
from loss_plot import loss_plot

# Number of epochs
epochs = 20
# Batchsize
batch_size = 128
# Optimizer for the generator
from keras.optimizers import Adam
optimizer = Adam(lr=0.0001)
# Shape of the input image
input_shape = (28,28,1)

(X_train, y_train), (X_test, y_test) = mnist.load_data()

X_train, X_val, y_train, y_val = train_test_split(X_train, y_train,
                                        stratify = y_train,
                                        test_size = 0.08333,
                                        random_state=42)

X_train = X_train.reshape(-1,28,28,1)
X_val = X_val.reshape(-1,28,28,1)
X_test = X_test.reshape(-1,28,28,1)

model = Sequential()
model.add(Conv2D(32, kernel_size=(3,3), input_shape=input_shape,
                activation = 'relu'))
model.add(MaxPool2D(2,2))
model.add(Dropout(0.2))
model.add(Conv2D(64, kernel_size=(3,3), activation = 'relu'))
model.add(MaxPool2D(2,2))
model.add(Dropout(0.2))
model.add(Conv2D(128, kernel_size=(3,3), activation = 'relu'))
model.add(MaxPool2D(2,2))
model.add(Dropout(0.2))
```

```
model.add(Flatten())
model.add(Dense(128, activation = 'relu'))
model.add(Dropout(0.2))
model.add(Dense(10, activation = 'softmax'))

model.compile(loss = 'sparse_categorical_crossentropy', optimizer=
optimizer,
             metrics = ['accuracy'])

history = model.fit(X_train, y_train, epochs = epochs,
batch_size=batch_size,
                    validation_data=(X_val, y_val))

loss,acc = model.evaluate(X_test, y_test)
print('Test loss:', loss)
print('Accuracy:', acc)

loss_plot(history)
```

Going deeper

The convolution classifier with max pooling and dropout seems to be the best classifier so far. However, we also noticed that there was a slight amount of overfitting on the train data.

Let's build a deeper model to see if we can create a classifier that is more accurate than the other models we have trained so far, and see if we can get it to reach an even better minima.

We will build a deeper model by adding two more convolution layers to our best model so far:

- The first layer is a convolution 2-D layer with 32 filters of size 3*3 with activation as relu, followed by downsampling with max pooling of size 2*2, followed by Dropout as the regularizer
- The second layer is a convolution 2-D layer with 64 filters of size 3*3 with activation as relu, followed by downsampling with max pooling of size 2*2, followed by Dropout as the regularizer
- The third layer is a convolution 2-D layer with 128 filters of size 3*3 with activation as relu, followed by downsampling with max pooling of size 2*2, followed by Dropout as the regularizer

Compiling the model

The following is the code for the deeper model:

```python
# model
model = Sequential()
model.add(Conv2D(32, kernel_size=(3,3), input_shape=input_shape, activation = 'relu'))
model.add(MaxPool2D(2,2))
model.add(Dropout(0.2))
model.add(Conv2D(64, kernel_size=(3,3), activation = 'relu'))
model.add(MaxPool2D(2,2))
model.add(Dropout(0.2))
model.add(Conv2D(128, kernel_size=(3,3), activation = 'relu'))
model.add(MaxPool2D(2,2))
model.add(Dropout(0.2))
model.add(Flatten())
model.add(Dense(128, activation = 'relu'))
model.add(Dropout(0.2))
model.add(Dense(10, activation = 'softmax'))

# compile model
model.compile(loss = 'sparse_categorical_crossentropy', optimizer=
optimizer, metrics = ['accuracy'])

# print model summary
model.summary()
```

The following is the output of the preceding code:

```
Layer (type)                    Output Shape              Param #
=================================================================
conv2d_20 (Conv2D)              (None, 26, 26, 32)        320

max_pooling2d_18 (MaxPooling    (None, 13, 13, 32)        0

dropout_21 (Dropout)            (None, 13, 13, 32)        0

conv2d_21 (Conv2D)              (None, 11, 11, 64)        18496

max_pooling2d_19 (MaxPooling    (None, 5, 5, 64)          0

dropout_22 (Dropout)            (None, 5, 5, 64)          0

conv2d_22 (Conv2D)              (None, 3, 3, 128)         73856

max_pooling2d_20 (MaxPooling    (None, 1, 1, 128)         0

dropout_23 (Dropout)            (None, 1, 1, 128)         0

flatten_12 (Flatten)            (None, 128)               0

dense_51 (Dense)                (None, 128)               16512

dropout_24 (Dropout)            (None, 128)               0

dense_52 (Dense)                (None, 10)                1290
=================================================================
Total params: 110,474
Trainable params: 110,474
Non-trainable params: 0
```

Figure 8.28: Summary of the deep convolution classifier

From the summary, we can see that the deeper model has only $110,474$ parameters. Now, let's see if a deeper model with fewer parameters can do a better job than we have done so far.

Fitting the model

Just like we did previously, fit the model, but with epochs set as 40 instead of 20, since the deeper model takes longer to learn. Try training the model for 20 epochs first to see what happens:

```
# fit model
history = model.fit(X_train, y_train, epochs = 40, batch_size=batch_size,
validation_data=(X_val, y_val))
```

The following is the output of the preceding code:

```
Train on 55000 samples, validate on 5000 samples
Epoch 1/40
55000/55000 [==============================] - 9s 172us/step - loss: 4.1928 - acc: 0.3508 - val_loss: 1.0419 - val_acc: 0.7016
Epoch 2/40
55000/55000 [==============================] - 8s 150us/step - loss: 1.2163 - acc: 0.5978 - val_loss: 0.5370 - val_acc: 0.8628
Epoch 3/40
55000/55000 [==============================] - 8s 150us/step - loss: 0.7717 - acc: 0.7507 - val_loss: 0.3267 - val_acc: 0.9118
```

The following is the output at the end of the code's execution:

```
Epoch 39/40
55000/55000 [==============================] - 8s 154us/step - loss: 0.0517 - acc: 0.9843 - val_loss: 0.0363 - val_acc: 0.9898
Epoch 40/40
55000/55000 [==============================] - 8s 154us/step - loss: 0.0510 - acc: 0.9838 - val_loss: 0.0370 - val_acc: 0.9884
```

Figure 8.29: Metrics printed out during the training of the deep convolution classifier

Evaluating the model

Now, evaluate the model with the following code:

```
# evaluate model
loss,acc = model.evaluate(X_test, y_test)
print('Test loss:', loss)
print('Accuracy:', acc)
```

The following is the output of the preceding code:

```
10000/10000 [====================================] - 1s 123us/step
Test loss: 0.03408890862933331
Accuracy: 0.9901
```

Figure 8.30: Printout of the evaluation of the deep convolution classifier

We can see that the model is 99.01% accurate on the test data, 98.84% on the validation data, and 98.38% on the train data. The deeper convolution model with pooling and dropout gives a much better performance with just 110,000 parameters. If you look at the loss as well, this model was able to reach a better minima than the other models that we trained previously:

Plot the metrics to understand how the training has progressed:

```
# plot training loss
loss_plot(history)
```

The following is the output of the preceding code:

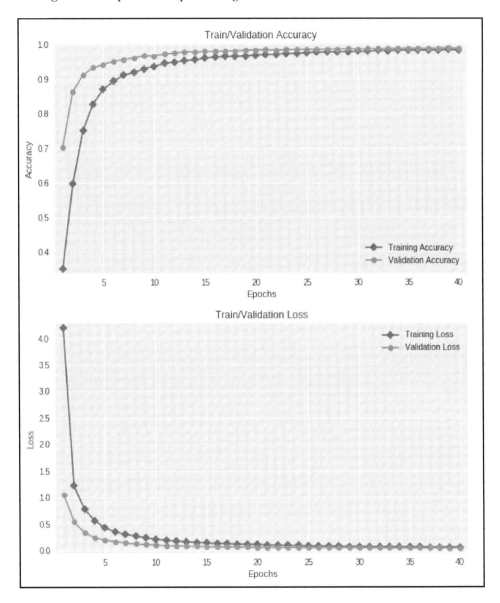

Figure 8.31: Loss/accuracy plot of the deep convolution classifier during training

This is one of the best training plots you can get. We can see no overfitting at all.

Convolution with pooling and Dropout – Python file

This module implements the training and evaluation of a deep convolution classifier with the max pool and `Dropout` operations:

```python
"""This module implements a deep conv classifier with max pool and
dropout."""
import numpy as np
from keras.datasets import mnist
from keras.models import Sequential
from keras.layers import Dense, Conv2D, Flatten, MaxPool2D, Dropout
import matplotlib.pyplot as plt

from sklearn.model_selection import train_test_split
from loss_plot import loss_plot

# Number of epochs
epochs = 20
# Batchsize
batch_size = 128
# Optimizer for the generator
from keras.optimizers import Adam
optimizer = Adam(lr=0.0001)
# Shape of the input image
input_shape = (28,28,1)

(X_train, y_train), (X_test, y_test) = mnist.load_data()

X_train, X_val, y_train, y_val = train_test_split(X_train, y_train,
                                        stratify = y_train,
                                        test_size = 0.08333,
                                        random_state=42)

X_train = X_train.reshape(-1,28,28,1)
X_val = X_val.reshape(-1,28,28,1)
X_test = X_test.reshape(-1,28,28,1)

model = Sequential()
model.add(Conv2D(32, kernel_size=(3,3), input_shape=input_shape,
                activation = 'relu'))
model.add(MaxPool2D(2,2))
model.add(Dropout(0.2))
model.add(Conv2D(64, kernel_size=(3,3), activation = 'relu'))
model.add(MaxPool2D(2,2))
model.add(Dropout(0.2))
model.add(Conv2D(128, kernel_size=(3,3), activation = 'relu'))
model.add(MaxPool2D(2,2))
model.add(Dropout(0.2))
```

```
model.add(Flatten())
model.add(Dense(128, activation = 'relu'))
model.add(Dropout(0.2))
model.add(Dense(10, activation = 'softmax'))

model.compile(loss = 'sparse_categorical_crossentropy', optimizer=
optimizer,
                metrics = ['accuracy'])

history = model.fit(X_train, y_train, epochs = epochs,
batch_size=batch_size,
                    validation_data=(X_val, y_val))

loss,acc = model.evaluate(X_test, y_test)
print('Test loss:', loss)
print('Accuracy:', acc)

loss_plot(history)
```

Data augmentation

Imagine a situation where you might want to build a convolution classifier on a small set of images. The problem here is that the classifier will easily overfit on this small set of data. The reason why the classifier will overfit is that there are very few images that are similar. That is, there are not a lot of variations for the model to capture within a specific class so that it can be robust and perform well on new data.

Keras provides a preprocessing utility called `ImageDataGenerator` that can be used to augment image data with simple configuration.

Its capabilities include the following:

- `zoom_range`: Randomly zoom in on images to a given zoom level
- `horizontal_flip`: Randomly flip images horizontally
- `vertical_flip`: Randomly flip images vertically
- `rescale`: Multiply the data with the factor provided

It also includes capabilities for random rotations, random shear, and many more.

 Visit the official Keras documentation (https://keras.io/preprocessing/image/) to learn more about some of the additional functionalities of the `image_data_generator` API.

Using ImageDataGenerator

The `image_data_generator` API transforms and augments the data in batches on the go, and is also super easy to use.

First, import the `ImageDataGenerator`:

```
from keras.preprocessing.image import ImageDataGenerator
```

Implement a random horizontal flip augmenter:

```
train_datagen = ImageDataGenerator(horizontal_flip=True)
```

Fit the augmenter on the train data:

```
# fit the augmenter
train_datagen.fit(X_train)
```

After the fit, we usually use the `transform` command. Here, instead of `transform`, we have the `flow` command. It accepts the images and its corresponding labels, and then generates batches of transformed data of the specified batch size.

Let's transform a bunch of images and look at the result:

```
# transform the data
for img, label in train_datagen.flow(X_train, y_train, batch_size=6):
    for i in range(0, 6):
        plt.subplot(2,3,i+1)
        plt.title('Label {}'.format(label[i]))
        plt.imshow(img[i].reshape(28, 28), cmap='gray')
    break
plt.tight_layout()
plt.show()
```

The following is the output of the preceding code:

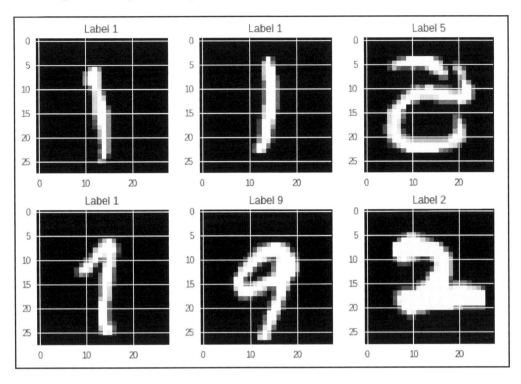

Figure 8.32: Digits after horizontal flip augmentation

Similarly, we can implement a random zoom augmenter, like so:

```
train_datagen = ImageDataGenerator(zoom_range=0.3)

#fit
train_datagen.fit(X_train)

#transform
for img, label in train_datagen.flow(X_train, y_train, batch_size=6):
    for i in range(0, 6):
        plt.subplot(2,3,i+1)
        plt.title('Label {}'.format(label[i]))
        plt.imshow(img[i].reshape(28, 28), cmap='gray')
    break
plt.tight_layout()
plt.show()
```

The following is the output of the preceding code:

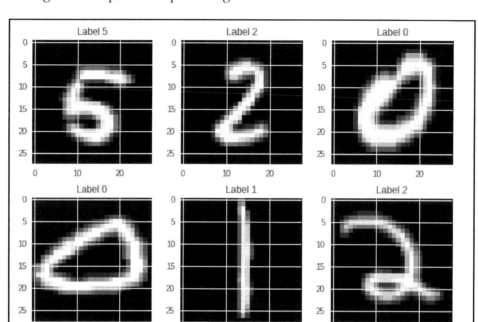

Figure 8.33: Digits after zoom augmentation

Fitting ImageDataGenerator

Now, let's build a classifier using the same architecture as the deep convolution model with pooling and Dropout, but on augmented data.

First, define the features of the ImageDataGenerator, as follows:

```
train_datagen = ImageDataGenerator(
        rescale = 1./255,
        zoom_range = 0.2,
        horizontal_flip = True)
```

We have defined that the ImageDataGenerator can perform the following operations

- Rescaling
- Random zoom
- Random horizontal flip

The rescaling operation scales the pixel values to a range between 0 and 1.

The next step is to fit this generator on the train data:

```
train_datagen.fit(X_train)
```

Compiling the model

We need to define and compile the deep convolution model like so:

```
# define model
model = Sequential()
model.add(Conv2D(32, kernel_size=(3,3), input_shape=input_shape, activation
= 'relu'))
model.add(MaxPool2D(2,2))
model.add(Dropout(0.2))
model.add(Conv2D(64, kernel_size=(3,3), activation = 'relu'))
model.add(MaxPool2D(2,2))
model.add(Dropout(0.2))
model.add(Conv2D(128, kernel_size=(3,3), activation = 'relu'))
model.add(MaxPool2D(2,2))
model.add(Dropout(0.2))
model.add(Flatten())
model.add(Dense(128, activation = 'relu'))
model.add(Dropout(0.2))
model.add(Dense(10, activation = 'softmax'))

# compile model
model.compile(loss = 'sparse_categorical_crossentropy', optimizer=
optimizer, metrics = ['accuracy'])
```

Fitting the model

Finally, we need to fit the model:

```
# fit the model on batches with real-time data augmentation
history = model.fit_generator(train_datagen.flow(X_train, y_train,
batch_size=128), steps_per_epoch=len(X_train) / 128, epochs=10,
validation_data=(train_datagen.flow(X_val, y_val)))
```

The following is the output of the preceding code:

```
Epoch 1/10
430/429 [==============================] - 18s 43ms/step - loss: 0.7970 - acc: 0.7317 - val_loss: 0.3087 - val_acc: 0.9038
Epoch 2/10
430/429 [==============================] - 17s 41ms/step - loss: 0.3466 - acc: 0.8902 - val_loss: 0.1981 - val_acc: 0.9412
Epoch 3/10
430/429 [==============================] - 18s 41ms/step - loss: 0.2568 - acc: 0.9203 - val_loss: 0.1654 - val_acc: 0.9486
```

The following is the output at the end of the code's execution:

```
Epoch 9/10
430/429 [==============================] - 18s 42ms/step - loss: 0.1367 - acc: 0.9578 - val_loss: 0.0953 - val_acc: 0.9720
Epoch 10/10
430/429 [==============================] - 17s 41ms/step - loss: 0.1289 - acc: 0.9602 - val_loss: 0.0916 - val_acc: 0.9718
```

Figure 8.34: Metrics printed out during the training of the deep convolution classifier on augmented data

Evaluating the model

Now, we need to evaluate the model:

```
# transform/augment test data
for test_img, test_lab in train_datagen.flow(X_test, y_test, batch_size =
X_test.shape[0]):
    break

# evaluate model on test data
loss,acc = model.evaluate(test_img, test_lab)
print('Test loss:', loss)
print('Accuracy:', acc)
```

The following is the output of the preceding code:

```
10000/10000 [==============================] - 1s 107us/step
Test loss: 0.07422855299189687
Accuracy: 0.9764
```

Figure 8.35: Printout of the evaluation of the deep convolution classifier on augmented data

Then, we need to plot the deep convolution classifier:

```
# plot the learning
loss_plot(history)
```

The following is the output of the preceding code:

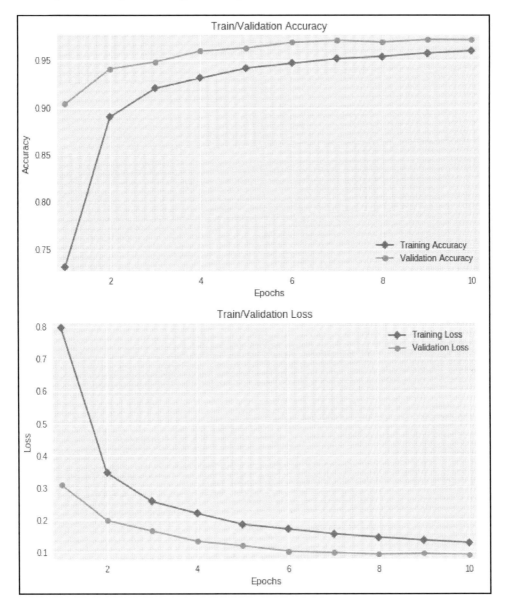

Figure 8.36: Loss/accuracy plot of the deep convolution classifier during training on augmented data

Augmentation – Python file

This module implements the training and evaluation of a deep convolution classifier on augmented data:

```python
"""This module implements a deep conv classifier on augmented data."""
import numpy as np
from keras.datasets import mnist
from keras.models import Sequential
from keras.layers import Dense, Conv2D, Flatten, MaxPool2D, Dropout
import matplotlib.pyplot as plt
from keras.preprocessing.image import ImageDataGenerator

from sklearn.model_selection import train_test_split
from loss_plot import loss_plot

# Number of epochs
epochs = 10
# Batchsize
batch_size = 128
# Optimizer for the generator
from keras.optimizers import Adam
optimizer = Adam(lr=0.001)
# Shape of the input image
input_shape = (28,28,1)

(X_train, y_train), (X_test, y_test) = mnist.load_data()

X_train, X_val, y_train, y_val = train_test_split(X_train, y_train,
                                                  stratify = y_train,
                                                  test_size = 0.08333,
                                                  random_state=42)

X_train = X_train.reshape(-1,28,28,1)
X_val = X_val.reshape(-1,28,28,1)
X_test = X_test.reshape(-1,28,28,1)

train_datagen = ImageDataGenerator(
        rescale=1./255,
        zoom_range=0.2,
        horizontal_flip=True)

train_datagen.fit(X_train)

model = Sequential()
model.add(Conv2D(32, kernel_size=(3,3), input_shape=input_shape,
                 activation = 'relu'))
model.add(MaxPool2D(2,2))
```

```
model.add(Dropout(0.2))
model.add(Conv2D(64, kernel_size=(3,3), activation = 'relu'))
model.add(MaxPool2D(2,2))
model.add(Dropout(0.2))
model.add(Conv2D(128, kernel_size=(3,3), activation = 'relu'))
model.add(MaxPool2D(2,2))
model.add(Dropout(0.2))
model.add(Flatten())
model.add(Dense(128, activation = 'relu'))
model.add(Dropout(0.2))
model.add(Dense(10, activation = 'softmax'))

model.compile(loss = 'sparse_categorical_crossentropy', optimizer=
optimizer,
             metrics = ['accuracy'])

# fits the model on batches with real-time data augmentation:
history = model.fit_generator(train_datagen.flow(X_train, y_train,
                                              batch_size=128),
                           steps_per_epoch=len(X_train) / 128,
epochs=epochs,
                           validation_data=(train_datagen.flow(X_val,
                                                          y_val)))

for test_img, test_lab in train_datagen.flow(X_test, y_test,
                                           batch_size = X_test.shape[0]):
    break

loss,acc = model.evaluate(test_img, test_lab)
print('Test loss:', loss)
print('Accuracy:', acc)

loss_plot(history)
```

Additional topic – convolution autoencoder

An autoencoder is a combination of two parts: an encoder and a decoder. The encoder and decoder of a simple autoencoder are usually made up of dense layers, whereas in a convolution autoencoder, they are made of convolution layers:

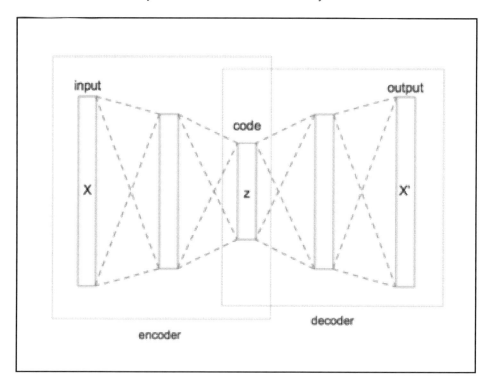

Figure 8.37: The structure of an autoencoder (image source: Wikipedia)

The encoder part of the autoencoder accepts an image and compresses it into a smaller size with the help of a pooling operation. In our case, this is max pooling. The decoder accepts the input of the encoder and learns to expand the image to our desired size by using convolution and upsampling.

Imagine a situation where you want to build high-resolution images out of blurred images:

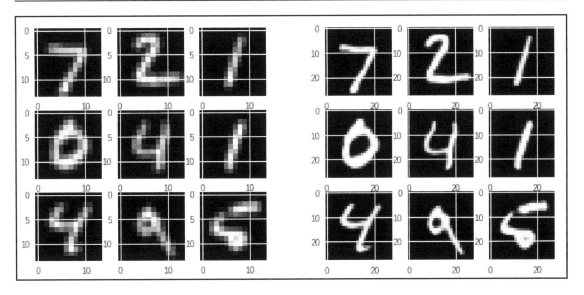

Figure 8.38: Low-resolution digits on the left and high-resolution digits on the right

Convolution autoencoders are capable of doing this job very well. The preceding high-resolution digits that you can see were actually generated using convolution autoencoders.

By the end of this section, you will have built a convolution autoencoder that accepts low-resolution 14*14*1 MNIST digits and generates high-resolution 28*28*1 digits.

Importing the dependencies

Consider restarting your session before starting this section:

```
import numpy as np
import matplotlib.pyplot as plt
%matplotlib inline

from keras.datasets import mnist
(X_train, y_train), (X_test, y_test) = mnist.load_data()

from keras.layers import Conv2D, MaxPooling2D, UpSampling2D
from keras.models import Model, Sequential
from keras.optimizers import Adam
from keras import backend as k

# for resizing images
from scipy.misc import imresize
```

Generating low-resolution images

To generate low-resolution images, define a function called `reshape()` that will resize the input image/digit to size `14*14`. After defining this, we will use the `reshape()` function to generate low-resolution train and test images:

```
def reshape(x):
    """Reshape images to 14*14"""
    img = imresize(x.reshape(28,28), (14, 14))
    return img

# create 14*14 low resolution train and test images
XX_train = np.array([*map(reshape, X_train.astype(float))])
XX_test = np.array([*map(reshape, X_test.astype(float))])
```

`XX_train` and `XX_test` will be the images that we will feed into the encoder, and `X_train` and `X_test` will be the targets.

Scaling

Scale the train input, test input, and target images to range between 0 and 1 so that the learning process is faster:

```
# scale images to range between 0 and 1
# 14*14 train images
XX_train = XX_train/255
# 28*28 train label images
X_train = X_train/255

# 14*14 test images
XX_test = XX_test/255
# 28*28 test label images
X_test = X_test/255
```

Defining the autoencoder

The convolution autoencoder we are going to build will accept 14*14*1 images as input with 28*28*1 images as the targets, and will have the following characteristics:

In the encoder:

- The first layer is a convolution 2-D layer with 64 filters of size 3*3, followed by batch normalization, with `activation` as `relu`, followed by downsampling with `MaxPooling2D` of size 2*2
- The second layer, or the final layer in this encoder part, is again a convolution 2-D layer with 128 filters of size 3*3, batch normalization, with `activation` as `relu`

In the decoder:

- The first layer is a convolution 2-D layer with 128 filters of size 3*3 with `activation` as `relu`, followed by upsampling that's performed with `UpSampling2D`
- The second layer is a convolution 2-D layer with 64 filters of size 3*3 with `activation` as `relu`, followed by upsampling with `UpSampling2D`
- The third layer, or the final layer in this decoder part, is again a convolution 2-D layer with 1 filter of size 3*3 with `activation` as `sigmoid`

The following is the code for our autoencoder:

```
batch_size = 128
epochs = 40
input_shape = (14,14,1)

# define autoencoder
def make_autoencoder(input_shape):
    generator = Sequential()
    generator.add(Conv2D(64, (3, 3), activation='relu', padding='same',
input_shape=input_shape))
    generator.add(MaxPooling2D(pool_size=(2, 2)))
    generator.add(Conv2D(128, (3, 3), activation='relu', padding='same'))
    generator.add(Conv2D(128, (3, 3), activation='relu', padding='same'))
    generator.add(UpSampling2D((2, 2)))
    generator.add(Conv2D(64, (3, 3), activation='relu', padding='same'))
    generator.add(UpSampling2D((2, 2)))
    generator.add(Conv2D(1, (3, 3), activation='sigmoid', padding='same'))

    return generator

autoencoder = make_autoencoder(input_shape)

# compile auto encoder
autoencoder.compile(loss='mean_squared_error', optimizer = Adam(lr=0.0002,
beta_1=0.5))
```

```
# auto encoder summary
autoencoder.summary()
```

The following is the output of the preceding code:

```
Layer (type)                  Output Shape            Param #
==================================================================
conv2d_6 (Conv2D)             (None, 14, 14, 64)      640

max_pooling2d_2 (MaxPooling2  (None, 7, 7, 64)        0

conv2d_7 (Conv2D)             (None, 7, 7, 128)       73856

conv2d_8 (Conv2D)             (None, 7, 7, 128)       147584

up_sampling2d_3 (UpSampling2  (None, 14, 14, 128)     0

conv2d_9 (Conv2D)             (None, 14, 14, 64)      73792

up_sampling2d_4 (UpSampling2  (None, 28, 28, 64)      0

conv2d_10 (Conv2D)            (None, 28, 28, 1)       577
==================================================================
Total params: 296,449
Trainable params: 296,449
Non-trainable params: 0
```

Figure 8.39: Autoencoder summary

We are using `mean_squared_error` as the `loss`, as we want the model to predict the pixel values.

If you take a look at the summary, the input image of size 14*14*1 is compressed along the width and the height dimensions to a size of 7*7, but is expanded along the channel dimension from 1 to 128. These small/compressed feature maps are then fed to the decoder to learn the mappings that are required to generate high-resolution images of the defined dimension, which in this case is 28*28*1.

If you have any questions about the usage of he Keras API, please visit the Keras official documentation at `https://keras.io/`.

Fitting the autoencoder

Like any regular model fit, fit the autoencoder:

```
# fit autoencoder
autoencoder_train = autoencoder.fit(XX_train.reshape(-1,14,14,1),
X_train.reshape(-1,28,28,1), batch_size=batch_size,
                            epochs=epochs, verbose=1,
                            validation_split = 0.2)
```

The following is the output of the preceding code:

```
Train on 48000 samples, validate on 12000 samples
Epoch 1/40
48000/48000 [==============================] - 13s 271us/step - loss: 0.0279 - val_loss: 0.0101
Epoch 2/40
48000/48000 [==============================] - 11s 226us/step - loss: 0.0081 - val_loss: 0.0065
Epoch 3/40
48000/48000 [==============================] - 11s 226us/step - loss: 0.0059 - val_loss: 0.0052
```

The following is the output at the end of the code's execution:

```
Epoch 39/40
48000/48000 [==============================] - 11s 227us/step - loss: 0.0017 - val_loss: 0.0018
Epoch 40/40
48000/48000 [==============================] - 11s 224us/step - loss: 0.0017 - val_loss: 0.0020
```

Figure 8.40: Printout during the training of the autoencoder

You will notice that inside the fit, we have specified a parameter called validation_split and that we have set it to 0.2. This will split the train data into train and validation data, with validation data having 20% of the original train data.

Loss plot and test results

Now, let's get to plotting the train and validation loss progression during training. We will also plot the high-resolution image result from the model by feeding the test images:

```
loss = autoencoder_train.history['loss']
val_loss = autoencoder_train.history['val_loss']
epochs_ = [x for x in range(epochs)]
plt.figure()
plt.plot(epochs_, loss, label='Training loss')
plt.plot(epochs_, val_loss, label='Validation loss')
plt.title('Training and validation loss')
plt.legend()
```

```
plt.show()

print('Input')
plt.figure(figsize=(5,5))
for i in range(9):
    plt.subplot(331 + i)
    plt.imshow(np.squeeze(XX_test.reshape(-1,14,14)[i]), cmap='gray')
plt.show()

# Test set results
print('GENERATED')
plt.figure(figsize=(5,5))
for i in range(9):
    pred = autoencoder.predict(XX_test.reshape(-1,14,14,1)[i:i+1],
verbose=0)
    plt.subplot(331 + i)
    plt.imshow(pred[0].reshape(28,28), cmap='gray')
plt.show()
```

The following is the output of the preceding code:

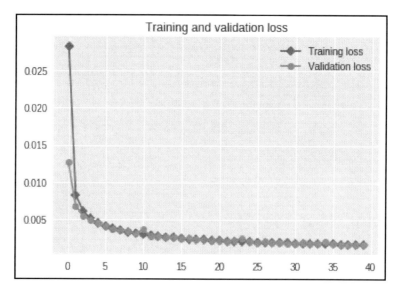

Figure 8.41: Train/val loss plot

The following is the output of high-resolution images that have been generated from low-resolution images:

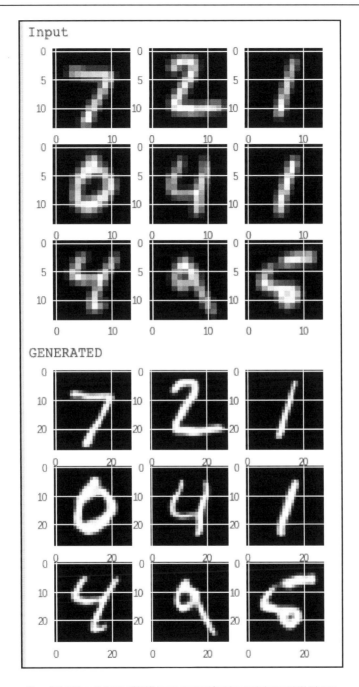

Figure 8.42: High-resolution test (28*28) images generated from low-resolution test (14*14) images

Autoencoder – Python file

This module implements training an autoencoder on MNIST data:

```python
"""This module implements a convolution autoencoder on MNIST data."""
import numpy as np
import matplotlib.pyplot as plt

from keras.datasets import mnist
(X_train, y_train), (X_test, y_test) = mnist.load_data()

from keras.layers import Conv2D, MaxPooling2D, UpSampling2D
from keras.models import Model, Sequential
from keras.optimizers import Adam
from keras import backend as k

# for resizing images
from scipy.misc import imresize

def reshape(x):
    """Reshape images to 14*14"""
    img = imresize(x.reshape(28,28), (14, 14))
    return img

# create 14*14 low resolution train and test images
XX_train = np.array([*map(reshape, X_train.astype(float))])
XX_test = np.array([*map(reshape, X_test.astype(float))])

# scale images to range between 0 and 1
#14*14 train images
XX_train = XX_train/255
#28*28 train label images
X_train = X_train/255

#14*14 test images
XX_test = XX_test/255
#28*28 test label images
X_test = X_test/255

batch_size = 128
epochs = 40
input_shape = (14,14,1)

def make_autoencoder(input_shape):

    generator = Sequential()
    generator.add(Conv2D(64, (3, 3), activation='relu', padding='same',
                         input_shape=input_shape))
```

```
    generator.add(MaxPooling2D(pool_size=(2, 2)))

    generator.add(Conv2D(128, (3, 3), activation='relu', padding='same'))

    generator.add(Conv2D(128, (3, 3), activation='relu', padding='same'))
    generator.add(UpSampling2D((2, 2)))

    generator.add(Conv2D(64, (3, 3), activation='relu', padding='same'))
    generator.add(UpSampling2D((2, 2)))

    generator.add(Conv2D(1, (3, 3), activation='sigmoid', padding='same'))

    return generator


autoencoder = make_autoencoder(input_shape)
autoencoder.compile(loss='mean_squared_error', optimizer = Adam(lr=0.0002,
beta_1=0.5))

autoencoder_train = autoencoder.fit(XX_train.reshape(-1,14,14,1),
                                    X_train.reshape(-1,28,28,1),
                                    batch_size=batch_size,
                                    epochs=epochs, verbose=1,
                                    validation_split = 0.2)

loss = autoencoder_train.history['loss']
val_loss = autoencoder_train.history['val_loss']
epochs_ = [x for x in range(epochs)]
plt.figure()
plt.plot(epochs_, loss, label='Training loss', marker = 'D')
plt.plot(epochs_, val_loss, label='Validation loss', marker = 'o')
plt.title('Training and validation loss')
plt.legend()
plt.show()

print('Input')
plt.figure(figsize=(5,5))
for i in range(9):
    plt.subplot(331 + i)
    plt.imshow(np.squeeze(XX_test.reshape(-1,14,14)[i]), cmap='gray')
plt.show()

# Test set results
print('GENERATED')
plt.figure(figsize=(5,5))
for i in range(9):
    pred = autoencoder.predict(XX_test.reshape(-1,14,14,1)[i:i+1],
verbose=0)
```

```
    plt.subplot(331 + i)
    plt.imshow(pred[0].reshape(28,28), cmap='gray')
plt.show()
```

Conclusion

This project was all about building a CNN classifier to classify handwritten digits better than we did in Chapter 2, *Training NN for Prediction Using Regression,* with a multilayer Perceptron.

Our deep convolution neural network classifier with max pooling and dropout hit 99.01% accuracy on a test set of 10,000 images/digits. This is good. This is almost 12% better than our multilayer Perceptron model.

However, there are some implications. What are the implications of this accuracy? It is important that we understand this. Just like we did in Chapter 2, *Training NN for Prediction Using Regression,* let's calculate the incidence of an error occurring that would result in a customer service issue.

Just to refresh our memory, in this hypothetical use case, we assumed that the restaurant has an average of 30 tables at each location, and that those tables turn over two times per night during the rush hour when the system is likely to be used, and finally that the restaurant chain has 35 locations. This means that each day of operation, there are approximately 21,000 handwritten numbers being captured (30 tables x 2 turns/day x 35 locations x 10-digit phone number).

The ultimate goal is to classify all of the digits properly, since even a single-digit misclassification will result in a failure. With the classifier that we have built, it would improperly classify 208 digits per day. If we consider the worst case scenario, out of the 2,100 patrons, 208 phone numbers would be misclassified. That is, even in the worst case, 90.09% ((2,100-208)/2,100) of the time, we would be sending the text to the right patron.

The best case scenario would be that if all ten digits were misclassified in each phone number, we would only be improperly classifying 21 phone numbers. This means that we would have a failure rate of ((2,100-21)/2,100) 1%. This is as good as it gets.

Unless you aim at reducing that 1% error...

Summary

In this chapter, we understood how to implement a convolution neural network classifier in Keras. You now have a brief understanding of what convolution, average, max pooling, and dropout are, and you also built a deep model. You understood how to reduce overfitting as well as how to generate more/validation in data to build a generalizable model when you have less data than you need. Finally, we assessed the model's performance on test data and determined that we succeeded in achieving our goal. We ended this chapter by introducing you to autoencoders.

9
Object Detection Using OpenCV and TensorFlow

Welcome to the second chapter focusing on computer vision in *Python Deep Learning Projects* (a data science pun to kick us off!). Let's think about what we accomplished in `Chapter 8`, *Handwritten Digits Classification Using ConvNets*, where we were able to train an image classifier with a **convolutional neural network** (**CNN**) to accurately classify handwritten digits in an image. What was a key characteristic of the raw data, and what was our business objective? The data was less complicated than it could have been because each image only had one handwritten digit in it and our goal was to accurately assign a digital label to the image.

What would have happened if each image had multiple handwritten digits in it? What would have happened if we had a video of the digits? What if we want to identify where the digits are in the image? These questions represent challenges that real-world data embodies, and they drive our data science innovation to new models and capabilities.

Let's expand our line of questions and imagination to the next (hypothetical) business use case for our Python deep learning project, where we're looking to build, train, and test an object detection and classification model to be used by an automobile manufacturer in their new line of self-driving cars. Autonomous vehicles need to have fundamental computer vision capabilities that you and I have organically by way of our physiology and experiential learning. We as humans can examine our field of vision and report whether or not a specific item is present and where in relation to other objects that item (if present) is located. So, if I were to ask you if you see a chicken, you'd likely say no, unless you live on a farm and are looking out your window. But if I ask you if you see a keyboard, you'd likely say yes, and could even say that the keyboard is different from other objects and is in front of the wall before you.

This is no trivial task for a computer. As Deep Learning Engineers, you are going to learn the intuition and model architecture that empowers you to build a powerful object detection and classification engine that we can envision being tested for use in autonomous vehicles. The data inputs that we're going to be working with in this chapter will be much more informationally complex than what we've had in previous projects, and the outcomes when we get them right will be that much more impressive.

So, let's get started!

Object detection intuition

When you need your application to find and name things in an image, you need to build a deep neural network for object detection. The visual field is very complex, and a camera for still images and video captures frames with many, many objects in them. Object detection is used in manufacturing for process automation in production lines; autonomous vehicles sensing pedestrians, other cars, the road, and signs, for example; and, of course, facial recognition. Computer vision solutions based on machine learning and deep learning require you, the Data Scientist, to build, train, and evaluate models that can differentiate one object from another and then accurately classify those detected objects.

As you've seen in other projects we've worked on, CNNs are very powerful models for image data. We need to look at expansions on the basic architecture that has performed so well on a single (still) image with simple information to see what works best for complex images and video.

Progress recently has been made with these networks: Faster R-CNN, **region-based fully convolutional network (R-FCN)**, MultiBox, **solid-state drive (SSD)**, and **you only look once (YOLO)**. We've seen the value of these models in common consumer applications such as Google Photos and Pinterest Visual Search. We are even seeing some of these that are lightweight and fast enough to perform well on mobile devices.

Recent progress in the field can be researched with the following list of references:

- *PVANET: Deep but Lightweight Neural Networks for Real-time Object Detection,* arXiv:1608.08021
- *R-CNN: Rich feature hierarchies for accurate object detection and semantic segmentation,* CVPR, 2014.
- *SPP: Spatial Pyramid Pooling in Deep Convolutional Networks for Visual Recognition,* ECCV, 2014.
- *Fast R-CNN,* arXiv:1504.08083.
- *Faster R-CNN: Towards Real-Time Object Detection with Region Proposal Networks,* arXiv:1506.01497.
- *R-CNN minus R,* arXiv:1506.06981.
- *End-to-end people detection in crowded scenes,* arXiv:1506.04878.
- *YOLO – You Only Look Once: Unified, Real-Time Object Detection,* arXiv:1506.02640
- *Inside-Outside Net: Detecting Objects in Context with Skip Pooling and Recurrent Neural Networks*
- *Deep Residual Network: Deep Residual Learning for Image Recognition*
- *R-FCN: Object Detection via Region-based Fully Convolutional Networks*
- *SSD: Single Shot MultiBox Detector,* arXiv:1512.02325

Also, following is the timeline of how the evolution of object detection has developed from 1999–2017:

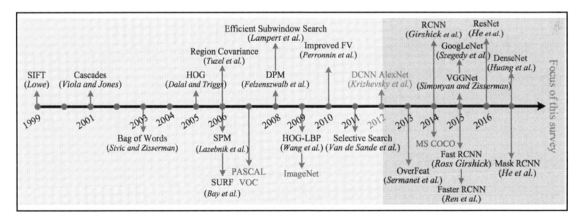

Figure 9.1: The timeline of the evolution of object detection from 1999 to 2017

The files for this chapter can be found at `https://github.com/`
`PacktPublishing/Python-Deep-Learning-Projects/tree/master/`
`Chapter09`.

Improvements in object detection models

Object detection and classification has been the subject of study for quite some time. The models that have been used build on the great success of previous researchers. A brief summary of progress history starts by highlighting the computer vision model called **Histogram of Oriented Gradients (HOG)** features that was developed by Navneet Dalal and Bill Triggs in 2005.

HOG features were fast and performed well. Interest in deep learning and the great success of CNNs that were more accurate classifiers due to their deep networks. But the problem was that the CNNs of the time were too slow in comparison.

The solution was to take advantage of the CNNs, improved classification capabilities and improve their speed with a technique and employ a selective search paradigm in what became known as R-CNN. Reducing the number of bounding boxes did show improvements in speed, but not sufficiently for the expectations.

SPP-net was a proposed solution, wherein a CNN representation for the whole image was calculated and drove CNN-calculated representations for each sub-section generated by selective search. Selective search uses image features to generate all the possible locations for an object by looking at pixel intensity, color, image texture, and a measure of insideness. These identified objects are then fed into the CNN model for classification.

This, in turn, saw improvements in a model named Fast R-CNN that trained end-to-end, and thereby fixed the primary problems with SPP-net and R-CNN. Advancing this technology further with a model named Faster R-CNN, the technique of using small regional proposal CNNs in place of the selective search performed very well.

Here is a quick overview of the Faster R-CNN object detection pipeline:

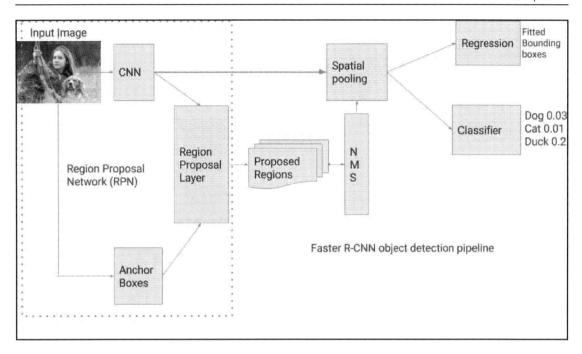

A quick benchmark comparison of the versions of R-CNN discussed previously shows the following:

	R-CNN	Fast R-CNN	Faster R-CNN
Average response time	~50 sec	~2 sec	~0.2 sec
Speed boost	1x	25x	250x

The performance improvement is impressive, with Faster R-CNN being one of the most accurate and fastest object detection algorithms deployed in real-time use cases. Other recent powerful alternatives include YOLO models, which we will look into in detail later in this chapter.

Object detection using OpenCV

Let's start our project with a basic or traditional implementation of **Open Source Computer Vision (OpenCV)**. This library is primarily targeted at real-time applications that need computer vision capabilities.

OpenCV has its API wrappers in various languages such as C, C++, Python, and so on, and the best way forward is to build a quick prototype using Python wrappers or any other language you are comfortable with, and once you are ready with your code, rewrite it in C/C++ for production.

In this chapter, we will be using the Python wrappers to create our initial object detection module.

So, let's do it.

A handcrafted red object detector

In this section, we will learn how to create a feature extractor that will be able to detect any red object from the provided image using various image processing techniques such as erosion, dilation, blurring, and so on.

Installing dependencies

First, we need to install OpenCV, which we do with this simple `pip` command:

```
pip install opencv-python
```

Then we will import it along with other modules for visualizations and matrix operations:

```
import cv2
import matplotlib
from matplotlib import colors
from matplotlib import pyplot as plt
import numpy as np
from __future__ import division
```

Also, let's define some helper functions that will help us to plot the images and the contours:

```
# Defining some helper function
def show(image):
    # Figure size in inches
    plt.figure(figsize=(15, 15))
    # Show image, with nearest neighbour interpolation
    plt.imshow(image, interpolation='nearest')
def show_hsv(hsv):
    rgb = cv2.cvtColor(hsv, cv2.COLOR_HSV2BGR)
    show(rgb)
```

```
def show_mask(mask):
    plt.figure(figsize=(10, 10))
    plt.imshow(mask, cmap='gray')
def overlay_mask(mask, image):
    rgb_mask = cv2.cvtColor(mask, cv2.COLOR_GRAY2RGB)
    img = cv2.addWeighted(rgb_mask, 0.5, image, 0.5, 0)
    show(img)


def find_biggest_contour(image):
    image = image.copy()
    im2,contours, hierarchy = cv2.findContours(image, cv2.RETR_LIST,
cv2.CHAIN_APPROX_SIMPLE)

    contour_sizes = [(cv2.contourArea(contour), contour) for contour in
contours]
    biggest_contour = max(contour_sizes, key=lambda x: x[0])[1]

    mask = np.zeros(image.shape, np.uint8)
    cv2.drawContours(mask, [biggest_contour], -1, 255, -1)
    return biggest_contour, mask

def circle_countour(image, countour):
    image_with_ellipse = image.copy()
    ellipse = cv2.fitEllipse(countour)

    cv2.ellipse(image_with_ellipse, ellipse, (0,255,0), 2)
    return image_with_ellipse
```

Exploring image data

The first thing in any data science problem is to explore and understand the data. This helps us to make our objective clear. So, let's first load the image and examine the properties of that image, such as the color spectrum and the dimensions:

```
# Loading image and display
image = cv2.imread('./ferrari.png')
show(image)
```

Following is the output:

Since the order of the image stored in the memory is **Blue Green Red** (**BGR**), we need to convert it into **Red Green Blue** (**RGB**):

```
image = cv2.cvtColor(image, cv2.COLOR_BGR2RGB)
show(image)
```

Following is the output:

Figure 9.2: The raw input image in RGB color format.

Normalizing the image

We will be scaling down the image dimensions, for which we will be using the
`cv2.resize()` function:

```
max_dimension = max(image.shape)
scale = 700/max_dimension
image = cv2.resize(image, None, fx=scale,fy=scale)
```

Now we will perform a blur operation to make the pixels more normalized, for which we
will be using the Gaussian kernel. Gaussian filters are very popular in the research field
and are used for various operations, one of which is the blurring effect that reduces the
noise and balances the image. The following code performs a blur operation:

```
image_blur = cv2.GaussianBlur(image, (7, 7), 0)
```

Then we will convert the RGB-based image into an HSV color spectrum, which will help us to extract other characteristics of the image using color intensity, brightness, and shades:

```
image_blur_hsv = cv2.cvtColor(image_blur, cv2.COLOR_RGB2HSV)
```

Following is the output:

Figure: 9.3: The raw input image in HSV color format.

Preparing a mask

We need to create a mask that can detect the specific color spectrum; let's say red in our case. Now we will create two masks that will be performing feature extraction using the color values and the brightness factors:

```
# filter by color
min_red = np.array([0, 100, 80])
max_red = np.array([10, 256, 256])
mask1 = cv2.inRange(image_blur_hsv, min_red, max_red)

# filter by brightness
min_red = np.array([170, 100, 80])
max_red = np.array([180, 256, 256])
mask2 = cv2.inRange(image_blur_hsv, min_red, max_red)
```

```
# Concatenate both the mask for better feature extraction
mask = mask1 + mask2
```

Following is how our mask looks:

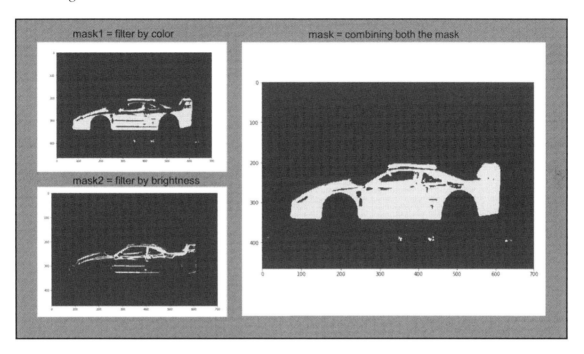

Post-processing of a mask

Once we are able to create our mask successfully, we need to perform some morphological operations, which are basic image processing operations used for the analysis and processing of geometrical structures.

First, we will create a kernel that will perform various morphological operations over the input image:

```
kernel = cv2.getStructuringElement(cv2.MORPH_ELLIPSE, (15, 15))
```

Closing: *Dilation followed by erosion* is helpful to close small pieces inside the foreground objects or small black points on the object.

Now let's perform the close operation over the mask:

```
mask_closed = cv2.morphologyEx(mask, cv2.MORPH_CLOSE, kernel)
```

The opening operation *erosion followed by dilation* is used to remove noise.

Then we perform the opening operation:

```
mask_clean = cv2.morphologyEx(mask_closed, cv2.MORPH_OPEN, kernel)
```

Following is the output:

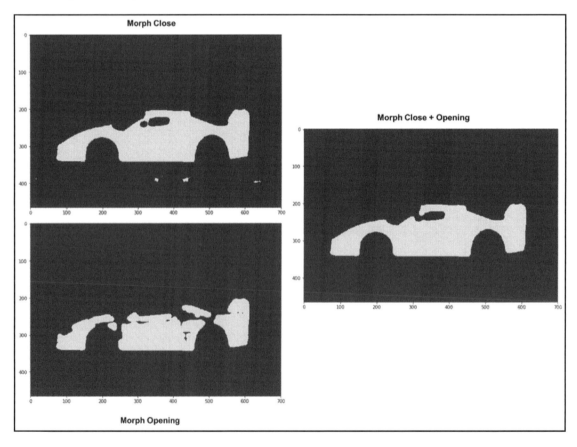

Figure 9.4: This figure illustrated the output of morphological close and open operation (left side) and we combine the both to get the final processed mask(right side).

In the preceding screenshot you can see (in the left part of the screenshot) how the morphological operation changes the structure of the mask and when combining both the operations (in the right side of the screenshot) you get a denoised cleaner structure.

Applying a mask

It's time to use the mask that we created to extract the object from the image. First, we will find the biggest contour using the helper function, which is the largest region of our object that we need to extract. Then apply the mask to the image and draw a circle bounding box on the extracted object:

```
# Extract biggest bounding box
big_contour, red_mask = find_biggest_contour(mask_clean)

# Apply mask
overlay = overlay_mask(red_mask, image)

# Draw bounding box
circled = circle_countour(overlay, big_contour)

show(circled)
```

Following is the output:

Figure 9.5: This figure shows that we have detected the red region (car body) from the image and plotted an ellipes around it.

Voila! So, we successfully extracted the image and also drew the bounding box around the object using simple image processing techniques.

Object detection using deep learning

In this section, we will learn how to build a world-class object detection module without much use of traditional handcrafting techniques. Here, will be using the deep learning approach, which is powerful enough to extract features automatically from the raw image and then use those features for classification and detection purposes.

First, we will build an object detector using a pre-baked Python library that can use most of the state-of-the-art pre-trained models, and later on, we will learn how to implement a really fast and accurate object detector using YOLO architecture.

Quick implementation of object detection

Object detection saw an increase in adoption as a result of the industry trend towards deep learning after 2012. Accurate and increasingly fast models such as R-CNN, Fast-RCNN, Faster-RCNN, and RetinaNet, and fast yet highly accurate ones like SSD and YOLO are in production today. In this section, we will use fully-functional pre-baked feature extractors in a Python library that can be used in just a few lines of code. Also, we will touch base regarding the production-grade setup for the same.

So, let's do it.

Installing all the dependencies

This is the same drill that we performed in the previous chapters. First let's install all the dependencies. Here, we are using a Python module called ImageAI (`https://github.com/OlafenwaMoses/ImageAI`), which is an effective way to start building your own object detection application from scratch in no time:

```
pip install tensorflow
pip install keras
pip install numpy
pip install scipy
pip install opencv-python
pip install pillow
pip install matplotlib
pip install h5py
```

```
# Here we are installing ImageAI
pip3 install
https://github.com/OlafenwaMoses/ImageAI/releases/download/2.0.2/imageai-2.
0.2-py3-none-any.whl
```

 We will be using the Python 3.x environment to run this module.

For this implementation, we are going to use a pre-trained ResNet model that is trained on the COCO dataset (`http://cocodataset.org/#home`) (a large-scale object detection, segmentation, and captioning dataset). You can also use other pre-trained models such as follows:

- `DenseNet-BC-121-32.h5` (`https://github.com/OlafenwaMoses/ImageAI/releases/download/1.0/DenseNet-BC-121-32.h5`) (31.7 MB)

- `inception_v3_weights_tf_dim_ordering_tf_kernels.h5` (`https://github.com/OlafenwaMoses/ImageAI/releases/download/1.0/inception_v3_weights_tf_dim_ordering_tf_kernels.h5`) (91.7 MB)

- `resnet50_coco_best_v2.0.1.h5` (`https://github.com/OlafenwaMoses/ImageAI/releases/download/1.0/resnet50_coco_best_v2.0.1.h5`) (146 MB)

- `resnet50_weights_tf_dim_ordering_tf_kernels.h5` (`https://github.com/OlafenwaMoses/ImageAI/releases/download/1.0/resnet50_weights_tf_dim_ordering_tf_kernels.h5`) (98.1 MB)

- `squeezenet_weights_tf_dim_ordering_tf_kernels.h5` (`https://github.com/OlafenwaMoses/ImageAI/releases/download/1.0/squeezenet_weights_tf_dim_ordering_tf_kernels.h5`) (4.83 MB)

- `yolo-tiny.h5` (`https://github.com/OlafenwaMoses/ImageAI/releases/download/1.0/yolo-tiny.h5`) (33.9 MB)

- `yolo.h5` (`https://github.com/OlafenwaMoses/ImageAI/releases/download/1.0/yolo.h5`): 237 MB

To get the dataset, use the following command:

```
wget
https://github.com/OlafenwaMoses/ImageAI/releases/download/1.0/resnet50_coc
o_best_v2.0.1.h5
```

Implementation

Now that we have all the dependencies and pre-trained models ready, we will implement a state-of-the-art object detection model. We will import the ImageAI's `ObjectDetection` class using the following code:

```
from imageai.Detection import ObjectDetection
import os
model_path = os.getcwd()
```

Then we create the instance for the `ObjectDetection` object and set the model type as `RetinaNet()`. Next, we set the part of the ResNet model that we downloaded and call the `loadModel()` function:

```
object_detector = ObjectDetection()
object_detector.setModelTypeAsRetinaNet()
object_detector.setModelPath( os.path.join(model_path ,
"resnet50_coco_best_v2.0.1.h5"))
object_detector.loadModel()
```

Once the model is loaded into the memory, we can feed a new image to the model, which can be of any popular image format, such as JPEG, PNG, and so on. Also, the function has no constraint on the size of the image, so, you can use any dimensional data and the model will handle it internally. We are using `detectObjectsFromImage()` to feed the input image. This method returns the image with some more information such as the bounding box coordinates of the detected object, the label of the detected object, and the confidence score.

Following are some images that are used as input into the model and to perform the object detection:

Figure 9.6: Since I was traveling to Asia (Malaysia/Langkawi) while writing this chapter. I decided to give it a shot and use some real images that I captured on the go.

The following code is used for inputting images into the model:

```
object_detections =
object_detector.detectObjectsFromImage(input_image=os.path.join(model_path
, "image.jpg"), output_image_path=os.path.join(model_path ,
"imagenew.jpg"))
```

Further, we iterate over the `object_detection` object to read all the objects that the model predicted with the respective confidence score:

```
for eachObject in object_detections:
    print(eachObject["name"] , " : " ,
eachObject["percentage_probability"])
```

Following are how the results look:

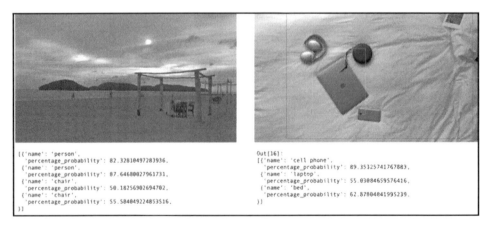

Figure 9.7: The results extracted from the object detection model with the bounding box around the detected object. Results contain the name of the object and the confidence score.

So, we can see that the pre-trained models performed well enough with very few lines of code.

Deployment

Now that we have all base code ready, let's deploy the `ObjectDetection` modules into production. In this section, we will write a RESTful service that will accept the image as an input and returns the detected object as a response.

We will define a `POST` function that accepts the image files with the PNG, JPG, JPEG, and GIF extensions. The uploaded image path is sent to the `ObjectDetection` module, which performs the detection and returns the following JSON results:

```python
from flask import Flask, request, jsonify, redirect
import os , json
from imageai.Detection import ObjectDetection

model_path = os.getcwd()

PRE_TRAINED_MODELS = ["resnet50_coco_best_v2.0.1.h5"]


# Creating ImageAI objects and loading models

object_detector = ObjectDetection()
object_detector.setModelTypeAsRetinaNet()
object_detector.setModelPath( os.path.join(model_path ,
PRE_TRAINED_MODELS[0]))
object_detector.loadModel()
object_detections =
object_detector.detectObjectsFromImage(input_image='sample.jpg')

# Define model paths and the allowed file extentions
UPLOAD_FOLDER = model_path
ALLOWED_EXTENSIONS = set(['png', 'jpg', 'jpeg', 'gif'])

app = Flask(__name__)
app.config['UPLOAD_FOLDER'] = UPLOAD_FOLDER


def allowed_file(filename):
    return '.' in filename and \
            filename.rsplit('.', 1)[1].lower() in ALLOWED_EXTENSIONS


@app.route('/predict', methods=['POST'])
```

```
def upload_file():
    if request.method == 'POST':
        # check if the post request has the file part
        if 'file' not in request.files:
            print('No file part')
            return redirect(request.url)
        file = request.files['file']
        # if user does not select file, browser also
        # submit a empty part without filename
        if file.filename == '':
            print('No selected file')
            return redirect(request.url)
        if file and allowed_file(file.filename):
            filename = file.filename
            file_path = os.path.join(app.config['UPLOAD_FOLDER'], filename)
            file.save(file_path)

    try:
        object_detections =
object_detector.detectObjectsFromImage(input_image=file_path)
    except Exception as ex:
        return jsonify(str(ex))
    resp = []
    for eachObject in object_detections :
        resp.append([eachObject["name"],
                    round(eachObject["percentage_probability"],3)
                    ]
                    )

    return json.dumps(dict(enumerate(resp)))
if __name__ == "__main__":
    app.run(host='0.0.0.0', port=4445)
```

Save the file as `object_detection_ImageAI.py` and execute the following command to run the web services:

```
python object_detection_ImageAI.py
```

Following is the output:

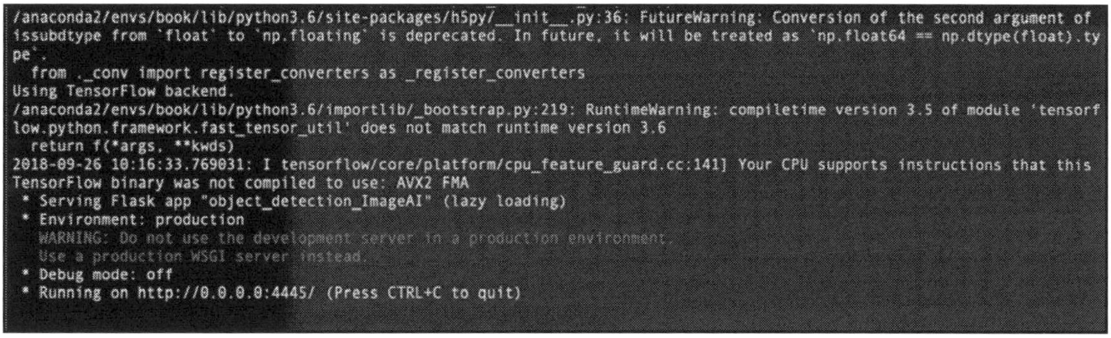

```
/anaconda2/envs/book/lib/python3.6/site-packages/h5py/__init__.py:36: FutureWarning: Conversion of the second argument of issubdtype from `float` to `np.floating` is deprecated. In future, it will be treated as `np.float64 == np.dtype(float).type`.
  from ._conv import register_converters as _register_converters
Using TensorFlow backend.
/anaconda2/envs/book/lib/python3.6/importlib/_bootstrap.py:219: RuntimeWarning: compiletime version 3.5 of module 'tensorflow.python.framework.fast_tensor_util' does not match runtime version 3.6
  return f(*args, **kwds)
2018-09-26 10:16:33.769031: I tensorflow/core/platform/cpu_feature_guard.cc:141] Your CPU supports instructions that this TensorFlow binary was not compiled to use: AVX2 FMA
 * Serving Flask app "object_detection_ImageAI" (lazy loading)
 * Environment: production
   WARNING: Do not use the development server in a production environment.
   Use a production WSGI server instead.
 * Debug mode: off
 * Running on http://0.0.0.0:4445/ (Press CTRL+C to quit)
```

Figure 9.8: Output on the Terminal screen after successful execution of the web service.

In a separate Terminal, you can now try to call the API, as shown in the following command:

```
curl -X POST \
  http://0.0.0.0:4445/predict \
  -H 'content-type: multipart/form-data; boundary=----
WebKitFormBoundary7MA4YWxkTrZu0gW' \
  -F file=@/Users/rahulkumar/Downloads/IMG_1651.JPG
```

Following will be the response output:

```
{
 "0": ["person",54.687],
 "1": ["person",56.77],
 "2": ["person",55.837],
 "3": ["person",75.93],
 "4": ["person",72.956],
 "5": ["bird",81.139]
}
```

So, this was awesome; with just a few hours' work, you are ready with a production-grade object detection module that is something close to state-of-the-art.

Object Detection In Real-Time Using YOLOv2

A great advancement in object detection and classification was made possible with a process where You Only Look Once (YOLO) at an input image. In this single pass, the goal is to set the coordinates for the corners of the bounding box to be drawn around the detected object and to then classify the object with a regression model. This process is capable of avoiding false positives because it takes into account contextual information from the whole image, and not just a smaller section as in a regional proposal of earlier described methods. The **convolutional neural network (CNN)** as follows can pass over the image once, and therefore be fast enough to function in applications where real-time processing is a requirement.

YOLOv2 predicts an N number of bounding boxes and associates a confidence level for the classification of the object for each individual grid in an S-by-S grid that is established in the immediately preceding step.

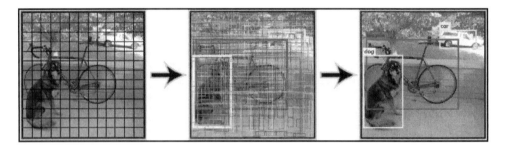

Figure 9.9: The overview of how YOLO works. The input image is divided into grids and then been sent into the detection process which results in lots of bounding boxes which is further been filtered by applying some thresholds.

The outcome of this process is to produce a total of S-by-S by N complement of boxes. For a great percentage of these boxes you'll get confidence scores that are quite low, and by applying a lower threshold (30% in this case), you can eliminate a majority of inaccurately classified objects as shown in the figure.

We will be using a pre-trained YOLOv2 model in this section for object detection and classification.

Preparing the dataset

In this part, we will explore the data preparation using the existing the COCO dataset and a custom dataset. If you want to train the YOLO model with lots of classes, then you can follow the instructions provided in the pre-existing part, or else if you want to build your custom object detector, then follow the instructions provided in the custom build section.

Using the pre-existing COCO dataset

For this implementation, we will be using the COCO dataset. This is a great resource dataset for training YOLOv2 to detect, segment, and caption images on a large scale. Download the dataset from `http://cocodataset.org` and run the following command in the terminal:

1. Get the training dataset:

```
wget http://images.cocodataset.org/zips/train2014.zip
```

2. Get the validation dataset:

```
wget http://images.cocodataset.org/zips/val2014.zip
```

3. Get the train and validation annotations:

```
wget
http://images.cocodataset.org/annotations/annotations_trainval2014.
zip
```

Now, let's convert the annotations in the COCO format to VOC format:

1. Install Baker:

```
pip install baker
```

2. Create the folders to store the images and annotations:

```
mkdir images annotations
```

3. Unzip `train2014.zip` and `val2014.zip` under the `images` folder:

```
unzip train2014.zip -d ./images/
unzip val2014.zip -d ./images/
```

4. Unzip `annotations_trainval2014.zip` into `annotations` folder:

```
unzip annotations_trainval2014.zip -d ./annotations/
```

5. Create a folder to store the converted data:

```
mkdir output
mkdir output/train
mkdir output/val

python coco2voc.py create_annotations /TRAIN_DATA_PATH train
/OUTPUT_FOLDER/train
```

```
python coco2voc.py create_annotations /TRAIN_DATA_PATH val
/OUTPUT_FOLDER/val
```

This is how the folder structure will look after the final transformation:

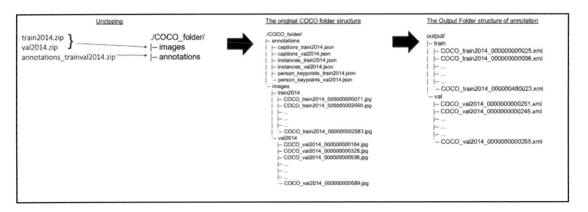

Figure 9.10: The illustration of the COCO data extraction and formatting process

 This establishes a perfect correspondence between the image and the annotation. When the validation set is empty, we will use a ratio of eight to automatically split the training and validation sets.

The result is that we will have two folders, `./images` and `./annotation`, for the training purpose.

Using the custom dataset

Now, if you want to build an object detector for your specific use case, then you will need to scrape around 100–200 images from the web and annotate them. There are lots of annotation tools available online, such as LabelImg (`https://github.com/tzutalin/labelImg`) or **Fast Image Data Annotation Tool** (**FIAT**) (`https://github.com/christopher5106/FastAnnotationTool`).

For you to play around with the custom object detector, we have provided some sample images with respective annotations. Look into the repository folder called `Chapter09/yolo/new_class/`.

Each image has its respective annotations, as shown in the following picture:

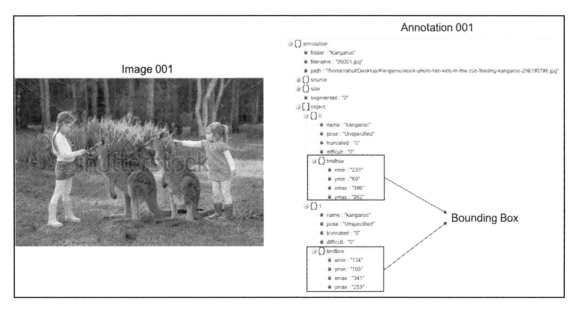

Figure 9.11: The relation between the image and the annotation which is shown here

Also, let's download the pre-trained weights from `https://pjreddie.com/darknet/yolo/`, which we will use to initialize our model, and which will train the custom object detector on top of these pretrained weights:

```
wget https://pjreddie.com/media/files/yolo.weights
```

Installing all the dependencies

We will be using the Keras APIs with a TensorFlow approach to create the YOLOv2 architecture. Let's import all the dependencies:

```
pip install keras tensorflow tqdm numpy cv2 imgaug
```

Following is the code for this:

```
from keras.models import Sequential, Model
from keras.layers import Reshape, Activation, Conv2D, Input, MaxPooling2D,
BatchNormalization, Flatten, Dense, Lambda
from keras.layers.advanced_activations import LeakyReLU
from keras.callbacks import EarlyStopping, ModelCheckpoint, TensorBoard
from keras.optimizers import SGD, Adam, RMSprop
```

```
from keras.layers.merge import concatenate
import matplotlib.pyplot as plt
import keras.backend as K
import tensorflow as tf
import imgaug as ia
from tqdm import tqdm
from imgaug import augmenters as iaa
import numpy as np
import pickle
import os, cv2
from preprocessing import parse_annotation, BatchGenerator
from utils import WeightReader, decode_netout, draw_boxes

#Setting GPU configs
os.environ["CUDA_DEVICE_ORDER"] = "PCI_BUS_ID"
os.environ["CUDA_VISIBLE_DEVICES"] = ""
```

It is always recommended to use GPUs to train any YOLO models.

Configuring the YOLO model

YOLO models are designed with the set of hyperparameter and some other configuration. This configuration defines the type of model to construct, as well as other parameters of the model such as the input image size and the list of anchors. You have two options at the moment: tiny YOLO and full YOLO. The following code defines the type of model to construct:

```
# List of object that YOLO model will learn to detect from COCO dataset

#LABELS = ['person', 'bicycle', 'car', 'motorcycle', 'airplane', 'bus',
'train', 'truck', 'boat', 'traffic light', 'fire hydrant', 'stop sign',
'parking meter', 'bench', 'bird', 'cat', 'dog', 'horse', 'sheep', 'cow',
'elephant', 'bear', 'zebra', 'giraffe', 'backpack', 'umbrella', 'handbag',
'tie', 'suitcase', 'frisbee', 'skis', 'snowboard', 'sports ball', 'kite',
'baseball bat', 'baseball glove', 'skateboard', 'surfboard', 'tennis
racket', 'bottle', 'wine glass', 'cup', 'fork', 'knife', 'spoon', 'bowl',
'banana', 'apple', 'sandwich', 'orange', 'broccoli', 'carrot', 'hot dog',
'pizza', 'donut', 'cake', 'chair', 'couch', 'potted plant', 'bed', 'dining
table', 'toilet', 'tv', 'laptop', 'mouse', 'remote', 'keyboard', 'cell
phone', 'microwave', 'oven', 'toaster', 'sink', 'refrigerator', 'book',
'clock', 'vase', 'scissors', 'teddy bear', 'hair drier', 'toothbrush']

# Label for the custom curated dataset.
```

```
LABEL = ['kangaroo']
IMAGE_H, IMAGE_W  = 416, 416
GRID_H,  GRID_W   = 13 , 13
BOX               = 5
CLASS             = len(LABELS)
CLASS_WEIGHTS     = np.ones(CLASS, dtype='float32')
OBJ_THRESHOLD     = 0.3
NMS_THRESHOLD     = 0.3
ANCHORS           = [0.57273, 0.677385, 1.87446, 2.06253, 3.33843, 5.47434,
7.88282, 3.52778, 9.77052, 9.16828]

NO_OBJECT_SCALE   = 1.0
OBJECT_SCALE      = 5.0
COORD_SCALE       = 1.0
CLASS_SCALE       = 1.0

BATCH_SIZE        = 16
WARM_UP_BATCHES   = 0
TRUE_BOX_BUFFER   = 50
```

Configure the path of the pre-trained model and the images, as in the following code:

```
wt_path = 'yolo.weights'
train_image_folder = '/new_class/images/'
train_annot_folder = '/new_class/anno/'
valid_image_folder = '/new_class/images/'
valid_annot_folder = '/new_class/anno/'
```

Defining the YOLO v2 model

Now let's have a look at the model architecture of the YOLOv2 model:

```
# the function to implement the organization layer (thanks to
github.com/allanzelener/YAD2K)
def space_to_depth_x2(x):
    return tf.space_to_depth(x, block_size=2)
input_image = Input(shape=(IMAGE_H, IMAGE_W, 3))
true_boxes  = Input(shape=(1, 1, 1, TRUE_BOX_BUFFER , 4))

# Layer 1
x = Conv2D(32, (3,3), strides=(1,1), padding='same', name='conv_1',
use_bias=False)(input_image)
x = BatchNormalization(name='norm_1')(x)
x = LeakyReLU(alpha=0.1)(x)
x = MaxPooling2D(pool_size=(2, 2))(x)

# Layer 2
```

```
x = Conv2D(64, (3,3), strides=(1,1), padding='same', name='conv_2',
use_bias=False)(x)
x = BatchNormalization(name='norm_2')(x)
x = LeakyReLU(alpha=0.1)(x)
x = MaxPooling2D(pool_size=(2, 2))(x)

# Layer 3
# Layer 4
# Layer 23
# For the entire architecture, please refer to the yolo/Yolo_v2_train.ipynb
notebook here:
https://github.com/PacktPublishing/Python-Deep-Learning-Projects/blob/maste
r/Chapter09/yolo/Yolo_v2_train.ipynb
```

The network architecture that we just created can be found here: `https://github.com/`
`PacktPublishing/Python-Deep-Learning-Projects/blob/master/Chapter09/Network_`
`architecture/network_architecture.png`

Following is the output:

```
Total params: 50,983,561
Trainable params: 50,962,889
Non-trainable params: 20,672
```

Training the model

Following are the steps to train the model:

1. Load the weights that we downloaded and use them to initialize the model:

```
weight_reader = WeightReader(wt_path)
weight_reader.reset()
nb_conv = 23
for i in range(1, nb_conv+1):
    conv_layer = model.get_layer('conv_' + str(i))
    if i < nb_conv:
        norm_layer = model.get_layer('norm_' + str(i))
        size = np.prod(norm_layer.get_weights()[0].shape)

        beta  = weight_reader.read_bytes(size)
        gamma = weight_reader.read_bytes(size)
        mean  = weight_reader.read_bytes(size)
        var   = weight_reader.read_bytes(size)

        weights = norm_layer.set_weights([gamma, beta, mean, var])
```

```
    if len(conv_layer.get_weights()) > 1:
        bias   =
weight_reader.read_bytes(np.prod(conv_layer.get_weights()[1].shape)
)
        kernel =
weight_reader.read_bytes(np.prod(conv_layer.get_weights()[0].shape)
)
        kernel =
kernel.reshape(list(reversed(conv_layer.get_weights()[0].shape)))
        kernel = kernel.transpose([2,3,1,0])
        conv_layer.set_weights([kernel, bias])
    else:
        kernel =
weight_reader.read_bytes(np.prod(conv_layer.get_weights()[0].shape)
)
        kernel =
kernel.reshape(list(reversed(conv_layer.get_weights()[0].shape)))
        kernel = kernel.transpose([2,3,1,0])
        conv_layer.set_weights([kernel])
```

2. Randomize the weights of the last layer:

```
layer   = model.layers[-4] # the last convolutional layer
weights = layer.get_weights()

new_kernel =
np.random.normal(size=weights[0].shape)/(GRID_H*GRID_W)
new_bias   =
np.random.normal(size=weights[1].shape)/(GRID_H*GRID_W)

layer.set_weights([new_kernel, new_bias])
```

3. Generate the configurations as in the following code:

```
generator_config = {
    'IMAGE_H' : IMAGE_H,
    'IMAGE_W' : IMAGE_W,
    'GRID_H' : GRID_H,
    'GRID_W' : GRID_W,
    'BOX' : BOX,
    'LABELS' : LABELS,
    'CLASS' : len(LABELS),
    'ANCHORS' : ANCHORS,
    'BATCH_SIZE' : BATCH_SIZE,
    'TRUE_BOX_BUFFER' : 50,
}
```

4. Create a training and validation batch:

```
# Training batch data
train_imgs, seen_train_labels =
parse_annotation(train_annot_folder, train_image_folder,
labels=LABELS)
train_batch = BatchGenerator(train_imgs, generator_config,
norm=normalize)

# Validation batch data
valid_imgs, seen_valid_labels =
parse_annotation(valid_annot_folder, valid_image_folder,
labels=LABELS)
valid_batch = BatchGenerator(valid_imgs, generator_config,
norm=normalize, jitter=False)
```

5. Set early stop and checkpoint callbacks:

```
early_stop = EarlyStopping(monitor='val_loss',
                           min_delta=0.001,
                           patience=3,
                           mode='min',
                           verbose=1)

checkpoint = ModelCheckpoint('weights_coco.h5',
                             monitor='val_loss',
                             verbose=1,
                             save_best_only=True,
                             mode='min',
                             period=1)
```

6. Use the following code to train the model:

```
tb_counter = len([log for log in
os.listdir(os.path.expanduser('~/logs/')) if 'coco_' in log]) + 1
tensorboard = TensorBoard(log_dir=os.path.expanduser('~/logs/') +
'coco_' + '_' + str(tb_counter),
                          histogram_freq=0,
                          write_graph=True,
                          write_images=False)

optimizer = Adam(lr=0.5e-4, beta_1=0.9, beta_2=0.999,
epsilon=1e-08, decay=0.0)
#optimizer = SGD(lr=1e-4, decay=0.0005, momentum=0.9)
#optimizer = RMSprop(lr=1e-4, rho=0.9, epsilon=1e-08, decay=0.0)
```

```
model.compile(loss=custom_loss, optimizer=optimizer)

model.fit_generator(generator = train_batch,
                    steps_per_epoch = len(train_batch),
                    epochs = 100,
                    verbose = 1,
                    validation_data = valid_batch,
                    validation_steps = len(valid_batch),
                    callbacks = [early_stop, checkpoint,
tensorboard],
                    max_queue_size = 3)
```

Following is the output:

```
Epoch 1/2
11/11 [==============================] – 315s 29s/step – loss: 3.6982 –
val_loss: 1.5416

Epoch 00001: val_loss improved from inf to 1.54156, saving model to
weights_coco.h5
Epoch 2/2
11/11 [==============================] – 307s 28s/step – loss: 1.4517 –
val_loss: 1.0636

Epoch 00002: val_loss improved from 1.54156 to 1.06359, saving model to
weights_coco.h5
```

Following is the TensorBoard plots output for just two epochs:

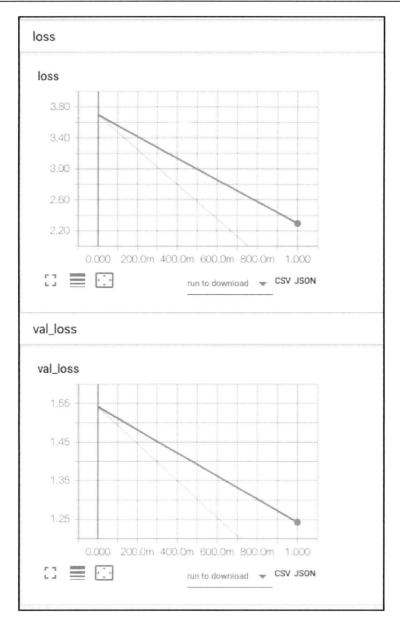

Figure 9.12: The figure represents the loss plots for 2 epochs

Evaluating the model

Once the training is complete, let's perform the prediction by feeding an input image into the model:

1. First we will load the model into the memory:

```
model.load_weights("weights_coco.h5")
```

2. Now set the test image path and read it:

```
input_image_path = "my_test_image.jpg"
image = cv2.imread(input_image_path)
dummy_array = np.zeros((1,1,1,1,TRUE_BOX_BUFFER,4))
plt.figure(figsize=(10,10))
```

3. Normalize the image:

```
input_image = cv2.resize(image, (416, 416))
input_image = input_image / 255.
input_image = input_image[:,:,::-1]
input_image = np.expand_dims(input_image, 0)
```

4. Make a prediction:

```
netout = model.predict([input_image, dummy_array])

boxes = decode_netout(netout[0],
                        obj_threshold=OBJ_THRESHOLD,
                        nms_threshold=NMS_THRESHOLD,
                        anchors=ANCHORS,
                        nb_class=CLASS)

image = draw_boxes(image, boxes, labels=LABELS)

plt.imshow(image[:,:,::-1]); plt.show()
```

So, here are some of the results:

```
Found 8 boxes for woman-1979272_1280.jpg
knife 0.37 (343, 606) (539, 637)
pottedplant 0.49 (1136, 488) (1275, 745)
knife 0.54 (734, 617) (851, 708)
bottle 0.57 (200, 489) (285, 746)
wine glass 0.58 (27, 562) (97, 758)
person 0.74 (225, 47) (663, 792)
pottedplant 0.79 (985, 356) (1136, 596)
person 0.82 (592, 0) (1053, 759)
```

```
Found 7 boxes for relay-race-655353_1280.jpg
person 0.41 (950, 143) (1092, 370)
person 0.42 (938, 185) (1119, 667)
person 0.66 (746, 218) (966, 801)
person 0.73 (65, 117) (307, 744)
person 0.77 (1085, 168) (1266, 699)
person 0.81 (246, 135) (541, 826)
person 0.82 (602, 150) (823, 802)
```

```
Found 3 boxes for water-3567092_1280.jpg
surfboard 0.34 (760, 466) (810, 498)
surfboard 0.35 (733, 443) (813, 505)
person 0.85 (704, 239) (797, 496)
```

```
Found 2 boxes for man-3694475_1280.jpg
person 0.90 (505, 198) (695, 825)
person 0.95 (696, 120) (910, 825)
```

Congratulations—you have developed a state-of-the-art object detector that is very fast and reliable.

We learned about building a world class object detection model using YOLO architecture and the results seems to be very promising. Now you can also deploy the same on other mobile devices or Raspberry Pi.

Image segmentation

Image segmentation is the process of categorizing what is in a picture at a pixel level. For example, if you were given a picture with a person in it, separating the person from the image is known as segmentation and is done using pixel-level information.

We will be using the COCO dataset for image segmentation.

Following is what you should do before executing any of the SegNet scripts:

```
cd SegNet
wget http://images.cocodataset.org/zips/train2014.zip
mkdir images
unzip train2014.zip -d images
```

When executing SegNet scripts, make sure that your present working directory is SegNet.

Importing all the dependencies

Make sure to restart the session before proceeding forward.

We will be using numpy, pandas, keras, pylab, skimage, matplotlib, and pycocotools, as in the following code:

```
from __future__ import absolute_import
from __future__ import print_function

import pylab
import numpy as np
import pandas as pd
import skimage.io as io
import matplotlib.pyplot as plt

from pycocotools.coco import COCO
pylab.rcParams['figure.figsize'] = (8.0, 10.0)
import cv2

import keras.models as models, Sequential
from keras.layers import Layer, Dense, Dropout, Activation, Flatten, Reshape, Permute
from keras.layers import Conv2D, MaxPool2D, UpSampling2D, ZeroPadding2D
from keras.layers import BatchNormalization

from keras.callbacks import ModelCheckpoint, ReduceLROnPlateau
from keras.optimizers import Adam
```

```
import keras
keras.backend.set_image_dim_ordering('th')

from tqdm import tqdm
import itertools
%matplotlib inline
```

Exploring the data

We will start off by defining the location of the annotation file we will be using for image segmentation, and then we will initialize the COCO API:

```
# set the location of the annotation file associated with the train images
annFile='annotations/annotations/instances_train2014.json'

# initialize COCO api with
coco = COCO(annFile)
```

Following should be the output:

```
loading annotations into memory...
Done (t=12.84s)
creating index...
index created!
```

Images

Since we are building a binary segmentation model, let us consider the images from the `images/train2014` folder that are only tagged with the person label so that we can segment the person out of the image. The COCO API provides us with easy-to-use methods, two of which are the `getCatIds` and `getImgIds`. The following snippet will help us extract the image IDs of all the images with the label `person` tagged to it:

```
# extract the category ids using the label 'person'
catIds = coco.getCatIds(catNms=['person'])

# extract the image ids using the catIds
imgIds = coco.getImgIds(catIds=catIds )

# print number of images with the tag 'person'
print("Number of images with the tag 'person' :" ,len(imgIds))
```

This should be the output:

```
Number of images with the tag 'person' : 45174
```

Now let us use the following snippet to plot an image:

```
# extract the details of image with the image id
img = coco.loadImgs(imgIds[2])[0]
print(img)

# load the image using the location of the file listed in the image
variable
I = io.imread('images/train2014/'+img['file_name'])

# display the image
plt.imshow(I)
```

Following should be the output:

```
{'height': 426, 'coco_url':
'http://images.cocodataset.org/train2014/COCO_train2014_000000524291.jpg',
'date_captured': '2013-11-18 09:59:07', 'file_name':
'COCO_train2014_000000524291.jpg', 'flickr_url':
'http://farm2.staticflickr.com/1045/934293170_d1b2cc58ff_z.jpg', 'width':
640, 'id': 524291, 'license': 3}
```

We get the following picture as an output:

Figure 9.13: The plot representation a sample image from the dataset.

In the previous code snippet, we feed in an image ID to the `loadImgs` method of COCO to extract the details of the image it corresponds to. If you look at the output of the `img` variable, one of the keys listed is the `file_name` key. This key holds the name of the image located in the `images/train2014/` folder.

Then we read the image using the `imread` method of the `io` module we have already imported and plot it using `matplotlib.pyplot`.

Annotations

Now let us load the annotation corresponding to the previous picture and plot the annotation on top of the picture. The `coco.getAnnIds()` function helps load the annotation info of an image using its ID. Then, with the help of the `coco.loadAnns()` function, we load the annotations and plot it using the `coco.showAnns()` function. It is important that you first plot the image and then perform the annotation operations as shown in the following code snippet:

```
# display the image
plt.imshow(I)

# extract the annotation id
annIds = coco.getAnnIds(imgIds=img['id'], catIds=catIds, iscrowd=None)

# load the annotation
anns = coco.loadAnns(annIds)

# plot the annotation on top of the image
coco.showAnns(anns)
```

Following should be the output:

Figure 9.14: Visualizing annotation on an image

To be able to obtain the annotation label array, use the `coco.annToMask()` function as shown in the following code snippet. This array will help us form the segmentation target:

```
# build the mask for display with matplotlib
mask = coco.annToMask(anns[0])

# display the mask
plt.imshow(mask)
```

Following should be the output:

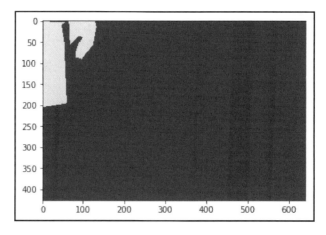

Figure 9.15: Visualizing just the annotation

Preparing the data

Let us now define a `data_list()` function that will automate the process of loading an image and its segmentation array into memory and resize them to the shape of 360*480 using OpenCV. This function returns two lists containing images and segmentation array:

```python
def data_list(imgIds, count = 12127, ratio = 0.2):
    """Function to load image and its target into memory."""
    img_lst = []
    lab_lst = []

    for x in tqdm(imgIds[0:count]):
        # load image details
        img = coco.loadImgs(x)[0]
        # read image
        I = io.imread('images/train2014/'+img['file_name'])
        if len(I.shape)<3:
            continue
        # load annotation information
        annIds = coco.getAnnIds(imgIds=img['id'], catIds=catIds,
iscrowd=None)
        # load annotation
        anns = coco.loadAnns(annIds)
        # prepare mask
        mask = coco.annToMask(anns[0])
        # This condition makes sure that we select images having only one
person
        if len(np.unique(mask)) == 2:
            # Next condition selects images where ratio of area covered by
the
            # person to the entire image is greater than the ratio
parameter
            # This is done to not have large class imbalance
            if (len(np.where(mask>0)[0])/len(np.where(mask>=0)[0])) > ratio
:
                # If you check, generated mask will have 2 classes i.e 0
and 2
                # (0 - background/other, 1 - person).
                # to avoid issues with cv2 during the resize operation
                # set label 2 to 1, making label 1 as the person.
                mask[mask==2] = 1
                # resize image and mask to shape (480, 360)
                I= cv2.resize(I, (480,360))
                mask = cv2.resize(mask, (480,360))

                # append mask and image to their lists
                img_lst.append(I)
```

```
                    lab_lst.append(mask)
        return (img_lst, lab_lst)

    # get images and their labels
    img_lst, lab_lst = data_list(imgIds)

    print('Sum of images for training, validation and testing :', len(img_lst))
    print('Unique values in the labels array :', np.unique(lab_lst[0]))
```

Following should be the output:

```
Sum of images for training, validation and testing : 1997
Unique values in the labels array : [0 1]
```

Normalizing the image

First, let's define the make_normalize() function, which accepts an image and performs the histogram normalization operation on it. The return object is a normalized array:

```
def make_normalize(img):
    """Function to histogram normalize images."""
    norm_img = np.zeros((img.shape[0], img.shape[1], 3),np.float32)

    b=img[:,:,0]
    g=img[:,:,1]
    r=img[:,:,2]

    norm_img[:,:,0]=cv2.equalizeHist(b)
    norm_img[:,:,1]=cv2.equalizeHist(g)
    norm_img[:,:,2]=cv2.equalizeHist(r)

    return norm_img

plt.figure(figsize = (14,5))
plt.subplot(1,2,1)
plt.imshow(img_lst[9])
plt.title(' Original Image')
plt.subplot(1,2,2)
plt.imshow(make_normalize(img_lst[9]))
plt.title(' Histogram Normalized Image')
```

Following should be the output:

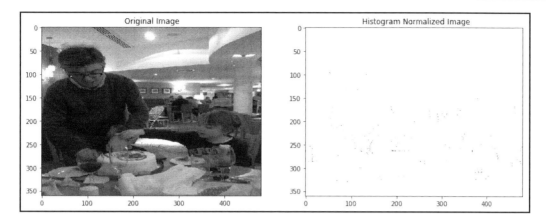

Figure 9.16: Before and After histogram normalization on an image

In the preceding screenshot, we see the original picture on the left, which is very visible, and on the right we see the normalized picture, which is not at all visible.

Encoding

With the `make_normalize()` function defined, let's now define a `make_target` function. This function accepts the segmentation array of shape (360,480) and then returns a segmentation target of shape (360,480,2). In the target, channel 0 represents the background and will have 1 in locations that represent the background in the image and zero elsewhere. Channel 1 represents the person and will have 1 in locations that represent the person in the image and 0 elsewhere. The following code implements the function:

```
def make_target(labels):
    """Function to one hot encode targets."""
    x = np.zeros([360,480,2])
    for i in range(360):
        for j in range(480):
            x[i,j,labels[i][j]]=1
    return x

plt.figure(figsize = (14,5))
plt.subplot(1,2,1)
plt.imshow(make_target(lab_lst[0])[:,:,0])
plt.title('Background')
plt.subplot(1,2,2)
plt.imshow(make_target(lab_lst[0])[:,:,1])
plt.title('Person')
```

Following should be the output:

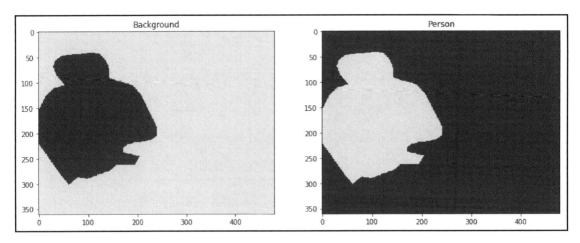

Figure 9.17: Visualizing the encoded target arrays

Model data

We will now define a function called `model_data()` that accepts a list of images and a list of labels. This function will apply the `make_normalize()` function on each image for the purpose of normalizing, and it will apply the `make_encode()` function on each label/segmentation array to obtain the encoded array.

The return of this function is two lists, one containing the normalized images and the other containing the corresponding target arrays:

```
def model_data(images, labels):
    """Function to perform normalize and encode operation on each image."""
    # empty label and image list
    array_lst = []
    label_lst=[]
    # apply normalize function on each image and encoding function on each
label
    for x,y in tqdm(zip(images, labels)):
        array_lst.append(np.rollaxis(normalized(x), 2))
        label_lst.append(make_target(y))
    return np.array(array_lst), np.array(label_lst)

# Get model data
train_data, train_lab = model_data(img_lst, lab_lst)
```

```
flat_image_shape = 360*480

# reshape target array
train_label = np.reshape(train_lab,(-1,flat_image_shape,2))

# test data
test_data = test_data[1900:]
# validation data
val_data = train_data[1500:1900]
# train data
train_data = train_data[:1500]

# test label
test_label = test_label[1900:]
# validation label
val_label = train_label[1500:1900]
# train label
train_label = train_label[:1500]
```

In the preceding snippet, we have also split the data into train, test, and validation sets, with the train set containing 1500 data points, the validation set containing 400 data points, and the test set containing 97 data points.

Defining hyperparameters

The following are some of the defined hyperparameters that we will be using throughout the code, and they are totally configurable:

```
# define optimizer
optimizer = Adam(lr=0.002)

# input shape to the model
input_shape=(3, 360, 480)

# training batchsize
batch_size = 6

# number of training epochs
nb_epoch = 60
```

To learn more about optimizers and their APIs in Keras, visit https://keras.io/optimizers/. Reduce batch_size if you get a resource exhaustion error with respect to the GPU.

Experiment with different learning rates, `optimizers,` and `batch_size` to see how these factors affect the quality of your model, and if you get better results, show them to the deep learning community.

Define SegNet

For the purpose of image segmentation, we will build a SegNet model, which is very similar to the autoencoder we built in `Chapter 8`: *Handwritten Digits Classification Using ConvNets*, as shown:

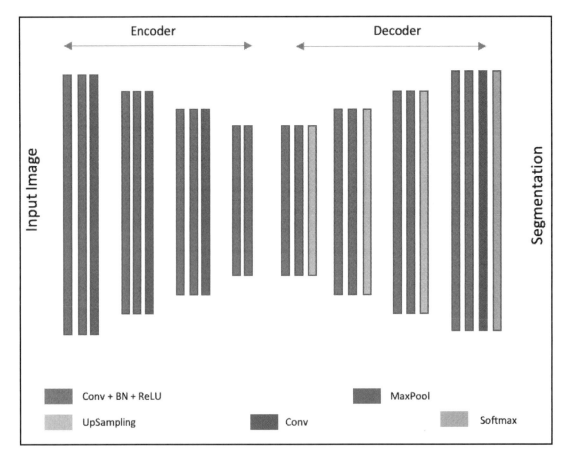

Figure 9.18: SegNet architecture used in this chapter

The SegNet model we'll define will accept (*3,360, 480*) images as input with (*172800, 2*) segmentation arrays as the targets, and it will have the following characteristics in the encoder:

- The first layer is a Convolution 2D layer with 64 filters of size 3*3, with `activation` as `relu`, followed by batch normalization, followed by downsampling with MaxPooling2D of size 2*2.
- The second layer is a Convolution 2D layer with 128 filters of size 3*3, with `activation` as `relu`, followed by batch normalization, followed by downsampling with MaxPooling2D of size 2*2.
- The third layer is a Convolution 2D layer with 256 filters of size 3*3, with `activation` as `relu`, followed by batch normalization, followed by downsampling with MaxPooling2D of size 2*2.
- The fourth layer is again a Convolution 2D layer with 512 filters of size 3*3, with `activation` as `relu`, followed by batch normalization.

And the model will have the following characteristics in the decoder:

- The first layer is a Convolution 2D layer with 512 filters of size 3*3, with `activation` as `relu`, followed by batch normalization, followed by downsampling with UpSampling2D of size 2*2.
- The second layer is a Convolution 2D layer with 256 filters of size 3*3, with `activation` as `relu`, followed by batch normalization, followed by downsampling with UpSampling2D of size 2*2.
- The third layer is a Convolution 2D layer with 128 filters of size 3*3, with `activation` as `relu`, followed by batch normalization, followed by downsampling with UpSampling2D of size 2*2.
- The fourth layer is a Convolution 2D layer with 64 filters of size 3*3 with `activation` as `relu`, followed by batch normalization.
- The fifth layer is a Convolution 2D layer with 2 filters of size 1*1, followed by Reshape, Permute and a `softmax` as `activation` layer for predicting scores.

The model is described with the following code:

```
model = Sequential()
# Encoder
model.add(Layer(input_shape=input_shape))
model.add(ZeroPadding2D())
model.add(Conv2D(filters=64, kernel_size=(3,3), padding='valid',
activation='relu'))
model.add(BatchNormalization())
model.add(MaxPool2D(pool_size=(2,2)))

model.add(ZeroPadding2D())
model.add(Conv2D(filters=128, kernel_size=(3,3), padding='valid',
activation='relu'))
model.add(BatchNormalization())
model.add(MaxPool2D(pool_size=(2,2)))

model.add(ZeroPadding2D())
model.add(Conv2D(filters=256, kernel_size=(3,3), padding='valid',
activation='relu'))
model.add(BatchNormalization())
model.add(MaxPool2D(pool_size=(2,2)))

model.add(ZeroPadding2D())
model.add(Conv2D(filters=512, kernel_size=(3,3), padding='valid',
activation='relu'))
model.add(BatchNormalization())

# Decoder
# For the remaining part of this section of the code refer to the
segnet.ipynb file in the SegNet folder. Here is the github link:
https://github.com/PacktPublishing/Python-Deep-Learning-Projects/tree/maste
r/Chapter09
```

Compiling the model

With the model defined, compile the model with `'categorical_crossentropy'` as `loss` and `optimizer` as `Adam`, as defined by the `optimizer` variable in the hyperparameters section. We will also define `ReduceLROnPlateau` to reduce the learning rate as needed when training, as follows:

```
# compile model
model.compile(loss="categorical_crossentropy", optimizer=Adam(lr=0.002),
metrics=["accuracy"])

# use ReduceLROnPlateau to adjust the learning rate
reduceLROnPlat = ReduceLROnPlateau(monitor='val_acc', factor=0.75,
patience=5,
                    min_delta=0.005, mode='max', cooldown=3, verbose=1)

callbacks_list = [reduceLROnPlat]
```

Fitting the model

With the model compiled, we will now fit the model on the data using the `fit` method of the model. Here, since we are training on a small set of data, it is important to set the parameter shuffle to `True` so that the images are shuffled after each epoch:

```
# fit the model
history = model.fit(train_data, train_label, callbacks=callbacks_list,
                    batch_size=batch_size, epochs=nb_epoch,
                    verbose=1, shuffle = True, validation_data = (val_data,
val_label))
```

This should be the output:

```
Train on 1500 samples, validate on 400 samples
Epoch 1/60
1500/1500 [==============================] - 351s 234ms/step - loss: 0.6338 - acc: 0.6610 - val_loss: 0.6201
- val_acc: 0.6631
Epoch 2/60
1500/1500 [==============================] - 339s 226ms/step - loss: 0.6016 - acc: 0.6678 - val_loss: 0.6049
- val_acc: 0.6673
Epoch 3/60
1500/1500 [==============================] - 337s 225ms/step - loss: 0.5941 - acc: 0.6751 - val_loss: 0.6468
- val_acc: 0.5983
```

Figure 9.19: Training output

The following shows the accuracy and loss plots:

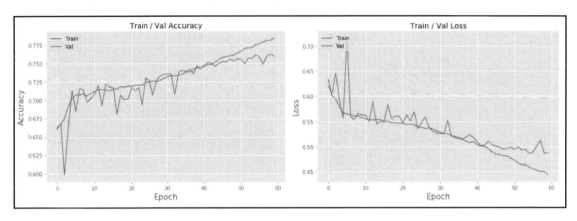

Figure 9.20: Plot showing training progression

Testing the model

With the model trained, evaluate the model on test data, as in the following:

```
loss,acc = model.evaluate(test_data, test_label)
print('Loss :', loss)
print('Accuracy :', acc)
```

This should be the output:

```
97/97 [==============================] - 7s 71ms/step
Loss : 0.5390811630131043
Accuracy : 0.7633129960482883
```

We see that the SegNet model we built has a loss of 0.539 and accuracy of 76.33 on test images.

Let's plot the test images and their corresponding generated segmentations to understand model learning:

```
for i in range(3):
    plt.figure(figsize = (10,3))
    plt.subplot(1,2,1)
    plt.imshow(img_lst[1900+i])
    plt.title('Input')
    plt.subplot(1,2,2)
    plt.imshow(model.predict_classes(test_data[i:(i+1)*1]).reshape(360,480))
    plt.title('Segmentation')
```

Following should be the output:

Figure 9.21: Segmentation generated on test images

From the preceding figure, we see that the model was able to segment the person from the image.

Conclusion

The first part of the project was to build an object detection classifier using YOLO architecture in Keras.

The second part of the project was to build a binary image segmentation model on COCO images that contain just a person, aside from the background. The goal was to build a good enough model to segment out the person from the background in the image.

The model we build by training on 1500 images, each of shape 360*480*3, has an accuracy of 79% on train data, and 78% on validation and test data. The model is successfully able to segment the person in the image, but the borders of the segmentations are slightly off from where they should be. This is due to using a small training set. Considering the number of images used for training, the model did a good job of segmenting.

There are more images available in this dataset that can be used for training, and it might take over a day to train on all of them using a Nvidia Tesla K80 GPU, but doing so will give you really good segmentation.

Summary

In the first part of this chapter, we learnt how to build a RESTful service for object detection using an existing classifier, and we also learned to build an accurate object detector using the YOLO architecture object detection classifier using Keras, while also implementing transfer learning. In the second part of the chapter, we understood what image segmentation is and built an image segmentation model on images from the COCO dataset. We also tested the performance of the object detector and the image segmenter on test data, and determined that we succeeded in achieving the goal.

10
Building Face Recognition Using FaceNet

In the previous chapter, we learned how to detect objects in an image. In this chapter, we will look into a specific use case of object detection—face recognition. Face recognition is a combination of two major operations: face detection, followed by face classification.

The (hypothetical) client that provides our business use case for us in this project is a high-performance computing data center Tier III, certified for sustainability. They have designed the facility to meet the very highest standards for protection against natural disasters, with many redundant systems.

The facility currently has ultra-high security protocols in place to prevent malicious, man-made disasters, and they are looking to augment their security profile with facial recognition for access to secure areas throughout the facility.

The stakes are high, as the servers they house and maintain process some of the most sensitive, valuable, and influential data in the world:

This facial recognition system would need to be able to accurately identify not only their own employees, but employees of their clients, who occasionally tour the data center for inspection.

They have asked us to provide a POC for this intelligence-based capability, for review and later inclusion throughout their data center.

So, in this chapter, we will learn how to build a world-class face recognition system. We will define the pipeline as follows:

1. **Face detection**: First, look at an image and find all the possible faces in it
2. **Face extraction**: Second, focus on each face image and understand it, for example if it is turned sideways or badly lit
3. **Feature extraction**: Third, extract unique features from the faces using convolutional neural networks (CNNs)
4. **Classifier training**: Finally, compare the unique features of that face to all the people already known, to determine the person's name

You will learn the main ideas behind each step, and how to build your own facial recognition system in Python using the following deep-learning technologies:

- **dlib** (http://dlib.net/): Provides a library that can be used for facial detection and alignment.
- **OpenFace** (https://cmusatyalab.github.io/openface/): A deep-learning facial recognition model, developed by Brandon Amos *et al* (http://bamos.github.io/). It is able to run on real-time mobile devices as well.
- **FaceNet** (https://arxiv.org/abs/1503.03832): A CNN architecture that is used for feature extraction. For a loss function, FaceNet uses triplet loss. Triplet loss relies on minimizing the distance from positive examples, while maximizing the distance from negative examples.

Setup environment

Since setup can get very complicated and take a long time, which is not on the agenda for this chapter, we will be building a Docker image that contains all the dependencies, including dlib, OpenFace, and FaceNet.

Getting the code

Fetch the code that we will use to build face recognition from the repository:

```
git clone https://github.com/PacktPublishing/Python-Deep-Learning-Projects
cd Chapter10/
```

Building the Docker image

Docker is a container platform that simplifies deployment. It solves the problem of installing software dependencies onto different server environments. If you are new to Docker, you can read more at https://www.docker.com/.

To install Docker on Linux machines, run the following command:

```
curl https://get.docker.com | sh
```

For other systems such as macOS and Windows, visit https://docs.docker.com/install/ . You can skip this step if you already have Docker installed.

Once Docker is installed, you should be able to use the `docker` command in the Terminal, as follows:

```
[rahulkumar@              $ docker

Usage:  docker COMMAND

A self-sufficient runtime for containers

Options:
      --config string      Location of client config files (default "/home/rahulkumar/.docker")
  -D, --debug              Enable debug mode
  -H, --host list          Daemon socket(s) to connect to
  -l, --log-level string   Set the logging level ("debug"|"info"|"warn"|"error"|"fatal") (default "info")
      --tls                Use TLS; implied by --tlsverify
      --tlscacert string   Trust certs signed only by this CA (default "/home/rahulkumar/.docker/ca.pem")
      --tlscert string     Path to TLS certificate file (default "/home/rahulkumar/.docker/cert.pem")
      --tlskey string      Path to TLS key file (default "/home/rahulkumar/.docker/key.pem")
      --tlsverify          Use TLS and verify the remote
  -v, --version            Print version information and quit

Management Commands:
  checkpoint  Manage checkpoints
  config      Manage Docker configs
  container   Manage containers
  image       Manage images
  network     Manage networks
  node        Manage Swarm nodes
  plugin      Manage plugins
  secret      Manage Docker secrets
  service     Manage services
  swarm       Manage Swarm
  system      Manage Docker
  trust       Manage trust on Docker images
  volume      Manage volumes

Commands:
  attach      Attach local standard input, output, and error streams to a running container
  build       Build an image from a Dockerfile
  commit      Create a new image from a container's changes
  cp          Copy files/folders between a container and the local filesystem
  create      Create a new container
  deploy      Deploy a new stack or update an existing stack
  diff        Inspect changes to files or directories on a container's filesystem
  events      Get real time events from the server
  exec        Run a command in a running container
  export      Export a container's filesystem as a tar archive
  history     Show the history of an image
  images      List images
  import      Import the contents from a tarball to create a filesystem image
  info        Display system-wide information
  inspect     Return low-level information on Docker objects
  kill        Kill one or more running containers
  load        Load an image from a tar archive or STDIN
  login       Log in to a Docker registry
  logout      Log out from a Docker registry
  logs        Fetch the logs of a container
  pause       Pause all processes within one or more containers
  port        List port mappings or a specific mapping for the container
  ps          List containers
  pull        Pull an image or a repository from a registry
```

Now we will create a `docker` file that will install all the dependencies, including OpenCV, dlib, and TensorFlow. This file is available in the repository at https://github.com/PacktPublishing/Python-Deep-Learning-Projects/tree/master/Chapter10/Dockerfile:

```
#Dockerfile for our env setup
FROM tensorflow/tensorflow:latest

RUN apt-get update -y --fix-missing
RUN apt-get install -y ffmpeg
RUN apt-get install -y build-essential cmake pkg-config \
                    libjpeg8-dev libtiff5-dev libjasper-dev libpng12-dev \
                    libavcodec-dev libavformat-dev libswscale-dev libv4l-
dev \
                    libxvidcore-dev libx264-dev \
                    libgtk-3-dev \
                    libatlas-base-dev gfortran \
                    libboost-all-dev \
                    python3 python3-dev python3-numpy

RUN apt-get install -y wget vim python3-tk python3-pip

WORKDIR /
RUN wget -O opencv.zip https://github.com/Itseez/opencv/archive/3.2.0.zip \
    && unzip opencv.zip \
    && wget -O opencv_contrib.zip
https://github.com/Itseez/opencv_contrib/archive/3.2.0.zip \
    && unzip opencv_contrib.zip

# install opencv3.2
RUN cd /opencv-3.2.0/ \
    && mkdir build \
    && cd build \
    && cmake -D CMAKE_BUILD_TYPE=RELEASE \
            -D INSTALL_C_EXAMPLES=OFF \
            -D INSTALL_PYTHON_EXAMPLES=ON \
            -D OPENCV_EXTRA_MODULES_PATH=/opencv_contrib-3.2.0/modules \
            -D BUILD_EXAMPLES=OFF \
            -D BUILD_opencv_python2=OFF \
            -D BUILD_NEW_PYTHON_SUPPORT=ON \
            -D CMAKE_INSTALL_PREFIX=$(python3 -c "import sys;
print(sys.prefix)") \
            -D PYTHON_EXECUTABLE=$(which python3) \
            -D WITH_FFMPEG=1 \
            -D WITH_CUDA=0 \
            .. \
    && make -j8 \
    && make install \
    && ldconfig \
```

```
        && rm /opencv.zip \
        && rm /opencv_contrib.zip


    # Install dlib 19.4
    RUN wget -O dlib-19.4.tar.bz2 http://dlib.net/files/dlib-19.4.tar.bz2 \
        && tar -vxjf dlib-19.4.tar.bz2

    RUN cd dlib-19.4 \
        && cd examples \
        && mkdir build \
        && cd build \
        && cmake .. \
        && cmake --build . --config Release \
        && cd /dlib-19.4 \
        && pip3 install setuptools \
        && python3 setup.py install \
        && cd $WORKDIR \
        && rm /dlib-19.4.tar.bz2



    ADD $PWD/requirements.txt /requirements.txt
    RUN pip3 install -r /requirements.txt


    CMD ["/bin/bash"]
```

Now execute the following command to build the image:

```
docker build -t hellorahulk/facerecognition -f Dockerfile
```

It will take approximately 20-30 mins to install all the dependencies and build the Docker image:

Downloading pre-trained models

We will download a few more artifacts, which we will use and discuss in detail later in this chapter.

Download dlib's face landmark predictor, using the following commands:

```
curl -O http://dlib.net/

files/shape_predictor_68_face_landmarks.dat.bz2
bzip2 -d shape_predictor_68_face_landmarks.dat.bz2
cp shape_predictor_68_face_landmarks.dat facenet/
```

Download the pre-trained Inception model:

```
curl -L -O https://www.dropbox.com/s/hb75vuur8olyrtw/Resnet-185253.pb
cp Resnet-185253.pb pre-model/
```

Once we have all the components ready, the folder structure should look roughly as follows:

The folder structure of the code

Make sure that you keep the images of the person you want to train the model with in the /data folder, and name the folder as
/data/<class_name>/<class_name>_000<count>.jpg.

The /output folder will contain the trained SVM classifier and all preprocessed images inside a subfolder /intermediate, using the same folder nomenclature as in the /data folder.

Pro tip: For better performance in terms of accuracy, always keep more than five samples of images for each class. This will help the model to converge faster and generalize better.

Building the pipeline

Facial recognition is a biometric solution that measures the unique characteristics of faces. To perform facial recognition, you'll need a way to uniquely represent a face.

The main idea behind any face recognition system is to break the face down into unique features, and then use those features to represent identity.

Building a robust pipeline for feature extraction is very important, as it will directly affect the performance and accuracy of our system. In 1960, Woodrow Bledsoe used a technique involving marking the coordinates of prominent features of a face. Among these features were the location of hairline, eyes, and nose.

Later, in 2005, a much robust technique was invented, **Histogram of Oriented Gradients (HOG)**. This captured the orientation of the dense pixels in the provided image.

The most advanced technique yet, outperforming all others at the time of writing, uses CNNs. In 2015, researchers from Google released a paper describing their system, FaceNet (https://arxiv.org/abs/1503.03832), which uses a CNN relying on image pixels to identify features, rather than extracting them manually.

To build the face recognition pipeline, we will devise the following flow (represented by orange blocks in the diagram):

- **Preprocessing**: Finding all the faces, fixing the orientation of the faces
- **Feature extraction**: Extracting unique features from the processed faces
- **Classifier training**: Training the SVM classifier with 128 dimensional features

The diagram is as follows:

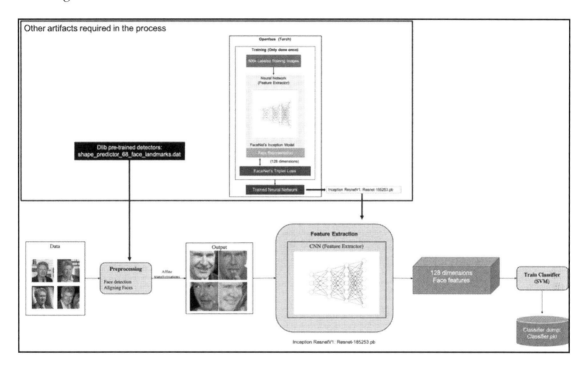

This image illustrates the end to end flow for face recognition pipeline

We will look into each of the steps, and build our world-class face recognition system.

Preprocessing of images

The first step in our pipeline is face detection. We will then align the faces, extract features, and then finalize our preprocessing on Docker.

Face detection

Obviously, it's very important to first locate the faces in the given photograph so that they can be fed into the later part of the pipeline. There are lots of ways to detect faces, such as detecting skin textures, oval/round shape detection, and other statistical methods. We're going to use a method called HOG.

 HOG is a feature descriptor that represents the distribution (histograms) of directions of gradients (oriented gradients), which are used as features. Gradients (x and y derivatives) of an image are useful, because the magnitude of gradients is large around edges and corners (regions of abrupt intensity changes), which are excellent features in a given image.

To find faces in an image, we'll convert the image into greyscale. Then we'll look at every single pixel in our image, one at a time, and try to extract the orientation of the pixels using the HOG detector. We'll be using `dlib.get_frontal_face_detector()` to create our face detector.

The following small snippet demonstrates the HOG-based face detector being used in the implementation:

```
import sys
import dlib
from skimage import io


# Create a HOG face detector using the built-in dlib class
face_detector = dlib.get_frontal_face_detector()

# Load the image into an array
file_name = 'sample_face_image.jpeg'
image = io.imread(file_name)

# Run the HOG face detector on the image data.
# The result will be the bounding boxes of the faces in our image.
detected_faces = face_detector(image, 1)

print("Found {} faces.".format(len(detected_faces)))
```

```
# Loop through each face we found in the image
for i, face_rect in enumerate(detected_faces):
    # Detected faces are returned as an object with the coordinates
    # of the top, left, right and bottom edges
    print("- Face #{} found at Left: {} Top: {} Right: {} Bottom:
{}".format(i+1, face_rect.left(), face_rect.top(), face_rect.right(),
face_rect.bottom()))
```

The output is as follows:

```
Found 1 faces.
-Face #1 found at Left: 365 Top: 365 Right: 588 Bottom: 588
```

Aligning faces

Once we know the region in which the face is located, we can perform various kinds of isolation techniques to extract the face from the overall image.

One challenge to deal with is that faces in images may be turned in different directions, making them look different to the machine.

To solve this issue, we will warp each image so that the eyes and lips are always in the sample place in the provided images. This will make it a lot easier for us to compare faces in the next steps. To do so, we are going to use an algorithm called **face landmark estimation**.

 The basic idea is we will come up with 68 specific points (called *landmarks*) that exist on every face—the top of the chin, the outside edge of each eye, the inner edge of each eyebrow, and so on. Then we will train a machine learning algorithm to be able to find these 68 specific points on any face.

The 68 landmarks we will locate on every face are shown in the following diagram:

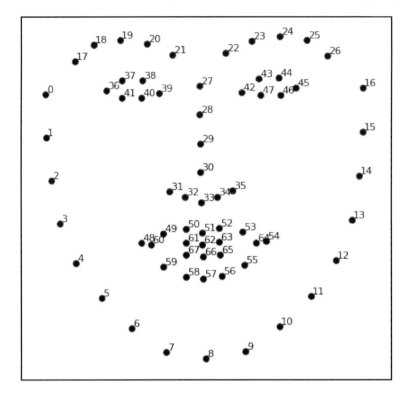

This image was created by Brandon Amos (`http://bamos.github.io/`), who works on OpenFace (`https://github.com/cmusatyalab/openface`).

Here is a small snippet demonstrating how to use face landmarks, which we downloaded in the *Setup environment* section:

```
import sys
import dlib
import cv2
import openface

predictor_model = "shape_predictor_68_face_landmarks.dat"

# Create a HOG face detector , Shape Predictor and Aligner
face_detector = dlib.get_frontal_face_detector()
face_pose_predictor = dlib.shape_predictor(predictor_model)
face_aligner = openface.AlignDlib(predictor_model)

# Take the image file name from the command line
```

```
file_name = 'sample_face_image.jpeg'

# Load the image
image = cv2.imread(file_name)

# Run the HOG face detector on the image data
detected_faces = face_detector(image, 1)

print("Found {} faces.".format(len(detected_faces))

# Loop through each face we found in the image
for i, face_rect in enumerate(detected_faces):

    # Detected faces are returned as an object with the coordinates
    # of the top, left, right and bottom edges
    print("- Face #{} found at Left: {} Top: {} Right: {} Bottom:
{}".format(i, face_rect.left(), face_rect.top(), face_rect.right(),
face_rect.bottom()))

    # Get the the face's pose
    pose_landmarks = face_pose_predictor(image, face_rect)

    # Use openface to calculate and perform the face alignment
    alignedFace = face_aligner.align(534, image, face_rect,
landmarkIndices=openface.AlignDlib.OUTER_EYES_AND_NOSE)

    # Save the aligned image to a file
    cv2.imwrite("aligned_face_{}.jpg".format(i), alignedFace)
```

Using this, we can perform various basic image transformations such as rotation and scaling while preserving parallel lines. These are also known as affine transformations (https://en.wikipedia.org/wiki/Affine_transformation).

The output is as follows:

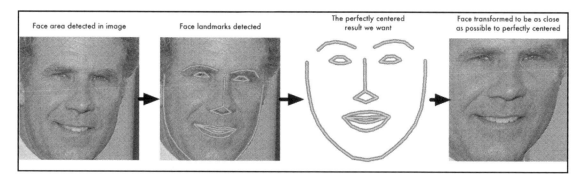

With segmentation, we solved finding the largest face in an image, and with alignment, we standardized the input image to be in the center based on the location of eyes and bottom lip.

Here is a sample from our dataset, showing the raw image and processed image:

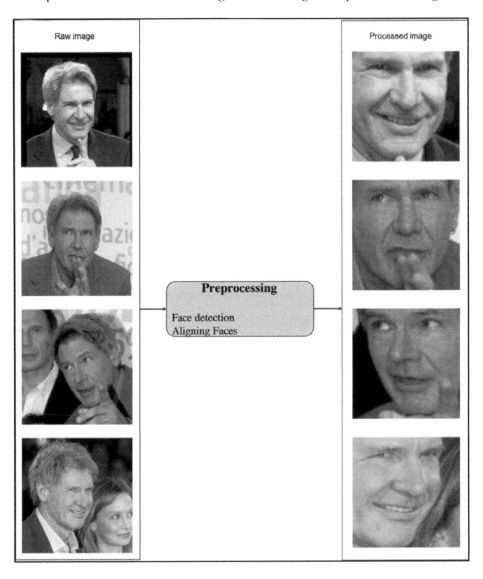

Feature extraction

Now that we've segmented and aligned the data, we'll generate vector embeddings of each identity. These embeddings can then be used as input to a classification, regression, or clustering task.

This process of training a CNN to output face embeddings requires a lot of data and computer power. However, once the network has been trained, it can generate measurements for any face, even ones it has never seen before! So this step only needs to be done once.

For convenience, we have provided a model that has been pre-trained on Inception-Resnet-v1, which you can run over any face image to get the 128 dimension feature vectors. We downloaded this file in the *Setup environment* section, and it's located in the /pre-model/Resnet-185253.pb directory.

 If you want to try this step yourself, OpenFace provides a Lua script (https://github.com/cmusatyalab/openface/blob/master/batch-represent/batch-represent.lua) that will generate embeddings for all images in a folder and write them to a CSV file.

The code to create the embeddings for the input images can be found further after the paragraph. The code is available in the repository at https://github.com/PacktPublishing/Python-Deep-Learning-Projects/blob/master/Chapter10/facenet/train_classifier.py.

In the process, we are loading trained components from the Resnet model such as embedding_layer, images_placeholder, and phase_train_placeholder, along with the images and the labels:

```
def _create_embeddings(embedding_layer, images, labels, images_placeholder,
phase_train_placeholder, sess):
    """
    Uses model to generate embeddings from :param images.
    :param embedding_layer:
    :param images:
    :param labels:
    :param images_placeholder:
    :param phase_train_placeholder:
    :param sess:
    :return: (tuple): image embeddings and labels
    """
    emb_array = None
    label_array = None
```

```
    try:
        i = 0
        while True:
            batch_images, batch_labels = sess.run([images, labels])
            logger.info('Processing iteration {} batch of size:
{}'.format(i, len(batch_labels)))
            emb = sess.run(embedding_layer,
                           feed_dict={images_placeholder: batch_images,
phase_train_placeholder: False})

            emb_array = np.concatenate([emb_array, emb]) if emb_array is
not None else emb
            label_array = np.concatenate([label_array, batch_labels]) if
label_array is not None else batch_labels
            i += 1

    except tf.errors.OutOfRangeError:
        pass

    return emb_array, label_array
```

Here is a quick view of the embedding creating process. We fed the image and the label data along with few components from the pre-trained model:

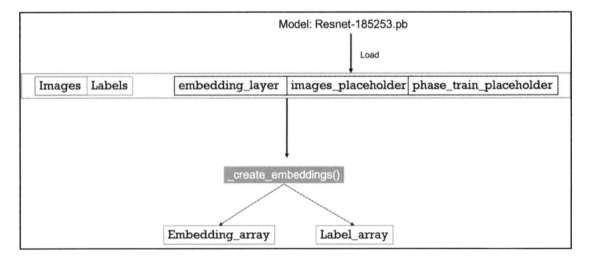

The output of the process will be a vector of 128 dimensions, representing the facial image.

Execution on Docker

We will implement preprocessing on our Docker image. We'll mount the `project` directory as a volume inside the Docker container (using a `-v` flag), and run the preprocessing script on the input data. The results will be written to a directory specified with command-line arguments.

The `align_dlib.py` file is sourced from CMU. It provides methods for detecting a face in an image, finding facial landmarks, and aligning these landmarks:

```
docker run -v $PWD:/facerecognition \
-e PYTHONPATH=$PYTHONPATH:/facerecognition \
-it hellorahulk/facerecognition python3
/facerecognition/facenet/preprocess.py \
--input-dir /facerecognition/data \
--output-dir /facerecognition/output/intermediate \
--crop-dim 180
```

In the preceding command we are setting the input data path using a `--input-dir` flag. This directory should contain the images that we want to process.

We are also setting the output path using a `--output-dir` flag, which will store the segmented aligned images. We will be using these output images as input for training.

The `--crop-dim` flag is to define the output dimensions of the image. In this case, all images will be stored at 180 × 180.

The outcome of this process will be an `/intermediate` folder being created inside the `/output` folder, containing all the preprocessed images.

Training the classifier

First, we'll load the segmented and aligned images from the `input` directory `--input-dir` flag. While training, we'll apply preprocessing to the image. This preprocessing will add random transformations to the image, creating more images to train on.

These images will be fed in a batch size of 128 into the pre-trained model. This model will return a 128-dimensional embedding for each image, returning a 128 x 128 matrix for each batch.

After these embeddings are created, we'll use them as feature inputs into a scikit-learn SVM classifier to train on each identity.

The following command will start the process, and train the classifier. The classifier will be dumped as a `pickle` file in the path defined in the `--classifier-path` argument:

```
docker run -v $PWD:/facerecognition \
-e PYTHONPATH=$PYTHONPATH:/facerecognition \
-it hellorahulk/facerecognition \
python3 /facerecognition/facenet/train_classifier.py \
--input-dir /facerecognition/output/intermediate \
--model-path /facerecognition/pre-model/Resnet-185253.pb \
--classifier-path /facerecognition/output/classifier.pkl \
--num-threads 16 \
--num-epochs 25 \
--min-num-images-per-class 10 \
--is-train
```

A few custom arguments are tunable:

- `--num-threads`: Modify according to the CPU/GPU config
- `--num-epochs`: Change according to your dataset
- `--min-num-images-per-class`: Change according to your dataset
- `--is-train`: Set the `True` flag for training

This process will take a while, depending on the number of images you are training on. Once the process is completed, you will find a `classifier.pkl` file inside the `/output` folder.

Now you can use the `classifier.pkl` file to make predictions, and deploy it on production.

Evaluation

We will evaluate the performance of the trained model. To do that, we will execute the following command:

```
docker run -v $PWD:/facerecognition \
-e PYTHONPATH=$PYTHONPATH:/facerecognition \
-it hellorahulk/facerecognition \
python3 /facerecognition/facenet/train_classifier.py \
--input-dir /facerecognition/output/intermediate \
--model-path /facerecognition/pre-model/Resnet-185253.pb \
```

```
--classifier-path /facerecognition/output/classifier.pkl \
--num-threads 16 \
--num-epochs 2 \
--min-num-images-per-class 10 \
```

Once the execution is completed, you will see predictions with a confidence score, as shown in the following screenshot:

```
INFO:__main__:Evaluating classifier on 22 images
    0   Abdullah_Gul: 0.997
    1   Abdullah_Gul: 1.000
    2   Abdullah_Gul: 0.999
    3   Abdullah_Gul: 1.000
    4   Abdullah_Gul: 0.998
    5   Adrien_Brody: 0.997
    6   Adrien_Brody: 0.963
    7   Adrien_Brody: 0.989
    8   Alejandro_Toledo: 1.000
    9   Alejandro_Toledo: 1.000
   10   Alejandro_Toledo: 0.993
   11   Alejandro_Toledo: 1.000
   12   Alejandro_Toledo: 1.000
   13   Alejandro_Toledo: 1.000
   14   Alejandro_Toledo: 0.505
   15   Alejandro_Toledo: 1.000
   16   Alejandro_Toledo: 0.995
   17   Alejandro_Toledo: 1.000
   18   Harrison_Ford: 0.945
   19   Alejandro_Toledo: 0.998
   20   Abdullah_Gul: 0.762
   21   Harrison_Ford: 0.987
Accuracy: 0.955
INFO:__main__:Completed in 7.507126092910767 seconds
```

We can see that the model is able to predict with 99.5% accuracy. It is also relatively fast.

Summary

We have successfully completed a world-class facial recognition POC for our hypothetical high-performance data center, utilizing the deep-learning technologies of OpenFace, dlib, and FaceNet.

We built a pipeline that included:

- **Face detection**: To examine an image and find all the faces it contains
- **Face extraction**: To focus on each face and understand its general qualities
- **Feature extraction**: To pull out unique features from the faces using CNNs
- **Classifier training**: To compare those unique features to all the people already known, and determine the person's name

The added security level of a robust facial recognition system for access control is in keeping with the high standards demanded by this Tier III facility. This project is a great example of the power of deep learning to produce solutions that make a meaningful impact on the business operations of our clients.

11
Automated Image Captioning

In the previous chapter, we learned about building an object detection and classification model, which was really exciting. But in this chapter, we are going to do something even more impressive by combining current state-of-the-art techniques in both computer vision and natural language processing to form a complete image description approach (https://www.cs.cmu.edu/~afarhadi/papers/sentence.pdf). This will be responsible for constructing computer-generated natural descriptions of any provided images.

Our team has been asked to build this model to generate natural language descriptions of images to be used as the core intelligence of a company that wants to help the visually impaired take advantage of the explosion of photo sharing that's done on the web. It's exciting to think that this deep learning technology could have the power to effectively bring image content alive to this community. People who are likely to enjoy the outcome of our work are those who are visually impaired from birth right up to our aging population. Each of these user types and many more could use an image captioning bot that could be based on the model in this project so that they can keep up with family by knowing the content of posted images, for example.

With this in mind, let's look at the deep learning engineering that we need to do. The idea is to replace the encoder (RNN layer) in an encoder-decoder architecture with a deep **convolutional neural network** (**CNN**) trained to classify objects in images.

Normally, the CNN's last layer is the softmax layer, which assigns the probability that each object might be in the image. But if we remove that softmax layer from CNN, we can feed the CNN's rich encoding of the image into the decoder (language generation RNN) designed to produce phrases. We can then train the whole system directly on images and their captions, so it maximizes the likelihood that the descriptions it produces best match the training descriptions for each image.

Here is the small illustration of the **Auto Image Captioning Model**. In the top left corner is the **Encoder-Decoder** architecture for sequence-to-sequence model which is combined with the **Object Detection model** as shown in the following diagram:

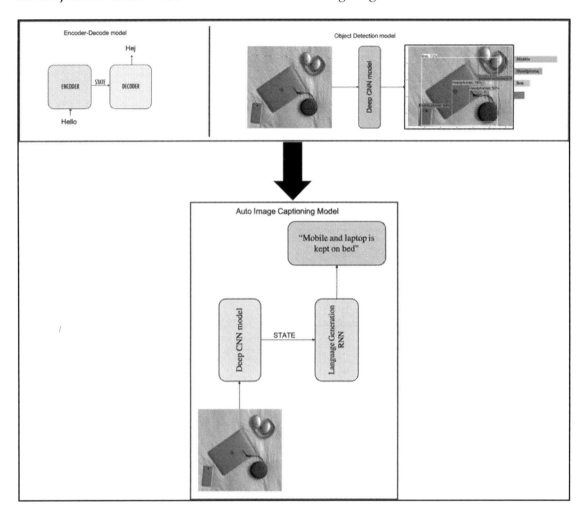

In this implementation, we will be using a pretrained Inception-v3 model as a feature extractor in an encoder trained on the ImageNet dataset.

Data preparation

Let's import all of the dependencies that we will need to build an auto-captioning model.

All of the Python files and the Jupyter Notebooks for this chapter can be found at `https://` `github.com/PacktPublishing/Python-Deep-Learning-Projects/tree/master/Chapter11`.

Initialization

For this implementation, we need a TensorFlow version greater than or equal to 1.9 and we will also enable the eager execution (`https://www.tensorflow.org/guide/eager`) mode, which will help us use the debug the code more effectively. Here is the code for this:

```python
# Import TensorFlow and enable eager execution
import tensorflow as tf
tf.enable_eager_execution()

import matplotlib.pyplot as plt

from sklearn.model_selection import train_test_split
from sklearn.utils import shuffle

import re
import numpy as np
import os
import time
import json
from glob import glob
from PIL import Image
import pickle
```

Download and prepare the MS-COCO dataset

We are going to use the MS-COCO dataset (`http://cocodataset.org/#home`) to train our model. This dataset contains more than 82,000 images, each of which has been annotated with at least five different captions. The following code will download and extract the dataset automatically:

```python
annotation_zip = tf.keras.utils.get_file('captions.zip',
cache_subdir=os.path.abspath('.'),
                                    origin =
'http://images.cocodataset.org/annotations/annotations_trainval2014.zip',
                                    extract = True)
annotation_file =
os.path.dirname(annotation_zip)+'/annotations/captions_train2014.json'

name_of_zip = 'train2014.zip'
if not os.path.exists(os.path.abspath('.') + '/' + name_of_zip):
```

```
image_zip = tf.keras.utils.get_file(name_of_zip,
                                cache_subdir=os.path.abspath('.'),
                                origin =
'http://images.cocodataset.org/zips/train2014.zip',
                                extract = True)
    PATH = os.path.dirname(image_zip)+'/train2014/'
else:
    PATH = os.path.abspath('.')+'/train2014/'
```

 This involves a large download ahead. We'll use the training set; it's a 13 GB file.

The following will be the output:

```
Downloading data from
http://images.cocodataset.org/annotations/annotations_trainval2014.zip
252878848/252872794 [==============================] - 6s 0us/step
Downloading data from http://images.cocodataset.org/zips/train2014.zip
13510574080/13510573713 [==============================] - 322s 0us/step
```

For this example, we'll select a subset of 40,000 captions and use these and the corresponding images to train our model. As always, captioning quality will improve if you choose to use more data:

```
# read the json annotation file
with open(annotation_file, 'r') as f:
    annotations = json.load(f)

# storing the captions and the image name in vectors
all_captions = []
all_img_name_vector = []

for annot in annotations['annotations']:
    caption = '<start> ' + annot['caption'] + ' <end>'
    image_id = annot['image_id']
    full_coco_image_path = PATH + 'COCO_train2014_' + '%012d.jpg' %
(image_id)
    all_img_name_vector.append(full_coco_image_path)
    all_captions.append(caption)

# shuffling the captions and image_names together
# setting a random state
train_captions, img_name_vector = shuffle(all_captions,
                                all_img_name_vector,
                                random_state=1)
```

```
# selecting the first 40000 captions from the shuffled set
num_examples = 40000
train_captions = train_captions[:num_examples]
img_name_vector = img_name_vector[:num_examples]
```

Once the data preparation is completed, we will have all of the image path stored in the `img_name_vector` list variable, and the associated captions are stored in `train_caption`, as shown in the following screenshot:

Data preparation for a deep CNN encoder

Next, we will use Inception-v3 (pretrained on ImageNet) to classify each image. We will extract features from the last convolutional layer. We will create a helper function that will transform the input image to the format that is expected by Inception-v3:

```
#Resizing the image to (299, 299)
#Using the preprocess_input method to place the pixels in the range of -1
to 1.

def load_image(image_path):
    img = tf.read_file(image_path)
    img = tf.image.decode_jpeg(img, channels=3)
    img = tf.image.resize_images(img, (299, 299))
    img = tf.keras.applications.inception_v3.preprocess_input(img)
    return img, image_path
```

Now let's initialize the Inception-v3 model and load the pretrained ImageNet weights. To do so, we'll create a `tf.keras` model where the output layer is the last convolutional layer in the Inception-v3 architecture.

While creating the `keras` model, you can see a parameter called `include_top=False` that indicates whether to include the fully connected layer at the top of the network or not:

```
image_model = tf.keras.applications.InceptionV3(include_top=False,
                                                weights='imagenet')
new_input = image_model.input
hidden_layer = image_model.layers[-1].output

image_features_extract_model = tf.keras.Model(new_input, hidden_layer)
```

The output is as follows:

```
Downloading data from
https://github.com/fchollet/deep-learning-models/releases/download/v0.5/inc
eption_v3_weights_tf_dim_ordering_tf_kernels_notop.h5
87916544/87910968 [==============================] - 40s 0us/step
```

So, the `image_features_extract_model` is our deep CNN encoder, which is responsible for learning the features from the given image.

Performing feature extraction

Now we will pre-process each image with the deep CNN encoder and dump the output to the disk:

1. We will load the images in batches using the `load_image()` helper function that we created before
2. We will feed the images into the encoder to extract the features
3. Dump the features as a `numpy` array:

```
encode_train = sorted(set(img_name_vector))
#Load images
image_dataset = tf.data.Dataset.from_tensor_slices(
encode_train).map(load_image).batch(16)
# Extract features
for img, path in image_dataset:
  batch_features = image_features_extract_model(img)
  batch_features = tf.reshape(batch_features,
                              (batch_features.shape[0], -1,
batch_features.shape[3]))
#Dump into disk
  for bf, p in zip(batch_features, path):
    path_of_feature = p.numpy().decode("utf-8")
    np.save(path_of_feature, bf.numpy())
```

Data prep for a language generation (RNN) decoder

The first step is to pre-process the captions.

We will perform a few basic pre-processing steps on the captions, such as the following:

- First, we'll tokenize the captions (for example, by splitting on spaces). This will help us to build a vocabulary of all the unique words in the data (for example, "playing", "football", and so on).
- Next, we'll limit the vocabulary size to the top 5,000 words to save memory. We'll replace all other words with the token unk (for unknown). You can obviously optimize that according to the use case.
- Finally, we will create a word --> index mapping and vice versa.
- We will then pad all sequences to be the same length as the longest one.

Here is the code for that:

```
# Helper func to find the maximum length of any caption in our dataset

def calc_max_length(tensor):
    return max(len(t) for t in tensor)


# Performing tokenization on the top 5000 words from the vocabulary
top_k = 5000
tokenizer = tf.keras.preprocessing.text.Tokenizer(num_words=top_k,
                                       oov_token="<unk>",
                                       filters='!"#$%&()*+.,-
/:;=?@[\]^_`{|}~ ')

# Converting text into sequence of numbers
tokenizer.fit_on_texts(train_captions)
train_seqs = tokenizer.texts_to_sequences(train_captions)

tokenizer.word_index = {key:value for key, value in
tokenizer.word_index.items() if value <= top_k}

# putting <unk> token in the word2idx dictionary
tokenizer.word_index[tokenizer.oov_token] = top_k + 1
tokenizer.word_index['<pad>'] = 0

# creating the tokenized vectors
train_seqs = tokenizer.texts_to_sequences(train_captions)
```

```
# creating a reverse mapping (index -> word)
index_word = {value:key for key, value in tokenizer.word_index.items()}

# padding each vector to the max_length of the captions
cap_vector = tf.keras.preprocessing.sequence.pad_sequences(train_seqs,
padding='post')

# calculating the max_length
# used to store the attention weights
max_length = calc_max_length(train_seqs)
```

So, the end result will be an array of a sequence of integers, as shown in the following screenshot:

```
In [68]:
        cap_vector[0]

Out[68]: array([  3,   2, 351, 687,   2, 280,   5,   2,  84, 339,   4,   0,   0,
                  0,   0,   0,   0,   0,   0,   0,   0,   0,   0,   0,   0,   0,
                  0,   0,   0,   0,   0,   0,   0,   0,   0,   0,   0,   0,   0,
                  0,   0,   0,   0,   0,   0,   0,   0,   0,   0], dtype=int32)
```

Now, we will split the data into training and validation samples using an 80:20 split ratio:

```
img_name_train, img_name_val, cap_train, cap_val =
train_test_split(img_name_vector,cap_vector,test_size=0.2,random_state=0)

# Checking the sample counts
print ("No of Training Images:",len(img_name_train))
print ("No of Training Caption: ",len(cap_train) )
print ("No of Training Images",len(img_name_val))
print ("No of Training Caption:",len(cap_val) )

No of Training Images: 24000
No of Training Caption:  24000
No of Training Images 6000
No of Training Caption: 6000
```

Setting up the data pipeline

Our images and captions are ready! Next, let's create a `tf.data` dataset (https://www.
tensorflow.org/api_docs/python/tf/data/Dataset) to use for training our model. Now
we will prepare the pipeline for an image and the text model by
performing transformations and batching on them:

```
# Defining parameters
BATCH_SIZE = 64
BUFFER_SIZE = 1000
embedding_dim = 256
units = 512
vocab_size = len(tokenizer.word_index)

# shape of the vector extracted from Inception-V3 is (64, 2048)
# these two variables represent that
features_shape = 2048
attention_features_shape = 64

# loading the numpy files
def map_func(img_name, cap):
    img_tensor = np.load(img_name.decode('utf-8')+'.npy')
    return img_tensor, cap

#We use the from_tensor_slices to load the raw data and transform them into
the tensors

dataset = tf.data.Dataset.from_tensor_slices((img_name_train, cap_train))

# Using the map() to load the numpy files in parallel
# NOTE: Make sure to set num_parallel_calls to the number of CPU cores you
have
# https://www.tensorflow.org/api_docs/python/tf/py_func
dataset = dataset.map(lambda item1, item2: tf.py_func(
        map_func, [item1, item2], [tf.float32, tf.int32]),
num_parallel_calls=8)

# shuffling and batching
dataset = dataset.shuffle(BUFFER_SIZE)
dataset = dataset.batch(BATCH_SIZE)
dataset = dataset.prefetch(1)
```

Defining the captioning model

The model architecture we are using to build the auto captioning is inspired by the *Show, Attend and Tell* paper (`https://arxiv.org/pdf/1502.03044.pdf`). The features that we extracted from the lower convolutional layer of Inception-v3 gave us a vector of a shape of (8, 8, 2048). Then, we squash that to a shape of (64, 2048).

This vector is then passed through the CNN encoder, which consists of a single fully connected layer. The RNN (GRU in our case) attends over the image to predict the next word:

```
def gru(units):
  if tf.test.is_gpu_available():
    return tf.keras.layers.CuDNNGRU(units,
                                return_sequences=True,
                                return_state=True,
                                recurrent_initializer='glorot_uniform')
  else:
    return tf.keras.layers.GRU(units,
                           return_sequences=True,
                           return_state=True,
                           recurrent_activation='sigmoid',
                           recurrent_initializer='glorot_uniform')
```

Attention

Now we will define the attention mechanism popularly known as Bahdanau attention (`https://arxiv.org/pdf/1409.0473.pdf`). We will need the features from the CNN encoder of a shape of (`batch_size`, 64, `embedding_dim`). This attention mechanism will return the context vector and the attention weights over the time axis:

```
class BahdanauAttention(tf.keras.Model):
  def __init__(self, units):
    super(BahdanauAttention, self).__init__()
    self.W1 = tf.keras.layers.Dense(units)
    self.W2 = tf.keras.layers.Dense(units)
    self.V = tf.keras.layers.Dense(1)
  def call(self, features, hidden):
    # hidden_with_time_axis shape == (batch_size, 1, hidden_size)
    hidden_with_time_axis = tf.expand_dims(hidden, 1)
    # score shape == (batch_size, 64, hidden_size)
    score = tf.nn.tanh(self.W1(features) + self.W2(hidden_with_time_axis))
    # attention_weights shape == (batch_size, 64, 1)
    # we get 1 at the last axis because we are applying score to self.V
    attention_weights = tf.nn.softmax(self.V(score), axis=1)
```

```
    # context_vector shape after sum == (batch_size, hidden_size)
    context_vector = attention_weights * features
    context_vector = tf.reduce_sum(context_vector, axis=1)
    return context_vector, attention_weights
```

CNN encoder

Now let's define the CNN encoder that will be the single, fully connected layer followed by the ReLU activation:

```
class CNN_Encoder(tf.keras.Model):
    # Since we have already extracted the features and dumped it using
pickle
    # This encoder passes those features through a Fully connected layer
    def __init__(self, embedding_dim):
        super(CNN_Encoder, self).__init__()
        # shape after fc == (batch_size, 64, embedding_dim)
        self.fc = tf.keras.layers.Dense(embedding_dim)
    def call(self, x):
        x = self.fc(x)
        x = tf.nn.relu(x)
        return x
```

RNN decoder

Here, we will define the RNN decoder which will take the encoded features from the encoder. The features are fed into the attention layer, which is concatenated with the input embedding vector. Then, the concatenated vector is passed into the GRU module, which is further passed through two fully connected layers:

```
class RNN_Decoder(tf.keras.Model):
  def __init__(self, embedding_dim, units, vocab_size):
    super(RNN_Decoder, self).__init__()
    self.units = units

    self.embedding = tf.keras.layers.Embedding(vocab_size, embedding_dim)
    self.gru = gru(self.units)
    self.fc1 = tf.keras.layers.Dense(self.units)
    self.fc2 = tf.keras.layers.Dense(vocab_size)
    self.attention = BahdanauAttention(self.units)
  def call(self, x, features, hidden):
    # defining attention as a separate model
    context_vector, attention_weights = self.attention(features, hidden)
    # x shape after passing through embedding == (batch_size, 1,
```

```
embedding_dim)
    x = self.embedding(x)
    # x shape after concatenation == (batch_size, 1, embedding_dim +
hidden_size)
    x = tf.concat([tf.expand_dims(context_vector, 1), x], axis=-1)
    # passing the concatenated vector to the GRU
    output, state = self.gru(x)
    # shape == (batch_size, max_length, hidden_size)
    x = self.fc1(output)
    # x shape == (batch_size * max_length, hidden_size)
    x = tf.reshape(x, (-1, x.shape[2]))
    # output shape == (batch_size * max_length, vocab)
    x = self.fc2(x)

    return x, state, attention_weights

  def reset_state(self, batch_size):
    return tf.zeros((batch_size, self.units))

encoder = CNN_Encoder(embedding_dim)
decoder = RNN_Decoder(embedding_dim, units, vocab_size)
```

Loss function

We are using the `Adam` optimizer to train the model and masking the loss calculated for the <PAD> key:

```
optimizer = tf.train.AdamOptimizer()

# We are masking the loss calculated for padding
def loss_function(real, pred):
    mask = 1 - np.equal(real, 0)
    loss_ = tf.nn.sparse_softmax_cross_entropy_with_logits(labels=real,
logits=pred) * mask
    return tf.reduce_mean(loss_)
```

Training the captioning model

Now, let's train the model. The first thing we need to do is to extract the features stored in the respective .npy files and then pass those features through the CNN encoder.

The encoder output, hidden state (initialized to 0) and the decoder input (which is the start token) are passed to the decoder. The decoder returns the predictions and the decoder hidden state.

The decoder hidden state is then passed back into the model and the predictions are used to calculate the loss. While training, we use the **teacher forcing technique** to decide the next input to the decoder.

 Teacher forcing is the technique where the target word is passed as the next input to the decoder. This technique helps to learn the correct sequence or correct statistical properties for the sequence, quickly.

The final step is to calculate the gradient and apply it to the optimizer and backpropagate:

```
EPOCHS = 20
loss_plot = []

for epoch in range(EPOCHS):
    start = time.time()
    total_loss = 0
    for (batch, (img_tensor, target)) in enumerate(dataset):
        loss = 0
        # initializing the hidden state for each batch
        # because the captions are not related from image to image
        hidden = decoder.reset_state(batch_size=target.shape[0])

        dec_input = tf.expand_dims([tokenizer.word_index['<start>']] *
BATCH_SIZE, 1)
        with tf.GradientTape() as tape:
            features = encoder(img_tensor)
            for i in range(1, target.shape[1]):
                # passing the features through the decoder
                predictions, hidden, _ = decoder(dec_input, features,
hidden)

                loss += loss_function(target[:, i], predictions)
                # using teacher forcing
                dec_input = tf.expand_dims(target[:, i], 1)
        total_loss += (loss / int(target.shape[1]))
        variables = encoder.variables + decoder.variables
        gradients = tape.gradient(loss, variables)
        optimizer.apply_gradients(zip(gradients, variables),
tf.train.get_or_create_global_step())
        if batch % 100 == 0:
            print ('Epoch {} Batch {} Loss {:.4f}'.format(epoch + 1,
                                                           batch,
```

```
                                                       loss.numpy() /
int(target.shape[1])))
    # storing the epoch end loss value to plot later
    loss_plot.append(total_loss / len(cap_vector))
    print ('Epoch {} Loss {:.6f}'.format(epoch + 1,
                                total_loss/len(cap_vector)))
    print ('Time taken for 1 epoch {} sec\n'.format(time.time() - start))
```

The following is the output:

```
Epoch 8 Batch 200 Loss 0.5677
Epoch 8 Batch 300 Loss 0.5790
Epoch 8 Loss 0.006937
Time taken for 1 epoch 2127.0434930324554 sec

Epoch 9 Batch 0 Loss 0.5392
Epoch 9 Batch 100 Loss 0.5242
Epoch 9 Batch 200 Loss 0.4697
Epoch 9 Batch 300 Loss 0.4957
Epoch 9 Loss 0.006584
Time taken for 1 epoch 3446.0260667800903 sec

Epoch 10 Batch 0 Loss 0.5271
Epoch 10 Batch 100 Loss 0.5373
Epoch 10 Batch 200 Loss 0.5161
Epoch 10 Batch 300 Loss 0.5193
Epoch 10 Loss 0.006244
Time taken for 1 epoch 4010.5842893123627 sec
```

After performing the training process over few epochs lets plot the Epoch vs Loss graph:

```
plt.plot(loss_plot)
plt.xlabel('Epochs')
plt.ylabel('Loss')
plt.title('Loss Plot')
plt.show()
```

The output is as follows:

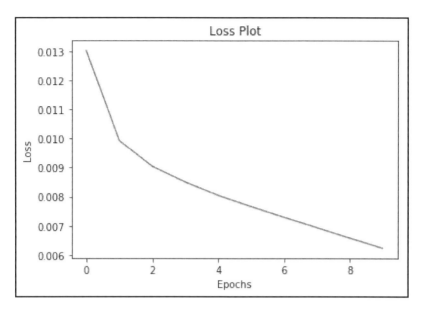

The loss vs Epoch plot during training process

Evaluating the captioning model

The evaluation function is similar to the training loop, except we don't use teacher forcing here. The input to the decoder at each time step is its previous predictions, along with the hidden state and the encoder output.

A few key points to remember while making predictions:

- Stop predicting when the model predicts the end token
- Store the attention weights for every time step

Let's define the `evaluate()` function:

```
def evaluate(image):
  attention_plot = np.zeros((max_length, attention_features_shape))

  hidden = decoder.reset_state(batch_size=1)

  temp_input = tf.expand_dims(load_image(image)[0], 0)
  img_tensor_val = image_features_extract_model(temp_input)
```

```
  img_tensor_val = tf.reshape(img_tensor_val, (img_tensor_val.shape[0], -1,
img_tensor_val.shape[3]))

  features = encoder(img_tensor_val)

  dec_input = tf.expand_dims([tokenizer.word_index['<start>']], 0)
  result = []

  for i in range(max_length):
  predictions, hidden, attention_weights = decoder(dec_input, features,
hidden)

  attention_plot[i] = tf.reshape(attention_weights, (-1, )).numpy()

  predicted_id = tf.argmax(predictions[0]).numpy()
  result.append(index_word[predicted_id])

  if index_word[predicted_id] == '<end>':
  return result, attention_plot

  dec_input = tf.expand_dims([predicted_id], 0)

  attention_plot = attention_plot[:len(result), :]
  return result, attention_plot
```

Also, let's create a `helper` function to visualize the attention points that predict the words:

```
def plot_attention(image, result, attention_plot):
    temp_image = np.array(Image.open(image))

    fig = plt.figure(figsize=(10, 10))
    len_result = len(result)
    for l in range(len_result):
        temp_att = np.resize(attention_plot[l], (8, 8))
        ax = fig.add_subplot(len_result//2, len_result//2, l+1)
        ax.set_title(result[l])
        img = ax.imshow(temp_image)
        ax.imshow(temp_att, cmap='gray', alpha=0.6,
extent=img.get_extent())

    plt.tight_layout()
    plt.show()

# captions on the validation set
rid = np.random.randint(0, len(img_name_val))
image = img_name_val[rid]
real_caption = ' '.join([index_word[i] for i in cap_val[rid] if i not in
[0]])
```

```
result, attention_plot = evaluate(image)

print ('Real Caption:', real_caption)
print ('Prediction Caption:', ' '.join(result))
plot_attention(image, result, attention_plot)
# opening the image
Image.open(img_name_val[rid])
```

The output is as follows:

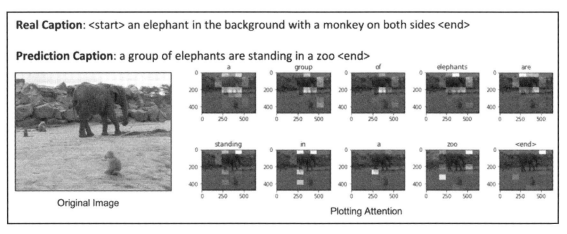

Real Caption: <start> an elephant in the background with a monkey on both sides <end>

Prediction Caption: a group of elephants are standing in a zoo <end>

Original Image

Plotting Attention

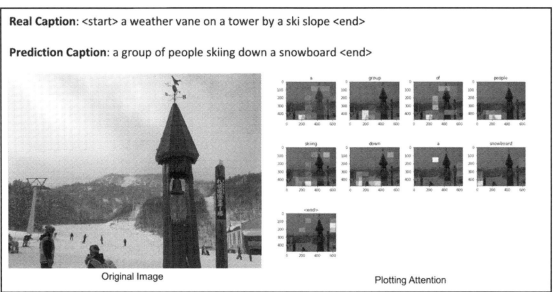

Real Caption: <start> a weather vane on a tower by a ski slope <end>

Prediction Caption: a group of people skiing down a snowboard <end>

Original Image

Plotting Attention

Deploying the captioning model

Now let's deploy the complete module as a RESTful service. To do so, we will write an inference code that loads the latest checkpoint and makes the prediction on the given image.

Look into the `inference.py` file in the repository. All the code is similar to the training loop except we don't use teacher forcing here. The input to the decoder at each time step is its previous predictions, along with the hidden state and the encoder output.

One important part is to load the model in memory for which we are using the `tf.train.Checkpoint()` method, which loads all of the learned weights for `optimizer`, `encoder`, `decoder` into the memory. Here is the code for that:

```
checkpoint_dir = './my_model'
checkpoint_prefix = os.path.join(checkpoint_dir, "ckpt")
checkpoint = tf.train.Checkpoint(
                            optimizer=optimizer,
                            encoder=encoder,
                            decoder=decoder,
                            )

checkpoint.restore(tf.train.latest_checkpoint(checkpoint_dir))
```

So, we will create an `evaluate()` function, which defines the prediction loop. To make sure that the prediction ends after certain words, we will stop predicting when the model predicts the end token, `<end>`:

```
def evaluate(image):
    attention_plot = np.zeros((max_length, attention_features_shape))

    hidden = decoder.reset_state(batch_size=1)

    temp_input = tf.expand_dims(load_image(image)[0], 0)
    # Extract features from the test image
    img_tensor_val = image_features_extract_model(temp_input)
    img_tensor_val = tf.reshape(img_tensor_val, (img_tensor_val.shape[0],
-1, img_tensor_val.shape[3]))
    # Feature is fed into the encoder
    features = encoder(img_tensor_val)

    dec_input = tf.expand_dims([tokenizer.word_index['<start>']], 0)
    result = []
    # Prediction loop
    for i in range(max_length):
        predictions, hidden, attention_weights = decoder(dec_input,
```

```
features, hidden)

        attention_plot[i] = tf.reshape(attention_weights, (-1, )).numpy()

        predicted_id = tf.argmax(predictions[0]).numpy()
        result.append(index_word[predicted_id])
        # Hard stop when end token is predicted
        if index_word[predicted_id] == '<end>':
            return result, attention_plot

        dec_input = tf.expand_dims([predicted_id], 0)

    attention_plot = attention_plot[:len(result), :]
    return result, attention_plot
```

Now let's use this `evaluate()` function in our web application code:

```python
#!/usr/bin/env python2
# -*- coding: utf-8 -*-
"""
@author: rahulkumar
"""

from flask import Flask , request, jsonify

import time
from inference import evaluate
import tensorflow as tf

app = Flask(__name__)

@app.route("/wowme")
def AutoImageCaption():
    image_url=request.args.get('image')
    print('image_url')
    image_extension = image_url[-4:]
    image_path =
tf.keras.utils.get_file(str(int(time.time()))+image_extension,
origin=image_url)
    result, attention_plot = evaluate(image_path)
    data = {'Prediction Caption:': ' '.join(result)}
    return jsonify(data)


if __name__ == "__main__":
    app.run(host = '0.0.0.0',port=8081)
```

Execute the following command in the Terminal to run the web app:

```
python caption_deploy_api.py
```

You should get the following output:

```
* Running on http://0.0.0.0:8081/ (Press CTRL+C to quit)
```

Now we request the API, as follows:

```
curl
0.0.0.0:8081/wowme?image=https://www.beautifulpeopleibiza.com/images/BPI/im
g_bpi_destacada.jpg
```

We should get our caption predicted, as shown in the following screenshot:

Make sure to train the model on the large image to get better predictions.

Voila! We just deployed the state-of-the-art automatic captioning module.

Summary

In this implementation, we used a pretrained Inception-v3 model as a feature extractor in an encoder trained on the ImageNet dataset as part of a deep learning solution. This solution combines current state-of-the-art techniques in both *computer vision* and *natural language processing,* to form a complete image description approach (`https://www.cs.cmu.edu/~afarhadi/papers/sentence.pdf`) able to construct computer-generated natural descriptions of any provided images. We've effectively broken the barrier between images and language with this trained model and we've provided a technology that could be used as part of an application, helping the visually impaired enjoy the benefits of the megatrend of photo sharing! Great work!

Pose Estimation on 3D models Using ConvNets

12

Welcome to our chapter on human pose estimation. In this chapter, we will be building a neural network that will predict 3D human poses using 2D images. We will do this with the help of transfer learning by using the VGG16 model architecture and modifying it accordingly for our current problem. By the end of this chapter, you will have a **deep learning (DL)** model that does a really good job of predicting human poses.

Visual effects (VFX) in movies are expensive. They involve using a lot of expensive sensors that will be placed on the body of the actor when shooting. The information from these sensors will then be used to build visual effects, all of which ends up being super expensive. We have been asked (in this hypothetical use case) by a major movie studio whether we can help their graphics department build cheaper and better visual effects by building a human pose estimator, which they will use to better estimate poses on the screen while editing.

For this task, we will be using images from **Frames Labeled In Cinema (FLIC)**. These images are not ready to be used for modeling just yet. So, get ready to spend a bit more time on preparing the image data in this chapter. Also, we will only be estimating the pose of arms, shoulders, and the head.

In this chapter, we'll learn about the following topics:

- Processing/preparing images for pose estimation
- The VGG16 model
- Transfer learning
- Building and understanding the training loop
- Testing the model

It would be better if you implement the code snippets as you go along in this chapter, either in a Jupyter notebook or any source code editor. This will make it easier for you to follow along, as well as understand what each part of the code does.

All of the Python files and the Jupyter Notebooks for this chapter can be found at `https://github.com/PacktPublishing/Python-Deep-Learning-Projects/tree/master/Chapter12`.

Code implementation

In this exercise, we will be using the Keras deep learning library, which is a high-level neural network API capable of running on top of TensorFlow, Theano, and CNTK.

 If you ever have a question related to Keras, refer to this easy-to-understand Keras documentation at `https://keras.io`.

Please download the `Chapter12` folder from GitHub before moving forward with this chapter.

This project involves downloading files from various sources that will be called inside the scripts. To make sure that the Python scripts or the Jupyter Notebook have no issues locating the downloaded files, follow these steps:

1. Open a Terminal and change your directory by using the `cd` command in the `Chapter12` folder.
2. Download the `FLIC-full` data file with the following command:

   ```
   wget http://vision.grasp.upenn.edu/video/FLIC-full.zip
   ```

3. Unzip the ZIP file with the following command:

   ```
   unzip FLIC-full.zip
   ```

4. Remove the ZIP file with the following command:

   ```
   rm -rf FLIC-full.zip
   ```

5. Change directories in the `FLIC-full` folder by using the following command:

   ```
   cd FLIC-full
   ```

6. Download the file containing the training indices:

```
wget http://cims.nyu.edu/~tompson/data/tr_plus_indices.mat
```

7. Change the directory back to the `Chapter12` folder.

8. Launch your Jupyter Notebook or run the Python scripts from the `Chapter12` directory.

 Further information on the `FLIC-full` data folder can be found at `https://bensapp.github.io/flic-dataset.html`.

Importing the dependencies

We will be using `numpy`, `matplotlib`, `keras`, `tensorflow`, and the `tqdm` package in this exercise. Here, TensorFlow is used as the backend for Keras. You can install these packages with `pip`. For the MNIST data, we will be using the dataset that's available in the `keras` module with a simple `import`:

```
import matplotlib.pyplot as plt
%matplotlib inline

import os
import random
import glob
import h5py
from scipy.io import loadmat
import numpy as np
import pandas as pd
import cv2 as cv
from __future__ import print_function

from sklearn.model_selection import train_test_split

from keras.models import Sequential, Model
from keras.layers.core import Flatten, Dense, Dropout
from keras.optimizers import Adam
from keras import backend as K
from keras import applications
K.clear_session()
```

It is important that you set `seed` for reproducibility:

```
# set seed for reproducibility
seed_val = 9000
np.random.seed(seed_val)
random.seed(seed_val)
```

Exploring and pre-processing the data

With the `FLIC-full` data folder downloaded and unpacked, inside the `FLIC-full` folder you should find the `tr_plus_indices.mat` and `examples.mat` MATLAB files, and also the folder named `images`, inside which are the images that will be used in this project.

You will find that the images have been captured from movies such as *2 Fast 2 Furious*, *Along Came Polly*, *American Wedding*, and a few others. Each of these images is 480*720 px in size. These images are nothing but screenshots of scenes involving actors from the selected movies, which we will use for pose estimation.

Let's load the MATLAB file `examples.mat`. We will do this with the help of the `loadmat` module, which we have imported already, along with other imports. Also, let's print out some of the information from this file:

```
# load the examples file
examples = loadmat('FLIC-full/examples.mat')

# print type of the loaded file
print('examples variable is of', type(examples))

# print keys in the dictionary examples
print('keys in the dictionary examples:\n', examples.keys())ut
```

Following is the output:

```
examples variable is of <type 'dict'>
keys in the dictionary examples:
  ['examples', '__version__', '__header__', '__globals__']
```

Figure 12.1: Example file information from printout 1

From the printout, we can see that the MATLAB file has been loaded as a dictionary with four keys, one of which is the one we need: the `examples` key. Let's see what this key holds:

```
# print type and shape of values in examples key
print('Shape of value in examples key: ',examples['examples'].shape)

# print examples
print('Type: ',type(examples['examples']))

# reshape the examples array
examples = examples['examples'].reshape(-1,)

# print shape of examples array
print("Shape of reshaped 'examples' array:", examples.shape)
```

Following is the output:

```
Shape of value in examples key:  (1, 20928)
Type:  <type 'numpy.ndarray'>
Shape of reshaped 'examples' array: (20928,)
```

Figure 12.2: Example file information from printout 1

The notable thing here is that the value of the `examples` key is a numpy array of shape (1, 20928). You will also see that the array has been reshaped to shape `(20928,)`. The `examples` key contains the IDs of the images (in the `images` folder) and the corresponding pose coordinates that can be used for modeling.

Let's print out an image ID and its corresponding coordinates array with its shape. The image ID we need is stored at index 3, and the corresponding coordinates are at index 2. Let's print these out:

```
print('Coordinates at location/index 3 of example 0:\n' ,examples[0][2].T)

print('\n Data type in which the coordinates are stored: ',type(examples[0][2]))

print('\n Shape of the coordinates:', examples[0][2].shape)

print('\n Name of the image file the above coordinates correspond to :\n ',examples[0][3][0])
```

Following is the output:

```
Coordinates at location 3 of example 0:
 [[436.58776855 195.15625    ]
 [446.54693604 286.796875   ]
 [456.50613403 322.65625    ]
 [265.28979492 203.125      ]
 [277.24081421 328.6328125  ]
 [380.81634521 336.6015625  ]
 [434.59591675 370.46875    ]
 [         nan          nan]
 [         nan          nan]
 [325.04492188 386.40625    ]
 [         nan          nan]
 [         nan          nan]
 [400.73471069 129.4140625  ]
 [374.84082031 125.4296875  ]
 [         nan          nan]
 [         nan          nan]
 [384.80001831 145.3515625  ]
 [         nan          nan]
 [         nan          nan]
 [         nan          nan]
 [         nan          nan]
 [         nan          nan]
 [         nan          nan]
 [         nan          nan]
 [         nan          nan]
 [         nan          nan]
 [         nan          nan]
 [         nan          nan]
 [         nan          nan]]

Data type in which the coordinates are stored:  <type 'numpy.ndarray'>

Shape of the coordinates: (2, 29)

Name of the image file the above coordinates correspond to :
 12-oclock-high-special-edition-00004151.jpg
```

Figure 12.3: Example file information from printout 2

---

[328]

From the preceding screenshot, we can see that the coordinates array is of shape (2,29):

```
# each coordinate corresponds to the the below listed body joints/locations
and in the same order
joint_labels = ['lsho', 'lelb', 'lwri', 'rsho', 'relb', 'rwri', 'lhip',
                'lkne', 'lank', 'rhip', 'rkne', 'rank', 'leye', 'reye',
                'lear', 'rear', 'nose', 'msho', 'mhip', 'mear', 'mtorso',
                'mluarm', 'mruarm', 'mllarm', 'mrlarm', 'mluleg', 'mruleg',
                'mllleg', 'mrlleg']

# print joint_labels
print(joint_labels)
```

Following is the output:

```
['lsho', 'lelb', 'lwri', 'rsho', 'relb', 'rwri', 'lhip', 'lkne', 'lank',
 'rhip', 'rkne', 'rank', 'leye', 'reye', 'lear', 'rear', 'nose', 'msho',
 'mhip', 'mear', 'mtorso', 'mluarm', 'mruarm', 'mllarm', 'mrlarm', 'mlule
g', 'mruleg', 'mllleg', 'mrlleg']
```

Figure 12.4: List of joint labels

But, if you look back at the coordinates array that we printed in the preceding screenshot, out of the 29 coordinates, we only have information on 11 of the body joints/locations. These are as follows:

```
# print list of known joints
known_joints = [x for i,x in enumerate(joint_labels) if i in np.r_[0:7, 9,
12:14, 16]]
print(known_joints)
```

Following is the output:

```
['lsho', 'lelb', 'lwri', 'rsho', 'relb', 'rwri', 'lhip', 'rhip', 'leye',
 'reye', 'nose']
```

Figure 12.5: List of joint labels with coordinates

For the purpose of this project, we only need information on the following body joints/locations:

```
# print needed joints for the task
target_joints = ['lsho', 'lelb', 'lwri', 'rsho', 'relb',
                 'rwri', 'leye', 'reye', 'nose']
print('Joints necessary for the project:\n', target_joints)
```

```
# print the indices of the needed joints in the coordinates array
joints_loc_id = np.r_[0:6, 12:14, 16]
print('\nIndices of joints necessary for the project:\n',joints_loc_id)
```

Following is the output:

```
Joints necessary for the project:
 ['lsho', 'lelb', 'lwri', 'rsho', 'relb', 'rwri', 'leye', 'reye', 'nose']

Indices of joints necessary for the project:
 [ 0  1  2  3  4  5 12 13 16]
```

Figure 12.6: Required joints and their indices in the array

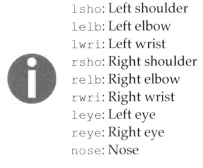

`lsho`: Left shoulder

`lelb`: Left elbow

`lwri`: Left wrist

`rsho`: Right shoulder

`relb`: Right elbow

`rwri`: Right wrist

`leye`: Left eye

`reye`: Right eye

`nose`: Nose

Now, let's define a function that takes in a dictionary of nine joint labels and coordinates and returns a list with seven coordinates (7 (*x*,*y*) pairs). The reason for seven coordinates is that the `leye`, `reye`, and the `nose` coordinates are converted into one head coordinate when we take the mean across them:

```
def joint_coordinates(joint):
    """Store necessary coordinates to a list"""
    joint_coor = []
    # Take mean of the leye, reye, nose to obtain coordinates for the head
    joint['head'] = (joint['leye']+joint['reye']+joint['nose'])/3
    joint_coor.extend(joint['lwri'].tolist())
    joint_coor.extend(joint['lelb'].tolist())
    joint_coor.extend(joint['lsho'].tolist())
    joint_coor.extend(joint['head'].tolist())
    joint_coor.extend(joint['rsho'].tolist())
    joint_coor.extend(joint['relb'].tolist())
    joint_coor.extend(joint['rwri'].tolist())
    return joint_coor
```

Now let's load the `tr_plus_indices.mat` MATLAB file, just like we did previously:

 The reason why we need to use the `tr_plus_indices.mat` file is because it contains indices of images that should only be used for training, as well as some unlisted ones for testing. The reason for such a split is to make sure that the train set and the test set have frames from completely different movies so as to avoid overfitting. More on this can be found at https://bensapp.github.io/flic-dataset.html.

```
# load the indices matlab file
train_indices = loadmat('FLIC-full/tr_plus_indices.mat')

# print type of the loaded file
print('train_indices variable is of', type(train_indices))

# print keys in the dictionary training_indices
print('keys in the dictionary train_indices:\n', train_indices.keys())
```

Following is the output:

```
train_indices variable is of <type 'dict'>
keys in the dictionary train_indices:
 ['__version__', 'tr_plus_indices', '__header__', '__globals__']
```

Figure 12.7: train_indices file information printout 1

From the preceding screenshot, you can see that the MATLAB file has been loaded as a dictionary with four keys, one of which is `tr_plus_indices`, which is the one we need. Let's look at the content of this key:

```
# print type and shape of values in tr_plus_indices key
print('Shape of values in tr_plus_indices key:
',train_indices['tr_plus_indices'].shape)

# print tr_plus_indices
print('Type: ',type(train_indices['tr_plus_indices']))

# reshape the training_indices array
train_indices = train_indices['tr_plus_indices'].reshape(-1,)

# print shape of train_indices array
print("Shape of reshaped 'train_indices' array:", train_indices.shape)
```

Following is the output:

```
Shape of values in tr_plus_indices key:  (17380, 1)
Type:  <type 'numpy.ndarray'>
Shape of reshaped 'train_indices' array: (17380,)
```

Figure 12.8: train_indices file information printout 2

We can see that the `tr_plus_indices` key corresponds to a (17380*1) shaped array. We will reshape this to `(17380, )` for convenience.

`tr_plus_indices` contains the indices of the data in the `examples` key of the `examples.mat` file, which should only be used for training. Using this information, we will subset the data into a train set and a test set:

```
# empty list to store train image ids
train_ids = []
# empty list to store train joints
train_jts = []
# empty list to store test image ids
test_ids = []
# empty list to store test joints
test_jts = []

for i, example in enumerate(examples):
    # image id
    file_name = example[3][0]
    # joint coordinates
    joint = example[2].T
    # dictionary that goes into the joint_coordinates function
    joints = dict(zip(target_joints, [x for k,x in enumerate(joint) if k in
joints_loc_id]))
    # obtain joints for the task
    joints = joint_coordinates(joints)
    # use train indices list to decide if an image is to be used for
training or testing
    if i in train_indices:
        train_ids.append(file_name)
        train_jts.append(joints)
    else:
        test_ids.append(file_name)
        test_jts.append(joints)


# Concatenate image ids dataframe and the joints dataframe and save it as a
csv
```

For the remaining part of this code snippet, please refer to the
`deeppose.ipynb` file here: https://github.com/PacktPublishing/
Python-Deep-Learning-Projects/blob/master/Chapter12/deeppose.
ipynb

We can see that the train data has 17,380 data points, with each data point having an image ID and 7(*x,y*) joint coordinates. Similarly, the test data has 3,548 data points.

In the preceding snippet, we first initialize four empty lists, two for saving train and test image IDs, and two for saving train and test joints. Then, for each data point in the `examples` key, we do the following:

1. Extract the file name.
2. Extract the joint coordinates.
3. ZIP the target joints (target joint labels) and the corresponding joint coordinates and convert them into a dictionary.
4. Feed the dictionary to the `joint_coordinates` function to obtain the joints needed for this task.
5. Append the image IDs and the resulting joints from the previous step to a train or test list by using the `train_indices` list.

Finally, convert the lists into train and test data frames and save them as a CSV file. Make sure that you don't set the index and header parameters to `False` when saving the data frame as a CSV file.

Let's load the `train_joints.csv` and `test_joints.csv` files we saved in the previous step and print out some details:

```
# load train_joints.csv
train_data = pd.read_csv('FLIC-full/train_joints.csv', header=None)

# load test_joints.csv
test_data = pd.read_csv('FLIC-full/test_joints.csv', header = None)

# train image ids
train_image_ids = train_data[0].values
print('train_image_ids shape', train_image_ids.shape)

# train joints
train_joints = train_data.iloc[:,1:].values
print('train_image_ids shape', train_joints.shape)

# test image ids
test_image_ids = test_data[0].values
```

```
print('train_image_ids shape', test_image_ids.shape)

# test joints
test_joints = test_data.iloc[:,1:].values
print('train_image_ids shape', test_joints.shape)
```

Following is the output:

```
train_image_ids shape (17380,)
train_image_ids shape (17380, 14)
train_image_ids shape (3548,)
train_image_ids shape (3548, 14)
```

Figure 12.9: Printout of image IDs and the joint's array shape

Now, let's load some images from the `images` folder and plot them to see what they look like:

```
import glob
image_list = glob.glob('FLIC-full/images/*.jpg')[0:8]

plt.figure(figsize=(12,5))
for i in range(8):
    plt.subplot(2,4,(i+1))
    img = plt.imread(image_list[i])
    plt.imshow(img, aspect='auto')
    plt.axis('off')
    plt.title('Shape: '+str(img.shape))

plt.tight_layout()
plt.show()
```

Following is the output:

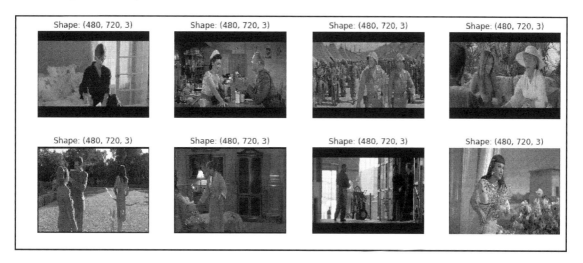

Figure 12.10: Plot of eight images from the images folder in the FLIC_full folder

We can see that each image is of shape (480*720*3). Our next task will be to crop the original image and focus on the person of interest by using the joint coordinates that are available to us. We do this by resizing the images into a shape of 224*24*3 so that we can feed them into the VGG16 model. Finally, we will also build a `plotting` function to plot the joints on the image:

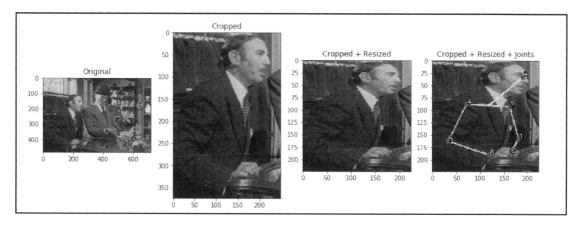

Figure 12.11: Plot showing the transformation each image has to go through

Preparing the data

Now let's implement the functions that will perform the tasks that we discussed when we ended the previous section.

Cropping

We will first start off with the `image_cropping()` function. This function accepts an image ID and its corresponding joint coordinates. It loads the image into memory and then crops the image so that it only includes the section of the image that's bound within the coordinates. The cropped image is then padded so that the joints and limbs are completely visible. For the added padding, the joint coordinates are also adjusted accordingly. When it has done this, the image is returned. This is the most important part of the transformation. Take your time and dissect the function to see exactly what is happening (the `crop_pad_inf` and `crop_pad_sup` parameters control the amount of padding):

```
def image_cropping(image_id, joints, crop_pad_inf = 1.4, crop_pad_sup=1.6,
shift = 5, min_dim = 100):
    """Function to crop original images"""
    ## image cropping
    # load the image
    image = cv.imread('FLIC-full/images/%s' % (image_id))
    # convert joint list to array
    joints = np.asarray([int(float(p)) for p in joints])
    # reshape joints to shape (7*2)
    joints = joints.reshape((len(joints) // 2, 2))
    # transform joints to list of (x,y) tuples
    posi_joints = [(j[0], j[1]) for j in joints if j[0] > 0 and j[1] > 0]
    # obtain the bounding rectangle using opencv boundingRect
    x_loc, y_loc, width, height =
cv.boundingRect(np.asarray([posi_joints]))
    if width < min_dim:
        width = min_dim
    if height < min_dim:
        height = min_dim

    ## bounding rect extending
    inf, sup = crop_pad_inf, crop_pad_sup
    r = sup - inf
    # define width padding
    pad_w_r = np.random.rand() * r + inf # inf~sup
    # define height padding
    pad_h_r = np.random.rand() * r + inf # inf~sup
    # adjust x, y, w and h by the defined padding
    x_loc -= (width * pad_w_r - width) / 2
```

```
y_loc -= (height * pad_h_r - height) / 2
width *= pad_w_r
height *= pad_h_r

## shifting
## clipping
## joint shifting
```

For the remaining part of this code snippet please refer to the file `deeppose.ipynb` **here**: `https://github.com/PacktPublishing/Python-Deep-Learning-Projects/blob/master/Chapter12/deeppose.ipynb`

Let's pass an image ID and its joints to the `image_cropping()` function and plot the output image:

```
# plot the original image
plt.figure(figsize = (15,5))
plt.subplot(1,2,1)
plt.title('Original')
plt.imshow(plt.imread('FLIC-full/images/'+train_image_ids[0]))

# plot the cropped image
image, joint = image_cropping(train_image_ids[0], train_joints[0])
plt.subplot(1,2,2)
plt.title('Cropped')
plt.imshow(image)
```

Following is the output:

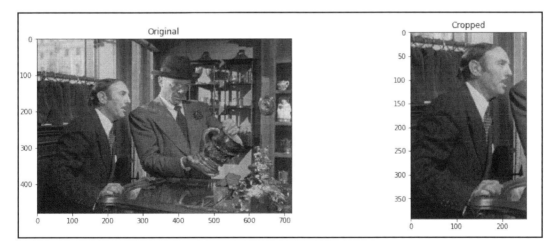

Figure 12.12: Plot of the resulting cropped image compared to the original image

Resizing

In the *Cropping* section, we saw that the original image of shape (480*720*3) is cropped to shape (393*254*3). However, the VGG16 architecture accepts images of shape (224*224*3). Hence, we will define a function called `image_resize()` that does the resizing for us. It accepts the cropped image and the joint resulting from the `image_cropping()` function as input and returns the resized image and its joint coordinates:

```
def image_resize(image, joints, new_size = 224):
    """Function resize cropped images"""
    orig_h, orig_w = image.shape[:2]
    joints[0::2] = joints[0::2] / float(orig_w) * new_size
    joints[1::2] = joints[1::2] / float(orig_h) * new_size
    image = cv.resize(image, (new_size, new_size),
interpolation=cv.INTER_NEAREST)
    return image, joints
# plot resized image
image, joint = image_resize(image, joint)
plt.title('Cropped + Resized')
plt.imshow(image)
```

Following is the output:

Figure 12.13: Plot of the resized image

After passing the cropped image to the `image_resize()` function, we can see that the resulting image is of shape (224*224*3). Now this image and its joints can be passed into the model for training.

Plotting the joints and limbs

Let's also define the plotting functions that will plot the limbs on the resized image. The following defined `plot_joints()` function accepts the resized image and its joints and returns an image of the same shape with the limbs plotted on top:

```
def plot_limb(img, joints, i, j, color):
    """Function to plot the limbs"""
    cv.line(img, joints[i], joints[j], (255, 255, 255), thickness=2,
lineType=16)
    cv.line(img, joints[i], joints[j], color, thickness=1, lineType=16)
    return img

def plot_joints(img, joints, groundtruth=True, text_scale=0.5):
    """Function to draw the joints"""
    h, w, c = img.shape
    if groundtruth:
        # left hand to left elbow
        img = plot_limb(img, joints, 0, 1, (0, 255, 0))
        # left elbow to left shoulder
        img = plot_limb(img, joints, 1, 2, (0, 255, 0))
        # left shoulder to right shoulder
        img = plot_limb(img, joints, 2, 4, (0, 255, 0))
        # right shoulder to right elbow
        img = plot_limb(img, joints, 4, 5, (0, 255, 0))
        # right elbow to right hand
        img = plot_limb(img, joints, 5, 6, (0, 255, 0))
        # neck coordinate
        neck = tuple((np.array(joints[2]) + np.array(joints[4])) // 2)
        joints.append(neck)
        # neck to head
        img = plot_limb(img, joints, 3, 7, (0, 255, 0))
        joints.pop()

    # joints
    for j, joint in enumerate(joints):
        # plot joints
        cv.circle(img, joint, 5, (0, 255, 0), -1)
        # plot joint number black
        cv.putText(img, '%d' % j, joint, cv.FONT_HERSHEY_SIMPLEX,
text_scale,
                   (0, 0, 0), thickness=2, lineType=16)
        # plot joint number white
        cv.putText(img, '%d' % j, joint, cv.FONT_HERSHEY_SIMPLEX,
text_scale,
                   (255, 255, 255), thickness=1, lineType=16)

    else:
```

For the remaining part of this code snippet please refer to the `deeppose.ipynb` file here: `https://github.com/PacktPublishing/Python-Deep-Learning-Projects/blob/master/Chapter12/deeppose.ipynb`

Following is the output:

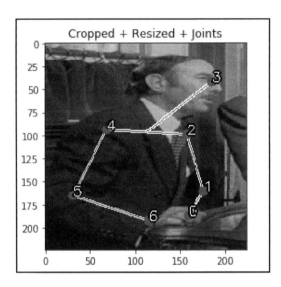

Figure 12.14: Plot showing the true joint coordinates on top of the image

Transforming the images

Now let's transform the images and their corresponding joints to the desired form by using the functions we have defined previously. We will do this with the help of the `model_data()` function, which is defined as follows:

```python
def model_data(image_ids, joints, train = True):
    """Function to generate train and test data."""
    if train:
        # empty list
        train_img_joints = []
        # create train directory inside FLIC-full
        if not os.path.exists(os.path.join(os.getcwd(), 'FLIC-
full/train')):
            os.mkdir('FLIC-full/train')

        for i, (image, joint) in enumerate(zip(image_ids, joints)):
            # crop the image using the joint coordinates
```

```
                image, joint = image_cropping(image, joint)
                # resize the cropped image to shape (224*224*3)
                image, joint = image_resize(image, joint)
                # save the image in train folder
                cv.imwrite('FLIC-full/train/train{}.jpg'.format(i), image)
                # store joints and image id/file name of the saved image in the
initialized list
                train_img_joints.append(['train{}.jpg'.format(i)] +
joint.tolist())
        # convert to a dataframe and save as a csv
            pd.DataFrame(train_img_joints).to_csv('FLIC-
full/train/train_joints.csv', index=False, header=False)
    else:
            # empty list
            test_img_joints = []
```

For the remaining part of this code snippet, please refer to the `deeppose.ipynb` file here: `https://github.com/PacktPublishing/Python-Deep-Learning-Projects/blob/master/Chapter12/deeppose.ipynb`

The preceding defined `model_data()` function accepts three parameters: `image_ids` (array of image IDs), `joints` (array of joints), and a Boolean parameter called `train`. Set the `train` parameter to `True` when transforming the training images and joints and to `False` when transforming the test images and joints.

When the `train` parameter is set to `True`, perform the following steps:

1. Initialize an empty list to store the ID of the transformed image and its joint coordinates.
2. A new directory called `train` will be created inside the `images` folder if the folder does not exist.
3. An image and its joint coordinates are first passed to the `image_cropping` function we defined previously, which will return the cropped image and joint coordinates.
4. The result of *Step 3* is passed to the `image_resize` function, which will then resize the image to the desired shape. In our case, this is 224*224*3.

5. The resized image is then written into the `train` folder via the OpenCV `imwrite()` function with a new image ID (for example, `train0.jpg`).

6. The new image ID and its joints are appended to the list initialized in *Step 1.*

7. *Step 3* through *Step 6* are repeated until all of the training images are transformed.

8. The list defined in *Step 1* now contains the new image IDs and the joint coordinates, which are then converted to a data frame and saved as a CSV file in the `train` folder.

For transforming the test data, the preceding procedure is repeated by setting the `train` parameter to `False` and feeding the test image IDs and the joints.

The train and test data frames that get generated inside the `model_data()` function are stored as a CSV file with no header and no index column. Take this into consideration when loading these files.

Defining hyperparameters for training

The following are some of the hyperparameters that have been defined that we will be using throughout our code. These are totally configurable:

```
# Number of epochs
epochs = 3

# Batchsize
batch_size = 128

# Optimizer for the model
optimizer = Adam(lr=0.0001, beta_1=0.5)

# Shape of the input image
input_shape = (224, 224, 3)

# Batch interval at which loss is to be stored
store = 40
```

Experiment with different learning rates, optimizers, batch size, as well as smoothing value to see how these factors affect the quality of your model. If you get better results, show these to the deep learning community.

Building the VGG16 model

The VGG16 model is a deep convolution neural network image classifier. The model uses a combination of Conv2D, MaxPooling2D, and Dense layers to form the final architecture, and the activation function that's used is ReLU. It accepts color images of shape 224*224*3, and is capable of predicting 1,000 classes. This means that the final Dense layer has 1,000 neurons, and it uses softmax activation to get scores for each class.

Defining the VGG16 model

In this project, we want to feed in images of shape 224*224*3 and be able to predict the joint coordinates for the body in the image. That is, we want to be able to predict 14 numerical values (7 (x,y) pairs). Therefore, we modify the final Dense layer to have 14 neurons and use ReLU activation instead of sigmoid.

Training a deep learning model such as VGG16 can take up to a week on a local machine. This is a lot of time. An alternative to this in our case is to use the weights of a trained VGG16 model through transfer learning.

We will do this with the help of the applications module in Keras that we imported in the beginning, along with the other imports.

In the following code, we will load part of the VGG16 model up to, but not including, the Flatten layer and the corresponding weights. Setting the `include_top` parameter to `False` does this for us:

 The first line of the following snippet will also download the VGG16 weights from the Keras server, so you don't have to worry about downloading the weights file from anywhere else.

```
# load the VGG16 model
model = applications.VGG16(weights = "imagenet", include_top=False,
input_shape = input_shape)

# print summary of VGG16 model
model.summary()
```

Following is the output:

```
Layer (type)                 Output Shape            Param #
=================================================================
input_1 (InputLayer)         (None, 224, 224, 3)     0

block1_conv1 (Conv2D)        (None, 224, 224, 64)    1792

block1_conv2 (Conv2D)        (None, 224, 224, 64)    36928

block1_pool (MaxPooling2D)   (None, 112, 112, 64)    0

block2_conv1 (Conv2D)        (None, 112, 112, 128)   73856

block2_conv2 (Conv2D)        (None, 112, 112, 128)   147584

block2_pool (MaxPooling2D)   (None, 56, 56, 128)     0

block3_conv1 (Conv2D)        (None, 56, 56, 256)     295168

block3_conv2 (Conv2D)        (None, 56, 56, 256)     590080

block3_conv3 (Conv2D)        (None, 56, 56, 256)     590080

block3_pool (MaxPooling2D)   (None, 28, 28, 256)     0

block4_conv1 (Conv2D)        (None, 28, 28, 512)     1180160

block4_conv2 (Conv2D)        (None, 28, 28, 512)     2359808

block4_conv3 (Conv2D)        (None, 28, 28, 512)     2359808

block4_pool (MaxPooling2D)   (None, 14, 14, 512)     0

block5_conv1 (Conv2D)        (None, 14, 14, 512)     2359808

block5_conv2 (Conv2D)        (None, 14, 14, 512)     2359808

block5_conv3 (Conv2D)        (None, 14, 14, 512)     2359808

block5_pool (MaxPooling2D)   (None, 7, 7, 512)       0
=================================================================
Total params: 14,714,688
Trainable params: 14,714,688
Non-trainable params: 0
```

Figure 12.15: Summary of the VGG16 model (up to Flatten)

From the summary, we can see that all of the layers of the VGG16 model up to, but not including, the Flatten layer have been loaded with their weights.

 To learn more about the additional functionality of the applications module of Keras, take a look at the official documentation at `https://keras.io/applications/`.

We don't want weights of any of these layers to be trained. So, in the following code, we need to set the `trainable` parameter of each layer to `False`:

```
# set layers as non trainable
for layer in model.layers:
    layer.trainable = False
```

As a next step, flatten the output of the preceding section of the model and then add three Dense layers, of which two layers have 1,024 neurons each with a dropout between them, and a final Dense layer with 14 neurons to obtain the 14 joint coordinates. We will only be training the weights of the layers defined in the following code snippet:

```
# Adding custom Layers
x = model.output
x = Flatten()(x)
x = Dense(1024, activation="relu")(x)
x = Dropout(0.5)(x)
x = Dense(1024, activation="relu")(x)

# Dense layer with 14 neurons for predicting 14 numeric values
predictions = Dense(14, activation="relu")(x)
```

Once all of the layers have been defined and configured, we will combine them by using the `Model` function in Keras, as follows:

```
# creating the final model
model_final = Model(inputs = model.input, outputs = predictions)

# print summary
model_final.summary()
```

Following is the output:

```
Layer (type)                  Output Shape              Param #
=================================================================
input_1 (InputLayer)          (None, 224, 224, 3)       0

block1_conv1 (Conv2D)         (None, 224, 224, 64)      1792

block1_conv2 (Conv2D)         (None, 224, 224, 64)      36928

block1_pool (MaxPooling2D)    (None, 112, 112, 64)      0

block2_conv1 (Conv2D)         (None, 112, 112, 128)     73856

block2_conv2 (Conv2D)         (None, 112, 112, 128)     147584

block2_pool (MaxPooling2D)    (None, 56, 56, 128)       0

block3_conv1 (Conv2D)         (None, 56, 56, 256)       295168

block3_conv2 (Conv2D)         (None, 56, 56, 256)       590080

block3_conv3 (Conv2D)         (None, 56, 56, 256)       590080

block3_pool (MaxPooling2D)    (None, 28, 28, 256)       0

block4_conv1 (Conv2D)         (None, 28, 28, 512)       1180160

block4_conv2 (Conv2D)         (None, 28, 28, 512)       2359808

block4_conv3 (Conv2D)         (None, 28, 28, 512)       2359808

block4_pool (MaxPooling2D)    (None, 14, 14, 512)       0

block5_conv1 (Conv2D)         (None, 14, 14, 512)       2359808

block5_conv2 (Conv2D)         (None, 14, 14, 512)       2359808

block5_conv3 (Conv2D)         (None, 14, 14, 512)       2359808

block5_pool (MaxPooling2D)    (None, 7, 7, 512)         0

flatten_1 (Flatten)           (None, 25088)             0

dense_1 (Dense)               (None, 1024)              25691136

dropout_1 (Dropout)           (None, 1024)              0

dense_2 (Dense)               (None, 1024)              1049600

dense_3 (Dense)               (None, 14)                14350
=================================================================
Total params: 41,469,774
Trainable params: 26,755,086
Non-trainable params: 14,714,688
```

Figure 12.16: Summary of the customized VGG16 model

From the summary, we can see that `26,755,086` parameters are trainable and that `14,714,688` parameters are untrainable, since we have set them as untrainable.

The model is then compiled with `mean_squared_error` as `loss`. The `optimizer` used here is Adam, which has a learning rate of 0.0001, as defined by the optimizer variable in the hyperparameter section:

```
# compile the model
model_final.compile(loss = "mean_squared_error", optimizer = optimizer)
```

Training loop

Now that the VGG16 model is all set to be used for training, let's load the `train_joints.csv` file from the `train` folder containing the IDs of the cropped and resized images with their joint coordinates.

Then, split the data into an 80:20 train and validation set by using the `train_test_split` module from `sklearn`. We imported it with the other imports at the beginning of this chapter. Since the validation data is small, load all of the corresponding images into memory:

 Be mindful of how many validation images you load into memory, as this may become an issue with systems that have less RAM.

```
# load the train data
train = pd.read_csv('FLIC-full/train/train_joints.csv', header = None)

# split train into train and validation
train_img_ids, val_img_ids, train_jts, val_jts =
train_test_split(train.iloc[:,0], train.iloc[:,1:], test_size=0.2,
random_state=42)

# load validation images
val_images = np.array([cv.imread('FLIC-full/train/{}'.format(x)) for x in
val_img_ids.values])

# convert validation images to dtype float
val_images = val_images.astype(float)
```

Explore the data with the pandas head, tail, and info functions. Please note that when loading the .csv file using pandas, set the header parameter to False so that pandas knows that the file has no header.

We will now define the training() function, which will train the VGG16 model on the train images. This function accepts the VGG16 model, train image IDs, train joints, validation images, and validation joints as parameters. The following steps define what is happening in the training() function:

1. The function defines empty lists by using loss_lst to store the train loss and val_loss_lst to store the validation loss. It also defines a counter count to keep track of the total number of batches.
2. It then creates a batch of train image IDs and their corresponding joints.
3. Using the batch image IDs, it loads the corresponding images into memory by using the OpenCV imread() function.
4. It then converts the loaded train images into a float, which it feeds along with the joint IDs to the train_on_batch() function of the model for the fit.
5. At every 40th batch, it evaluates the model on the validation data and stores the train and validation loss in the defined lists.
6. It then repeats *Steps* 2 through 5 for the desired number of epochs.

Following is the code:

```python
def training(model, image_ids, joints ,val_images, val_jts, batch_size =
128, epochs=3, store = 40):
    # empty train loss list
    loss_lst = []
    # empty validation loss list
    val_loss_lst = []
    # counter
    count = 0
    count_lst = []
    # create shuffled batches
    batches = np.arange(len(image_ids)//batch_size)
    data_idx = np.arange(len(image_ids))
    random.shuffle(data_idx)
    print('......Training......')
    for epoch in range(epochs):
        for batch in (batches):
            # batch of training image ids
            imgs = image_ids[data_idx[batch*batch_size :
(batch+1)*batch_size:]]
            # corresponding joints for the above images
```

```
        jts = joints[data_idx[batch*batch_size :
(batch+1)*batch_size:]]
        # load the training image batch
        batch_imgs = np.array([cv.imread('FLIC-
full/train/{}'.format(x)) for x in imgs])

        # fit model on the batch
        loss = model.train_on_batch(batch_imgs.astype(float), jts)
        if batch%store==0:
```

 For the remaining part of this code snippet, please refer to the `deeppose.ipynb` file here: https://github.com/PacktPublishing/Python-Deep-Learning-Projects/blob/master/Chapter12/deeppose.ipynb

The output is as follows:

```
......Training......
Epoch:1, End of batch:1, loss:15108.95, val_loss:13433.66
Epoch:1, End of batch:2, loss:13351.67
Epoch:1, End of batch:3, loss:10308.54
Epoch:1, End of batch:4, loss:6844.49
Epoch:1, End of batch:5, loss:4493.11
Epoch:1, End of batch:6, loss:2447.66
Epoch:1, End of batch:7, loss:2385.18
Epoch:1, End of batch:8, loss:2414.53
Epoch:1, End of batch:9, loss:2691.82
Epoch:1, End of batch:10, loss:2248.67
Epoch:1, End of batch:11, loss:2093.94
Epoch:1, End of batch:12, loss:2028.02
Epoch:1, End of batch:13, loss:1771.39
Epoch:1, End of batch:14, loss:1956.56
Epoch:1, End of batch:15, loss:1816.25
```

The following is the output at the end of the code's execution:

```
Epoch:3, End of batch:101, loss:439.03
Epoch:3, End of batch:102, loss:461.61
Epoch:3, End of batch:103, loss:410.48
Epoch:3, End of batch:104, loss:472.89
Epoch:3, End of batch:105, loss:426.41
Epoch:3, End of batch:106, loss:460.95
Epoch:3, End of batch:107, loss:482.03
Epoch:3, End of batch:108, loss:467.63
Epoch:3, End of batch:108, VAL LOSS:503.85
```

Figure 12.17: Loss output when training the model

If you are using a small GPU for training, reduce the batch size to avoid GPU memory issues. Also, remember that a smaller batch size may or may not result in the same fit that this chapter indicates.

Plot training and validation loss

With `loss_lst` and `val_loss_lst` containing the train and validation MSE loss at intervals of 40 batches, let's plot this and see how the learning has progressed:

```
plt.style.use('ggplot')
plt.figure(figsize=(10, 6))
plt.plot(count_lst, loss_lst, marker='D', label = 'training_loss')
plt.plot(count_lst, val_loss_lst, marker='o', label = 'validation_loss')
plt.ylabel('Mean Squared Error')
plt.title('Plot of MSE over time')
plt.legend(loc = 'upper right')
plt.show()
```

Following is the output:

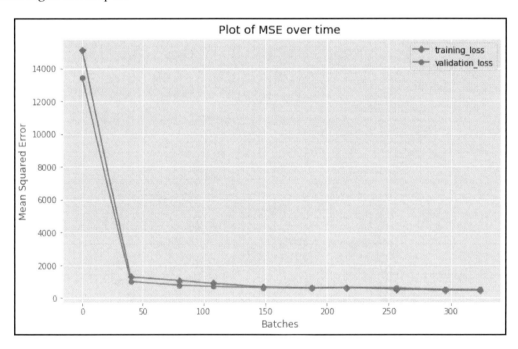

Figure 12.18: Plot of train and validation loss

A smoother train validation loss plot can be obtained by reducing the store hyperparameter. A small store value will result in a longer training time.

Predictions

This is what we have been waiting for...

Making test predictions!

We will define a function that takes the model as input and tests the model on the test data we have preprocessed and saved in the test folder. Along with predictions, it will also save test images with the true and predicted joints plotted on it by using the plot_limb() and the plot_joints() functions we defined in the preceding section:

```
def test(model, nrows=200, batch_size=128):
    # load the train data
    test = pd.read_csv('FLIC-full/test/test_joints.csv', header = None,
nrows=nrows)
    test_img_ids = test.iloc[:,0].values
    # load validation images
    test_images = np.array([cv.imread('FLIC-full/test/{}'.format(x)) for x
in test_img_ids])

    # convert validation images to dtype float
    test_images = test_images.astype(float)
    # joints
    test_joints = test.iloc[:,1:].values
    # evaluate
    test_loss = model.evaluate(test_images, test_joints, verbose = 0,
batch_size=batch_size)
    # predict
    predictions = model.predict(test_images, verbose = 0,
batch_size=batch_size)

    # folder to save the results
    if not os.path.exists(os.path.join(os.getcwd(), 'FLIC-
full/test_plot')):
        os.mkdir('FLIC-full/test_plot')
    for i, (ids, image, joint, pred) in enumerate(zip(test_img_ids,
test_images, test_joints, predictions)):
        joints = joint.tolist()
        joints = list(zip(joints[0::2], joints[1::2]))
        # plot original joints
```

```
        image = plot_joints(image.astype(np.uint8), joints,
groundtruth=True, text_scale=0.5)
        pred = pred.astype(np.uint8).tolist()
        pred = list(zip(pred[0::2], pred[1::2]))
        # plot predicted joints
        image = plot_joints(image.astype(np.uint8), pred,
groundtruth=False, text_scale=0.5)
        # save resulting images with the same id
        plt.imsave('FLIC-full/test_plot/'+ids, image)
    return test_loss

# test and save results
test_loss = test(m, batch_size)

# print test loss
print('Test Loss:', test_loss)
```

Following is the output:

```
Test Loss: 454.8094494628906
```

Figure 12.19: Test loss

On a test set with 200 images, the test MSE loss is 454.80, which is very close to the validation MSE loss of 503.85, indicating that the model is not overfitting on the train data.

 Train the model for a few more epochs if possible, and check if a better fit is possible. Be mindful of how many test images you want to load into memory for evaluation since it might become a problem on machines with RAM limitations.

Now let's plot the images we saved during testing to get a measure of how the true joints compare to the predicted joints:

```
image_list = glob.glob('FLIC-full/test_plot/*.jpg')[8:16]

plt.figure(figsize=(16,8))
for i in range(8):
    plt.subplot(2,4,(i+1))
    img = cv.imread(image_list[i])
    plt.imshow(img, aspect='auto')
    plt.axis('off')
    plt.title('Green-True/Red-Predicted Joints')

plt.tight_layout()
plt.show()
```

Following is the output:

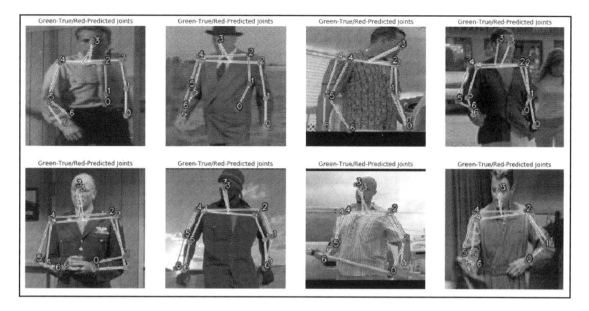

Figure 12.20: Test images with true and predicted joints plotted on top

From the preceding picture, we can see that the model is doing a really good job of predicting the seven joints on unseen images.

Scripts in modular form

The entire script can be split into four modules named `train.py`, `test.py`, `plotting.py`, and `crop_resize_transform.py`. You should be able to find these scripts in the `Chapter12` folder. Follow the instructions under the *Code implementation* section of this chapter to run the scripts. Set `Chapter12` as the project folder in your favorite source code editor and just run the `train.py` file.

The `train.py` Python file will import functions from all of the other modules in places where they are needed for execution.

Now let's walk through the contents of each file.

Module 1 – crop_resize_transform.py

This Python file contains the `image_cropping()`, `image_resize()`, and `model_data()` functions, as shown:

```python
"""This module contains functions to crop and resize images."""

import os
import cv2 as cv
import numpy as np
import pandas as pd


def image_cropping(image_id, joints, crop_pad_inf=1.4, crop_pad_sup=1.6,
                   shift=5, min_dim=100):
    """Crop Function."""
    # # image cropping
    # load the image
    image = cv.imread('FLIC-full/images/%s' % (image_id))
    # convert joint list to array
    joints = np.asarray([int(float(p)) for p in joints])
    # reshape joints to shape (7*2)
    joints = joints.reshape((len(joints) // 2, 2))
    # transform joints to list of (x,y) tuples
    posi_joints = [(j[0], j[1]) for j in joints if j[0] > 0 and j[1] > 0]
    # obtain the bounding rectangle using opencv boundingRect
    x_loc, y_loc, width, height =
cv.boundingRect(np.asarray([posi_joints]))
    if width < min_dim:
        width = min_dim
    if height < min_dim:
        height = min_dim

    # # bounding rect extending
    inf, sup = crop_pad_inf, crop_pad_sup
    r = sup - inf
    # define width padding
    pad_w_r = np.random.rand() * r + inf # inf~sup
    # define height padding
    pad_h_r = np.random.rand() * r + inf # inf~sup
    # adjust x, y, w and h by the defined padding
    x_loc -= (width * pad_w_r - width) / 2
    y_loc -= (height * pad_h_r - height) / 2
    width *= pad_w_r
    height *= pad_h_r

    # # shifting
    x_loc += np.random.rand() * shift * 2 - shift
```

```
    y_loc += np.random.rand() * shift * 2 - shift

    # # clipping
    x_loc, y_loc, width, height = [int(z) for z in [x_loc, y_loc,
                                                    width, height]]
    x_loc = np.clip(x_loc, 0, image.shape[1] - 1)
    y_loc = np.clip(y_loc, 0, image.shape[0] - 1)
    width = np.clip(width, 1, image.shape[1] - (x_loc + 1))
    height = np.clip(height, 1, image.shape[0] - (y_loc + 1))
    image = image[y_loc: y_loc + height, x_loc: x_loc + width]

    # # joint shifting
    # adjust joint coordinates onto the padded image
    joints = np.asarray([(j[0] - x_loc, j[1] - y_loc) for j in joints])
    joints = joints.flatten()

    return image, joints


def image_resize(image, joints, new_size=224):
    """Resize Function."""
    orig_h, orig_w = image.shape[:2]
    joints[0::2] = joints[0::2] / float(orig_w) * new_size
    joints[1::2] = joints[1::2] / float(orig_h) * new_size
    image = cv.resize(image, (new_size, new_size),
                      interpolation=cv.INTER_NEAREST)
    return image, joints


def model_data(image_ids, joints, train=True):
    """Function to generate train and test data."""
    if train:
        # empty list
        train_img_joints = []
        # create train directory inside FLIC-full
        if not os.path.exists(os.path.join(os.getcwd(), 'FLIC-
full/train')):
            os.mkdir('FLIC-full/train')

        for i, (image, joint) in enumerate(zip(image_ids, joints)):
            # crop the image using the joint coordinates
            image, joint = image_cropping(image, joint)
            # resize the cropped image to shape (224*224*3)
            image, joint = image_resize(image, joint)
            # save the image in train folder
            cv.imwrite('FLIC-full/train/train{}.jpg'.format(i), image)
            # store joints and image id/file name of the saved image in
            # the initialized list
```

```
                    train_img_joints.append(['train{}.jpg'.format(i)] +
joint.tolist())

            # convert to a dataframe and save as a csv
            pd.DataFrame(train_img_joints
                        ).to_csv('FLIC-full/train/train_joints.csv',
                                index=False, header=False)
        else:
            # empty list
            test_img_joints = []
            # create test directory inside FLIC-full
            if not os.path.exists(os.path.join(os.getcwd(), 'FLIC-full/test')):
                os.mkdir('FLIC-full/test')

            for i, (image, joint) in enumerate(zip(image_ids, joints)):
                # crop the image using the joint coordinates
                image, joint = image_cropping(image, joint)
                # resize the cropped image to shape (224*224*3)
                image, joint = image_resize(image, joint)
                # save the image in test folder
                cv.imwrite('FLIC-full/test/test{}.jpg'.format(i), image)
                # store joints and image id/file name of the saved image
                # in the initialized list
                test_img_joints.append(['test{}.jpg'.format(i)] +
joint.tolist())

            # convert to a dataframe and save as a csv
            pd.DataFrame(test_img_joints).to_csv('FLIC-
full/test/test_joints.csv',
                                            index=False, header=False)
```

Module 2 – plotting.py

This Python file contains two functions, namely `plot_limb()` and `plot_joints()`, as shown:

```
"""This module contains functions to plot the joints and the limbs."""
import cv2 as cv
import numpy as np


def plot_limb(img, joints, i, j, color):
    """Limb plot function."""
    cv.line(img, joints[i], joints[j], (255, 255, 255), thickness=2,
            lineType=16)
    cv.line(img, joints[i], joints[j], color, thickness=1, lineType=16)
    return img
```

```python
def plot_joints(img, joints, groundtruth=True, text_scale=0.5):
    """Joint and Limb plot function."""
    h, w, c = img.shape
    if groundtruth:
        # left hand to left elbow
        img = plot_limb(img, joints, 0, 1, (0, 255, 0))

        # left elbow to left shoulder
        img = plot_limb(img, joints, 1, 2, (0, 255, 0))

        # left shoulder to right shoulder
        img = plot_limb(img, joints, 2, 4, (0, 255, 0))

        # right shoulder to right elbow
        img = plot_limb(img, joints, 4, 5, (0, 255, 0))

        # right elbow to right hand
        img = plot_limb(img, joints, 5, 6, (0, 255, 0))

        # neck coordinate
        neck = tuple((np.array(joints[2]) + np.array(joints[4])) // 2)
        joints.append(neck)
        # neck to head
        img = plot_limb(img, joints, 3, 7, (0, 255, 0))
        joints.pop()

    # joints
    for j, joint in enumerate(joints):
        # plot joints
        cv.circle(img, joint, 5, (0, 255, 0), -1)
        # plot joint number black
        cv.putText(img, '%d' % j, joint, cv.FONT_HERSHEY_SIMPLEX, text_scale,
                   (0, 0, 0), thickness=2, lineType=16)
        # plot joint number white
        cv.putText(img, '%d' % j, joint, cv.FONT_HERSHEY_SIMPLEX, text_scale,
                   (255, 255, 255), thickness=1, lineType=16)

    else:
        # left hand to left elbow
        img = plot_limb(img, joints, 0, 1, (0, 0, 255))

        # left elbow to left shoulder
        img = plot_limb(img, joints, 1, 2, (0, 0, 255))

        # left shoulder to right shoulder
        img = plot_limb(img, joints, 2, 4, (0, 0, 255))
```

```
        # right shoulder to right elbow
        img = plot_limb(img, joints, 4, 5, (0, 0, 255))

        # right elbow to right hand
        img = plot_limb(img, joints, 5, 6, (0, 0, 255))

        # neck coordinate
        neck = tuple((np.array(joints[2]) + np.array(joints[4])) // 2)
        joints.append(neck)

        # neck to head
        img = plot_limb(img, joints, 3, 7, (0, 0, 255))
        joints.pop()

    # joints
    for j, joint in enumerate(joints):
        # plot joints
        cv.circle(img, joint, 5, (0, 0, 255), -1)
        # plot joint number black
        cv.putText(img, '%d' % j, joint, cv.FONT_HERSHEY_SIMPLEX,
text_scale,
                   (0, 0, 0), thickness=3, lineType=16)
        # plot joint number white
        cv.putText(img, '%d' % j, joint, cv.FONT_HERSHEY_SIMPLEX,
text_scale,
                   (255, 255, 255), thickness=1, lineType=16)

    return img
```

Module 3 – test.py

This module contains the `test()` function that will be called in the `train_dqn.py` script so that it can test the performance of the trained model, as shown:

```
"""This module contains the function to test the vgg16 model
performance."""
from plotting import *

import os
import pandas as pd
import numpy as np
import cv2 as cv
import matplotlib.pyplot as plt


def test(model, nrows=200, batch_size=128):
    """Test trained vgg16."""
```

```
# load the train data
test = pd.read_csv('FLIC-full/test/test_joints.csv', header=None,
                   nrows=nrows)
test_img_ids = test.iloc[:, 0].values

# load validation images
test_images = np.array(
        [cv.imread('FLIC-full/test/{}'.format(x)) for x in
test_img_ids])

# convert validation images to dtype float
test_images = test_images.astype(float)

# joints
test_joints = test.iloc[:, 1:].values

# evaluate
test_loss = model.evaluate(test_images, test_joints,
                           verbose=0, batch_size=batch_size)

# predict
predictions = model.predict(test_images, verbose=0,
batch_size=batch_size)

# folder to save the results
if not os.path.exists(os.path.join(os.getcwd(), 'FLIC-
full/test_plot')):
    os.mkdir('FLIC-full/test_plot')

for i, (ids, image, joint, pred) in enumerate(zip(test_img_ids,
                                                  test_images,
                                                  test_joints,
                                                  predictions)):
    joints = joint.tolist()
    joints = list(zip(joints[0::2], joints[1::2]))

    # plot original joints
    image = plot_joints(image.astype(np.uint8), joints,
                        groundtruth=True, text_scale=0.5)

    pred = pred.astype(np.uint8).tolist()
    pred = list(zip(pred[0::2], pred[1::2]))

    # plot predicted joints
    image = plot_joints(image.astype(np.uint8), pred,
                        groundtruth=False, text_scale=0.5)

    # save resulting images with the same id
```

```
        plt.imsave('FLIC-full/test_plot/'+ids, image)
    return test_loss
```

Module 4 – train.py

In this module, we have the `joint_coordinates()` and `training()` functions, as well as the calls to train and test the VGG16 model:

```
"""This module imports other modules to train the vgg16 model."""
from __future__ import print_function

from crop_resize_transform import model_data
from test import test

import matplotlib.pyplot as plt

import random
from scipy.io import loadmat
import numpy as np
import pandas as pd
import cv2 as cv
import glob

from sklearn.model_selection import train_test_split

from keras.models import Model
from keras.optimizers import Adam
from keras.layers import Flatten, Dense, Dropout
from keras import backend as K
from keras import applications
K.clear_session()


# set seed for reproducibility
seed_val = 9000
np.random.seed(seed_val)
random.seed(seed_val)

# load the examples file
examples = loadmat('FLIC-full/examples.mat')
# reshape the examples array
examples = examples['examples'].reshape(-1,)

# each coordinate corresponds to the the below listed body joints/locations
# in the same order
joint_labels = ['lsho', 'lelb', 'lwri', 'rsho', 'relb', 'rwri', 'lhip',
                'lkne', 'lank', 'rhip', 'rkne', 'rank', 'leye', 'reye',
```

```
                        'lear', 'rear', 'nose', 'msho', 'mhip', 'mear', 'mtorso',
                        'mluarm', 'mruarm', 'mllarm', 'mrlarm', 'mluleg', 'mruleg',
                        'mllleg', 'mrlleg']

# print list of known joints
known_joints = [x for i, x in enumerate(joint_labels) if i in np.r_[0:7, 9,
                                                                      12:14,
16]]
target_joints = ['lsho', 'lelb', 'lwri', 'rsho', 'relb',
                 'rwri', 'leye', 'reye', 'nose']
# indices of the needed joints in the coordinates array
joints_loc_id = np.r_[0:6, 12:14, 16]


def joint_coordinates(joint):
    """Store necessary coordinates to a list."""
    joint_coor = []
    # Take mean of the leye, reye, nose to obtain coordinates for the head
    joint['head'] = (joint['leye']+joint['reye']+joint['nose'])/3
    joint_coor.extend(joint['lwri'].tolist())
    joint_coor.extend(joint['lelb'].tolist())
    joint_coor.extend(joint['lsho'].tolist())
    joint_coor.extend(joint['head'].tolist())
    joint_coor.extend(joint['rsho'].tolist())
    joint_coor.extend(joint['relb'].tolist())
    joint_coor.extend(joint['rwri'].tolist())
    return joint_coor


# load the indices matlab file
train_indices = loadmat('FLIC-full/tr_plus_indices.mat')
# reshape the training_indices array
train_indices = train_indices['tr_plus_indices'].reshape(-1,)

# empty list to store train image ids
train_ids = []
# empty list to store train joints
train_jts = []
# empty list to store test image ids
test_ids = []
# empty list to store test joints
test_jts = []

for i, example in enumerate(examples):
    # image id
    file_name = example[3][0]
    # joint coordinates
    joint = example[2].T
```

```
    # dictionary that goes into the joint_coordinates function
    joints = dict(zip(target_joints,
                      [x for k, x in enumerate(joint) if k in
joints_loc_id]))
    # obtain joints for the task
    joints = joint_coordinates(joints)
    # use train indices list to decide if an image is to be used for
training
    # or testing
    if i in train_indices:
        train_ids.append(file_name)
        train_jts.append(joints)
    else:
        test_ids.append(file_name)
        test_jts.append(joints)

# Concatenate image ids dataframe and the joints dataframe and save it as a
csv
train_df = pd.concat([pd.DataFrame(train_ids), pd.DataFrame(train_jts)],
                     axis=1)
test_df = pd.concat([pd.DataFrame(test_ids), pd.DataFrame(test_jts)],
axis=1)
train_df.to_csv('FLIC-full/train_joints.csv', index=False, header=False)
test_df.to_csv('FLIC-full/test_joints.csv', index=False, header=False)

# load train_joints.csv
train_data = pd.read_csv('FLIC-full/train_joints.csv', header=None)
# load test_joints.csv
test_data = pd.read_csv('FLIC-full/test_joints.csv', header=None)

# train image ids
train_image_ids = train_data[0].values
# train joints
train_joints = train_data.iloc[:, 1:].values
# test image ids
test_image_ids = test_data[0].values
# test joints
test_joints = test_data.iloc[:, 1:].values

model_data(train_image_ids, train_joints, train=True)
model_data(test_image_ids, test_joints, train=False)

# Number of epochs
epochs = 3
# Batchsize
batch_size = 128
# Optimizer for the model
optimizer = Adam(lr=0.0001, beta_1=0.5)
```

```
# Shape of the input image
input_shape = (224, 224, 3)
# Batch interval at which loss is to be stores
store = 40

# load the vgg16 model
model = applications.VGG16(weights="imagenet", include_top=False,
                           input_shape=input_shape)

# set layers as non trainable
for layer in model.layers:
    layer.trainable = False

# Adding custom Layers
x = model.output
x = Flatten()(x)
x = Dense(1024, activation="relu")(x)
x = Dropout(0.5)(x)
x = Dense(1024, activation="relu")(x)

# Dense layer with 14 neurons for predicting 14 numeric values
predictions = Dense(14, activation="relu")(x)
# creating the final model
model_final = Model(inputs=model.input, outputs=predictions)
# compile the model
model_final.compile(loss="mean_squared_error", optimizer=optimizer)
# load the train data
train = pd.read_csv('FLIC-full/train/train_joints.csv', header=None)
# split train into train and validation
train_img_ids, val_img_ids, train_jts, val_jts = train_test_split(
        train.iloc[:, 0], train.iloc[:, 1:], test_size=0.2,
random_state=42)

# load validation images
val_images = np.array(
    [cv.imread('FLIC-full/train/{}'.format(w)) for w in
val_img_ids.values])

# convert validation images to dtype float
val_images = val_images.astype(float)


def training(model, image_ids, joints, val_images, val_jts,
            batch_size=128, epochs=2):
    """Train vgg16."""
    # empty train loss and validation loss list
    loss_lst = []
    val_loss_lst = []
```

```
        count = 0 # counter
        count_lst = []

        # create shuffled batches
        batches = np.arange(len(image_ids)//batch_size)
        data_idx = np.arange(len(image_ids))
        random.shuffle(data_idx)
        print('......Training......')
        for epoch in range(epochs):
            for batch in (batches):
                # batch of training image ids
                imgs =
image_ids[data_idx[batch*batch_size:(batch+1)*batch_size:]]
                # corresponding joints for the above images
                jts = joints[data_idx[batch*batch_size:(batch+1)*batch_size:]]
                # load the training image batch
                batch_imgs = np.array(
                        [cv.imread('FLIC-full/train/{}'.format(x)) for x in
imgs])
                # fit model on the batch
                loss = model.train_on_batch(batch_imgs.astype(float), jts)
                if batch % 40 == 0:
                    # evaluate model on validation set
                    val_loss = model.evaluate(val_images, val_jts, verbose=0,
                                            batch_size=batch_size)
                    # store train and val loss
                    loss_lst.append(loss)
                    val_loss_lst.append(val_loss)
                    print('Epoch:{}, End of batch:{},
loss:{:.2f},val_loss:{:.2f}\
                    '.format(epoch+1, batch+1, loss, val_loss))

                    count_lst.append(count)
                else:
                    print('Epoch:{}, End of batch:{}, loss:{:.2f}\
                    '.format(epoch+1, batch+1, loss))
                count += 1
        count_lst.append(count)
        loss_lst.append(loss)
        val_loss = model.evaluate(val_images, val_jts, verbose=0,
                            batch_size=batch_size)
        val_loss_lst.append(val_loss)
        print('Epoch:{}, End of batch:{}, VAL_LOSS:{:.2f}\
        '.format(epoch+1, batch+1, val_loss))
        return model, loss_lst, val_loss_lst, count_lst


m, loss_lst, val_loss_lst, count_lst = training(model_final,
```

```
                                          train_img_ids.values,
                                          train_jts.values,
                                          val_images,
                                          val_jts.values,
                                          epochs=epochs,
                                          batch_size=batch_size)

# plot the learning
plt.style.use('ggplot')
plt.figure(figsize=(10, 6))
plt.plot(count_lst, loss_lst, marker='D', label='training_loss')
plt.plot(count_lst, val_loss_lst, marker='o', label='validation_loss')
plt.xlabel('Batches')
plt.ylabel('Mean Squared Error')
plt.title('Plot of MSE over time')
plt.legend(loc='upper right')
plt.show()

# test and save results
test_loss = test(m)

# print test_loss
print('Test Loss:', test_loss)

image_list = glob.glob('FLIC-full/test_plot/*.jpg')[8:16]

plt.figure(figsize=(16, 8))
for i in range(8):
    plt.subplot(2, 4, (i+1))
    img = cv.imread(image_list[i])
    plt.imshow(img, aspect='auto')
    plt.axis('off')
    plt.title('Green-True/Red-Predicted Joints')

plt.tight_layout()
plt.show()
```

Conclusion

This project was all about building a **convolutional neural network** (**CNN**) classifier to solve the problem of estimating 3D human poses using frames captured from movies. Our hypothetical use case was to enable visual effects specialists to easily estimate the pose of actors (from their shoulders, necks, and heads from the frames in a video. Our task was to build the intelligence for this application.

The modified VGG16 architecture we built using transfer learning has a test mean squared error loss of 454.81 squared units over 200 test images for each of the 14 coordinates (that is, the $7(x, y)$ pairs). We can also say that the test root mean squared error over 200 test images for each of the 14 coordinates is 21.326 units. What does this mean?

The **root mean squared error** (**RMSE**), in this case, is a measure of how far off the predicted joint coordinates/joint pixel location are from the actual joint coordinate/joint pixel location.

An RMSE loss of 21.32 units is equivalent to having each predicted coordinate off by 21.32 pixels within an image of shape 224*224*3. The test results plotted in *Figure 13.20* represent this measure.

Each coordinate being off by 21.32 pixels is good at a general level, but we want to build a product that will be used in movies for which the margin for error is much less, and being off by 21 pixels is not acceptable.

To improve the model, you can do the following:

- Try using a lower learning rate for a larger number of epochs
- Try using a different loss function (for example, **mean absolute error** (**MAE**))
- Try using an even deeper model, such as RESNET50 or VGG19
- Try centering and scaling the data
- Get more data

These are some of the additional steps you should take if you are interested in becoming an expert in this specific area once you are done with this chapter.

Summary

In this chapter, we successfully built a deep convolution neural network/VGG16 model in Keras on FLIC images. We got hands-on experience in preparing these images for modeling. We successfully implemented transfer learning, and understood that doing so will save us a lot of time. We defined some key hyperparameters as well in some places, and reasoned about why we used what we used. Finally, we tested the modified VGG16 model performance on unseen data and determined that we succeeded in achieving our goals.

13
Image Translation Using GANs for Style Transfer

Welcome to the chapter on **Generative Adversarial Networks** (**GANs**). In this chapter, we will be building a neural network that fills in the missing part of a handwritten digit. Previously, we have built a digit classifier for the restaurant chain. But they have also noticed that sometimes, when customers write in their phone number, small sections/regions of the digits are missing. This may be a combination of the customer not having a smooth flow when writing on the iPad application, as well as issues with the iPad application not processing the complete user gesture on the screen. This makes it hard for the handwritten digit classifier to predict the correct digit corresponding to the handwritten number. Now, they want us to reconstruct (generate back) the missing parts of the handwritten numbers so that the classifier receives clear handwritten numbers for conversion into digits. With this, the classifier will be able to do a much more accurate job of classifying handwritten digits and the notice gets sent to the right hungry customer!

We will mostly focus on the generation/reconstruction of the missing sections of a digit and we will do this with the help of neural inpainting with GANs; see the following flowchart:

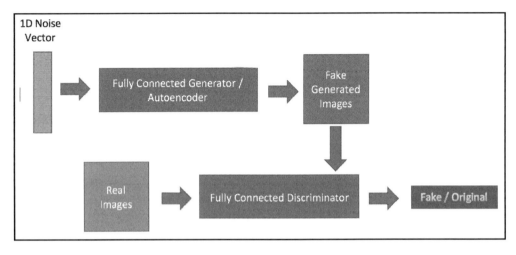

Figure 13.1: GAN flowchart

What we'll learn in this chapter is the following:

- What is a GAN
- What is a generator and a discriminator
- Coding the model and defining hyperparameters
- Building and understanding the training loop
- Testing the model
- Extending the model to new datasets

In this chapter, you will implement the following:

- Build an MNIST digit classifier
- Simulate a dataset of handwritten digits with sections of the handwritten numbers missing
- Use the MNIST classifier to predict on noised/masked MNIST digits dataset (simulated dataset)
- Implement GAN to generate back the missing regions of the digit
- Use the MNIST classifier to predict on the generated digits from GAN
- Compare performance between masked data and generated data

It would be better if you implement the code snippets as you go along in this chapter, either in a Jupyter Notebook or any source code editor. This will make it easier for you to follow along, as well as understand what each part of the code does.

All of the Python files and Jupyter Notebook files for this chapter can be found here: https://github.com/PacktPublishing/Python-Deep-Learning-Projects/tree/master/Chapter13.

Let's code the implementation!

In this exercise, we will be using the Keras deep learning library, which is a high-level neural network API, capable of running on top of Tensorflow, Theano, or Cognitive Toolkit (CNTK).

 Know the code! We will not spend time on understanding how Keras works but, if you are interested, refer to this easy-to-understand Keras official documentation at https://keras.io/.

Importing all of the dependencies

We will be using numpy, matplotlib, keras, tensorflow, and the tqdm package in this exercise. Here, TensorFlow is used as the backend for Keras. You can install these packages with pip. For the MNIST data, we will be using the dataset available in the keras module with a simple import:

```
import numpy as np
import random
import matplotlib.pyplot as plt
%matplotlib inline

from tqdm import tqdm

from keras.layers import Input, Conv2D
from keras.layers import AveragePooling2D, BatchNormalization
from keras.layers import UpSampling2D, Flatten, Activation
from keras.models import Model, Sequential
from keras.layers.core import Dense, Dropout
from keras.layers.advanced_activations import LeakyReLU
from keras.optimizers import Adam
from keras import backend as k
```

```
from keras.datasets import mnist
```

It is important that you set `seed` for reproducibility:

```
# set seed for reproducibility
seed_val = 9000
np.random.seed(seed_val)
random.seed(seed_val)
```

Exploring the data

We will load the MNIST data into our session from the `keras` module with
`mnist.load_data()`. After doing so, we will print the shape and the size of the dataset, as
well as the number of classes and unique labels in the dataset:

```
(X_train, y_train), (X_test, y_test) = mnist.load_data()

print('Size of the training_set: ', X_train.shape)
print('Size of the test_set: ', X_test.shape)
print('Shape of each image: ', X_train[0].shape)
print('Total number of classes: ', len(np.unique(y_train)))
print('Unique class labels: ', np.unique(y_train))
```

We have a dataset with 10 different classes and 60,000 images, with each image having a
shape of 28*28 and each class having 6,000 images.

Let's plot and see what the handwritten images look like:

```
# Plot of 9 random images
for i in range(0, 9):
    plt.subplot(331+i) # plot of 3 rows and 3 columns
    plt.axis('off') # turn off axis
    plt.imshow(X_train[i], cmap='gray') # gray scale
```

The output is as follows:

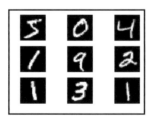

Figure 13.2: Plot of nine MNIST digits from the training set

Let's plot a handwritten digit from each class:

```
# plotting image from each class
fig=plt.figure(figsize=(8, 4))
columns = 5
rows = 2
for i in range(0, rows*columns):
    fig.add_subplot(rows, columns, i+1)
    plt.title(str(i)) # label
    plt.axis('off') # turn off axis
    plt.imshow(X_train[np.where(y_train==i)][0], cmap='gray') # gray scale
plt.show()
```

The output is as follows:

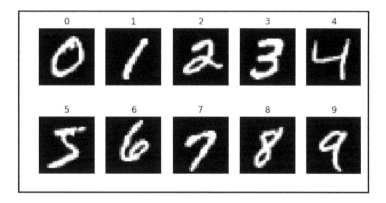

Figure 13.3: Plot of an MNIST digit from each class

Look at the maximum and the minimum pixel value in the dataset:

```
print('Maximum pixel value in the training_set: ', np.max(X_train))
print('Minimum pixel value in the training_set: ', np.min(X_train))
```

The output is as follows:

```
('Maximum pixel value in the training_set: ', 255)
('Minimum pixel value in the training_set: ', 0)
```

Figure 13.5: Plot of nine noised/masked MNIST digits

We see that the maximum pixel value in the dataset is 255 and the minimum is 0.

Preparing the data

Type conversion, centering, scaling, and reshaping are some of the pre-processing we will implement in this chapter.

Type conversion, centering, and scaling

Set the type to `np.float32`.

Important: One of the main reasons for doing this is that the weights will all be of the `float` type, and multiplication between floating numbers is much faster than between an integer and a float. So it's better to convert the input into the `float` type.

For centering, we subtract the dataset by 127.5. The values in the dataset will now range between -127.5 to 127.5.

For scaling, we divide the centered dataset by half of the maximum pixel value in the dataset, that is, *255/2*. This will result in a dataset with values ranging between -1 and 1:

```
# Converting integer values to float types
X_train = X_train.astype(np.float32)
X_test = X_test.astype(np.float32)

# Scaling and centering
X_train = (X_train - 127.5) / 127.5
X_test = (X_test - 127.5)/ 127.5
print('Maximum pixel value in the training_set after Centering and Scaling:
', np.max(X_train))
print('Minimum pixel value in the training_set after Centering and Scaling:
', np.min(X_train))
```

Let's define a function to rescale the pixel values of the scaled image to range between 0 and 255:

```
# Rescale the pixel values (0 and 255)
def upscale(image):
    return (image*127.5 + 127.5).astype(np.uint8)

# Lets see if this works
z = upscale(X_train[0])
print('Maximum pixel value after upscaling scaled image: ',np.max(z))
print('Maximum pixel value after upscaling scaled image: ',np.min(z))
```

Matplotlib tip: Rescaling needs to be done so that you avoid errors with Matplotlib if you were to use the scaled image as is without upscaling.

A plot of 9 centered and scaled images after upscaling:

```
for i in range(0, 9):
    plt.subplot(331+i) # plot of 3 rows and 3 columns
    plt.axis('off') # turn off axis
    plt.imshow(upscale(X_train[i]), cmap='gray') # gray scale
```

The output is as follows:

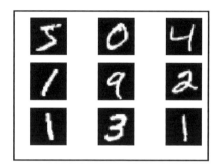

Figure 13.4: Plot of nine centered and scaled MNIST digits after upscaling

Masking/inserting noise

For the needs of this project, we need to simulate a dataset of incomplete digits. So, let's write a function to mask small regions in the original image to form the noised dataset.

The idea is to mask an 8*8 region of the image with the top-left corner of the mask falling between the 9th and 13th pixel (between index 8 and 12) along both the x and y axis of the image. This is to make sure that we are always masking around the center part of the image:

```
def noising(image):
    array = np.array(image)
    i = random.choice(range(8,12)) # x coordinate for the top left corner
of the mask
    j = random.choice(range(8,12)) # y coordinate for the top left corner
of the mask
    array[i:i+8, j:j+8]=-1.0 # setting the pixels in the masked region to
-1
```

```
        return array

noised_train_data = np.array([*map(noising, X_train)])
noised_test_data = np.array([*map(noising, X_test)])
print('Noised train data Shape/Dimension : ', noised_train_data.shape)
print('Noised test data Shape/Dimension : ', noised_train_data.shape)
```

 The bigger the size of the mask, the harder it will be for the MNIST classifier to predict the right digit.

 Feel free to experiment with the size of the masked region, that is, try smaller/bigger, as well as the location of the mask on the image.

A plot of 9 scaled noised images after upscaling:

```
# Plot of 9 scaled noised images after upscaling
for i in range(0, 9):
    plt.subplot(331+i) # plot of 3 rows and 3 columns
    plt.axis('off') # turn off axis
    plt.imshow(upscale(noised_train_data[i]), cmap='gray') # gray scale
```

The output is as follows:

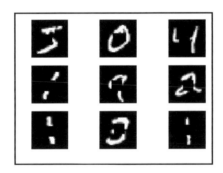

Figure 13.5: Plot of nine noised/masked MNIST digits

Reshaping

Reshape the original dataset and the noised dataset to a shape of 60000*28*28*1. This is important since the 2D convolutions expect to receive images of a shape of 28*28*1:

```
# Reshaping the training data
X_train = X_train.reshape(X_train.shape[0], X_train.shape[1],
X_train.shape[2], 1)
print('Size/Shape of the original training set: ', X_train.shape)

# Reshaping the noised training data
noised_train_data = noised_train_data.reshape(noised_train_data.shape[0],
                                              noised_train_data.shape[1],
                                              noised_train_data.shape[2],
1)
print('Size/Shape of the noised training set: ', noised_train_data.shape)

# Reshaping the testing data
X_test = X_test.reshape(X_test.shape[0], X_test.shape[1], X_test.shape[2],
1)
print('Size/Shape of the original test set: ', X_test.shape)

# Reshaping the noised testing data
noised_test_data = noised_test_data.reshape(noised_test_data.shape[0],
                                            noised_test_data.shape[1],
                                            noised_test_data.shape[2], 1)
print('Size/Shape of the noised test set: ', noised_test_data.shape)
```

> If you are doing multiple training runs on the GPU, it is always a good idea to clear space on the GPU after each run so that your next run executes efficiently without errors related to **resource exhaustion**, which is pretty common with GPUs. This can be done with the following code:
> ```
> from keras import backend as k
> k.clear_session()
> ```

MNIST classifier

To start off with modeling, let's build a simple **convolutional neural network (CNN)** digit classifier.

The first layer is a convolution layer that has 32 filters of a shape of 3*3, with `relu` activation and `Dropout` as the regularizer. The second layer is a convolution layer that has 64 filters of a shape of 3*3, with `relu` activation and `Dropout` as the regularizer. The third layer is a convolution layer that has 128 filters of a shape of 3*3, with `relu` activation and `Dropout` as the regularizer, which is finally flattened. The fourth layer is a `Dense` layer of 1024 neurons with `relu` activation. The final layer is a `Dense` layer with 10 neurons corresponding to the 10 classes in the MNIST dataset, and the activation used here is `softmax`, `batch_size` is set to 128, the `optimizer` used is `adam`, and `validation_split` is set to 0.2. This means that 20% of the training set will be used as the validation set:

```
# input image shape
input_shape = (28,28,1)

def train_mnist(input_shape, X_train, y_train):
    model = Sequential()
    model.add(Conv2D(32, (3, 3), strides=2, padding='same',
                     input_shape=input_shape))
    model.add(Activation('relu'))
    model.add(Dropout(0.2))

    model.add(Conv2D(64, (3, 3), strides=2, padding='same'))
    model.add(Activation('relu'))
    model.add(Dropout(0.2))

    model.add(Conv2D(128, (3, 3), padding='same'))
    model.add(Activation('relu'))
    model.add(Dropout(0.2))
    model.add(Flatten())

    model.add(Dense(1024, activation = 'relu'))
    model.add(Dense(10, activation='softmax'))
    model.compile(loss = 'sparse_categorical_crossentropy',
                  optimizer = 'adam', metrics = ['accuracy'])
    model.fit(X_train, y_train, batch_size = 128,
              epochs = 3, validation_split=0.2, verbose = 1 )
    return model

mnist_model = train_mnist(input_shape, X_train, y_train)
```

The output is as follows:

```
Train on 48000 samples, validate on 12000 samples
Epoch 1/3
48000/48000 [==============================] - 10s 213us/step - loss: 0.2327 - acc: 0.9269 -
val_loss: 0.0682 - val_acc: 0.9802
Epoch 2/3
48000/48000 [==============================] - 9s 184us/step - loss: 0.0705 - acc: 0.9780 - v
al_loss: 0.0516 - val_acc: 0.9856
Epoch 3/3
48000/48000 [==============================] - 9s 185us/step - loss: 0.0496 - acc: 0.9839 - v
al_loss: 0.0410 - val_acc: 0.9884
```

Figure 13.6: MNIST CNN classifier training for three epochs

Use the built CNN digit classifier on the masked images to get a measure of its performance on digits that are missing small sections:

```
# prediction on the masked images
pred_labels = mnist_model.predict_classes(noised_test_data)
print('The model model accuracy on the masked images
is:',np.mean(pred_labels==y_test)*100)
```

On the masked images, the CNN digit classifier is 74.9% accurate. It might be slightly different when you run it, but it will still be very close.

We have not used maxpooling in the preceding classifier. Try building the same classifier with maxpooling or other pooling options.

Defining hyperparameters for GAN

The following are some of the hyperparameters defined that we will be using throughout the code and are totally configurable:

```
# Smoothing value
smooth_real = 0.9

# Number of epochs
epochs = 5

# Batchsize
batch_size = 128

# Optimizer for the generator
optimizer_g = Adam(lr=0.0002, beta_1=0.5)

# Optimizer for the discriminator
optimizer_d = Adam(lr=0.0004, beta_1=0.5)

# Shape of the input image
input_shape = (28,28,1)
```

 Experiment with different learning rates, optimizers, batch sizes, and smoothing values to see how these factors affect the quality of your model and, if you get better results, show it to the deep learning community.

Building the GAN model components

With the idea that the final GAN model will be able to fill in the part of the image that is missing (masked), let's define the generator.

Defining the generator

The generator that we are using here is a simple convolution autoencoder that is a combination of two parts—an encoder and a decoder.

In the encoder, we have the following:

- The first layer is a convolution 2D layer with 32 filters of a size of 3*3, followed by batch normalization, with activation as relu, followed by downsampling done with AveragePooling2D of size 2*2
- The second layer is a convolution 2D layer with 64 filters of a size of 3*3, followed by batch normalization, with activation as relu, followed by downsampling with AveragePooling2D of a size of 2*2
- The third layer or the final layer in this encoder part is again a convolution 2D layer with 128 filters of a size of 3*3, batch normalization, with activation as relu

In the decoder, we have the following:

- The first layer is a convolution 2D layer with 128 filters of a size of 3*3 with activation as relu, followed by upsampling done with UpSampling2D
- The second layer is a convolution 2D layer with 64 filters of a size of 3*3 with activation as relu, followed by upsampling with UpSampling2D
- The third layer or the final layer in this decoder part is again a convolution 2D layer with 1 filters of a size of 3*3 with activation as tanh

Remember, in the encoder, if you have 32, 64, 128 filters, it should be followed by 128, 64, image_channels filters in the decoder. image_channels is the number of channels in the input image, which is one in the MNIST dataset. If you have 64, 128, 256, 512 filters in the first, second, third, and fourth layers of the encoder, the following filters in the decoder should be 256, 128, 64, image_channels:

```
def img_generator(input_shape):
    generator = Sequential()
    generator.add(Conv2D(32, (3, 3), padding='same,
input_shape=input_shape)) # 32 filters
    generator.add(BatchNormalization())
    generator.add(Activation('relu'))
    generator.add(AveragePooling2D(pool_size=(2, 2)))
    generator.add(Conv2D(64, (3, 3), padding='same')) # 64 filters
    generator.add(BatchNormalization())
    generator.add(Activation('relu'))
    generator.add(AveragePooling2D(pool_size=(2, 2)))
```

```
        generator.add(Conv2D(128, (3, 3), padding='same')) # 128 filters
        generator.add(BatchNormalization())
        generator.add(Activation('relu'))
        generator.add(Conv2D(128, (3, 3), padding='same')) # 128 filters
        generator.add(Activation('relu'))
        generator.add(UpSampling2D((2,2)))
        generator.add(Conv2D(64, (3, 3), padding='same')) # 64 filters
        generator.add(Activation('relu'))
        generator.add(UpSampling2D((2,2)))
        generator.add(Conv2D(1, (3, 3), activation='tanh', padding='same')) # 1
    filter
        return generator
```

Two important things to remember here about the final convolution layer in the generator. One is to use `tanh` as the activation function since the dataset range is between -1 and 1, and the other is, to use the same number of filter(s) as the number of channels in the input image. This is to make sure that the image being generated has the same number of channels as the input image.

 If you decide to center and scale your data like we have done in this exercise, you need to use batch normalization in the generator during downsampling, otherwise, the loss will not converge. You can witness the effects of not using the batch normalization by training the generator without the batch normalization layer.

In the following `summary` of the generator, if you refer to the output shape, you see the downscaling or compression of the image in the first half of the network and the upscaling of the images in the second half of the network:

```
# print generator summary
img_generator(input_shape).summary()
```

The output is as follows:

```
Layer (type)                     Output Shape            Param #
=================================================================
conv2d_4 (Conv2D)                (None, 28, 28, 32)      320

batch_normalization_1 (Batch     (None, 28, 28, 32)      128

activation_4 (Activation)        (None, 28, 28, 32)      0

average_pooling2d_1 (Average     (None, 14, 14, 32)      0

conv2d_5 (Conv2D)                (None, 14, 14, 64)      18496

batch_normalization_2 (Batch     (None, 14, 14, 64)      256

activation_5 (Activation)        (None, 14, 14, 64)      0

average_pooling2d_2 (Average     (None, 7, 7, 64)        0

conv2d_6 (Conv2D)                (None, 7, 7, 128)       73856

batch_normalization_3 (Batch     (None, 7, 7, 128)       512

activation_6 (Activation)        (None, 7, 7, 128)       0

conv2d_7 (Conv2D)                (None, 7, 7, 128)       147584

activation_7 (Activation)        (None, 7, 7, 128)       0

up_sampling2d_1 (UpSampling2     (None, 14, 14, 128)     0

conv2d_8 (Conv2D)                (None, 14, 14, 64)      73792

activation_8 (Activation)        (None, 14, 14, 64)      0

up_sampling2d_2 (UpSampling2     (None, 28, 28, 64)      0

conv2d_9 (Conv2D)                (None, 28, 28, 1)       577
=================================================================
Total params: 315,521
Trainable params: 315,073
Non-trainable params: 448
```

Figure 13.7: Summary of the generator (autoencoder)

Consider the following when you are not obtaining good results with the autoencoder. Use `AveragePooling2D` first and then check out `MaxPooling2D` for downsampling. Use `LeakyReLU` first and then `relu` next. For all of the convolution layers except the final one, use either `LeakyReLU` or `relu` activation. Try using a deeper autoencoder. Feel free to use more filters in the convolution layers, play with the filter sizes and the pooling sizes.

Defining the discriminator

The discriminator is a simple CNN binary classifier that takes in the image generated by the generator and tries to classify the image as original or fake.

The first layer is a convolution 2D layer with 64 filters of a size of 3*3 with the activation as `LeakyReLU` and `Dropout` as the regularizer. The second and third layers are the same as the first layer except the second layer has 128 filters and the third layer has 256 filters. The final layer is a `Dense` layer with `sigmoid` activation since we are doing a binary classification:

```
def img_discriminator(input_shape):
    discriminator = Sequential()
    discriminator.add(Conv2D(64, (3, 3), strides=2, padding='same',
input_shape=input_shape, activation = 'linear'))
    discriminator.add(LeakyReLU(0.2))
    discriminator.add(Dropout(0.2))
    discriminator.add(Conv2D(128, (3, 3), strides=2, padding='same',
activation = 'linear'))
    discriminator.add(LeakyReLU(0.2))
    discriminator.add(Dropout(0.2))
    discriminator.add(Conv2D(256, (3, 3), padding='same', activation =
'linear'))
    discriminator.add(LeakyReLU(0.2))
    discriminator.add(Dropout(0.2))
    discriminator.add(Flatten())
    discriminator.add(Dense(1, activation='sigmoid'))

    return discriminator

# print summary of the discriminator
img_discriminator(input_shape).summary()
```

The output is as follows:

```
Layer (type)                  Output Shape              Param #
=================================================================
conv2d_7 (Conv2D)             (None, 14, 14, 64)        640
_____
leaky_re_lu_1 (LeakyReLU)     (None, 14, 14, 64)        0
_____
dropout_1 (Dropout)           (None, 14, 14, 64)        0
_____
conv2d_8 (Conv2D)             (None, 7, 7, 128)         73856
_____
leaky_re_lu_2 (LeakyReLU)     (None, 7, 7, 128)         0
_____
dropout_2 (Dropout)           (None, 7, 7, 128)         0
_____
conv2d_9 (Conv2D)             (None, 7, 7, 256)         295168
_____
leaky_re_lu_3 (LeakyReLU)     (None, 7, 7, 256)         0
_____
dropout_3 (Dropout)           (None, 7, 7, 256)         0
_____
flatten_1 (Flatten)           (None, 12544)             0
_____
dense_1 (Dense)               (None, 1)                 12545
=================================================================
Total params: 382,209
Trainable params: 382,209
Non-trainable params: 0
```

Figure 13.8: Summary of the discriminator

 Play around with the parameters of the discriminator to suit the needs of the problem you are trying to solve. Include a `MaxPooling` layer in the model if needed.

Defining the DCGAN

The following function pipes the input followed by the generator, which is then followed by the discriminator to form the DCGAN architecture:

```
def dcgan(discriminator, generator, input_shape):
    # Set discriminator as non trainable before compiling GAN
    discriminator.trainable = False
```

```
# Accepts the noised input
gan_input = Input(shape=input_shape)
# Generates image by passing the above received input to the generator
gen_img = generator(gan_input)
# Feeds the generated image to the discriminator
gan_output = discriminator(gen_img)
# Compile everything as a model with binary crossentropy loss
gan = Model(inputs=gan_input, outputs=gan_output)
return gan
```

If you have not seen how to use the `Model` function API before, please visit the detailed documentation by Keras on using the `Model` function API and compiling it at `https://keras.io/models/model/`.

Training GAN

We've built the components of the GAN. Let's train the model in the next steps!

Plotting the training – part 1

During each epoch, the following function plots 9 generated images. For comparison, it will also plot the corresponding 9 original target images and 9 noised input images. We need to use the `upscale` function we've defined when plotting to make sure the images are scaled to range between 0 and 255, so that you do not encounter issues when plotting:

```
def generated_images_plot(original, noised_data, generator):
    print('NOISED')
    for i in range(9):
        plt.subplot(331 + i)
        plt.axis('off')
        plt.imshow(upscale(np.squeeze(noised_data[i])), cmap='gray') # upscale for plotting
    plt.show()
    print('GENERATED')
    for i in range(9):
        pred = generator.predict(noised_data[i:i+1], verbose=0)
        plt.subplot(331 + i)
        plt.axis('off')
        plt.imshow(upscale(np.squeeze(pred[0])), cmap='gray') # upscale to avoid plotting errors
    plt.show()
    print('ORIGINAL')
    for i in range(9):
        plt.subplot(331 + i)
```

```
        plt.axis('off')
        plt.imshow(upscale(np.squeeze(original[i])), cmap='gray') # upscale
for plotting
    plt.show()
```

The output of this function is as follows:

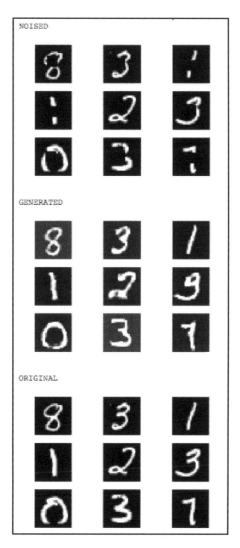

Figure 13.9: Sample/expected output of the generated_images_plot function

Plotting the training – part 2

Let's define another function that plots the images generated during each epoch. To reflect the difference, we will also include the original and the masked/noised images in the plot.

The top row contains the original images, the middle row contains the masked images, and the bottom row contains the generated images.

The plot has 12 rows with the sequence, row 1 - original, row 2 - masked, row3 - generated, row 4 - original, row5 - masked,..., row 12 - generated.

Let's take a look at the code for the same:

```python
def plot_generated_images_combined(original, noised_data, generator):
    rows, cols = 4, 12
    num = rows * cols
    image_size = 28

    generated_images = generator.predict(noised_data[0:num])
    imgs = np.concatenate([original[0:num], noised_data[0:num],
generated_images])
    imgs = imgs.reshape((rows * 3, cols, image_size, image_size))
    imgs = np.vstack(np.split(imgs, rows, axis=1))
    imgs = imgs.reshape((rows * 3, -1, image_size, image_size))
    imgs = np.vstack([np.hstack(i) for i in imgs])
    imgs = upscale(imgs)
    plt.figure(figsize=(8,16))
    plt.axis('off')
    plt.title('Original Images: top rows, '
              'Corrupted Input: middle rows, '
              'Generated Images: bottom rows')
    plt.imshow(imgs, cmap='gray')
    plt.show()
```

The output is as follows:

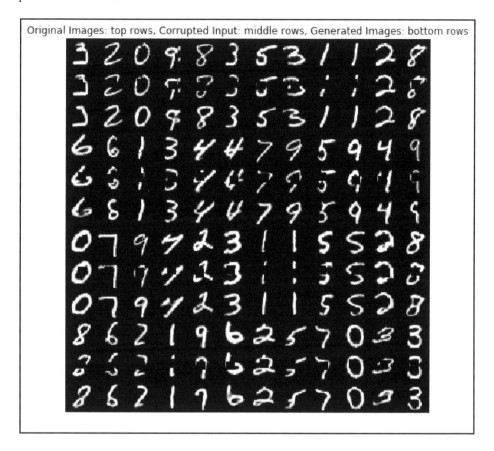

Figure 13.10: Sample/expected output from the plot_generated_images_combined function

Training loop

Now we are at the most important part of the code; the part where all of the functions we previously defined will be used. The following are the steps:

1. Load the generator by calling the `img_generator()` function.

2. Load the discriminator by calling the `img_discriminator()` function and compile it with the binary cross-entropy loss and optimizer as `optimizer_d`, which we have defined under the hyperparameters section.

3. Feed the generator and the discriminator to the `dcgan()` function and compile it with the binary cross-entropy loss and optimizer as `optimizer_g`, which we have defined under the hyperparameters section.

4. Create a new batch of original images and masked images. Generate new fake images by feeding the batch of masked images to the generator.

5. Concatenate the original and generated images so that the first 128 images are all original and the next 128 images are all fake. It is important that you do not shuffle the data here, otherwise it will be hard to train. Label the generated images as `0` and original images as `0.9` instead of 1. This is one-sided label smoothing on the original images. The reason for using label smoothing is to make the network resilient to adversarial examples. It's called one-sided because we are smoothing labels only for the real images.

6. Set `discriminator.trainable` to `True` to enable training of the discriminator and feed this set of 256 images and their corresponding labels to the discriminator for classification.

7. Now, set `discriminator.trainable` to `False` and feed a new batch of 128 masked images labeled as 1 to the GAN (DCGAN) for classification. It is important to set `discriminator.trainable` to `False` to make sure the discriminator is not getting trained while training the generator.

8. Repeat steps 4 through 7 for the desired number of epochs.

Batch size used here is 128.

We have placed the `plot_generated_images_combined()` function and the `generated_images_plot()` function so that we get a plot generated by both functions after the first iteration in the first epoch and after the end of each epoch.

Feel free to place these plot functions according to the frequency of plots you need displayed:

```
def train(X_train, noised_train_data,
          input_shape, smooth_real,
          epochs, batch_size,
          optimizer_g, optimizer_d):

    # define two empty lists to store the discriminator
    # and the generator losses
    discriminator_losses = []
    generator_losses = []
    # Number of iteration possible with batches of size 128
    iterations = X_train.shape[0] // batch_size

    # Load the generator and the discriminator
    generator = img_generator(input_shape)
    discriminator = img_discriminator(input_shape)
    # Compile the discriminator with binary_crossentropy loss
    discriminator.compile(loss='binary_crossentropy',optimizer=optimizer_d)
    # Feed the generator and the discriminator to the function dcgan
    # to form the DCGAN architecture
    gan = dcgan(discriminator, generator, input_shape)
    # Compile the DCGAN with binary_crossentropy loss
    gan.compile(loss='binary_crossentropy', optimizer=optimizer_g)

    for i in range(epochs):
        print ('Epoch %d' % (i+1))
        # Use tqdm to get an estimate of time remaining
        for j in tqdm(range(1, iterations+1)):
            # batch of original images (batch = batchsize)
            original = X_train[np.random.randint(0, X_train.shape[0],
size=batch_size)]
            # batch of noised images (batch = batchsize)
            noise = noised_train_data[np.random.randint(0,
noised_train_data.shape[0], size=batch_size)]

            # Generate fake images
            generated_images = generator.predict(noise)
            # Labels for generated data
            dis_lab = np.zeros(2*batch_size)
            # data for discriminator
            dis_train = np.concatenate([original, generated_images])
```

```
            # label smoothing for original images
            dis_lab[:batch_size] = smooth_real
            # Train discriminator on original images
            discriminator.trainable = True
            discriminator_loss = discriminator.train_on_batch(dis_train,
    dis_lab)

            # save the losses
            discriminator_losses.append(discriminator_loss)
            # Train generator
            gen_lab = np.ones(batch_size)
            discriminator.trainable = False
            sample_indices = np.random.randint(0, X_train.shape[0],
    size=batch_size)
            original = X_train[sample_indices]
            noise = noised_train_data[sample_indices]
            generator_loss = gan.train_on_batch(noise, gen_lab)
            # save the losses
            generator_losses.append(generator_loss)
            if i == 0 and j == 1:
                print('Iteration - %d', j)
                generated_images_plot(original, noise, generator)
                plot_generated_images_combined(original, noise, generator)
        print("Discriminator Loss: ", discriminator_loss,\
            ", Adversarial Loss: ", generator_loss)
        # training plot 1
        generated_images_plot(original, noise, generator)
        # training plot 2
        plot_generated_images_combined(original, noise, generator)
    # plot the training losses
    plt.figure()
    plt.plot(range(len(discriminator_losses)), discriminator_losses,
            color='red', label='Discriminator loss')
    plt.plot(range(len(generator_losses)), generator_losses,
            color='blue', label='Adversarial loss')
    plt.title('Discriminator and Adversarial loss')
    plt.xlabel('Iterations')
    plt.ylabel('Loss (Adversarial/Discriminator)')
    plt.legend()
    plt.show()
    return generator

generator = train(X_train, noised_train_data,
                input_shape, smooth_real,
                epochs, batch_size,
                optimizer_g, optimizer_d)
```

The output is as follows:

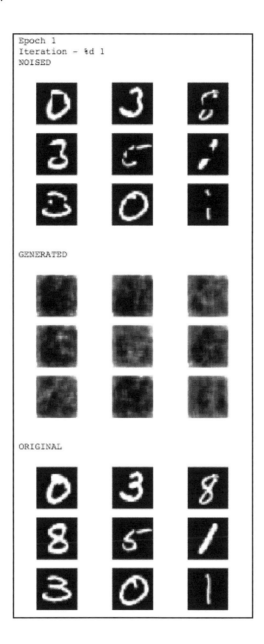

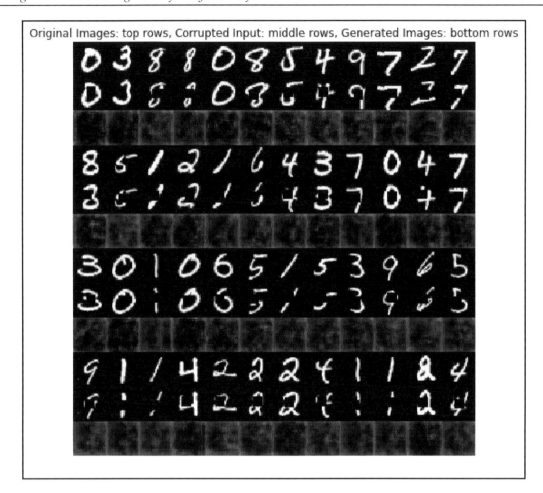

Figure 13.11.1: Generated images plotted with training plots at the end of the first iteration of epoch 1

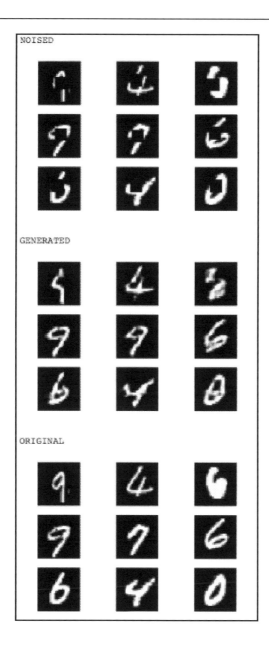

Figure 13.11.2: Generated images plotted with training plots at the end of epoch 2

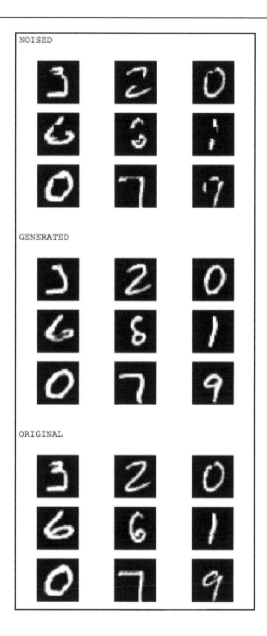

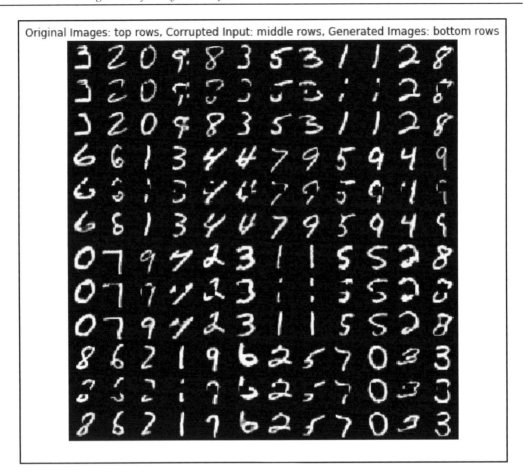

Figure 13.11.3: Generated images plotted with training plots at the end of epoch 5

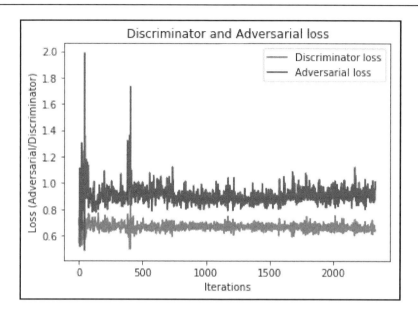

Figure 13.12: Plot of discriminator and adversarial loss during training

Play around with the learning rate for both the generator and the discriminator to find the optimal values for your use case. In general, when training GANs, you train it for a large number of epochs and then use the preceding loss versus iteration plot to identify the minimum spot you would like for the training to stop.

Predictions

This is what we've been building to: making predictions!

CNN classifier predictions on the noised and generated images

Now, we will call the generator on the masked MNIST test data to generate images, that is, fill in the missing part of the digits:

```
# restore missing parts of the digit with the generator
gen_imgs_test = generator.predict(noised_test_data)
```

Then, we will pass the generated MNIST digits to the digit classifier we have modeled already:

```
# predict on the restored/generated digits
gen_pred_lab = mnist_model.predict_classes(gen_imgs_test)
print('The model model accuracy on the generated images
is:',np.mean(gen_pred_lab==y_test)*100)
```

The MNIST CNN classifier is 87.82% accurate on the generated data.

The following is a plot showing 10 generated images by the generator, the actual label of the generated image, and the label predicted by the digit classifier after processing the generated image:

```
# plot of 10 generated images and their predicted label
fig=plt.figure(figsize=(8, 4))
plt.title('Generated Images')
plt.axis('off')
columns = 5
rows = 2
for i in range(0, rows*columns):
    fig.add_subplot(rows, columns, i+1)
    plt.title('Act: %d, Pred: %d'%(gen_pred_lab[i],y_test[i])) # label
    plt.axis('off') # turn off axis
    plt.imshow(upscale(np.squeeze(gen_imgs_test[i])), cmap='gray') # gray
scale
plt.show()
```

The output is as follows:

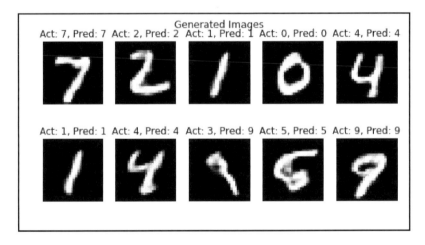

Figure 13.13: Plot of MNIST classifier predictions on the generated images

Scripts in modular form

The entire script can be split into four modules named `train_mnist.py`, `training_plots.py`, `GAN.py`, and `train_gan.py`. Store these in a folder of your choice, for example, `gan`. Set `gan` as the project folder in your favorite source code editor and just run the `train_gan.py` file.

The `train_gan.py` Python file will import functions from all of the other modules in places where they're needed for execution.

Now, let's walk through the contents of each file.

Module 1 – train_mnist.py

This Python file contains the `train_mnist()` function that we have used previously to train a CNN classifier on MNIST digits:

```python
"""This module is used to train a CNN on mnist."""
from keras.layers import Conv2D
from keras.layers import Flatten, Activation
from keras.models import Sequential
from keras.layers.core import Dense, Dropout


def train_mnist(input_shape, X_train, y_train):
    """Train CNN on mnist data."""
    model = Sequential()
    model.add(Conv2D(32, (3, 3), strides=2, padding='same',
                     input_shape=input_shape))
    model.add(Activation('relu'))
    model.add(Dropout(0.2))
    model.add(Conv2D(64, (3, 3), strides=2, padding='same'))
    model.add(Activation('relu'))
    model.add(Dropout(0.2))
    model.add(Conv2D(128, (3, 3), padding='same'))
    model.add(Activation('relu'))
    model.add(Dropout(0.2))
    model.add(Flatten())
    model.add(Dense(1024, activation='relu'))
    model.add(Dense(10, activation='softmax'))
    model.compile(loss='sparse_categorical_crossentropy',
                  optimizer='adam', metrics=['accuracy'])
    model.fit(X_train, y_train, batch_size=128,
              epochs=3, validation_split=0.2, verbose=1)
    return model
```

Module 2 – training_plots.py

This Python file contains the four functions, `upscale()`, `generated_images_plot()`, `plot_generated_images_combined()`, and `plot_training_loss()`:

```python
"""This module contains functions to plot image generated when training
GAN."""

import matplotlib.pyplot as plt
import numpy as np


def upscale(image):
    """Scale the image to 0-255 scale."""
    return (image*127.5 + 127.5).astype(np.uint8)


def generated_images_plot(original, noised_data, generator):
    """Plot subplot of images during training."""
    print('NOISED')
    for i in range(9):
        plt.subplot(331 + i)
        plt.axis('off')
        plt.imshow(upscale(np.squeeze(noised_data[i])), cmap='gray')
    plt.show()
    print('GENERATED')
    for i in range(9):
        pred = generator.predict(noised_data[i:i+1], verbose=0)
        plt.subplot(331 + i)
        plt.axis('off')
        plt.imshow(upscale(np.squeeze(pred[0])), cmap='gray')
    plt.show()
```

For the remaining part of this code, please visit: `https://github.com/PacktPublishing/Python-Deep-Learning-Projects/blob/master/Chapter13/training_plots.py`

Module 3 – GAN.py

This module contains the DCGAN components, namely `img_generator()`, `img_discriminator()`, and `dcgan()`:

```python
"""This module contains the DCGAN components."""
from keras.layers import Input, Conv2D, AveragePooling2D
from keras.layers import UpSampling2D, Flatten, Activation,
```

```
BatchNormalization
from keras.models import Model, Sequential
from keras.layers.core import Dense, Dropout
from keras.layers.advanced_activations import LeakyReLU


def img_generator(input_shape):
    """Generator."""
    generator = Sequential()
    generator.add(Conv2D(32, (3, 3), padding='same',
input_shape=input_shape))
    generator.add(BatchNormalization())
    generator.add(Activation('relu'))
    generator.add(AveragePooling2D(pool_size=(2, 2)))
    generator.add(Conv2D(64, (3, 3), padding='same'))
    generator.add(BatchNormalization())
    generator.add(Activation('relu'))
    generator.add(AveragePooling2D(pool_size=(2, 2)))
    generator.add(Conv2D(128, (3, 3), padding='same'))
    generator.add(BatchNormalization())
    generator.add(Activation('relu'))
    generator.add(Conv2D(128, (3, 3), padding='same'))
    generator.add(Activation('relu'))
    generator.add(UpSampling2D((2, 2)))
    generator.add(Conv2D(64, (3, 3), padding='same'))
    generator.add(Activation('relu'))
    generator.add(UpSampling2D((2, 2)))
    generator.add(Conv2D(1, (3, 3), activation='tanh', padding='same'))
    return generator
```

For the remaining part of this code, please visit: `https://github.com/`
`PacktPublishing/Python-Deep-Learning-Projects/blob/master/`
`Chapter13/GAN.py`

Module 4 – train_gan.py

In this module, we will include the hyperparameters, pre-process the data, generate synthetic data, train the GAN, train the CNN classifier, and import all of the necessary functions from other modules:

```
import numpy as np
from training_plots import upscale, generated_images_plot,
plot_training_loss
from training_plots import plot_generated_images_combined
from keras.optimizers import Adam
```

```
from keras import backend as k
import matplotlib.pyplot as plt
from tqdm import tqdm

from GAN import img_generator, img_discriminator, dcgan

from keras.datasets import mnist
from train_mnist import train_mnist

%matplotlib inline
# Smoothing value
smooth_real = 0.9
# Number of epochs
epochs = 5
# Batchsize
batch_size = 128
# Optimizer for the generator
optimizer_g = Adam(lr=0.0002, beta_1=0.5)
# Optimizer for the discriminator
optimizer_d = Adam(lr=0.0004, beta_1=0.5)
# Shape of the input image
input_shape = (28, 28, 1)
```

For the remaining part of this module, please visit: `https://github.com/PacktPublishing/Python-Deep-Learning-Projects/blob/master/Chapter13/train_gan.py`

You can use the same modules you have created to train on fashion MNIST data. All you have to do is replace line 11 in the `train_gan.py` file with (`from keras.datasets import fashion_mnist`) and replace line 28 with (`(X_train, y_train), (X_test, y_test) = fashion_mnist.load_data()`). The results will be good but not excellent since the parameters set here work best on the MNIST digit data. This will be a good exercise for you to get incredible results without much effort.

Here is a resource on tips to train GANs that you must check out:

`https://github.com/soumith/ganhacks`.

The Jupyter Notebook code files for the preceding DCGAN MNIST inpainting can be found at `https://github.com/PacktPublishing/Python-Deep-Learning-Projects/blob/master/Chapter%2014/DCGAN_MNIST.ipynb`. The Jupyter Notebook code files for the DCGAN Fashion MNIST inpainting can be found at `https://github.com/PacktPublishing/Python-Deep-Learning-Projects/blob/master/Chapter%2014/DCGAN_Fashion_MNIST.ipynb`.

The conclusion to the project

The goal of this project was to build a GAN to solve the problem of regenerating missing parts/regions of handwritten digits. In the initial chapters, we applied deep learning to enable customers of a restaurant chain to write their phone numbers in a simple iPad application to get a text notification that their party could be seated. The use case of this chapter was to apply deep learning to generate missing parts of the digits of the phone number so that a text notification can be sent to the right person.

The CNN digit classifier model accuracy hit 98.84% on the MNIST validation data. With the data we generated to simulate missing parts of a digit when fed to the CNN digit classifier, the model was only 74.90% accurate.

The same dataset with missing sections of the digit was passed to the generator to recover the missing parts. The resulting digits were then passed to the CNN classifier and the model was 87.82% accurate. See if you can tweak both the CNN classifier and the GAN to generate clearer digits, as well as much higher accuracy on these generated images.

Let's follow the same technique we have been following in the previous chapters for evaluating the performance of the models from the restaurant chain point of view.

What are the implications of this accuracy? Let's calculate the incidence of an error occurring that would result in a customer service issue (that is, the customer not getting the text that their table is ready and getting upset for an excessively long wait time at the restaurant).

Each customer's phone number is ten digits long. Let's assume our hypothetical restaurant has an average of 30 tables at each location and those tables turn over two times per night during the rush hour when the system is likely to be used, and finally, the restaurant chain has 35 locations. This means that each day of operation there are approximately 21,000 handwritten numbers captured (30 tables x 2 turns/day x 35 locations x 10 digit phone number).

Obviously, all digits must be correctly classified for the text to get to the proper waiting restaurant patron. So any single digit misclassification causes a failure. With the simulated data, the model accuracy was 74.90%, which means a total of 5,271 digits are misclassified. With the recovered data (on the simulated data) from the generator of the trained GAN, the model accuracy was 87.82%, which would improperly classify 2,558 digits per day in our example. The worst case for the hypothetical scenario would be if there occurred only one improperly classified digit in each phone number. Since there are only 2,100 patrons and corresponding phone numbers, this would mean that every phone number had an error in classification (100% failure) and not a single customer would get their text notification that their party could be seated! The best case scenario would be if all 10 digits were misclassified in each phone number and that would result in 263 wrong phone numbers out of 2,100 (12.5% failure rate). Still not a level of performance the restaurant chain would be likely to be happy with, so you can see why we'd need to continue fine-tuning the models to get the maximum performance possible.

Summary

In the project in this chapter, we have successfully built a deep convolution GAN in Keras on handwritten MNIST digits. We understood the function of the generator and the discriminator component of the GAN. We have defined some key hyperparameters, as well as, in some places, reasoned with why we used what we did. Finally, we tested the GAN's performance on unseen data and determined that we succeeded in achieving our goals.

14
Develop an Autonomous Agent with Deep R Learning

Welcome to the chapter on reinforcement learning. In the previous chapters, we have worked on solving supervised learning problems. In this chapter, we will learn to build and train a deep reinforcement learning model capable of playing games.

 Reinforcement learning is often a new paradigm for deep learning engineers and this is why we're using the framework of a game for this training. The business use cases that we should be looking out for are typified by process optimization. Reinforcement learning is great for gaming, but also applicable in use cases ranging from drone control (https://arxiv.org/pdf/1707.05110.pdf) and navigation to optimizing file downloads over mobile networks (http://anrg.usc.edu/www/papers/comsnets_2017.pdf).

We will do this with something called deep Q-learning and deep **State-Action-Reward-State-Action** (**SARSA**) learning. The idea is that we will build a deep learning model, also called an agent in reinforcement learning terms, that interacts with the game environment and learns how to play the game while maximizing rewards after several attempts at playing. Here is a diagram illustrating reinforcement learning:

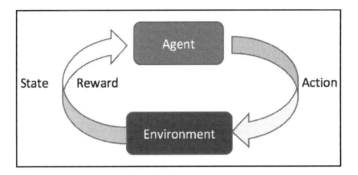

Figure 14.1: Reinforcement learning

For the purpose of this chapter, we will be using the CartPole game from OpenAI Gym.

What we'll learn in this chapter is the following:

- How to interact with the Gym toolkit
- What is Q-learning and SARSA learning
- Coding the RL model and defining hyperparameters
- Building and understanding the training loop
- Testing the model

It would be better if you implement the code snippets as you go along in this chapter, either in a Jupyter Notebook or any source code editor. This will make it easier for you to follow along, as well as understand what each part of the code does.

All of the Python and the Jupyter Notebook files for this chapter can be found
at `https://github.com/PacktPublishing/Python-Deep-Learning-Projects/tree/master/Chapter14`.

Let's get to the code!

In this exercise, we will be using the Gym toolkit from OpenAI for developing reinforcement learning models. It supports teaching agents such as CartPole and pinball games.

 To know more about the Gym toolkit from OpenAI and the games it supports, visit `http://gym.openai.com/`.

We will also be using the Keras deep learning library, which is a high-level neural network API capable of running on top of TensorFlow, Theano, or Cognitive Toolkit (CNTK).

 To learn more about Keras and its functionalities visit `https://keras.io/`.

Deep Q-learning

In this segment, we will implement deep Q-learning with a deep learning model built using the Keras deep learning library as the function approximator.

We will start off this segment with a gentle introduction as to how to use the Gym module and then move on to understanding what Q-learning is, and finally, implement the deep Q-learning. We will be using the CartPole environment from OpenAI Gym.

To follow along, refer to the Jupyter Notebook code file for the deep Q-learning section at `https://github.com/PacktPublishing/Python-Deep-Learning-Projects/blob/master/Chapter%2015/DQN.ipynb`.

Importing all of the dependencies

We will be using `numpy`, `gym`, `matplotlib`, `keras`, and `tensorflow` packages in this segment of the exercise. Here, TensorFlow will be used as the backend for Keras. You can install these packages using `pip`:

```
import random
import numpy as np
import matplotlib.pyplot as plt
```

```
from keras.layers import Dense, Dropout, Activation
from keras.models import Sequential
from keras.optimizers import Adam
from keras import backend as k
from collections import deque
import gym
```

deque is a list-like container with fast appends and pops on either end.

Exploring the CartPole game

In the CartPole game, you will find a pole attached by an unattached joint to the cart, which moves on a frictionless track. At the beginning of each game, the pole starts in the upright position and the goal is to hold it in the upright position as long as possible or for a given number of time steps. You can control the CartPole system by applying a force of +1 and -1 (to move the cart either to the right or to the left) and prevent the pole from falling over. The game/episode ends when the cart moves more than 2.4 units from the center or when the pole is more than 45 degrees from the vertical.

Interacting with the CartPole game

OpenAI Gym makes it super easy to interact with the game. In this section, we will cover how to load, reset, and play the CartPole game.

Loading the game

Let's load the `CartPole-v1` game from the `gym` module. It's very simple. All you have to do is feed the `gym.make()` function the name of the game. In our case, the game is `CartPole-v1`. Gym then loads the game into your workspace:

```
env = gym.make('CartPole-v1')
```

It is important that you set `seed` for reproducibility:

```
# Set seed for reproducibility
seed_val = 456
np.random.seed(seed_val)
env.seed(seed_val)
random.seed(seed_val)
```

Let's explore how many variables we have in the CartPole game:

```
states = env.observation_space.shape[0]
print('Number of states/variables in the cartpole environment', states)
```

The following is the output:

```
Number of states/variables in the cartpole environment 4
```

We can see that the CartPole has 4 variables and these are namely the position (x), velocity (x_dot), angular position (theta), and the angular velocity (theta_dot).

Let's explore how many possible responses we have in this game using the following code:

```
actions = env.action_space.n
print('Number of responses/classes in the cartpole environment', actions)
```

The following is the output:

```
Number of responses/classes in the cartpole environment 2
```

We see that the CartPole environment has 2 possible responses/buttons, namely move left and move right.

Resetting the game

You can reset the game with the following code:

```
state = env.reset() # reset the game
print('State of the Cart-Pole after reset', state)
print('Shape of state of the Cart-Pole after reset', state.shape)
```

The preceding snippet will reset the game and also return you the state (x, x_dot, theta, theta_dot) of the CartPole after the reset, which will be an array of the shape of (4,).

Playing the game

Now, once you have reset the game, all there is to do is play. You can feed your actions/responses to the game with the use of the following code:

```
action = 0
new state, reward, done, info = env.step(action)
print((new_state, reward, done, info))
```

The `env.step` function accepts your response/action (move left or right) and generates the `new_state`/orientation (x, x_dot, theta, theta_dot) of the CartPole system. Along with the new state, the `env.step` function also returns the `reward`, which indicates the score you receive for the `action` you just took; `done`, which indicates if the game has finished; and `info`, which has system-related information.

When the game begins, `done` is set to `False`. Only when the CartPole orientation exceeds the game rules will `done` be set to `True`, indicating that either the cart moved 2.4 units from the center or the pole was more than 45 degrees from the vertical.

As long as every step you take is within the game over limits, the reward for that step will be 1 unit, otherwise zero.

Let's play the game by making random actions:

```
def random_actions_game(episodes):
    for episode in range(episodes):
        state = env.reset() # reset environment
        done = False # set done to False
        score = 0
        while not done:
            #env.render() # Display cart pole game on the screen
            action = random.choice([0,1]) # Choose between 0 or 1
            new_state, reward, done, info = env.step(action) # perform the
action
            score+=1
        print('Episode: {} Score: {}'.format(episode+1, score))

# play game
random_actions_game(10)
```

The following is the Terminal output:

```
Episode: 1  Score:  14
Episode: 2  Score:  17
Episode: 3  Score:  10
Episode: 4  Score:  16
Episode: 5  Score:  20
Episode: 6  Score:  17
Episode: 7  Score:  14
Episode: 8  Score:  23
Episode: 9  Score:  23
Episode: 10 Score:  47
```

Figure 14.2: Scores from random actions game

The following is the CartPole game output:

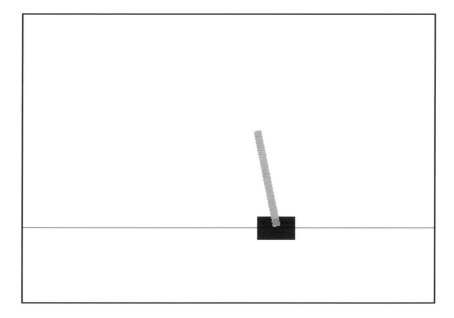

Figure 14.3: Snapshot of the CartPole game that gets displayed on the screen when rendered

 random.choice returns a randomly selected item from a non-empty sequence such as a list/array.

Q-learning

Q-learning is a policy-based reinforcement learning technique where the goal of Q-learning is to learn an optimal policy that helps an agent decide what action to take under which circumstances of the environment.

To implement Q-learning, you need to understand what a *Q* function is.

A *Q* function accepts a state and a corresponding action as input and yields the total expected reward. It can be expressed as *Q(s, a)*. When at the *s* state, an optimal *Q* function indicates to the agent how good of a choice is picking an action, *a*.

For a single state, *s*, and an action, *a*, *Q(s, a)* can be expressed in terms of the *Q* value of the next state, *s'*, given by using the following equation:

$$Q(s, a) = r + \gamma * max(Q(s', a'))$$

This is known as the Bellman equation. It tells us that the maximum reward is the sum of the reward the agent received for entering the current state, *s*, and the discounted maximum future reward for the next state, *s'*.

The following is the pseudocode for the Q-learning algorithm from the book *Reinforcement Learning: An Introduction,* by Richard S. Sutton and Andrew G. Barto:

```
Initialize Q(s, a) arbitrarily
Repeat (for each episode):
    Initialize s
    Choose a from s using policy derived from Q (e.g., ε-greedy)
    Repeat (for each step of episode):
        Take action a, observe r, s'
        Choose a' from s' using policy derived from Q (e.g., ε-greedy)
        Q(s, a) ← Q(s, a) + α[r + γQ(s', a') − Q(s, a)]
        s ← s'; a ← a';
    until s is terminal
```

Figure 14.4: Pseudocode for Q-learning

Reinforcement Learning: An Introduction by Richard S. Sutton and Andrew G. Barto (http://incompleteideas.net/book/ebook/the-book.html).

Defining hyperparameters for Deep Q Learning (DQN)

The following are some of the hyperparameters defined that we will be using throughout the code and are totally configurable:

```
# Discount in Bellman Equation
gamma = 0.95

# Epsilon
epsilon = 1.0

# Minimum Epsilon
epsilon_min = 0.01

# Decay multiplier for epsilon
epsilon_decay = 0.99

# Size of deque container
deque_len = 20000

# Average score needed over 100 epochs
target_score = 200

# Number of games
episodes = 2000

# Data points per episode used to train the agent
batch_size = 64

# Optimizer for training the agent
optimizer = 'adam'

# Loss for training the agent
loss = 'mse'
```

The following are the parameters used:

- gamma : Discount parameter in the Bellman equation
- epsilon_decay: Multiplier by which you want to discount the value of epsilon after each episode/game
- epsilon_min: Minimum value of epsilon beyond which you do not want to decay it
- deque_len: Size of the deque container used to store the training examples (state, reward, done, and action)

- `target_score`: The average score over 100 epochs that you want the agent to score after which you stop the learning process
- `episodes`: Maximum number of games you want the agent to play
- `batch_size`: Size of the batch of training data (stored in the `deque` container) used to train the agent after each episode
- `optimizer`: Optimizer of choice for training the agent
- `loss`: Loss of choice for training the agent

Experiment with different learning rates, optimizers, batch sizes as well as `epsilon_decay` values to see how these factors affect the quality of your model and, if you get better results, show it to the deep learning community.

Building the model components

In this section, we will define all of the functions that go into training the reinforcement learning agent. These functions are as follows:

- Agent
- Agent action
- Memory
- Performance plot
- Replay
- Training and testing to train and test the agent

Defining the agent

Let's define an agent/function approximator.

The agent is nothing but a simple deep neural network that takes in the state (four variables) of the CartPole system and returns the maximum possible reward for each of the two actions.

The first, second, and third layers are simple `Dense` layers with 16 neurons and with activation as `relu`.

The final layer is a `Dense` layer with two neurons equal to the number of possible `actions`:

```python
def agent(states, actions):
    """Simple Deep Neural Network."""
    model = Sequential()
    model.add(Dense(16, input_dim=states))
    model.add(Activation('relu'))
    model.add(Dense(16))
    model.add(Activation('relu'))
    model.add(Dense(16))
    model.add(Activation('relu'))
    model.add(Dense(actions))
    model.add(Activation('linear'))
    return model

# print summary of the agent
print(agent(states, actions).summary())
```

The following is the output:

```
Layer (type)                 Output Shape              Param #
=================================================================
dense_1 (Dense)              (None, 16)                80

activation_1 (Activation)    (None, 16)                0

dense_2 (Dense)              (None, 16)                272

activation_2 (Activation)    (None, 16)                0

dense_3 (Dense)              (None, 16)                272

activation_3 (Activation)    (None, 16)                0

dense_4 (Dense)              (None, 2)                 34

activation_4 (Activation)    (None, 2)                 0
=================================================================
Total params: 658
Trainable params: 658
Non-trainable params: 0

None
```

Figure 14.5: Summary of the agent

Play around with the parameters of the agent to suit the needs of the problem you are trying to solve. Try using leaky `relu` in the model if needed.

Defining the agent action

Let's define a function that, when called, will return the action that needs to be taken for that specific state:

```
def agent_action(model, epsilon, state, actions):
    """Define action to be taken."""
    if np.random.rand() <= epsilon:
        act = random.randrange(actions)
    else:
        act = np.argmax(model.predict(state)[0])
    return act
```

For any value from the uniform distribution (between 0 and 1), less than or equal to `epsilon`, the action returned will be `random`. For any value greater than `epsilon`, the action chosen will be that predicted by the agent we have defined in the preceding code.

The `numpy.random.rand` function generates a random number from a uniform distribution over 0 and 1. `numpy.argmax` returns the index of the maximum value in the sequence. `random.randrange` returns a randomly selected item from `range()`.

Defining the memory

Let's define a `deque` object to store the information (`state`, `action`, `reward`, and `done`) related to every relevant step we take when playing the game. We will then be using the data stored in this `deque` object for training:

```
training_data = deque(maxlen=deque_len)
```

We have defined the `deque` object to be of a size of `20000`. Once this container is filled with 20,000 data points, every new append being made at one end will result in popping a data point at the other end. Then, we will end up retaining only the latest information over time.

We will define a function called `memory`, which, when called during the game, will accept the information related to `action`, `state`, `reward`, and `done` as input at that time step, and then will store it in the training data `deque` container we have defined in the preceding code. You will see that we are storing these five variables as a tuple entry at each timestep:

```
def memory(state, new_state, reward, done, action):
    """Function to store data points in the deque container."""
    training_data.append((state, new_state, reward, done, action))
```

Defining the performance plot

The following `performance_plot` function plots the performance of the model over time. This function has been placed such that it is only plotted once our target of 200 points has been reached. You can also place this function to plot the progress after every 100 episodes during training:

```
def performance_plot(scores, target_score):
    """Plot the game progress."""
    scores_arr = np.array(scores) # convert list to array
    scores_arr[np.where(scores_arr > target_score)] = target_score # scores
    plt.figure(figsize=(20, 5)) # set figure size to 20 by 5
    plt.title('Plot of Score v/s Episode') # title
    plt.xlabel('Episodes') # xlabel
    plt.ylabel('Scores') # ylabel
    plt.plot(scores_arr)
    plt.show()
```

A sample plot output of the function (after the goal has been achieved) is shown in the following screenshot:

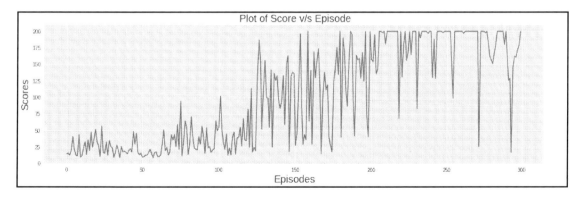

Figure 14.6: Sample plot output of performance_plot function

Defining replay

The following `replay` function is called inside the `train` function (defined in the next section) at the end of the game for training the agent. It is in this function that we define the targets for each state using the *Q* function Bellman equation:

```
def replay(epsilon, gamma, epsilon_min, epsilon_decay, model,
training_data, batch_size=64):
    """Train the agent on a batch of data."""
    idx = random.sample(range(len(training_data)), min(len(training_data),
batch_size))
    train_batch = [training_data[j] for j in idx]
    for state, new_state, reward, done, action in train_batch:
        target = reward
        if not done:
            target = reward + gamma * np.amax(model.predict(new_state)[0])
        #print('target', target)
        target_f = model.predict(state)
        #print('target_f', target_f)
        target_f[0][action] = target
        #print('target_f_r', target_f)
        model.fit(state, target_f, epochs=1, verbose=0)
    if epsilon > epsilon_min:
        epsilon *= epsilon_decay
    return epsilon
```

It is inside this function that we train the agent compiled with mean squared error loss to learn to maximize the reward. We have done so because we are predicting the numerical value of the reward possible for the two actions. Remember that the agent accepts the state as input that is of a shape of 1*4. The output of this agent is of shape 1*2, and it basically contains the expected reward for the two possible actions.

So, when an episode ends, we use a batch of data stored in the `deque` container to train the agent.

In this batch of data, consider the 1st tuple:

```
state = [[-0.07294358 -0.94589796 0.03188364 1.40490844]]
new_state = [[-0.09186154 -1.14140094 0.05998181 1.70738606]]
reward = 1
done = False
action = 0
```

For the `state`, we know the `action` that needs to be taken to enter the `new_state` and `reward` for doing so. We also have `done`, which indicates whether the `new_state` entered is within the game rules.

As long as the new state, s' ,being entered is within the game rules, that is, `done` is `False`, the total `reward` according to the Bellman equation for entering the new state s' form state s by taking an `action` can be written in Python as follows:

```
target = reward + gamma * np.amax(model.predict(new_state)[0])
```

Output of `model.predict(new_state)[0]` be `[-0.55639267, 0.37972435]`. The `np.amax([-0.55639267, 0.37972435])` will be `0.37972435`.

With the discount/`gamma` as 0.95 and the `reward` as 1, this gives us the following value. The `reward + gamma * np.amax(model.predict(new_state)[0])` end us up as `1.36073813587427`.

This is the value of the target defined previously.

Using the model, let's predict the reward for the two possible actions for the current state. `target_f = model.predict(state)` will be `[[-0.4597198 0.31523475]]`.

Since we already know the `action` that needs to be taken for the `state`, which is 0, to maximize the reward for the next state, we will set the `reward` at index zero of `target_f` equal to the `reward` computed using the Bellman equation, which is, `target_f[0][action] = 1.3607381358742714`.

Finally, `target_f` will be equal to `[[1.3607382 0.31523475]]`.

We will use the state as `input` and the `target_f` as the target reward and fit the agent/model on it.

This process will be repeated for all of the data points in the batch of training data. Also, for each call of the replay function, the value of epsilon is reduced by the multiplier epsilon decay.

`random.sample` samples *n* elements from a population set. `np.amax` returns the maximum value in an array.

Training loop

Now, let's put all of the pieces we have formed until now together to implement training of the agent using the `train()` function that we have defined here:

1. Load the agent by calling the `agent()` function and compile it with the loss as `loss` and with the optimizer as `optimizer`, which we have defined in the *Defining hyperparameters for Deep Q Learning (DQN)* section.
2. Reset the environment and reshape the initial state.
3. Call the `agent_action` function by passing the `model`, `epsilon`, and `state` information and obtain the next action that needs to be taken.
4. Take the action obtained in *Step 3* using the `env.step` function. Store the resulting information in the `training_data` deque container by calling the `memory` function and passing the required arguments.
5. Assign the new state obtained in *Step 4* to the `state` variable and increment the time step by 1 unit.
6. Until done resulting in *Step 4* turns `True`, repeat *Step 3* through *Step 5*.
7. Call the `replay` function to train the agent on a batch of the training data at the end of the episode/game.
8. Repeat *Step 2* through *Step 7* until the target score has been achieved:

Following code shows the implementation of the `train()` function:

```
def train(target_score, batch_size, episodes,
optimizer, loss, epsilon,
gamma, epsilon_min, epsilon_decay, actions, render=False):
    """Training the agent on games."""
    print('----Training----')
    k.clear_session()

    # define empty list to store the score at the end of each
    episode
    scores = []

    # load the agent
    model = agent(states, actions)

    # compile the agent with mean squared error loss
    model.compile(loss=loss, optimizer=optimizer)

    for episode in range(1, (episodes+1)):
    # reset environment at the end of each episode
    state = env.reset()
```

```
# reshape state to shape 1*4
state = state.reshape(1, states)

# set done value to False
done = False
```

For the remaining part of this code snippet, please refer to the `DQN.ipynb` file here: `https://github.com/PacktPublishing/Python-Deep-Learning-Projects/blob/master/Chapter14/DQN.ipynb`

To view the CartPole game on your screen when training, set the `render` argument to `True` inside the `train` function. Also, visualizing the game will slow down the training.

The following two images are the outputs generated during training of DQN:

```
----Training----
episode 100, score 76, epsilon 0.366
Avg Score over last 100 epochs 30.07
episode 200, score 203, epsilon 0.134
Avg Score over last 100 epochs 145.86
episode 300, score 238, epsilon 0.04904
Avg Score over last 100 epochs 281.42
------ Goal Achieved After 300 Episodes ------
```

Figure 14.7: Scores output when training the agent

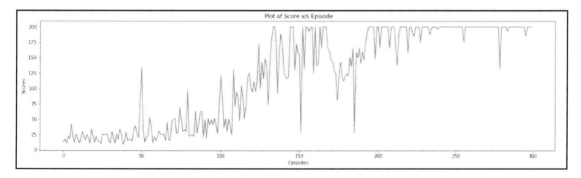

Figure 14.8: Plot of scores v/s episodes when training the agent

We can see that, when training the agent, our target score of 200 points averaging over 100 latest episodes was reached at the end of 300 games.

We have been using the epsilon-greedy policy to train the agent. Feel free to use other policies listed at `https://github.com/keras-rl/keras-rl/blob/master/rl/policy.py`, once you have finished mastering the training of DQN.

It is not always necessary that, when you give a try at training the agent, it takes you just 300 games. In some cases, it might even take more than 300. Refer to the notebook at `https://github.com/PacktPublishing/Python-Deep-Learning-Projects/blob/master/Chapter%2015/DQN.ipynb` to see the five tries made at training the agent and the number of episodes it took to train it.

Testing the DQN model

Now, let's test how our trained DQN model performs on new games. The following `test` function uses the trained DQN model to play ten games and see whether our average target of 200 points will be achieved:

```python
def test(env, model, states, episodes=100, render=False):
    """Test the performance of the DQN agent."""
    scores_test = []
    for episode in range(1, (episodes+1)):
        state = env.reset()
        state = state.reshape(1, states)

        done = False
        time_step = 0

        while not done:
            if render:
                env.render()
            action = np.argmax(model.predict(state)[0])
            new_state, reward, done, info = env.step(action)
            new_state = new_state.reshape(1, states)
            state = new_state
            time_step += 1
        scores_test.append(time_step)
        if episode % 10 == 0:
            print('episode {}, score {} '.format(episode, time_step))
    print('Average score over 100 test games: {}'.format(np.mean(scores_test)))
```

```
test(env, model, states, render=False)
```

 To view the CartPole game on your screen when testing, set the `render` argument to `true` inside the `test` function.

The following is the output:

```
episode 10, score 252
episode 20, score 241
episode 30, score 256
episode 40, score 265
episode 50, score 208
episode 60, score 237
episode 70, score 241
episode 80, score 284
episode 90, score 225
episode 100, score 268
Average score over 100 test games: 277.88
```

Figure 14.9: Test scores with the trained Q agent

When the agent is tested on the new 100 CartPole games, it is averaging a score of `277.88`.

 Remove the threshold of 200 points and aim at training the agent to consistently score an average of 450 points or more.

Deep Q-learning scripts in modular form

The entire script can be split into four modules named `train_dqn.py`, `agent_reply_dqn.py`, `test_dqn.py`, and `hyperparameters_dqn.py`. Store these in a folder of your choice, for example `chapter_15`. Set `chapter_15` as the project folder in your favorite source code editor and just run the `train_dqn.py` file.

The `train_dqn.py` Python file will import functions from all of the other modules in places where they are needed for execution.

Now let's walk through the contents of each file.

Module 1 – hyperparameters_dqn.py

This Python file contains the hyperparameters of the DQN model:

```python
"""This module contains hyperparameters for the DQN model."""

# Discount in Bellman Equation
gamma = 0.95
# Epsilon
epsilon = 1.0
# Minimum Epsilon
epsilon_min = 0.01
# Decay multiplier for epsilon
epsilon_decay = 0.99
# Size of deque container
deque_len = 20000
# Average score needed over 100 epochs
target_score = 200
# Number of games
episodes = 2000
# Data points per episode used to train the agent
batch_size = 64
# Optimizer for training the agent
optimizer = 'adam'
# Loss for training the agent
loss = 'mse'
```

Module 2 – agent_replay_dqn.py

This Python file contains the four functions, namely `agent()`, `agent_action()`, `performance_plot()`, and `replay()`:

```python
"""This module contains."""
import random
import numpy as np
import matplotlib.pyplot as plt
from keras.layers import Dense, Dropout, Activation
from keras.models import Sequential
from keras.optimizers import Adam


def agent(states, actions):
    """Simple Deep Neural Network."""
    model = Sequential()
    model.add(Dense(16, input_dim=states))
    model.add(Activation('relu'))
```

```
model.add(Dense(16))
model.add(Activation('relu'))
model.add(Dense(16))
model.add(Activation('relu'))
model.add(Dense(actions))
model.add(Activation('linear'))
return model
```

For the remaining part of this file, please visit here: `https://github.com/PacktPublishing/Python-Deep-Learning-Projects/blob/master/Chapter14/agent_replay_dqn.py`

Module 3 – test_dqn.py

This module contains the `test()` function, which will be called in the `train_dqn.py` script to test the performance of the DQN agent:

```python
"""This module contains function to test the performance of the DQN
model."""
import numpy as np


def test(env, model, states, episodes=100, render=False):
    """Test the performance of the DQN agent."""
    scores_test = []
    for episode in range(1, (episodes+1)):
        state = env.reset()
        state = state.reshape(1, states)

        done = False
        time_step = 0

        while not done:
            if render:
                env.render()
            action = np.argmax(model.predict(state)[0])
            new_state, reward, done, info = env.step(action)
            new_state = new_state.reshape(1, states)
            state = new_state
            time_step += 1
        scores_test.append(time_step)
        if episode % 10 == 0:
            print('episode {}, score {} '.format(episode, time_step))
    print('Average score over 100 test games:
{}'.format(np.mean(scores_test)))
```

Module 4 – train_dqn.py

In this module, we include the memory() and train() functions and also the calls to train and test the reinforcement learning model:

```
"""This module is used to train and test the DQN agent."""
import random
import numpy as np
from agent_replay_dqn import agent, agent_action, replay, performance_plot
from hyperparameters_dqn import *
from test_dqn import test
from keras import backend as k
from collections import deque
import gym

env = gym.make('CartPole-v1')

# Set seed for reproducibility
seed_val = 456
np.random.seed(seed_val)
env.seed(seed_val)
random.seed(seed_val)

states = env.observation_space.shape[0]
actions = env.action_space.n
training_data = deque(maxlen=deque_len)


def memory(state, new_state, reward, done, action):
    """Function to store data points in the deque container."""
    training_data.append((state, new_state, reward, done, action))


def train(target_score, batch_size, episodes,
          optimizer, loss, epsilon,
          gamma, epsilon_min, epsilon_decay, actions, render=False):
    """Training the agent on games."""
    print('----Training----')
    k.clear_session()
```

For the remaining part of this code, please visit here: https://github.com/PacktPublishing/Python-Deep-Learning-Projects/blob/master/Chapter14/train_dqn.py

Deep SARSA learning

In this segment, we will implement deep SARSA learning with the `keras-rl` library. The `keras-rl` library is a simple neural network API that allows simple and easy implementation of reinforcement learning models (Q, SARSA, and others). To learn more about the `keras-rl` library, visit the documentation at `https://keras-rl.readthedocs.io/en/latest/`.

We will be using the same CartPole environment we have been using so far from OpenAI Gym.

A Jupyter Notebook code example for deep SARSA learning can be found at `https://github.com/PacktPublishing/Python-Deep-Learning-Projects/blob/master/Chapter14/Deep%20SARSA.ipynb`.

SARSA learning

SARSA learning, like Q-learning, is also a policy-based reinforcement learning technique. Its goal is to learn an optimal policy, which helps an agent decide on the action that needs to be taken under various possible circumstances.

SARSA and Q-learning are very similar to each other, except Q-learning is an off-policy algorithm and SARSA is an on-policy algorithm. The Q value learned by SARSA is not based on a greedy policy like in Q-learning but is based on the action performed under the current policy.

For a single state, *s*, and an action, *a*, Q(s, a) can be expressed in terms of the Q value of the next state, *s'*, and action, *a'*, given by the following formula:

$$Q(s,a) = r + \gamma * Q(s',a')$$

The following is the pseudocode for the SARSA learning algorithm from the book, *Reinforcement Learning: An Introduction,* by Richard S. Sutton and Andrew G. Barto:

Initialize $Q(s, a)$ arbitrarily
Repeat (for each episode):
    Initialize s
    Choose a from s using policy derived from Q (e.g., ε-greedy)
    Repeat (for each step of episode):
        Take action a, observe r, s'
        Choose a' from s' using policy derived from Q (e.g., ε-greedy)
        $Q(s, a) \leftarrow Q(s, a) + \alpha \left[r + \gamma Q(s', a') - Q(s, a) \right]$
        $s \leftarrow s'; a \leftarrow a';$
    until s is terminal

Figure 14.10: Pseudocode for SARSA learning

Importing all of the dependencies

We will be using `numpy`, `gym`, `matplotlib`, `keras`, `tensorflow`, and the `keras-rl` package in this segment of the exercise. Here, TensorFlow will be used as the backend for Keras. You can install these packages with `pip`:

```
import numpy as np
import gym
from keras.models import Sequential
from keras.layers import Dense, Activation, Flatten
from keras.optimizers import Adam
from rl.agents import SARSAAgent
from rl.policy import EpsGreedyQPolicy
```

Loading the game environment

Just like we loaded the game in the DQN segment, we will load the game into the workspace and set `seed` for reproducibility:

```
env = gym.make('CartPole-v1')

# set seed
seed_val = 456
env.seed(seed_val)
np.random.seed(seed_val)
```

```
states = env.observation_space.shape[0]
actions = env.action_space.n
```

Defining the agent

For deep SARSA learning, we will be using the same agent we used in the Deep Q-learning segment:

```
def agent(states, actions):
    """Simple Deep Neural Network."""
    model = Sequential()
    model.add(Flatten(input_shape=(1,states)))
    model.add(Dense(16))
    model.add(Activation('relu'))
    model.add(Dense(16))
    model.add(Activation('relu'))
    model.add(Dense(16))
    model.add(Activation('relu'))
    model.add(Dense(actions))
    model.add(Activation('linear'))
    return model

model = agent(states, actions)
```

Training the agent

Training an agent using the `keras-rl` library is very easy:

1. Define the policy you want the training to follow. We will be using the epsilon-greedy policy. The equivalent of this in the DQN section would be the agent `action` function. To know more about other policies, visit `https://github.com/keras-rl/keras-rl/blob/master/rl/policy.py`.

2. Load the agent you would like to use. In this case, the SARSA agent has a lot of parameters of which the important ones that need to be defined are `model`, `nb_actions`, and `policy`. `model` is the deep learning agent you have defined in the preceding code, `nb_actions` is the number of possible actions in the system, and `policy` is your preferred choice of policy to train the SARSA agent.

3. We compile the SARSA agent with loss and optimizer of choice.

4. We fit the SARSA agent by feeding the `.fit` function the arguments environment and number of steps to train:

To get complete details on the usage of agents from the `keras-rl` library and their parameter definitions, visit this documentation by Keras at `http://keras-rl.readthedocs.io/en/latest/agents/sarsa/ #sarsaagent`.

```
# Define the policy
policy = EpsGreedyQPolicy()

# Loading SARSA agent by feeding it the policy and the model
sarsa = SARSAAgent(model=model, nb_actions=actions, policy=policy)

# compile sarsa with mean squared error loss
sarsa.compile('adam', metrics=['mse'])

# train the agent for 50000 steps
sarsa.fit(env, nb_steps=50000, visualize=False, verbose=1)
```

To view the CartPole game on your screen when training, set visualize argument to true inside the `.fit` function. But visualizing the game will slow down the training.

Here is the scores output when training the SARSA agent:

```
Training for 50000 steps ...
Interval 1 (0 steps performed)
10000/10000 [==============================] - 95s 10ms/step - reward: 1.0000
319 episodes - episode_reward: 30.984 [8.000, 500.000] - loss: 7.445 - mean_squared_error: 552.109 - mean_q: 29.475

Interval 2 (10000 steps performed)
10000/10000 [==============================] - 93s 9ms/step - reward: 1.0000
122 episodes - episode_reward: 82.467 [9.000, 435.000] - loss: 6.987 - mean_squared_error: 831.830 - mean_q: 39.221

Interval 3 (20000 steps performed)
10000/10000 [==============================] - 89s 9ms/step - reward: 1.0000
81 episodes - episode_reward: 122.617 [14.000, 500.000] - loss: 10.447 - mean_squared_error: 1416.096 - mean_q: 52.41
1

Interval 4 (30000 steps performed)
10000/10000 [==============================] - 95s 9ms/step - reward: 1.0000
75 episodes - episode_reward: 133.933 [15.000, 500.000] - loss: 6.933 - mean_squared_error: 1527.035 - mean_q: 54.172

Interval 5 (40000 steps performed)
10000/10000 [==============================] - 99s 10ms/step - reward: 1.0000
done, took 470.141 seconds
```

Figure 14.11: Scores output when training SARSA agent

Testing the agent

Once the agent has been trained, we evaluate its performance over 100 new episodes. This can be done by calling the `.test` function and feeding the arguments environment and number of episodes on which to test:

```
# Evaluate the agent on 100 new episodes
scores = sarsa.test(env, nb_episodes=100, visualize=False)

print('Average score over 100 test games:
{}'.format(np.mean(scores.history['episode_reward'])))
```

To view the CartPole game on your screen when testing, set the `visualize` argument to `True` inside the `.test` function.

The following is the output after testing 100 episodes:

```
Testing for 100 episodes ...
Episode 1: reward: 350.000, steps: 350
Episode 2: reward: 383.000, steps: 383
Episode 3: reward: 316.000, steps: 316
Episode 4: reward: 371.000, steps: 371
Episode 5: reward: 356.000, steps: 356
Episode 6: reward: 399.000, steps: 399
Episode 7: reward: 317.000, steps: 317
Episode 8: reward: 370.000, steps: 370
Episode 9: reward: 364.000, steps: 364
Episode 10: reward: 432.000, steps: 432
```

Following the the output at the end of the code execution:

```
Episode 90: reward: 334.000, steps: 334
Episode 91: reward: 392.000, steps: 392
Episode 92: reward: 393.000, steps: 393
Episode 93: reward: 359.000, steps: 359
Episode 94: reward: 370.000, steps: 370
Episode 95: reward: 363.000, steps: 363
Episode 96: reward: 349.000, steps: 349
Episode 97: reward: 338.000, steps: 338
Episode 98: reward: 387.000, steps: 387
Episode 99: reward: 367.000, steps: 367
Episode 100: reward: 425.000, steps: 425
Average score over 100 test games: 365.67
```

Figure 14.12: Test scores with trained SARSA agent

Deep SARSA learning script in modular form

For SARSA learning, we have only one script, which implements both the training and testing of the SARSA agent:

```python
"""This module implements training and testing of SARSA agent."""
import gym
import numpy as np
from keras.layers import Dense, Activation, Flatten
from keras.models import Sequential
from rl.agents import SARSAAgent
from rl.policy import EpsGreedyQPolicy

# load the environment
env = gym.make('CartPole-v1')

# set seed
seed_val = 456
env.seed(seed_val)
np.random.seed(seed_val)

states = env.observation_space.shape[0]
actions = env.action_space.n


def agent(states, actions):
    """Agent/Deep Neural Network."""
```

```
    model = Sequential()
    model.add(Flatten(input_shape=(1, states)))
    model.add(Dense(16))
    model.add(Activation('relu'))
    model.add(Dense(16))
    model.add(Activation('relu'))
    model.add(Dense(16))
    model.add(Activation('relu'))
    model.add(Dense(actions))
    model.add(Activation('linear'))
    return model


model = agent(states, actions)

# Define the policy
policy = EpsGreedyQPolicy()
# Define SARSA agent by feeding it the policy and the model
sarsa = SARSAAgent(model=model, nb_actions=actions, nb_steps_warmup=10,
                   policy=policy)
# compile sarsa with mean squared error loss
sarsa.compile('adam', metrics=['mse'])
# train the agent for 50000 steps
sarsa.fit(env, nb_steps=50000, visualize=False, verbose=1)

# Evaluate the agent on 100 new episodes.
scores = sarsa.test(env, nb_episodes=100, visualize=False)
print('Average score over 100 test games: {}'
      .format(np.mean(scores.history['episode_reward'])))
```

The conclusion to the project

This project was to build a deep reinforcement learning model to successfully play the game of CartPole-v1 from OpenAI Gym. The use case of this chapter is to build a reinforcement learning model on a simple game environment and then extend it to other complex games such as Atari.

In the first half of this chapter, we built a deep Q-learning model to play the CartPole game. The DQN model during testing scored an average of 277.88 points over 100 games.

In the second half of this chapter, we built a deep SARSA learning model (using the same epsilon-greedy policy as Q-learning) to play the CartPole game. The SARSA model during testing scored an average of 365.67 points over 100 games.

Now, let's follow the same technique we have been following in the previous chapters for evaluating the performance of the models from the restaurant chain point of view.

What are the implications of this score?

An average score of 277.88 with Q-learning means that we have successfully solved the game of CartPole as defined on the OpenAI site. It also means that our model survives slightly more than half the length of the game with the total game length being 500 points.

As regards SARSA learning, on the other hand, an average score of 365.67 with Q-learning means that we have successfully solved the game of CartPole as defined on the OpenAI site and that our model survives more than 70% the length of the game, with the total game length being 500 points.

It is still not a level of performance you should be happy with because the goal should not just be to solve the problem but to train a model that is really good at scoring a consistent 500 points at each game, so you can see why we'd need to continue fine-tuning the models to get the maximum performance possible.

Summary

In this chapter, we have successfully built a deep reinforcement learning model, each with Q-learning and SARSA learning in Keras using the CartPole game from OpenAI Gym. We understood Q-learning, SARSA learning, how to interact with game environments from Gym, and the function of the agent (deep learning model). We defined some key hyperparameters, as well as, in some places, reasoned with why we used what we did. Finally, we tested the performance of our reinforcement learning on new games and determined that we succeeded in achieving our goals.

15
Summary and Next Steps in Your Deep Learning Career

This has been a fantastic journey and you've been quite productive as a member of the team! We hope that you've enjoyed our practical approach to teaching *Python Deep Learning Projects*. Furthermore, it was our intention to provide you with thought-provoking and exciting experiences that will further your intuition and form the technical foundation for your career in deep learning engineering.

Each chapter was structured similarly to participating as a member of our Intelligence Factory team, where, by going through the material, we achieved the following:

- Saw the big picture of the real-world use case and identified the success criteria
- Got focused and into the code, loaded dependencies and data, and built, trained, and evaluated our models
- Expanded back out to the big picture to confirm that we achieved our goal

We love solving problems and building smart solutions, insights, and people! Let's review some key learning, summarize some of our intuition, and look at what could be next in your deep learning career.

Python deep learning – building the foundation – two projects

The foundation of a common working environment enables us to work together, and empowers our learning of cool and powerful deep learning technologies in the fields of **computer vision** (**CV**) and **natural language processing** (**NLP**). The first two chapters in this book provide the establishing experience that you will use time and again in your professional career as a data scientist.

Chapter 1 – Building the Deep Learning Environment

The main goal in this chapter was to standardize the toolset for our work together to achieve consistently accurate results. We want to establish a process for building applications using deep learning algorithms that can scale for production. Towards the end, we identified the components of our common deep learning environment, and initially set up a local deep learning environment, which expanded to a cloud-based environment. Throughout the projects that followed, you gained experience with Ubuntu, Anaconda, Python, TensorFlow, Keras, and **Google Cloud Platform** (**GCP**), to highlight but a few core technologies. These will continue to be of value to you in your deep learning engineering career!

Chapter 2 – Training NN for Prediction Using Regression

In `Chapter 2`, *Training NN for Prediction Using Regression*, we identified our first business use case—one that would become a theme for a number of projects: that of a restaurant chain seeking to automate some of its processes. Specifically, in this chapter, the business use case was to build a deep learning classifier using a **multi-layer perceptron** (**MLP**), the basic building block in deep learning, to accurately classify handwritten digits of a customer's phone number. If you recall, the goal was to accurately classify (digitize) the handwritten phone number on an iPad so that the patron could receive a text that their table was ready.

We built a two-layer (minimally deep) neural network in TensorFlow and trained it on the classic MNIST dataset. This project provided us the opportunity to address overfitting, underfitting, hyperparameter tuning, and activation functions in our exploration of the model's performance. What we found particularly interesting was the impact of the business use case on interpreting the utility of the model's performance. Our accuracy with this simple model initially seemed adequate, until we thought about what a single digit error in a phone number would mean to the accurate delivery of a text to the right patron. In this context, we quickly understood we would need to do much better. Fortunately, we had an opportunity later in the book to take a second run at the problem, and in `Chapter 8`, *Handwritten Digits Classification Using ConvNets*, we employed a more complex deep learning model that performed much better!

Python deep learning – NLP – 5 projects

A third of our *Python Deep Learning Projects* are in the field of computational linguistics. Unstructured text data is everywhere, and is being generated at an astonishing rate. We split up the approaches and technologies employed into five parts, to adequately handle the breadth of information. Let's review how the projects in Chapters 3, *Word Representation Using word2vec*, through Chapter 8, *Handwritten Digits Classification Using ConvNets*, relate and build on one another.

Chapter 3 – Word Representations Using word2vec

Core to computational linguistics is an effective representation of words and the features they embody. word2vec was used to transform the words into dense vectors (that is, tensors), creating embedding representations for the corpus. We then created a **convolutional neural network** (**CNN**) to build a language model for sentiment analysis. To help us frame this task we envisioned the hypothetical use case of our restaurant chain client asking us to make sense of the response texts that they were receiving from their patrons getting the notification that their table was ready. Particularly interesting was the realization that CNNs can be applied to more than just image data! We also took this project as an opportunity to explore data visualization with **t-distributed stochastic neighbor embedding** (**t-SNE**) and TensorBoard.

Chapter 4 – Build an NLP Pipeline for Building Chatbots

We dive deeper into computational linguistics in this project by exploring the deep learning techniques (building blocks) for language models. word2vec models like ours in Chapter 3, *Word Representation Using word2vec*, are made possible by NLP pipelines. Our task was to create a natural language pipeline that would power a chatbot for open-domain question-answering. We pictured our (hypothetical) restaurant chain as having a website with their menu, history, location, hours, and other information, and that they would like the added ability for a website visitor to ask a question in a query box, and for our deep-learning NLP chatbot to find the relevant information and present that back.

The NLP pipeline tokenized the corpus, tagged parts of speech, determined the relationship between words with dependency parsing, and conducted **named entity recognition** (**NER**). This prepared us to use TF-IDF to vectorize the features in the document to create a simple FAQ-type chatbot. We enhanced this with NER and the implementation of Rasa NLU. We were then able to build a bot that understood the context (intent) of a piece of text, and could also extract the entities, because we created an NLP pipeline that could perform intent classification, along with NER extraction, to allow it to provide an accurate response.

Chapter 5 – Sequence-to-Sequence Models for Building Chatbots

This chapter builds directly on `Chapter 4`, *Build NLP Pipeline for Building Chatbots* to build a more advanced chatbot for our hypothetical restaurant chain to automate the process of fielding call in orders. We combined our learning on a number of technologies to make a chatbot that is more contextually aware and robust. We avoided some of the limitations of CNNs in chatbots by building a **recurrent neural network** (**RNN**) model with **long short-term memory** (**LSTM**) units, specifically designed to capture the signal represented in sequences of characters or words.

We implemented a language model, with an encoder-decoder RNN based on the LSTM unit, for a simple sequence-to-sequence question-answer task. This model was able to handle inputs and outputs of different sizes, preserve the state of information, and adequately handle complex context. An additional learning of ours was that of the importance of obtaining a sufficient amount of the right training data as the outputs of the model are put up against a very high standard for speech interpretability. However, with the right training data, it would be possible to use this model to achieve the hypothetical restaurant chain's goal of building a robust chatbot (in combination with other computational linguistic technologies we've explored) that could automate the over-the-phone process of ordering food.

Chapter 6 – Generative Language Model for Content Creation

In this project, we not only take the next step in our computational linguistics journey; we take a profound leap to generate new content! We defined the business use case goal of providing a deep learning solution that generates new content that can be used in movie scripts, song lyrics, and music. We asked ourselves: how can we leverage our experience in solving problems for restaurant chains and apply it to different industries? Upon reflection on what we learned in past projects regarding the inputs and outputs of the models, we gained confidence that novel content was just another type of output. We demonstrated that we could take an image as input, and output a class label (Chapter 2, *Training NN for Prediction Using Regression*). We trained a model to take inputs of text and output sentiment classifications (Chapter 3, *Word Representation Using word2vec*), and we built a NLP pipeline for an open-domain question-answering chatbot, where we took text as input, and identified text in a corpus to present the appropriate output (Chapter 4, *Build NLP Pipeline for Building Chatbots*). We then expanded that chatbot functionality to be able to serve a restaurant with an automated ordering system (Chapter 5, *Sequence-to-Sequence Models for Building Chatbots*).

In this chapter, we implemented a generative model to generate content using the **long short-term memory (LSTM)**, variational autoencoders, and **generative adversarial networks (GANs)**. We effectively implemented models, for both text and music, that can generate song lyrics, scripts, and music for artists and various creative businesses.

Chapter 7 – Building Speech Recognition with DeepSpeech2

This project on building speech recognition with DeepSpeech2 is the capstone in the *Natural Language Processing* section of the *Python Deep Learning Projects* book. So far, we've explored chatbots, natural language processing, and speech recognition with RNNs (both uni- and bi-directional, with and without LSTM components) and CNNs. We've seen the power of these technologies to provide intelligence to existing business processes, as well as to create entirely new and smart systems. This is exciting work at the cutting edge of applied AI using deep learning!

The goal of this project was to build and train an **automatic speech recognition** (ASR) system to take in and convert an audio call to text, which could then be used as the input for a text-based chatbot that was capable of parsing the input and responding appropriately. We made a deep dive into speech data, performing feature engineering to allow us to extract various kinds of features from the data, to then build a speech recognition system which can detect a users voice. In the end, we demonstrated mastery by building a system, using the DeepSpeech2 model, that recognizes English speech. We worked with speech and spectograms to build an end-to-end speech recognition system using the **connectionist temporal classification** (CTC) loss function, batch normalization, and SortaGrad for the RNNs.

Deep learning – computer vision – 6 projects

The following six Python deep learning projects, focusing on CV, represent the largest portion of the content of this book. We've already seen how some of the deep learning technologies we explore in detail, with reference to CV, have some applicability to other types of data, and in particular, to text-based data. In no small part, that is because of the enormous utility of CNNs in feature extraction and hierarchical representation. There is no magic tool that is perfect for all jobs—being a deep learning engineer in data science is no exception. But you should not underestimate the familiarity you'll get with CNNs, as you'll find yourself using them time and again, across many different datasets and business use cases. Being a data scientist without CNN skills is like being a carpenter without a hammer. The obvious caveat is that not everything in data science is the equivalent of a nail!

Chapter 8 – Handwritten Digit Classification Using ConvNets

This chapter reminds us of the first deep neural net we created in Chapter 2, *Training NN for Prediction Using Regression*, and the business use case to which it was applied. The purpose of that chapter was to provide a foundation for our understanding of deep neural networks and how they operate. The complexity of the math underlying deep learning was highlighted when we compared the model architecture with the more advanced techniques afforded when we build deeper and more robust models. Complexity isn't cool just because it's complex; in this case, it's cool because of the improvement in realized performance utility that it provides.

We spent a considerable amount of time examining the convolution operation, pooling, and dropout regularization. These are the levers you'll adjust in tuning your models in your career, so getting a solid understanding of them early is essential. In reference to the business use case, we see the value of deploying a more complex model, in that the performance gain supports the parent product implementation. The error rate obtained in Chapter 2, *Training NN for Prediction Using Regression*, was such that, in the worse case, not a single text would have been appropriately delivered to the right patron at the hypothetical restaurant chain (and in the best case, it was still dismal and effectively not functional). The CNN model on the same dataset produces results that mean that, in the new worst-case scenario, 90% of the patrons would receive the text notifications, and in the best case, 99% would get the text!

Chapter 9 – Object Detection Using OpenCV and TensorFlow

Let's think about what we accomplished in Chapter 8, *Handwritten Digits Classification Using ConvNets*, where we were able to train an image classifier, with a CNN, to accurately classify handwritten digits in an image. The data was less complicated than it could have been, because each image only had one handwritten digit in it, and our goal was to accurately assign a class label to the image. What would have happened if each image had multiple handwritten digits in it, or different types of objects? What if we had a video? What if we want to identify *where* the digits are in the image? These questions represent the challenges that real-world data embodies, and drives our data science innovation toward new models and capabilities.

Object detection and classification is no trivial task for a computer, particularly at scale and hitting speed requirements. We employed data inputs in this project that were much more informationally complex than what we've had in previous projects, and the outcomes, when we got them right, were that much more impressive. We found that the deep learning package YOLOv2 performed very well, and saw our model architecture get deeper and more complex with good results.

Chapter 10 – Building Facial Recognition Using OpenFace

In `Chapter 9`, *Object Detection Using OpenCV and TensorFlow*, we demonstrated mastery in the skills needed to build a deep learning object detection and classification model. Building on that, we set our objective at a refinement of that classification operation: is the object identical to another? In our case, we were looking to build a facial recognition system of the kind that we see in spy movies, and now in high tech security systems. Facial recognition is a combination of two major operations: face detection, followed by face classification.

Using OpenFace in this project, we built a model that looked at a picture and identified all the possible faces in it, then performed face extraction to understand the quality of the part of the image containing faces. We then performed feature extraction on the face, identifying parts of the image that gave us the basis for comparison with another data point (a labeled image of the person's face). This Python deep learning project demonstrates the exciting potential for this technology, and the future for the engineers that excel at working on these applications.

Chapter 11 – Automated Image Captioning

In `Chapter 9`, *Object Detection Using OpenCV and TensorFlow*, we learned how to detect and classify objects in an image, and in `Chapter 10`, *Building Face Recognition Using FaceNet*, we learned how to detect, classify, and identify objects as being the same thing (for example, identifying the same person from two different facial images). In this project, we did something even more complicated and cool! We combined the current state-of-the-art techniques that we've learned so far in our Python deep learning projects, in both CV and NLP, to form a complete image description approach. This model was capable of constructing computer-generated natural language descriptions of any image provided.

The clever idea that made this possible was to replace the encoder (the RNN layer) in an encoder-decoder architecture with a deep CNN, trained to classify objects in images. Normally, the CNN's last layer is the softmax layer, which assigns the probability that each object might be in the image. But when we remove that softmax layer from the CNN, we can feed the CNN's rich encoding of the image into the decoder (the language generation component of the RNN) designed to produce phrases. We can then train the whole system directly on images and their captions, maximizing the likelihood that the descriptions it produces best match the training descriptions for each image. This deep learning technology is the backbone of many intelligence factory solutions!

Chapter 12 – Pose Estimation on 3D Models Using ConvNets

Data that we apply to our models are representations of the real world. This is the fundamental truth that unites computational linguistics and CV. With respect to CV, we need to remember that 2D images represent a 3D world, in the same way that video represents 4D, with the added aspects of time and movement. Recalling this obvious fact lets us ask ever more interesting questions and develop deep learning technologies with increasing utility. Our hypothetical use case was to enable visual effects specialists to easily estimate the pose of actors (particularly the shoulders, neck, and head) on frames of a video. Our task was to build the intelligence for this application.

We successfully built a deep CNN/VGG16 model in Keras on **frames labeled in cinema** (**FLIC**) images. We got hands-on experience in preparing the images for modeling. We successfully implemented transfer learning, and understood that doing so will save us a lot of time. We defined some key hyperparameters, as well as understanding why we did what we did. Finally, we tested the modified VGG16 model performance on unseen data, and determined that we succeeded in achieving our goals.

Chapter 13 – Image Translation Using GANs for Style Transfer

GANs are just downright cool. When we look back at the skills and intuition we've built throughout these projects, we had an interesting idea. Could we predict missing information? Or, stated in a different way: can we create data that should be in an image, but that's not there? If we can take text input and generate novel text output, and if we can take a 2D image and generate or predict a 3D positional output, then it would seem possible that, if we have a 2D image that's missing some information, maybe we ought to be able to generate the missing information? So, in this chapter, we built a neural network that fills in the missing part of a handwritten digit. We previously built a digit classifier for a hypothetical restaurant chain client. Error rates could be attributable to the digits not being accurately captured, and the resulting image having incompletely drawn digits. We focused our efforts on the new part of the model creation—the generation/reconstruction of the missing sections of a digit with the help of neural inpainting with GANs. We then reconstructed the missing parts of the handwritten numbers, so that the classifier received clear handwritten numbers for conversion into digits. With this, the classifier was able to do a much more accurate job of classifying the handwritten digits (and our mythical restaurant patrons were able to receive their notification texts and get seated promptly).

Python deep learning – autonomous agents – 1 project

The final project in our book is unlike anything we've done so far, and deserves its own treatment. Robotic process automation and optimization, and autonomous agents, such as drones and vehicles, require our deep learning models to learn from environmental cues in a reinforcement learning paradigm. Unlike previous projects, where we've been primarily focused on solving supervised learning problems, in this chapter, we learned to build and train a deep reinforcement learning model capable of playing games.

We employed a deep Q-learning and deep **state-action-reward-state-action** (**SARSA**) learning model. Unlike programming simple models by defining heuristics, deep learning models mapping A-B in a supervised learning environment, or determining decision boundaries in cluster analysis in unsupervised learning, it is the rules of the game or environment (as expressed in the delivery of reinforcement) that provide the feedback for training in reinforcement learning. The deep learning model, also called the agent in reinforcement-learning terms, interacts with the game environment and learns how to play the game, seeking to maximize rewards after several attempts at playing.

Chapter 14 – Develop an Autonomous Agent with Deep Reinforcement Learning

In this project, we built a deep reinforcement learning model to successfully play the game of CartPole-v1, from OpenAI Gym. Demonstrating mastery here first, we could then extend it to other complex games, such as those by Atari.

We learned how to interact with the Gym toolkit, Q-learning, and SARSA learning; how to code the reinforcement learning model and define hyperparameters; and how to build the training loop and test the model. We found that our SARSA model performed quite a bit better than the Q-learning model. Further training and tuning of hyperparameters, and our own capture of reinforcement units (better scores by our models), should shape our behavior to build better models that ultimately result in the nearly perfect performance of our agent!

Next steps – AI strategy and platforms

Throughout this book, you've gained experiences that form the technical foundations for professional work in deep learning projects. However, the scope of the book was such that our focus could only be on a subset of the entire production-scale data science pipeline. We spent our time in the context of a business use case to ground our thinking on the domain and success criteria, but quickly dove into deep-learning model training, evaluation, and validation. These components, comprising the bulk of the training in our projects, are certainly the core of a data science pipeline for an enterprise, but cannot function in a vacuum. Additional considerations and training in AI strategy and data science platforms are the natural next steps in your education and career.

AI strategy

AI strategy is about gaining knowledge from the client that empowers you to determine the following:

- The client's grand vision for an intelligence-based competitive advantage
- How to translate that vision into an effective production-scale data science pipeline:
  - Take into account the current and near-term digital maturity of the client
  - Processes of data ingestion, analysis, and transformation
  - Technology and engineering resources and constraints
  - The analytics team's current capabilities
  - Model selection, customization, training, evaluation, validation, and serving
- Achievement of KPIs and ROI that meets the objectives of the client's leadership

AI strategy consulting uncovers goals and expectations, while aligning outcomes with machine learning and deep learning technologies. Building an AI solution architecture must take all of this into account to be successful. You should look to mentors in the industry, read available case studies, and keep this in mind as your career advances, and you are called in to provide guidance and opinions earlier and earlier in the solution-building process.

Deep learning platforms – TensorFlow Extended (TFX)

Data science platforms, designed to meet the demands for production-scale deployment, require significant engineering support. At the Intelligence Factory and Skejul, we've built deep learning platforms that take in live feeds of constantly updating data to produce intelligence-based outputs within milliseconds, to be delivered via a cloud-based web application using API gateways. It's extraordinarily complex and rewarding, once you get all the pieces to come together!

One technology that will aid in your deep learning and data science career is TFX. This is Google's TensorFlow-based production-scale machine learning platform. The first few lines from their abstract from the article
TFX: A TensorFlow-Based Production-Scale Machine Learning Platform (`https://ai.google/research/pubs/pub46484`) summarize the potential of the TFX and similar platforms:

> *"Creating and maintaining a platform for reliably producing and deploying machine learning models requires careful orchestration of many components—a learner for generating models based on training data, modules for analyzing and validating both data as well as models, and finally infrastructure for serving models in production. This becomes particularly challenging when data changes over time and fresh models need to be produced continuously."*

Data science platform engineering that's based on a smartly crafted AI strategy is our next step in training, and we look forward to the opportunity to share those experiences with you too!

Conclusion and thank you!

We want to thank you for choosing our book, *Python Deep Learning Projects*, as part of your data science education! It's our hope that you found the projects and the business use cases intriguing and informative, and that you feel more professionally prepared than when you started. We look forward to the opportunity to engage with you via our respective blogs, on social media, and possibly even at conferences or on working together on delivering AI-based solutions to clients around the world.

We've been happy to have you in our weekly AI team meetings in these projects. Now that we've learned a bunch of stuff, and had some fun with really cool and powerful data science technologies, let's go out to do great work based on these Python deep learning projects!

Other Books You May Enjoy

If you enjoyed this book, you may be interested in these other books by Packt:

Python Deep Learning Cookbook
Indra den Bakker

ISBN: 978-1-78712-519-3

- Implement different neural network models in Python
- Select the best Python framework for deep learning such as PyTorch, Tensorflow, MXNet and Keras
- Apply tips and tricks related to neural networks internals, to boost learning performances
- Consolidate machine learning principles and apply them in the deep learning field
- Reuse and adapt Python code snippets to everyday problems
- Evaluate the cost/benefits and performance implication of each discussed solution

Hands-On Natural Language Processing with Python

Rajesh Arumugam, Rajalingappaa Shanmugamani

ISBN: 978-1-78913-949-5

- Implement semantic embedding of words to classify and find entities
- Convert words to vectors by training in order to perform arithmetic operations
- Train a deep learning model to detect classification of tweets and news
- Implement a question-answer model with search and RNN models
- Train models for various text classification datasets using CNN
- Implement WaveNet a deep generative model for producing a natural-sounding voice
- Convert voice-to-text and text-to-voice
- Train a model to convert speech-to-text using DeepSpeech

Leave a review - let other readers know what you think

Please share your thoughts on this book with others by leaving a review on the site that you bought it from. If you purchased the book from Amazon, please leave us an honest review on this book's Amazon page. This is vital so that other potential readers can see and use your unbiased opinion to make purchasing decisions, we can understand what our customers think about our products, and our authors can see your feedback on the title that they have worked with Packt to create. It will only take a few minutes of your time, but is valuable to other potential customers, our authors, and Packt. Thank you!

Index

A

affine transformations
  about 293
  reference 293
AI strategy 445
Anaconda installation
  DL libraries, installing 12
  performing 11
automated image captioning
  attention 310
  CNN encoder, defining 311
  data preparation 302
  feature extraction, performing 306
  loss function 312
  model, defining 310
  model, deploying 318, 320
  model, evaluating 315
  RNN decoder, defining 311
  training 312, 313

B

basic RNNs implementation
  basic RNN cell model, defining 94, 95, 97
  dataset, preparing 92, 93, 94
  dependencies, importing 92
  hyperparameters 94
  RNN model, evaluating 99, 100
  RNN model, training 97

C

CartPole game
  exploring 408
  interacting with 408
  loading 408
  playing 410
  Q-learning 412

resetting 409
centering 372
chatbots
  building, with NER 77
  dataset, preparing 79
  deploying 81
  serving 83, 84
  training 80, 81
cloud platforms, for deployment
  about 14
  GCP, setting up 14
  prerequisites 14
CNN classifier predictions
  on noised and generated images 397
CNN model
  accuracy 60
  convolution layer 59
  data format 61, 62
  deploying, into production 64
  dropout layer 60
  embedding layer 58
  executing 63, 64
  exploring 55, 56, 57
  placeholders, for inputs 58
  predictions 60
  word2vec, integrating with 63
code implementation
  about 324, 325
  data, exploring 326
  data, pre-processing 326, 327, 329, 331, 332, 333, 334, 335
  data, preparing 336
  dependencies, importing 325
  hyperparameters, defining for training 342
  images, transforming 340
  joints, plotting 339
  limbs, plotting 339

predictions 351, 353
  scripts, in modular form 353
  VGG16 model, building 343
common DL environment
  building 9, 10
  local DL environment, setting up 10
computer vision (CV) 435
Conv2D API
  reference 182
conversational bots
  advanced chatbots, with NER 77
  building 74
convolution autoencoder
  about 216
  defining 218, 219
  dependencies, importing 217
  fitting 221
  loss plot 221
  low-resolution images, generating 218
  Python file 224
  scaling 218
  test results 221
convolution neural networks (ConvNets) 169
convolution
  implementing 181
  in Keras 181, 183
  model, evaluating 184, 185
  model, fitting 184
  Python file 186
  with pooling 194
convolutional neural networks (CNNs) 42

D

data augmentation
  about 207
  ImageDataGenerator, fitting 210, 211
  ImageDataGenerator, using 208, 209, 210
  model, compiling 211
  model, evaluating 212, 213
  model, fitting 211, 212
  Python file 214
data exploring, in image segmentation
  annotations 267
  images 265
data preparation, automated image captioning

about 302
  data pipeline, setting up 309
  for deep CNN encoder 305, 306
  for language generation (RNN) decoder 307
  initialization 303
  MS-COCO dataset, downloading 303
  MS-COCO dataset, preparing 303
data preparing, code implementation
  cropping 336
  resizing 338
data preparing, image segmentation
  about 269
  encode 271
  model data 272
  normalize 270, 271
data
  exploring 370, 371
  preparing 372
dataset
  reshaping 375
DCGAN
  defining 383
deep learning (DL) technologies
  computer vision (CV) 9
  natural language processing (NLP) 9
deep learning (DL)
  for computational linguistics 41
Deep Q Learning (DQN)
  CartPole game, exploring 408
  conclusion 433
  dependencies, importing 407
  hyperparameters, defining 413
  implementing 407
  in modular form 423
  model components, building 414
  reference 407
DeepSpeech2 (DS2) model
  building 150
  corpus exploration 151, 152, 153
  data preprocessing 150
  data transformation 157
  defining 158, 159, 160
  evaluating 167
  feature engineering 153, 155
  testing 167

training 162, 163, 164, 166
dependencies
  importing 369, 370
dependency parsing 73
discriminator
  defining 382, 383
DL environment local setup
  about 10
  Anaconda, downloading 11
  Anaconda, installing 11
DL environment
  setting up, in cloud 13
dlib
  reference 282
Docker
  reference 283
DQN scripts, modular form
  agent_replay_dqn.py module 424
  hyperparameters_dqn.py module 424
  test_dqn.py module 425
  train_dqn.py module 426
dropout
  about 195, 196, 197
  convolution, with pooling 200
  model, evaluating 198, 199
  model, fitting 197, 198
DS2 architecture
  implementation 159

E

eager execution
  reference 303
embedding plot
  building, in TensorBoard 52

F

face detection
  classifier, training 297, 298
  code, obtaining 283
  Docker image, building 283, 284, 286
  Docker image, preprocessing 297
  environment, setting up 283
  faces, aligning 291, 292, 294
  feature extraction 295
  images, preprocessing 290

  model, evaluation 298
  pre-trained models, downloading 286, 287, 288
face landmark estimation 291
FaceNet
  reference 282
facial recognition
  about 288
  pipeline, building 288, 289
Fast Image Data Annotation Tool (FIAT) 252
Frames Labeled In Cinema (FLIC) 323

G

GAN model components
  building 378
  DCGAN 383
  discriminator 382, 383
  generator 379, 381
GCP setup
  firewall settings, modifying 15
  project, creating 14
  VM instance, spinning 14
  VM, booting 15
Generative Adversarial Networks (GANs)
  about 367
  parameters, defining for 378
  training 384
  training loop 388, 389, 391
  training, plotting 384, 386, 387
generator
  defining 379, 381
Google Cloud Platform (GCP) 13
Google Cloud
  reference 14
Google Colab
  reference 13
Google Compute Engine (GCE) 13
Gym toolkit
  reference 407

H

handcrafted red object detector 234
handwritten digits classification
  code, implementation 170
  convolution, defining 180, 181
  data augmentation 207

data, exploring 170, 171, 172
deep neural network, building 173, 174, 176
deep neural network, training 173, 174, 176
deeper model, building 201
dependencies, importing 170
dropout, defining 195, 196, 197
hyperparameters, defining 172
MLP 179
model, compiling 202
model, evaluating 177, 204, 205
model, fitting 176, 203, 204
pooling, defining 187, 188, 189, 190
with pooling and Dropout 206
Hierarchical Dirichlet Process (HDP) 43
Histogram of Oriented Gradients (HOG) 232, 288
hyperparameters
about 57
defining 25
defining, for GAN 378
embedding_size 57
filter_sizes 57
num_classes 57
num_filters 57
pre_trained 57
sequence_length 57
vocab_size 57

I

image segmentation
about 264
data, exploring 265
data, preparing 269
dependencies, importing 264
hyperparameters, defining 273
SegNet, defining 274
ImageAI
reference 242
implementation
coding 25
inference
building 36, 38
inverse document frequency (IDF) 74

K

Keras Dense API
reference 173
Keras Model API
reference 173
keras-rl library
reference 427
Keras
reference 170, 174, 207, 220, 369, 407

L

language models
building, with CNN and word2vec 54
Latent Dirichlet Allocation (LDA) 43
LSTM architecture 100, 101
LSTM model, for generating lyrics
building 124
data pre-processing 125, 127
deep TensorFlow-based LSTM model, training 130, 132
defining 129
inference 133
output 134
LSTM model, for generating music
building 135, 136
data pre-processing 136, 138, 139
defining 141
music, generating 144, 145
training 141, 143
LSTM model, for text generation
about 118
building 119
data pre-processing 119
defining 121
inference 123
output 123
training 121, 122
LSTM model
defining 102
evaluating 106
implementing 102
training 103, 105

M

masking 373
MNIST classifier 375, 376, 377
MNIST dataset
  exploring 21, 22, 23
model components, DQN
  agent action, defining 416
  agent, defining 414
  building 414
  loop, training 420, 422
  memory, defining 416
  performance plot, defining 417
  replay, defining 418, 419
  testing 422
model definition 26, 29
modelSegNet model
  fitting 277
modules
  about 353
  crop_resize_transform.py 354
  plotting.py 356
  test.py 358
MS-COCO dataset
  reference 303
multi-layer perceptron (MLP) 20

N

Named Entity Recognition (NER) 67, 73
Natural Language Processing (NLP) 67
natural language processing (NLP) 42, 435
Natural Language Toolkit (NLTK) package 69
Natural Language Toolkit (NLTK) tokenizer
  reference 44
Neural Machine Translation (NMT) 107
NLP pipelines
  basics 68
  dependency parsing 73
  NER 73
  Part-of-Speech tagging 70
  tokenization 69
noise
  inserting 373

O

object detection in real-time, with YOLOv2
  about 250
  custom dataset, using 252, 253
  dataset, preparing 250
  dependencies, installing 253
  model, evaluating 261
  model, training 256, 258
  pre-existing COCO dataset, using 251
  YOLO model, configuring 254
  YOLOv2 model, defining 255
object detection intuition
  about 230
  object detection models, improving 232
object detection, using OpenCV
  about 233
  dependencies, installing 234
  handcrafted red object detector 234
  image data, exploring 235, 236
  image, normalizing 237, 238
  mask, applying 241
  mask, post-processing 239, 240
  mask, preparing 238
object detection, with deep learning
  about 242
  dependencies, installing 242
  deployment 247, 249
  implementation 244, 245
  implementing 242
OpenFace
  reference 282, 292
optimization 34
optimizers, Keras
  reference 172
Out Of Vocab (OOV) 113

P

Part-of-Speech (POS) tagging
  about 70
  nouns, extracting 71
  verbs, extracting 72
pooling
  about 187, 188, 189, 190
  model, evaluating 192, 193

model, fitting 191, 192
  Python file 194
predictions 397
Project Gutenberg website
  reference 44
project structure
  defining 24

R

Rasa NLU 78
Rasa
  installing 78
rectified linear unit (ReLU) function 159
region-based fully convolutional network (R-FCN)
  230
regression model
  building for predictions, MLP used 20, 21
regression
  defining 24
RNN architectures
  about 90, 91
  many to many 90
  many to one 90
  one to many 90
RNNs
  about 88, 89
  basic RNNs implementation 91

S

SARSA learning
  about 427, 428
  agent, defining 429
  agent, testing 431
  agent, training 429
  dependencies, importing 428
  reference 427
  script, implementing in modular form 432
scaling 372
scripts, in modular form
  about 399
  GAN.py 400
  train_gan.py 401
  train_mnist.py 399
  training_plots.py 400
SegNet model

compiling 277
  defining 274, 275
  testing 278
sequence-to-sequence (seq2seq) model
  about 90, 106
  data preparation 108, 109
  defining 109, 110
  evaluating 113
  hyperparameters 111
  implementing 107
  training 112
setup process
  automating 15, 16, 17
solid-state drive (SSD) 230
speech recognition
  building, with DeepSpeech2 (DS2) 149
State-Action-Reward-State-Action (SARSA) 406

T

t-Distributed Stochastic Neighbor Embedding (t-SNE) algorithm
  about 43
  reference 49
  used, for plotting word cluster 49
teacher forcing technique 313
TensorBoard 51
TensorFlow Extended (TFX) 446
TensorFlow
  reference 12
term frequency (TF) 74
TF-IDF
  about 74
  dataset, preparing 74
  implementing 75
  query, processing 77
  rank results 77
  vectorizer, creating 76
tokenization 69
training loop
  building 29, 30, 33, 34
  overfitting 34
  underfitting 35
type conversion 372

V

VGG16 model
  building 343
  defining 343, 345, 347
  plot training 350
  training loop 347, 348, 349
  validation loss 350
visual effects (VFX) 323

W

word embedding model
  dependencies, loading 43
  embedding space, visualizing 51
  text corpus, preparing 44, 45

word2vec model, defining 45
word embeddings 42
word vectors
  learning 42
word2vec 42, 43
word2vec model
  analyzing 47
  defining 45, 46
  training 47
  word cluster, plotting with t-SNE algorithm 49

Y

YOLOv2 250
you only look once (YOLO) 230

Made in the USA
Coppell, TX
05 December 2019